BECOMING LEAN

BECOMING LEAN

Inside Stories of U.S. Manufacturers

JEFFREY K. LIKER, EDITOR

Productivity Press

New York

Additional copies of this book are available from the publisher. Discounts are available for multiple copies through the Sales Department (888-319-5852). Address all other inquiries to:

Productivity Press
444 Park Avenue South, 7th Floor
New York, NY 10016
United States of America
Telephone: 212-686-5900
Telefax: 212-686-5411
E-mail: info@productivitypress.com
ProductivityPress.com

Cover design by Chris Hanis
Text design by Bill Stanton
Page composition by William H. Brunson, Typography Services
Printed and bound by Malloy Lithographing in the United States of America

Library of Congress Cataloging-in-Publication Data

Becoming lean : inside stories of U.S. manufacturers / Jeffrey K.
   Liker, editor.
      p. cm.
   Includes bibliographical references and index.
   ISBN 978-1-56327-173-1
   1. Manufacturing industries—United States—Management—Case
studies. 2. Automobile industry and trade—United States—Management—
Case studies. 3. Manufacturing industries—Management—Case studies.
4. Automobile industry and trade—Management—Case studies.
I. Liker, Jeffrey K.
HD9725.B4   1997
658.5′0973—dc21   97-31995
                                                                CIP

10 09 08 07 06   11 10 9 8 7

To Debbie, Emma, and Jesse,
who support me every day, and who
put up with many hours of my mind focused
on work instead of on them.

Contents

PART THREE: Managing the Change Process

Publisher's Message

In *The Machine That Changed the World*, James Womack coined the term *lean production* to describe the profound revolution in manufacturing that was initiated by the Toyota Production System, and which is rapidly replacing *mass production*. Lean production focuses on eliminating waste in processes, including the waste of work-in-progress and finished goods inventories, which are the earmark of mass production. Lean is not about eliminating people but about expanding capacity by reducing costs and shortening cycle time between customer order and ship date.

The Toyota Production System (TPS) is an ongoing evolution of solutions designed to achieve the "lean" ideal. Lean is much more than techniques. It is a way of thinking. It is a whole-systems approach that creates a culture in which everyone is continuously improving processes and production. It is a human system—customer focused and customer driven—wherein employees within and outside the workplace are the customers of their upstream colleagues. This creates a *pull* system from the customer all the way through the production process to the product design teams and the strategists who determine the direction of the company.

Lean production leads to, indeed demands, lean management—that is, the integration of vision, culture, and strategy to serve the customer with high quality (Q), low cost (C), and short delivery times (D). Those Japanese companies who adopted lean production methods twenty years ago are world leaders in their industries today! In looking over the past decade, it is safe to say that implementing lean manufacturing has not been an easy task for U.S. companies.

Becoming Lean: Inside Stories of U.S. Manufacturers is the first book to use the personal voices of U.S. manufacturers to lay before the reader the raw numbers as well as the necessary ingredients for becoming lean in the U.S. It is a book that will take the reader on an inside journey to the heart of lean's philosophy, techniques, and applications. When you finish reading this book you'll no longer be confused about the meaning of TPS, lean manufacturing, or lean thinking. Instead, you'll be sold on them—sold, because for the first time you'll know what it takes to succeed in implementing the lean revolution.

In *Becoming Lean* Jeffrey Liker digs beyond the principles and techniques of lean and by using the power of the manufacturer's own voice, tells the inside story on the ups and downs of becoming lean. Readers will hear personal stories from CEO's, consultants, and plant managers. They will encounter a variety of case studies on manufacturers ranging from automobile makers to birdhouse builders. These inside stories will bring everyone from top management to plant managers to front line employees up to speed on the principles and techniques they need to become lean, show them the obstacles they might encounter, and tell what it takes to overcome them. The case studies are especially valuable for those plant managers all across the U.S. that have received the word from upstairs to "go lean." (For one very thorough step-by-step case study, see Chapter 10.) And as for top management, they'll clearly and repeatedly hear the message on the kind of commitment they'll need to give if their employees are to succeed in implementing lean.

We are grateful to Jeffrey Liker for choosing Productivity Press for his fifth book. Jeffrey has done a tremendous editorial job in pulling together these different stories into a cohesive, instructive, and exciting book. We're certain that *Becoming Lean* will spread the important concepts of lean manufacturing (and TPS) to an ever wider audience.

We wish to thank all those who participated in shaping this manuscript and bringing it to bound book: Jessica Letteney, prepress manager; Gary Peurasaari, developmental editor; Suzanne Cophenhagen copyeditor, Sheryl Rose proofreader; Mary Junewick, production editor; Bill Stanton, text designer; Bill Brunson, type-setter; Gordon Ekdahl, art designer; and Chris Hanis, cover designer.

Diane Asay
Editor in Chief

Steven Ott
President & Publisher

Foreword

James P. Womack

Henry Ford—as every child once knew but which most adults have now forgotten—was the first truly lean thinker. His breakthrough at Highland Park in 1914 not only placed assembly in continuous flow with no "fitting" of parts, but also lined up machines for fabricating component parts in process sequence, separated by short gravity slides with a few pieces of work-in-process inventory.[1]

The problem with the Ford system was that it worked properly only in very special conditions. He planned from the beginning for very high production volumes (reaching more than two million units in the early 1920s) and he presumed that there would be no model changeovers. After all, he had designed the ideal car in 1908! In addition, Ford offered no options to his basic chassis, believing that low purchase cost—not options, features, or fit-and-finish—was the overwhelming consideration of first-time car buyers. (As a result there were no machine changeovers in the Ford Motor Company in 1914. Every machine was permanently dedicated to a specific part number!)

Perhaps most remarkably, Ford presumed that customers would always want more than he could make, so his main challenge in drawing up the production schedule was to capacitize all machines for the same output and hope (in an age long before total productive maintenance [TPM]) that most machines would meet their production targets most of the time. They didn't, of course, so an army of parts expediters was needed at Highland Park, but in concept, shortage chasers could be eliminated as soon as machine reliability was perfected.

In the mid-1920s, when all of these presumptions proved erroneous, Ford made a dramatic wrong turn at his new Rouge complex. He maintained the assembly track but rearranged his fabrication machinery into process villages. He proceeded to run a push schedule in which growing fluctuations in end-customer demand and persistent hiccups in upstream production were buffered by a vast bank of finished units forced on the dealer network and equally vast buffers of parts at every stage of production upstream from assembly. Thus "flow" production—as Ford termed it in 1914—became mass production (a term he also coined, in 1926, without realizing the difference), and the opportunity to carry lean thinking to its logical conclusion was lost.

The great genius of Taiichi Ohno and his Toyota colleagues in post-war Japan was to see that Ford had discovered only the special case for lean thinking—high production volume with zero product variety, infinite model life, and completely stable demand. They saw that a general case could be perfected that worked with extraordinary results in conditions of rapid model changeover, wide product variety, and fluctuating demand. Perhaps most remarkably, they discovered that the Toyota Production System (TPS) was vastly superior to mass production in productivity, quality, and customer response at volumes ranging from thousands per day down to only a few per year.

In looking back on the history of this general case, captured in Ohno's *Toyota Production System* (Productivity Press, 1988), it is striking that the basic ideas of *jidoka*, with multi-machine working of equipment arranged in process sequence, standard work, and pull scheduling, were first introduced nearly 50 years ago. What is more, the companion breakthroughs in organization—the Toyota supplier group, dedicated product development teams, and "aggressive selling" to smooth demand and create customers for life—were in place by around 1950. How, then, can the need arise, a half century later, for a book on how to implement lean thinking?

The answer, quite simply, is that lean thinking has always been difficult to introduce. It was difficult for Ohno himself, who worked for 25 years to push it through Toyota and the first-tier suppliers, and it has been hard for the Japanese transplants who have been able to sustain only a very moderate rate of expansion at greenfield sites. (Toyota has required 10 years to deploy 500,000 units of capacity at its Georgetown, Kentucky complex, whereas Ford scaled up Highland Park almost instantly.)

For Western managers, who almost always deal with long-established "brownfields" rather than greenfields, the going has been even tougher since making the first serious efforts independent of the Japanese at the end of the 1980s. (By contrast, Henry Ford was able to convert the entire Ford Motor Company to flow production between the fall of 1913 and the end of 1914!)

Why is lean thinking and lean manufacturing so challenging to implement? It is not—as many early commentators believed—a set of isolated techniques, but a complete business system, a way of designing, selling, and manufacturing complex products that requires the cooperation of thousands of people and hundreds of independent organizations. A successful "lean leap" requires "change agent" leadership, a *sensei* (teacher) to demonstrate the techniques, a long-term commitment to the work force to inspire their best efforts, proactive development of the supply base, aggressive management of the distribution and sales system to smooth demand, and a score-keeping system (accounting methods plus individual compensation) that motivates managers to do the right thing every time.

Putting all this in place is clearly a tall order. Fortunately, *Becoming Lean* fills an urgent need by describing in great detail the initial steps taken by a number of pioneering American firms in a range of industries to introduce lean thinking. The change agents actually leading the efforts describe precisely what worked (and what didn't) and document measurable, dramatic improvements on key metrics—cost, throughput time, defects that escape to customers, inventories, capital spending, space utilization, job-related injuries, and responsiveness to changing customer needs. Their experiences are then generalized to teach us how to manage the change process step by step.

None of these stories will make the lean leap seem easy; indeed, this is why they are so believable! But they all clearly illustrate the sequence of steps taken by change-minded American leaders to produce dramatic, sustainable progress in a short time. Your job is to study their examples and advice carefully, and to look in the mirror to see whether you are that change agent who will make the future better than the past. Then, in keeping with the command of Taiichi Ohno (years before Nike picked up the phrase): "Just do it!"

Notes

1. The curious reader should find a copy of Horace Arnold and Fay Faurote, *Ford Methods and the Ford Shops*, New York: Engineering Magazine Press, 1915, for a remarkably detailed account of how Ford laid out fabrication machinery and ran his schedule.

Acknowledgments

This book was supported by the Japan Technology Management Program at the University of Michigan (funded by the Air Force Office of Scientific Research, DOD G-F49620-93-1-0612). I would also like to thank the Tauber Manufacturing Institute for supporting my research on Japanese manufacturing in the United States. An important part of my education in the Toyota Production System that helped me to write this book came from visits to the Toyota Supplier Support Center arranged by Mr. Hajime Ohba. I am very grateful to Toyota for their openness in sharing TPS. Finally, I would like to thank the fine staff at Productivity Press, particularly Diane Asay and Gary Peurasaari, who worked to shape the pieces of the book into a finished, integrated product.

PART ONE

Lean Manufacturing– Is It Transferrable?

 **Jeffrey K. Liker** *is Associate Professor of Industrial and Operations Engineering at the University of Michigan, Ann Arbor. He has been on the faculty since 1982 and has been studying Japanese design and manufacturing methods. In 1991 he cofounded the Japan Technology Management Program at the University of Michigan. Dr. Liker has authored or co-authored 50 articles and book chapters, and four books. He has received three Shingo Prizes for Excellence in Manufacturing Research in 1995, 1996, and 1997—one for a book he lead edited titled* Engineered in Japan: Japanese Technology Management Practices. *Other books about to be released by Dr. Liker are* Remade in America: Transplanting and Transforming Japanese Production Systems *(with Mark Fruin and Paul Adler) and* Concurrent Engineering Effectiveness: Integrating Product Development Across Organizations *(with Mitch Fleischer). Professor Liker has consulted on Japanese design and manufacturing methods for companies such as Whirlpool, Chrysler, Ford, LTV Steel, Renault, Peugeot, Mack Truck, Solar Turbine, and the Industrial Technology Institute.*

1

Introduction: Bringing Lean Back to the U.S.A.

by Jeffrey K. Liker

Some people imagine that Toyota has put on a smart new set of clothes, the kanban system, so they go out and purchase the same outfit and try it on. They quickly discover that they are much too fat to wear it! They must eliminate waste and make fundamental improvements in their production system before techniques like kanban can be of any help.

SHIGEO SHINGO[1]

Everybody is doing it—becoming lean, that is. Or are they just talking about doing it? Toyota started it in Japan out of necessity. They did not have space, they did not have money to hold a lot of inventory, they could not afford to integrate vertically into all their parts businesses, and they needed to build vehicles for a relatively small market demanding a large variety of vehicles. Under those conditions, it was simply impractical to follow the lead of Henry Ford and make large volumes of black Model Ts. So Taichi Ohno had to innovate, and innovate he did—on the shop floor through trial and error, eventually discovering that building cars and parts in a one-piece flow in a leveled and mixed production sequence was vastly superior to large batch and queue production. Over time, the Toyota Production System (TPS) was created (Womack and Jones, 1996; Monden, 1983; Ohno, 1988; Toyota Motor, 1995). With very lean inventory banks, Toyota soon discovered that their outside parts suppliers, which made the vast majority of components, were shutting them down. Suppliers also needed the Toyota Production System, so Toyota started training their suppliers and set up an organization to do this. TPS was developed inside Toyota over about a decade, and at least another decade was needed to teach it to their suppliers. Toyota has been improving the system ever since.

We all know the story of the 1977 oil embargo, the long gas lines in the United States, the shift by Americans to small Japanese cars, and the wake-up call that sent to the U.S. auto industry. What is less known is that the oil embargo also sent Japan into a recession and had at least as profound an effect on Japanese industry. When the oil embargo rocked Japan and most automakers were struggling to stay afloat, Toyota bounced right back because of their low inventories and internal flexibility to make multiple models on the same line. The rest of Japanese industry looked on with awe, and soon TPS was being taught to much of Japanese industry. It was implemented to varying degrees in many companies, though none carried it as far as Toyota and their closely knit band of affiliated suppliers.

TPS has continually been under challenge in Japan ever since. Whenever there are indications that the just-in-time (JIT) system has weaknesses—for example, in the aftermath of the great Kobe earthquake or the 1996 fire in Aisin Seiki that shut down all of Toyota's assembly plants—the Japanese press has been quick to conclude that Toyota's system is history. Yet what seems more impressive to me than the vulnerability of the system to these catastrophes is its resilience. In both cases, Toyota was up and running within one week and at full force within a couple of weeks. The glee with which the Japanese press seems willing to declare TPS dead suggests a resentment and nervousness about Toyota's system. Why? When it works it is a frighteningly powerful competitive advantage, but to accomplish it and keep it going is very difficult!

In the 1980s, Toyota brought TPS over to the United States in a joint venture with GM called New United Motor Manufacturing, Inc. (NUMMI). The success of NUMMI has become legendary in the auto industry because most of a very militant work force known for wildcat strikes returned to a renovated plant, were taught TPS, were treated well under Toyota's management philosophy, and broke all of General Motor's records for cost, quality, and delivery (Adler, 1993). Toyota then did it again in Georgetown, Kentucky—this time at a greenfield site with a nonunionized work force. The plants in Georgetown have won just about every quality award and are regularly at the top of The Harbour Report on productivity in stamping, assembly, and engine manufacture.

Discovering Lean in the United States

U.S. industry was not standing still in the 1980s. When the Japanese competitive threat became apparent to all, we aggressively worked on improving our quality. No customer would put up with 5–10 percent defect levels when Japanese plants were shipping a handful of defects per million units. We saw that Japanese workers participated in problem solving through quality circles, and we saw that good Japanese companies built quality in, rather than trying to inspect it in after the fact. Quality consultants made a fortune teaching about employee problem solving and statistical quality methods. We learned to focus on the customer, customer, customer! Good stuff? You bet. Was it enough? Not nearly—because competing on quality is not enough. We also need to compete on cost and timely delivery.

For some reason, which I do not claim to understand, it took us at least a decade from the early 1980s to the early 1990s to figure out that there was more to Japanese manufacturing than individual techniques like quality circles, statistical process control (SPC), and preventative maintenance. Probably we were in denial and saw what we wanted to see. It also took us that long to realize that not all Japanese companies were created equal and that Toyota was the leader of the pack in manufacturing excellence—certainly in automobiles, and their model applies to other industries as well. Womack and Jones finally revealed in *Lean Thinking* (1996: pp. 238–239) that most of the Japanese advantages they wrote about in *The Machine That Changed the World* (1990) were attributable to Toyota, which stood out in their data above other excellent Japanese auto companies.

A small number of U.S. companies woke up sooner than others. For example, Jacobs Vehicle Equipment Company ("Jake Brake"), discussed by George Koenigsaeker in Chapter 13, first began the journey to TPS in 1986 while working with former members of the Toyota Group's production engineering staff. Within three years, the performance improvements were astounding. There are other stories of U.S. companies that successfully adopted Toyota methods with outstanding results in the 1980s (cf. Womack and Jones, 1996; Schonberger, 1986), though the number is few, and by the end of the 1980s one had to travel far and wide to find these few living examples in the United States outside of Toyota or other Japanese ventures.

Toyota did much to bring TPS to the United States. For a variety of reasons, including the fact that they had committed to the U.S. government to source parts locally as much as possible, they set up a separate corporation to give free help to U.S. companies wishing to learn TPS. The Toyota Supplier Support Center (TSSC) was set up in September 1992 with a few TPS experts from Toyota and some group leaders from Toyota, Georgetown to help U.S. suppliers implement TPS. John Shook was an assistant general manager of TSSC at that time and gives a personalized account of the experience in Chapter 2. The approach was the same one used successfully by Toyota's Operations Management Consulting Group with Japanese suppliers in Japan: Set up a model line with as much of TPS as possible over a period of months, and then expect the plant management to proliferate TPS throughout the rest of the plant. The model lines were fantastic and showed the same triple-digit improvements that had been experienced time after time when TPS was implemented in Japanese suppliers. One of the first companies TSSC worked with was Garden State Tanning. Sean Traynor, who led the company through this transformation, tells that story in Chapter 6. The only problem was that in many of the plants they worked with, TPS never got much farther than the model line. It did not proliferate.

Later in the 1990s, the Big Three got religion. For example, beginning in 1995 we ran an annual conference on lean manufacturing in Dearborn, Michigan, which was sponsored by the University of Michigan. By the 1997 conference, all of the Big Three declared unequivocally that they were transforming all of their manufacturing to their own versions of TPS. In speech after speech, Toyota was touted as the best manufacturing company in the world because of their production system. This led Jim Womack, a discussant, to query: "So we are all Toyota guys now. What does that mean?"

What Is Lean?

What does it mean to get religion and say, "We are doing TPS"? What is the essence of TPS? How would we know if we were doing it? What does it take to do it? The essence of TPS is discussed by John Shook in Chapter 2, so I will not go into detail here, but I will relate the definition I learned from John Shook, who brought it from Toyota: "A manufacturing philosophy that shortens the time line between the customer order and the shipment by eliminating waste." This does not mean that you keep a large supply of inventory in a warehouse and ship immediately when the customer orders. It means that you build what the customer orders as soon as possible after the order and that the total lead time is as short as possible. Any time a product is sitting, just waiting in a queue somewhere, this is waste.

In their latest book, *Lean Thinking,* James Womack and Daniel Jones reduce this to three elements: flow, pull, and striving for excellence. To be a lean manufacturer requires a way of thinking that focuses on making the product flow through production without interruption, a pull system that cascades back from customer demand by replenishing what the next operation takes away at short intervals, and a culture in which everyone is striving continuously to improve. It's that simple! But is that simple? The answer is clearly no! After watching decades of success by Toyota—and Japanese companies that learned from Toyota—U.S. companies are only now beginning to implement TPS on a large scale. Even when Toyota installed TPS for some of their U.S. suppliers on model production lines and demonstrated levels of performance that the suppliers never thought possible, U.S. companies still were often unable to spread the system effectively to their other lines. General Motors watched NUMMI outperform all other GM production facilities for ten years and still did not substantially introduce TPS in their other plants. For some reason, TPS is not easy for U.S. automakers to implement.

Why All the Fuss About Implementation?

So what is so difficult? TPS is a system, not a set of isolated practices, and some of its fundamental principles fly in the face of common sense—mass production thinking. It is easy to understand that we want to build in quality and that we want reliable equipment. Who would argue that a messy, disorganized workplace is better than a clean, organized workplace? But focusing on quality, machine reliability, and workplace organization/visual factory (5S) does not get you to continuous flow, pull, and striving for excellence. What is less easy to see under mass production thinking is why we would want to shut a machine down after we have made just enough production, or why we would want to get rid of that safety stock on the floor, or why we might want five smaller machines dedicated to separate product lines rather than a single large machine that provides economies of scale, or why we would want to change over a machine several times in a shift instead of running one product flat out for a shift to improve our equipment utilization. Our accounting systems and mass production sensibilities tell us that these things may have made sense to Toyota when they lacked space and money and sufficient demand to justify mass production, but they do not make sense in today's mass production environment.

Throughout *Becoming Lean* we adhere to the lean concept as exemplified by the Toyota Production System. We chose the word "becoming" because we have learned from Toyota that lean manufacturing (or whatever we choose to call it) is a process, a journey, not an end state. The focus is on reducing non-value-added waste. Waste is anything that impedes the flow of product as it is being transformed in the value chain. It means getting product where it is needed, when it is needed, in the quantity needed—not more or less. Quality problems impede flow, as do inventory buffers and time spent in transit. While some of this waste is necessary (for example, product must be moved), the goal is to drive out as much of the non-valued activity as possible. Only if we are doing this are we "becoming lean."

Many books are available that tell us in great detail what the Toyota Production System is and how it works (cf. Suzaki, 1983; Shingo, 1989; Monden, 1983; numerous Productivity Press books). These are all valuable. Obviously, we need to understand the system to implement it. But time after time at conferences for manufacturing managers, I have been struck by the heightened interest of the audience when someone talks about implementation. Through stories about the travails of implementation, the system comes alive. Because we can see ourselves in these stories, I decided to bring some of them to print. This book is a kind of tour of implementation at lean plants.

Ford's Transition from Lean to Mass to Becoming Lean

It is impossible to discuss the genesis of lean manufacturing seriously without acknowledging its roots in Henry Ford's production system, as Jim Womack pointed out in his foreword. Ford went through a historical transformation when Henry Ford used the moving assembly line to build automobiles and raised the daily wage to $5. As I am putting the finishing touches on this book, Ford is busily attempting another historical transformation to lean manufacturing worldwide. I was hoping to include an entire chapter on Ford's transformation, but Ford executives felt it was too early in their implementation process to publish a detailed account. However, it is still instructive to consider the historical evolution of Ford and examine, at an admittedly superficial level based on public sources,[1] Ford's version of TPS and their approach to lean. This sets the stage for the more detailed accounts of factory transformations in Part Two of this book.

Ask a Toyota executive about the genesis of the Toyota Production System and he will probably tell you it all started with Henry Ford. In 1908, as the first producer of economical motor cars, Ford's best strategy was to satisfy that demand with mass production of the Model T. This required producing cheaply one simple car in one color in mass quantities. The conditions faced by Henry Ford could not have been more different from those faced by Toyota when they developed TPS.

On the other hand, as we look more deeply into Henry Ford's book, we are struck by his visions of continuous flow and the elimination of waste. For example, the following quote from Henry Ford's book, *Today and Tomorrow* (p. 112) could have been written by Ohno himself:

Ordinarily, money put into raw materials or into finished stock is thought of as live money. It is money in the business, it is true, but having a stock of raw material or finished goods in excess of requirements is waste—which, like every other waste, turns up in high prices and low wages.

At the time, Henry Ford went farther than anyone in creating flow in his company. The River Rouge complex was the model for Toyota City. Henry Ford's vision for the Rouge was to bring in raw materials and drive out finished cars. To make this as efficient as possible, he put all the plants he needed together in one complex. Delivery and manufacturing were done on a just-in-time basis. The engineers and managers worked diligently to drive out waste. Work methods analysis was an evolving science applied to all manual labor. He then replicated this model in Cologne, Germany and Dagenham, England. Clearly, Henry Ford went much further than the moving assembly line in his vision of continuously flowing materials:

> The thing is to keep everything in motion and take the work to the man and not the man to the work. That is the real principle of our production, and conveyors are only one of many means to an end. (Henry Ford, *Today and Tomorrow*, p. 103)

If this was Henry Ford's vision, and to a large degree the practice in the early days of Ford Motor Company, how did the U.S. auto industry find itself in such dismal shape in the 1970s—little growth in productivity, massive inventories from raw material to finished goods, poor quality, and adversarial union-management relationships? The obvious answer is in the economic conditions of the times. It has now become old hat to point to America's hunger for cars in a market in which the Big Three were the only game in town. Anything built could be sold, so the focus was on getting product out the door. Of course, in the chaos of a push-based mass production system, getting products out the door is not a trivial matter—it takes fire fighting, tough managers, and pressure on everyone. As James Womack points out in his foreword to this book, Henry Ford's vision of flow production quickly became mass production as equipment was grouped by type of process in what he calls "process villages" and batches were pushed from operation to operation and from plant to plant.

Ford's mass production system brought them to where they are today—the second largest automaker and one of the largest corporations in the world. But their success is also their challenge—to take their mega-company with its mega-plants and convert it from mass production to lean production. Ford, like Chrysler and General Motors, has concluded that they must become lean and they are modeling the "Ford Production System" after the Toyota Production System, which they regard as the best in the world.

The easy part of creating the vision for the Ford Production System (FPS) has been completed. The challenge lies ahead at the time of this writing. In the new global economy, Ford faces a challenge never faced in manufacturing history. The challenge is to transform about 140 Ford plants (excluding joint ventures) employing 280,000 people represented by more than 60 unions speaking more than 100 languages and dialects to a new system of production. In this section, I briefly review some of the progress Ford made even before embarking on FPS, and then discuss the Ford Production System and first steps toward implementation.

The Transition to FPS Through a Focus on Quality and People

Few people are aware that in the early 1980s Ford went through a crisis as severe as Chrysler's. Ford never got to the point of a federal bailout, but the need for change was urgent and widely felt within Ford. Ford had a crisis mentality, as vividly illustrated by one executive vice president:[2]

> You can never overestimate how scared we were in 1980–1981. We *really* believed Ford could die. From top executives through middle management and down to the hourly employees, a lot of people got religion. It enabled us to deal with the turf, the egos, and the "not invented here" attitudes that were killing us. This shared sense of impending disaster was so deeply etched that we did not lose intensity in 1984 when things began to look better.

The Japanese challenge hit Ford fast and furiously. Ford suddenly realized that the Japanese were doing something fundamentally different across the ocean, and focused on two things: the Japanese approach to building in quality and their emphasis on continuous improvement through operator involvement. Edward Deming's teachings had a profound effect on the management of Ford. Ford executives listened intently to his philosophy of building in quality. They took seriously his emphasis on using statistics to manage by facts. They believed Ford needed to drive out fear and involve all employees in improvement. The programs initiated in the 1980s and into the 1990s are too numerous to list, but Ford's Employee Involvement program warrants mention.

Employee Involvement (EI) was a radical move for a company with a history of autocratic management. It got a jump-start from the strong support of then CEO Philip Caldwell. His 1979 policy memo (the twenty-first in Ford history) encouraging EI let everyone know that this was a serious change. The letter of agreement with the UAW that followed gave EI support from both sides of the house. The idea of paying hourly people to have meetings and solve problems was revolutionary for Ford. Hourly people in all Ford plants were paid full-time as EI coordinators. In 1982, Ford funded a development and training program contributing five cents for each blue-collar hour worked (the "nickel" fund). These funds, later increased, could only be spent with UAW concurrence, and Ford could not redirect these funds. Ford trained everyone in its plants in teamwork and problem solving and also taught them statistical techniques. EI is not talked about very much at Ford these days, but it was a critical stage in Ford's evolution and a foundation for the current emphasis on shopfloor work groups under FPS. The skills gained, the changes in management philosophy, and the personal growth of the work force and management through that period were phenomenal and lasting.

During the 1980s Ford made remarkable progress on quality and productivity. Ford's success was driven by quality improvements. From 1980 to 1988 the quality of Ford cars and trucks improved by 65 percent, mainly due to the efforts of people, not through improvements in automation.[3] Between 1978 and 1986, the company closed eight plants in North America (and fifteen world-wide), reduced the hourly work force in North America by 45 percent, lowered its break-even volume by 40 percent, and increased productivity 6 percent per year.[4] In 1979, Ford sold 5.8 million vehicles worldwide or about 11.7 per worker; by 1988 Ford sold more than 6.5 million cars and trucks, or more than 18.2 per worker. Ford earned $2,400 per employee in 1979 and more than six times that much ($14,800 per worker) in 1988.

We now read in the popular press that quality is no longer a competitive advantage but a requirement for being in the game. J. D. Power is even questioning whether their Initial Quality Survey is still valuable, since all the leading automotive companies are so close on things gone wrong. For Ford this means that a major challenge is convincing people of the urgent need for change at a time when Ford has been successful in narrowing, and in some cases erasing, the gap in delivered quality to customers. For example, based on an internal Customer New Vehicle Quality Survey in 1986, Ford had about 72 percent customer satisfaction compared to Toyota's 87 percent. By 1995 Ford had 83 percent and Toyota was still at 87 percent, and in 1995 Ford was ahead of GM and Chrysler. So where was the urgent need for change?

There was a similar problem with the data on labor productivity in the *Harbour Report* on labor hours per vehicle.[5] It made Ford look good. In the 1995 report, Ford assembly plants in Atlanta and Chicago were just under Toyota's Georgetown assembly plant in productivity (ranking 4 and 5 after Georgetown's 2 and 3 ranking). Ford's engine plant in Dearborn was neck and neck with Toyota's engine plant in Georgetown (.35 workers per vehicle at Ford compared to Toyota's .34). In the 1996 report Ford slipped a bit on assembly—moving to 9 and 12 for Atlanta and Chicago, respectively. But Toyota also slipped to number 8 for one of the Georgetown plants and to number 11 for NUMMI. Dearborn Engine was still number 2, just shy of Toyota, prompting Harbour to write: "This plant is for real."

So why is there a need to change? The popular press would lead us to believe the gap is closed and the U.S. "Big 3" have caught up with their Japanese competitors. The bottom line is Ford management decided that despite many favorable indicators, their plants are not good enough. It costs too much to produce at the quality levels customers see because there is too much waste in the system. With Ford 2000, management was announcing to the world that Ford wanted to be the best, and to be the best meant fundamental improvements in all core processes within Ford. The next stage of successful manufacturers will focus on eliminating non-value-added waste, creating continuous flow wherever possible, pulling from the customer back through the system, and continually improving all products and processes.

What Is the Ford Production System?

All of the principles of FPS are completely consistent with TPS. Ford heavily benchmarked Toyota and hired some of the best TPS experts in the field. But Ford needed to create its own version of a lean manufacturing system. I describe the system only briefly here since it is consistent with all of the principles outlined in John Shook's chapter in this book.

The main shift is captured by the new FPS operating philosophy. In the past it was *de facto* to "produce the number of scheduled units each day at the lowest plant cost with the highest quality." The key terms here are *scheduled* and *lowest plant cost*. Under the old paradigm, Ford (and others) believed that if it used fancy enough computer systems, central staff could schedule all of its assembly plants, stamping plants, powertrain plants, and parts suppliers, and, as long as everyone built to that schedule, everything would be okay. Unfortunately nobody was building to the schedule. A myriad of unexpected events (machine downtime, defective parts, supplier problems, and on and on) meant that plants never made exactly what was scheduled. Instead, plant management huddled together in morning meetings and figured out what parts were on hand, what machines were running, and what they could build that day. This is the fate of a push system. To control costs, Ford management focused on controllable plant costs, which meant labor and overhead. Plant managers were tasked year after year to reduce costs by reducing labor and overhead, which is only one element in total cost.

By contrast, FPS starts with the customers and the intent is to build what they want based on total cost, thus eliminating the gamesmanship of labor and overhead. The new philosophy is to "build a customer driven product sequence in a predictable and stable manner at the lowest total cost and time with the highest quality." Total cost includes the cost of supplied parts, the cost of engineering, capital costs, and anything else entering into the delivered cost of the product. I discuss the new Ford measurables driving FPS in more detail further on in the chapter. First let's review the guts of FPS.

The Ford Production System

The overall vision that drove the development of the Ford Production System was stated in one sentence as follows:

> A *lean flexible* and *disciplined common production system* that is defined by a set of principles and processes that employs *groups of capable* and *empowered people* who are *learning* and *working safely together* to produce and deliver products that consistently *exceed customers' expectations* in quality, cost, and time.

Within this sentence the highlighted keywords are very powerful. Worthy of note is the vision of a *common* production system. This means that whether in England, Spain, Mexico, the United States, or Brazil, a plant should be following a common system of production—not a trivial matter in a company as big and complex as Ford. Also noteworthy is the central place of people in the vision. The creators and supporters of FPS believe that winning not only the minds but the hearts of everyone involved in manufacturing at Ford was an essential condition for long-term success.

The FPS design team selected a gear assembly (Figure 1-1) for the most visible symbol of FPS. It shows the pinion gears that do the work in a ring gear. This symbol provided a succinct model that was selected to emphasize that FPS is a system of production. Nonalignment of any of the teeth or damage to any part will lead to an inefficient gear system, noise, and roughness that will turn off the customer. But when all the gears are the right size and shape and in working order, we see a smooth flow that is at the heart of

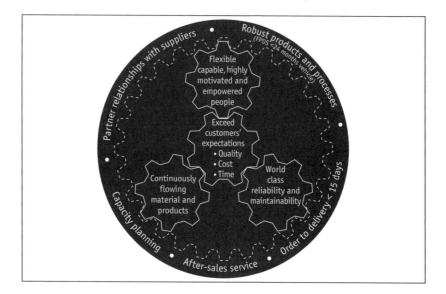

Figure 1-1. Ford Production System (FPS) Gear Model

any vehicle. At the center of this system of gears is the goal—exceeding customers' expectations in quality, cost, and timing.

The three, central, pinion gears needed in a production system that builds products exceeding customer expectations are continuously flowing material and products; world class reliability and maintainability; and flexible, capable, highly motivated and empowered people. The ring gear on the outside encapsulates the supporting systems that tie the production system together:

- Robust products and processes
- An efficient order-to-delivery system
- After-sales service to surprise and delight the customer
- Capacity planning consistent with lean principles
- Partner relationships with suppliers

The gear model provided a vision of how FPS should function, but it did not provide the drivers on which everyone could focus to reach this vision. One more step was needed. This led to breaking down the gear model into seven integrated processes that would be the focus of implementing FPS (see Figure 1-2). Training courses and entire books are written on each of these seven processes, so I discuss them only briefly here and in a somewhat different order from that in Figure 1-2.

1. *Material flow*. Throughout this book you will see how lean manufacturing focuses on reducing the time line by eliminating any wastes that prevent the continuous flow of material. FPS returns to Henry Ford's original vision of continually flowing materials in the entire value chain from raw material suppliers, component plants, and powertrain and stamping plants to final assembly plants. There are many opportunities to improve flow in Ford's external logistics process and inside the four walls of the plant. The vision for material flow includes continuous flow or, where this is not possible, small batch sizes, more frequent deliveries, a pull system, and the flexibility to make every part every day. Ford has separated these initiatives into external logistics (for example, use of third-party logistics providers) and internal logistics. Internally, there is a need to realign capacity across the plant. This means taking out monuments and creating continuous flowing product lines wherever possible, using pull systems for scheduling production, and, most of all, developing a mind-set that says overproduction is waste—stop producing when you have built what is needed.

2. *In-station process control (ISPC)*. This is Ford's version of *jidoka*. Workers at the workstation must immediately detect and contain problems in-station and then immediately take action. They must never pass defects on to the next operation. There are many tools to make this happen—mistake-proofing, built-in process checks, statistical process control, automatic or manual line-stopping, and *Andon* boards. But these are just tools. What is important is that everyone at every station in the value chain understands and acts according to the philosophy of process control.

3. *Ford total productive maintenance (FTPM)*. Keeping material flowing and building in quality depends on equipment that is functioning properly. In the past, Ford scheduled production around which machines were running. When a machine was operational, supervisors wanted it running flat-out to build up inventory stockpiles because they could not be sure when the machine would next go down. Under FPS, excellent productive maintenance is a requirement to support a smooth material flow and ISPC. Moreover, without reliable equipment, a pull system with minimal inventory will simply bring the entire production system to a screeching halt. FTPM was an ongoing program throughout Ford before they developed FPS. Unfortunately, it was hard to motivate people to practice the disciplines diligently as long as there were large inventory buffers and no threat of shutting down the assembly operation when equipment failed. So reducing inventories and FTPM go hand-in-hand.

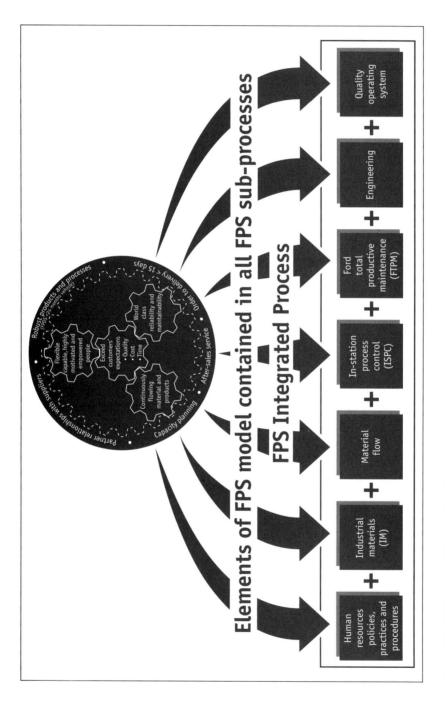

Figure 1-2. FPS Integrated Process Model

4. *Quality operating system*. Even before FPS, Ford had implemented quality operating systems for all of its processes on the shop floor and in the office. This included a detailed accounting of the critical dimensions that needed to be controlled and a "dynamic control plan" for each attribute. This plan included collecting statistical data to manage by fact. What FPS adds is that this is now part of a total production system to support material flow and in-station process control.

5. *Engineering*. The first pass at implementing FPS in about 140 manufacturing plants typically means retrofitting existing equipment and processes. In the future, process engineers need to be thinking about lean manufacturing in the earliest engineering phases. Product engineers need to design robust products and think about things like reducing assembly complexity and error proofing: for example, designing the left and right parts so they do not get confused. This requires a level of product-process integration far beyond usual practice. Process engineers also need to design error-proofing into all equipment, which often means working closely with outside equipment vendors and appropriately specifying this. FPS is based on flexible equipment designed for quick changeover, equipment that is smaller, simpler, and fits in line to minimize large monuments that produce in large batches. FPS also calls for designing generic equipment that can be reused and standardized across many plants. Reliability engineering needs to become a more integral part of the design process. Capacity planning needs to change to reflect balanced capacity across the value chain so that all operations in the value stream produce to *takt* time (the pace at which customers buy the product).

6. *Industrial materials*. Ford is applying the same disciplines they use for production materials, like lean material flow, pull systems, and workplace organization, to indirect industrial materials like cleaners, gloves, lubricants, and tools.

7. *People*. All of these systems depend on people to maintain the disciplined procedures and continually improve them lest they become stagnant and degrade. At one location or another, Ford has experimented with just about every form of employee involvement and team concept imaginable, but they have not had a consistent approach to work groups. Often a work group meant a bunch of employees sitting together in a meeting room each week and then going back to working as individuals during the normal work day. Ford management has worked closely with its union leadership to develop a standard model of work groups that empower people on the shop floor to make decisions historically reserved for management. A harder issue has been working out a reward system that rewards workers for learning and contributing to improvement, without pitting worker against worker to win individual suggestion awards. The ultimate goal is for the work group to own their manufacturing process and

manage it as a business. This requires far-reaching changes in standard human resource practices. The main challenge is to build trust that implementing FPS is a joint process between management and labor, a process in which everyone wins.

How Is Ford Changing?

I'm afraid to count the number of times the term "system" is used in this book. A system should be implemented all at once, right? The dilemma of implementing a system in an existing operation is that implementing only pieces gives you limited benefits as well as runs the risk of failing because it does not yet have the support of other essential system elements that need to be in place. But you cannot shut production down for months to change physical systems, implement procedures, and train people. In an existing operation you must develop a staged process to implement lean, one that is specifically designed to meet your particular needs and goals—as all the case studies in this book illustrate. The five-phase process Ford developed is not unusual in the lean manufacturing business and in fact is virtually the same as the process used by the Toyota Supplier Support Center (though its actual implementation differs between Ford and Toyota). The five phases are

1. Stability
2. Continuous flow
3. Synchronous production
4. Pull system
5. Level production

The five phases of implementation refer to the process inside the plant. But this process is supported by external logistics that the corporate material logistics group is handling and that were launched very quickly. External logistics focus on moving materials between plants with more frequent deliveries in smaller quantities, using returnable containers and racks, and also supporting the plant in workstation design to minimize inventory. But the changes inside the plant are still the biggest challenge. Starting with pilot lines, all Ford plants are expected to go through the following five-phase process:

Phase 1: Stability. This phase is a problem-solving activity aimed at creating stable workstations capable of consistent production. It includes total productive maintenance, reducing changeover times, developing Ford's version of standardized work sheets, developing mistake-proofing procedures, solving quality problems, and using 5S procedures to clean up and organize the workplace. (The 5S's are sort, straighten, sanitize, sweep, and sustain—sometimes referred to as sort, set in order, shine, standardize, and sustain.) None of this is new to Ford plants or unique to lean manufacturing. But the FPS team realized that they needed some level of stability before plants can reduce inventories without the risk of shutting the plant down. A result of success in stability is visible improvement and support from others in the plant who begin to see FPS as helpful rather than threatening. This stability phase is used to train employees and communicate what FPS is to the entire plant. Because Ford sees the need to get everyone on board upfront, this stability phase tends to take considerable time. There is a danger of getting stuck in this phase and never getting beyond it.

Phase 2: Continuous flow. The goal is to improve product flow from station to station, ideally in a continuous flow, while maximizing flexibility for changeovers. When continuous flow is not possible, the focus is on reducing batch sizes and in-process buffers: for example, by setting minimum and maximum levels.

Phase 3: Synchronous production. In this phase the goal is stable workstations operating in synchronous time. A key part of this phase is to implement sequenced delivery for selected commodities so that these parts come to the assembly line in the exact sequence in which they will be needed. The goal is to provide six days' firm and sequenced part-level requirements to participating suppliers.

Phase 4: Pull system. Ford intends to establish formal pull systems in this phase so that material is replenished by upstream processes. (To some degree, the minimum and maximum levels in phase 2 will be moving toward a pull system.) They will use various pull signals ranging from physical cards to electronic signals. Electronic broadcasts will be used for replenishment by suppliers.

Phase 5: Level production. The ultimate goal is to produce customer orders at a leveled quantity and mix. Production should be leveled throughout the value chain, which means that all processes must be capable of quick changeover and making "every part every day."

Education and Training: Down, Up, and Sideways

Education has been emphasized by Ford because they believe in the importance of getting support from every group within the plant.

They started at the top of the manufacturing organization by training Ford vice presidents, who were then expected to lead a training session of their direct reports, ultimately cascading the training down to the plant level.

When the training hit the plants the goal was to get the entire management team and bargaining committee on board. This was followed up by additional training and consultation. More intensive training on the first step, stability, is provided to full-time "FPS coordinators" from each plant who come to Dearborn for several weeks. The word that comes to mind for this training process is "massive." With 140 plants and 280,000 people, there is no choice but to treat this training as a mass production activity (though for the purpose of lean production).

Using New Measurables

In a large, multinational corporation, one of the major ways the central offices have control over the distributed plants is through performance measures. For years plant managers were evaluated based on how well they did at reducing labor and overhead based on predetermined targets (called "tasks" within Ford). This was not consistent with all of the tenets of FPS: for example, building only what is needed when it is needed. If you stop production when a maximum inventory level is reached, it means amortizing labor hours over a smaller number of units, which makes the plant look bad. If plant managers were told to implement lean manufacturing but the company only measured on labor and overhead, it was clear that the measures would win out over the vague directives of FPS.

To broaden the set of measurements used to judge plant performance the FPS measurables team first looked at the operating principles for FPS. What was FPS expected to achieve? They then developed measurables corresponding to each principle (see Figure 1-3). What is most critical about these measures is that they drive behaviors consistent with the Ford Production System. By design they are multiple measures, as there is no one behavior that by itself will lead to the creation of a new system of production. They are not all bottom-line cost measures, as the point is to reward behaviors consistent with the new production philosophy, which in the long

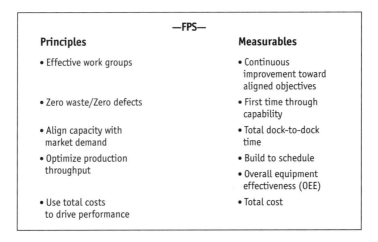

Figure 1-3. Ford Production System (FPS) Key Measurables

run will clearly pay benefits in cost, quality, and delivery. Each measure can be briefly defined as follows:

1. *Work group effectiveness.* This is the most difficult to measure but there are a variety of measures being used, including surveys of employees' perceptions of openness, teamwork, work groups' influence on decisions, and the like. Other measures include formal employee suggestions and a very elaborate approach to the measurement of workplace health and safety.

2. *First-time through capability.* What percentage of parts go through the plant from start to finish without being scrapped, rerun, retested, returned, or diverted? This measure is multiplicative, not additive. For example, if 77 percent of the components are getting through workstation A with no defects and 65 percent are getting through workstation B, the first-time through capability of this two-station system is the product, or 50 percent. In long-linked technologies like engine assembly or vehicle assembly, this means even having a small percentage of defects in individual workstations can affect the ultimate capability of the production line dramatically.

3. *Dock-to-dock time.* This is the elapsed time between unloading of raw materials and the release of finished goods from the plant. How much time did materials spend along the way sitting around waiting for something to happen? Clearly, as you reduce dock-to-dock time, value-added time goes way up. This is the single most important measure for driving plants to eliminate non-value-added wastes associated with large batch production—it defines lean manufacturing. It is heavily dependent

on first-time through capability and on overall equipment effectiveness (defined below).

4. *Build-to-schedule*. It is one thing to build a product quickly and correctly and get it out the door; it is quite another to build what the customer wants. Build-to-schedule is the percentage of units scheduled for a given day that are produced on the correct day and in the correct sequence. It means building the right amount at the right time—as many points are taken away for overbuilding as for underbuilding.

5. *Overall equipment effectiveness*. This is a measure of how well the equipment is performing. It is measured at the constraint operation. It is a product term of equipment availability times performance efficiency times quality rate. This means it goes beyond simple downtime measures and considers what percentage of the time the equipment is running at its rated capacity producing quality parts. It takes into account all of the seven losses associated with total productive maintenance (equipment breakdowns, setup and adjustment losses, tooling losses, startup losses, etc.). This is one measure that goes immediately to the bottom line.

6. *Total cost*. This is the total unit cost of material, labor, overhead, freight, inventory, fixed costs, assessments, and other associated costs. Total cost is the most important overall system driver and requires the biggest cultural shift for management. Labor and overhead are elements that managers can easily grasp and measure, even though they are not always the right ones to measure. Total cost is more amorphous and includes all the direct and allocated costs associated with getting the product out the door and to the customer. It includes many elements outside of the immediate control of the plant manager. This means that to reduce total cost requires a cooperative effort among the plant manager, purchasing, finance, the hourly work force, and engineering. To make this work, the cross-functional team must be judged on total cost, not on labor cost of any particular individual on the team. So working to total cost means putting labor costs in a broader perspective, taking some of the heat off of the team members, and allowing the workers' contributions to quality and elimination of waste to be meaningfully captured in a key measure.

Managing Change in a Large Corporation

Unfortunately, I can only describe the beginnings of this historical transformation at Ford Motor Company to lean manufacturing. Ford is still at the very beginning stages, having recently just crossed the starting line. In fact, some would say the "stability phase" is just preparation to get up to the starting line. The transformation of existing operations is clearly a challenging task, made even more difficult when trying to change so many plants around the world at once. Change means fighting historical patterns and habits that grew from decades of success with the old mass production system. Can you teach old dogs new tricks? When it comes to lean, we believe the answer is yes. When it comes down to the basics, there are three things people care about: 1. providing for their families, 2. getting something out of the job personally to enhance their self-esteem and gain the feeling they are making a contribution, and 3. the success of their companies. Regardless of how different people weigh these necessities, the fact remains that to overcome natural resistance to change, people must feel they are getting more than they are losing. As you read this book you will see that one of the great changes resulting from becoming lean is "employee satisfaction"—workers feel that they are in a much better place than they were when they first started out in the change process.

Unlike a big company like Ford, most of the cases in this book are small companies in which the top leadership could play a direct role in the transformation at each plant. The one exception is the Delphi steering plant in Saginaw. As I read the Delphi case, I could see some similarities to Ford that distinguish these two from the small companies. In Ford and Delphi, the changes are being made to a big company with a history of labor-management struggles. In both cases, a new approach to quality management was discovered in the 1980s with a lot of emphasis placed on employee involvement. Both are unionized companies that have expended a lot of effort (often with mixed success) to work jointly with the union on major change programs. In the shift to lean manufacturing, larger companies naturally place a major emphasis on getting the people in the plant to buy in through intense communication and broad up-front training of the work force. This seems like a natural approach to any major change, but we will see that most of the successful cases in this book used a more action-oriented approach—jumping to shopfloor changes before a great deal of education and training was done. We return to this theme in the Conclusion when we consider lessons learned across the cases in this book.

Preview of Book

The book centers on a set of case studies of plants that are on the journey to becoming lean. The stories focus on the transformations of individual plants. Womack and Jones (1996) make a compelling case for the future of "lean enterprises" that take lean beyond their individual plants. But it has been my experience that U.S. companies have a long way to go to implement lean inside the four walls of the plant, a prerequisite to a lean enterprise. I selected authors who were intimately involved in the implementation process to describe that process in detail. Some of them are managers with operational responsibility, others are executives who took a very hands-on role, and still others are consultants who were at the center of the action. I wanted to provide the reader with the opportunity to hear stories of becoming lean through multiple voices, and I specifically asked authors to tell the story of the process, the struggles, the ups, and the downs. I did not simply want testimonials as to what it was like before and after the miraculous change to lean. I took the lead in writing the Donnelly case, but the rest of the chapters were written by colleagues and associates. I asked that the chapters be written informally, without jargon and academic pontification.

In the following section I provide a preview of each chapter and highlight what I think are the major contributions of each story. Though each story is unique, in a conclusion I revisit what we have learned and try to identify the themes across the different case studies.

Part One: What Is Lean, and Is It Transferable?

In the first section of the book, we discuss what lean manufacturing is and consider whether it can work in the United States, even though the large number of success stories shows us that it can. We elaborate on the definition of lean and Toyota's experiences in transferring it to the United States in Chapter 2, consider the cultural advantages that the Japanese may have in developing lean systems as a result of their unique educational system in Chapter 3, and attempt to quantify statistically the performance benefits of lean methods in a large sample of small U.S. automotive suppliers in Chapter 4.

John Shook tells the story of "Bringing the Toyota Production System to the United States: A Personal Perspective" (Chapter 2), from his perspective as the first American employee at Toyota's world headquarters in Japan. He worked for Toyota from December 1983 until 1994. During that time, he was instrumental in the launch of NUMMI, Toyota Motor Manufacturing/ Georgetown, the Toyota Technical Center, and the Toyota Supplier Support Center. The first person whom many Americans going to Japan to learn about TPS met when they got off the plane was John Shook. He was the tour guide, translator, and teacher to many people from GM when NUMMI was in the planning stages. His personal account of TPS history has never appeared before in print. John Shook argues persuasively that TPS is not simply a collection of techniques, but a way of thinking—a paradigm. He worked with many American suppliers through TSSC, and in a new role as Director of the Japan Technology Management Program at the University of Michigan he has worked with many other American companies struggling to introduce TPS. Throughout these experiences he remains steadfastly optimistic that TPS can and does work very effectively in the United States, but only if a company is willing to make the serious, long-term commitment needed to a new way of thinking about manufacturing.

Most American managers I talk to agree that the early learning and socialization experiences we get going back to kindergarten are not only fundamental in shaping our language and math skills, but also our value systems and behavior patterns. There have been heavy investments by American companies in education. For example, Motorola set up their own university and has been committed to influencing the K-12 system to support their total quality management system. In "Japanese Education and Its Role in Kaizen" (Chapter 3), Jennifer Yukiko Orf, who is Japanese-American, tells of her unique experiences in attending both Japanese and U.S. schools. This chapter started as a paper for a course I taught on "Japanese Technology Management." I quickly discovered that I had a student who knew far more than I did about the Japanese educational system. As Jennifer Orf studied industrial engineering at the University of Michigan and learned about Japanese kaizen, it became clear to her that her Japanese education had prepared her perfectly to participate in kaizen activities. In her experience, Japanese children from kindergarten on learn to work in small groups (*han*), solve problems, follow standardized procedures, document their processes, improve their processes, collect and analyze data, and most importantly, self-manage within a peer group. From this very personal chapter, American managers can better understand how intricately connected the socialization of Japanese children is with their later kaizen roles in Japanese corporations.

I was concerned that this chapter might send the wrong message—that because the Japanese are raised differently from kindergarten on, we cannot implement lean manufacturing unless we change our entire education system to match theirs. Obviously, I believe it is possible for Americans to follow standard methods and to contribute to continuous improvement or I would not have bothered with this book. Nonetheless, this chapter does provide a warning. The part of lean manufacturing that depends on people "striving for excellence" will be more difficult in the United States than it has been in Japan. To "get it" and actively participate in continuous improvement of lean manufacturing, Americans will clearly need significant compensatory education to achieve a level of experience that Japanese students have gained throughout their educational lives.

Do we really have hard evidence that lean manufacturing works in the United States? We have a lot of case studies with dramatic before and after measures, as illustrated by the case studies in this book, in Womack and Jones (1996), and other books (for example, Schonberger, 1986). If you still need more convincing, read Steven Rasch's "Lean Manufacturing Practices at Small and Medium-Sized U.S. Parts Suppliers—Does It Work?" (Chapter 4). Steve Rasch's work is based on statistical analysis of data from 249 small suppliers of automotive component parts in the Midwest and looks in the aggregate at the relationship between various facets of lean manufacturing and performance outcomes. There have been other studies like this that rely heavily on opinions based on five-point scale ratings—"Do you agree or disagree?" Steve Rasch uses hard numbers wherever possible (inventory turns, for example). His results show convincingly that each of the major aspects of lean is associated with performance improvements, including built-in quality systems, JIT production, high-involvement team-based organization, and lean supply systems. Moreover, he finds a significant interaction between production worker involvement and authority on the one hand, and the use of JIT and preventative maintenance (PM) on the other. That is, the technical features of JIT and PM lead to improvement, and the social features of employee involvement and influence lead to improvement. In combination, these technical and social features have a multiplier effect that is more than the sum of the parts. Rasch's analysis comes the closest to quantifying the "systems" benefits of TPS that we have been claiming.

Part Two: Case Studies of Implementing Lean

The case studies section, with its stories of the process of transforming individual factories, is the heart of the book. In selecting these cases, I could have focused on only the most complete implementations of TPS—the TPS stars. But most American companies do not have the luxury of daily mentorship by Toyota experts. I did not want this book to be like the weight-loss commercials that show Cindy Crawford and Arnold Schwarzenegger working out. Unfortunately, most of us are not built like these natural wonders. What you will read about instead is a range of plants making different products in various industries and experiencing a variety of problems in their struggle to become lean. If lean sounds like anything other than a struggle, someone is glossing over the details. Talk to the workers if you want to learn about the real story; it is seldom one of straightforward, linear improvement. A close look at Toyota, Georgetown reveals some of the early struggles that even they had with implementing kanban (for example, losing cards) and teaching Americans the importance of standardized work. Keeping the system at a high level of performance and discipline is an ongoing struggle at Georgetown.

We begin with a General Motors internal parts plant in Delphi Saginaw Steering Systems and get a picture of implementing lean in a large, old-line, mass production operation. We then describe the transformation of plants in three external auto parts suppliers. But we do not want to give the impression that TPS started in automotive and ends in automotive, or that it only applies to relatively large-size and large-volume manufacturers. We examine three cases outside of automotive, all relatively small companies making small filtration devices, cedar birdhouses, and large cables used for underwater geophysical exploration, respectively.

Most of what I had heard about General Motors managers going to NUMMI (GM's joint venture with Toyota) for training and returning to GM to implement the system suggested very little transfer of the Toyota Production System, but Mike Husar proved me wrong, at least in Plant No. 6 of Delphi Saginaw Steering Systems. In "Transforming a Plant to Lean in a Large, Traditional Company: Delphi Saginaw Steering Systems, GM" (Chapter 5), we learn how Mike Husar, who had spent time at NUMMI, became plant manager of a traditional, existing United Auto Workers (UAW) plant staffed with highly senior employees (half the plant had more than 25 years at that plant), and over a five-year period made substantial progress in transforming most of the plant toward lean manufacturing. Customer rejects went from almost 2,000 parts per million in 1993 to 75 ppm in 1997. Cost reductions have ranged from 6 to 11 percent most years. Productivity has improved by almost 8 percent per year. Whereas in 1991 less than half of employees made improvement suggestions, this was increased to 90 percent by 1997. And Occupational Safety and Health Administration (OSHA) reportable accidents have declined significantly. This was all accomplished through extensive employee involvement and a close working relationship with the union. The story is told by Daniel Woolson, a University of Michigan student who worked in Plant No. 6, and cowritten with Mike Husar.

In Chapter 2, we learn from John Shook about his experiences in helping to establish the Toyota Supplier Support Center. TSSC was set up to help U.S. manufacturers implement TPS. One of the first companies they worked with was Garden State Tanning (GST). As CEO, Sean Traynor was the executive sponsor for the transformation to lean at GST. In "Making Leather Leaner: The

Garden State Tanning Story" (Chapter 6), Sean Traynor tells us about the fascinating process of making tanned leather from cow hides. Quality is critical, as this is a product purchased exclusively for its esthetic quality. Each hide is unique and contains some defects. When GST was fortunate enough to get a large order from Lexus in 1991, they quickly found that they could not keep up with the order quantity and before long were several months behind in fulfilling orders. Within Toyota's JIT system, this was devastating. The result was expensive air freight deliveries overseas to Japan and an unhappy customer. Rather than drop GST as a supplier, Toyota helped teach and implement TPS, at first through their purchasing department and later through TSSC.

Although it seemed initially to Sean Traynor that hides were by necessity a large batch operation that could not be made into a continuous flow operation, once again a doubter was proven wrong. A shift was made from a process-oriented approach to cells including cutters, packers, inspectors, etc. The work load was balanced. The result was a reduction in lead time of cutting and packing tanned leather for shipment from 10 days to two hours. Through this and other changes to lean manufacturing over two years, inventories were cut in half, and despite the reduced inventory, better scheduling through kanban resulted in virtual elimination of emergency air freight. Quality defects were cut from 1 percent to .05 percent (one-twentieth of the former level). Productivity in the cutting operation was increased by almost two-thirds, and lost-time accidents were reduced from 242 to 2 per year.

The wide range of approaches to implementation used by different companies is striking in these case studies. Freudenberg-NOK, the largest manufacturer of sealing components in the world, is by now quite well known for their impressive continuous improvement process led by Joseph Day, CEO. Unlike the Toyota approach of focusing on implementing the total system on one model line, they managed significant progress toward lean manufacturing through thousands of individual kaizen events. Joe Day took a struggling company and after some false starts began religiously applying repeated kaizen events to part after part of plant after plant, and eventually transformed much of the company.

He learned about the kaizen process from Wiremold, Inc., which is discussed in detail by Womack and Jones (1996). He tells this story in "Learning About Lean Systems at Freudenberg-NOK: Where Continuous Improvement Is a Way of Life" (Chapter 7). Between September 1992, when their GROWTTH program was launched, and 1996, sales grew from $200 million to $600 million with unprecedented profit levels. Joe Day attributes this to their dramatic improvements in quality, delivery times, and cost reductions through about 2,500 kaizen events in 15 manufacturing plants involving 90 percent of their 3,500 employees. A key factor of this success was the personal involvement of Joe Day and all of his top executives as members of kaizen teams. For the first two years of GROWTTH, Joe Day reports spending 30 percent of his work week on nothing but kaizen implementation.

Donnelly Mirrors went through many phases of becoming lean, including a series of radical kaizen events similar to what the GROWTTH program advocates. Donnelly, the world's leading manufacturer of automotive mirrors and known as a pioneer in human relations, has been moving toward lean manufacturing throughout its operations. Keith Allman, the plant manager, and I write about "The Donnelly Production System: Lean at Grand Haven" (Chapter 8). Donnelly has been named among the top ten companies in the book *The 100 Best Companies to Work for in America*, and Grand Haven exemplifies the people-oriented policies that won them this honor. This nonunion company has no time clocks, a no-layoff policy, job sharing, and a nursery service. Hourly associates meet each year to decide how big their pay raises will be.

Donnelly also demonstrates, however, that strong employee involvement does not necessarily equate to high quality and efficiency. The Grand Haven plant was launched in 1988 to provide exterior mirrors to Honda. From the start it had difficulty in meeting Honda's high quality expectations. The plant struggled over the years, trying quality program after quality program. It had some good years and some bad years. By 1995, the plant was in a crisis. Because of late shipments and poor quality, the message from Honda was to either shape up or lose their business. Donnelly embarked on a process based on externally led kaizen events averaging one four-day event every two weeks over a period of a year. Donnelly managed to "stop the bleeding" and get back on track with Honda, but at the cost of a major loss of employee morale and subsequent attempts to unionize.

In 1996, Grand Haven shifted toward a systems-oriented approach led by an hourly operator–staffed continuous improvement team. Over less than two years, Grand Haven shifted from a batch-and-queue process to a comparatively lean operation, reducing customer shipped defects by 80 percent, cutting internal scrap rates in half, almost eliminating premium freight, reducing inventory on hand by a factor of five, and improving productivity by 29 percent. The Grand Haven plant raises an important question: Does the transformation to lean need to be fast and furious and imposed from the outside on the work force, or can it be a gradual, incremental process with substantial employee involvement from the start? This case provides the question but not the answer, though it seems that some blend of "just do it!" and genuine employee involvement is needed.

The first non-auto example we take up is in the medical products industry. In "Implementing Lean Manufacturing at Gelman Sciences, Inc." (Chapter 9), we hear from Matt Zayko and Doug Broughman of Pall Gelman Sciences in Ann Arbor, Michigan and Professor Walt Hancock of the University of Michigan. Pall Gelman Sciences is a rapidly growing, small company that was performing reasonably well as a business before embarking on the journey to lean manufacturing. In February 1997, Gelman merged with Pall Corporation, a world leader in microfiltration and separations with sales of over $1 billion. This chapter provides a detailed historical view that starts with their attempts to focus on process control and work teams, which had only limited direct benefits until Gelman began to focus on flow. After engineers attended a workshop on the design of cells, all of the work teams were trained and asked to submit an ideal vision of a one-piece flow cell, though it took a trigger event to move the plant into implementation. The trigger event was a visit by the new parent company to see the manufacturing cells. Only one team volunteered to display their cell, and only if their plans were implemented as they had proposed.

The implementation happened almost overnight. In this lead manufacturing cell, inventory was cut by almost two-thirds, lead times were cut in half, and inventory turns increased 185 percent. The result has been major improvements in on-time deliveries, increased productivity, and improved quality. This plant quickly became a model for manufacturing practice within the rest of Gelman and indeed for all of Pall Corporation. At the time this chapter was written, Gelman's lead plant was still in the early stages of transformation to lean. The authors give a very detailed description of the process of change, the resistance they faced, and the results they were able to achieve.

"Cedar Works: Making the Transition to Lean" (Chapter 10) was written by Bill Costantino of RWD Consulting, who learned TPS first-hand at Toyota, Georgetown as a group leader responsible for several teams of associates. He decided to leave Toyota to help spread TPS to American manufacturers. One of his first clients was Cedar Works, a manufacturer of a variety of outdoor cedar products such as elaborate birdhouses. One might imagine this to be more of a small-batch craft operation to which lean concepts do not apply, and that was also the first reaction of many managers at Cedar Works. Bill Costantino was also concerned as to whether his automotive experience would transfer to making birdhouses. The impressive performance improvements in this company demonstrate that the lean system indeed does work quite effectively in this very different context. Bill Costantino gives us a blow-by-blow description of the process of selling the plan to management, as well as describing the training processes that followed the plan-do-check-act (PDCA) cycle, with hands-on application of everything taught, and takes us through the stages of development. At the end of each stage, he reflects on what worked, what did not work, and what might help other plants progress more rapidly up the learning curve. The chapter is filled with useful charts and tools for analysis and training.

Our final case study is "Operational Excellence: A Manufacturing Metamorphosis at Western Geophysical Exploration Products" (Chapter 11), by Mark F. McGovern and Brian J. Andrews of the Phoenix Consulting Group. Western Geophysical Exploration

Products manufactures seismic exploration equipment in Texas. Mark McGovern was hired as a consultant to help implement lean manufacturing and in this chapter focuses on the successful transformation of the Bay Cable manufacturing area of one plant. These cables are 1,250 feet in length, 1.5 inches in diameter, and weigh about 1,500 pounds. They are used by seismic data collection crews working in shallow water less than 200 feet deep. When the transformation process started, the Bay Cable manufacturing process was in desperate need of improvement. It experienced 50 percent more demand than it ever produced, first-run yields below 50 percent, high field failure rates, poor on-time delivery, high inventory levels, frequent material shortages, and high cable costs. By redesigning the flow from a process-oriented layout to product-oriented cells, Bay Cable movement was reduced from almost 1 mile to .3 mile and floor space was reduced by 30 percent. Cellular manufacturing also led to immediate quality feedback among workers on adjacent processes. Through this feedback, combined with cross-training and problem-solving training, responsibility for quality was spread throughout the cell. As a result, first-time yields increased from less than 50 percent to over 90 percent and final yields increased from 75 percent to almost 100 percent. Other improvements were aimed at controlling work in progress (WIP) through kanban, adding visual controls, and using kanban for supplied parts. WIP went from over 60 cables to 12 cables, lead time was reduced from over 30 days to less than 5 days, and material shortages became almost nonexistent.

Part Three: Managing the Change Process

In this last section of the book, we step back and take a broader look at the change process. The chapters still include case examples but with less focus on a blow-by-blow description of individual plants. Rather, the authors consider more general lessons learned about the change process.

In this book we focus on success stories, but not all companies are able to take the first critical steps to lean manufacturing successfully. In "The Successes and Failures of Implementing Continuous Improvement Programs: Cases of Seven Automotive Parts Suppliers"

(Chapter 12), Thomas Choi of Bowling Green State University conducts a systematic, comparative study of seven small automotive parts plants that launched continuous improvement programs at the same time. We do not wish to imply that these companies were focused on true lean manufacturing as described in this book. In fact, most of the focus of the companies was on workplace organization, and most of the companies never got to the point of continuous flow or pull systems. These cases are instructive because they show us how some small companies with limited resources can get derailed in their early stages of implementation and how others can progress rapidly through work organization and begin to move toward lean manufacturing. Tom Choi followed these companies for the first two years of their efforts. He found that out of seven, only three had any degree of success; the other four got little out of their efforts. He gives a detailed account of the successes and failures and extrapolates lessons for the implementation of continuous improvement programs.

We next hear from a veteran of lean manufacturing implementation in the United States. You may have read about George Koenigsaecker in *Lean Thinking*. In their vivid description of the transformation of Jake Brake, Jim Womack and Daniel Jones described George Koenigsaecker as one of the executives (actually president at the time) at first called a "hopeless concrete head" by Mr. Iwata of Shingijutsu (a consulting firm of former Ohno disciples). Although several times Iwata refused to help Jake Brake, George was extremely persistent and eventually convinced Iwata he was serious about transforming Jake Brake to TPS. One of Iwata's requirements was that they do whatever he told them to do. In "Lean Production—The Challenge of Multidimensional Change" (Chapter 13), George Koenigsaecker tells about the "just-do-it" mind-set that transformed his outlook on manufacturing transformation. Jake Brake became one of the great American success stories in the transformation to lean manufacturing, and George has gone on to work his magic as the president of The Hon Company. He reflects on what he learned at Jake Brake and considers the technical skills, the psychological aspects, and the management styles that are necessary for successful "multidimensional change."

Mike Rother, a consultant with TWI Network and manager of lean manufacturing outreach in the University of Michigan's Japan Technology Management Program, has worked with well over 100 companies in different parts of the country to help them implement lean manufacturing, ranging from tiny mom-and-pop shops to multinational corporations. As a consultant to these companies, he has amassed a range of experiences from out-and-out failure to considerable success. If one were to list the places in the country where we would expect Mike Rother to have the most success, we probably would not put the Mississippi Delta region at the top of the list. Yet this is exactly where a surprising number of manufacturers are having great success introducing lean concepts. Mike Rother has found receptive ears from executives who have the interest, drive, and commitment to implement new approaches to manufacturing. In "Crossroads: Which Way Will You Turn on the Road to Lean?" (Chapter 14), Mike Rother divides his experiences along two distinct paths, "superficial lean" and "true lean." He shares some succinct lessons regarding the challenges of implementing true lean manufacturing and illustrates his points with entertaining cartoons.

I wrap up the book in "Conclusion: What We Have Learned About Becoming Lean" (Chapter 15). Of course, I cannot summarize in a few short pages all the rich lessons that come through in the 14 chapters of detailed case studies and thoughtful reflections, but we can identify some common themes as well as differences in approaches across plants. There is no systematic, scientific way of resolving differences. We cannot conclude that one way is the best way, nor can we say definitively that all ways are equally good, but we can raise the questions that you will need to answer as you embark on becoming lean.

Notes

1. Shingo, Shigeo, *A Study of the Toyota Production System*, Portland, Oregon: Productivity Press, 1989, p. 64.

References

1. This section on the Ford Production System is based on public seminars put on by the University of Michigan in Dearborn, Michigan (May 1997) and Traverse City, Michigan (August 1997), on presentations to classes at UM by Hank Lenox and Ron Holcomb of Ford, and on published reports.

2. These quotes and much of this section on Ford's transformation were based on a Harvard Business School Case, "Transformation at Ford," by Mark Pelofsky, Harvard University, 1989, p. 5.

3. See "Transformation at Ford," by Mark Pelofsky, Harvard University, 1989.

4. Beverly Geber, "The Resurrection of Ford," *Training*, April 1989, p. 24.

5. *Harbour Report*, Troy, Mich.: Harbour Publications, 1995, 1996.

Bibliography

Adler, P. "Time-and-Motion Regained." *Harvard Business Review*. Jan.-Feb. 1993: 97-108.

Ford, Henry. *Today and Tomorrow*. Portland: Productivity Press reprint edition, 1988.

The Harbour Report: Manufacturing Productivity Company by Company—Plant by Plant. Troy, Michigan: Harbour Publications, 1995, 1996, 1997.

Monden, Y. *The Toyota Production System*. Atlanta: Institute of Industrial Engineers, 1983.

Ohno, T. *The Toyota Production System: Beyond Large-Scale Production*. Portland, Oregon: Productivity Press, 1988.

Schonberger, R.J. *World Class Manufacturing: The Lessons of Simplicity Applied*. New York: Free Press, 1986.

Shingo, S. *A Study of the Toyota Production System from an Industrial Engineering Viewpoint*. Portland, Oregon: Productivity Press, 1989.

Suzaki, K. *The New Manufacturing Challenge*. New York: Free Press, 1983.

Toyota Motor Corporation. *The Toyota Production System*. Operations Management Consulting Division and International Public Affairs Division. Toyota City: Toyota Motor Corporation, 1995.

Womack, J.P., and D.T. Jones. *Lean Thinking: Banish Waste and Create Wealth in Your Corporation*. New York: Simon & Schuster, 1996.

Womack, J., Jones, D., and Roos, D. *The Machine That Changed the World*. New York: Rawson Associates, 1990.

 **John Y. Shook** *is Director of the Japan Technology Management Program at the University of Michigan and teaches in the Department of Industrial and Operations Engineering. John divides his time between university work and consulting with auto industry companies and others on how to understand and implement lean manufacturing through TWI Network, a network of lean manufacturing consultants.*

For 11 years John worked for Toyota in Japan and the United States. He joined Toyota in 1983 in Toyota City to help with the process of transferring the company's management and production systems to NUMMI, and subsequently to other manufacturing facilities around the world. His first encounter with the Toyota Production System came from building Corollas at the Takaoka Plant in Toyota City. He later created internal TPS training manuals and led TPS training sessions. During his seven-year stay at Toyota's worldwide headquarters, he became the company's first (and still only) American "Kacho" (manager) in Japan.

In the United States, John became a part of Toyota's North American engineering and R&D center in Ann Arbor in 1991. As general manager of administration, his responsibilities included planning, purchasing, public affairs, and general administration. His last position with Toyota was as senior American manager with the Toyota Supplier Support Center in Lexington, Kentucky. It was the company's newly established organization to assist the efforts of U.S. companies to implement the Toyota Production System.

John has a B.A. from the University of Tennessee, an M.A. from the University of Hawaii, and is a graduate of the Japan-America Institute of Management Science. He is a frequent presenter at academic and industry forums and is often cited in major publications such as Fortune, Business Week, Time, Automotive News, *the* Nikkei Shinbun, *and others.*

2

Bringing the Toyota Production System to the United States: A Personal Perspective

by John Y. Shook

Editor's prologue: In December 1983, John Shook became the first U.S. employee to work at Toyota's world headquarters in Japan. He would work for them until 1994. During that time, he was instrumental in the launch of New United Motors Manufacturing, Inc. (NUMMI), TMM/Georgetown, the Toyota Technical Center, and the Toyota Supplier Support Center. John helped Toyota formalize their model of the Toyota Production System (TPS) so they could teach it to others. He has personally taught TPS to thousands of Americans throughout the auto industry. In this chapter, John provides his personal perspective on what TPS or "lean manufacturing" is, and tells us the story of his role in bringing TPS to the United States and its unique adaptation to the GM Fremont plant (NUMMI). But before that could happen, there were several lessons he had to experience to really understand the "system." What it boils down to is that TPS is not simply a collection of techniques, but a way of thinking, a philosophy—a paradigm. Herein lies one of the greater challenges in implementing TPS in the United States; while we're good at "putting out fires" and reacting to a "crisis," we still don't get it that it takes a whole-system approach to prevent problems and continuously improve our processes and products. In this chapter, John addresses the challenges of implementing TPS in the United States. He defines the major techniques and principles of TPS, like *jidoka, just-in-time, heijunka, kanban,* *one-piece flow*, *takt time*, and *kaizen*. You will encounter these same techniques and principles throughout this book as you read about how other U.S. manufacturers have faced the challenge of becoming lean.

In 1984, the International Motor Vehicle Program at MIT began its now-famous five-year, five-million-dollar study of the world auto industry, the findings of which were summarized in the best-seller, *The Machine That Changed the World*. The researchers concluded that the system of manufacturing pioneered by Taiichi Ohno at Toyota differed so fundamentally from mass production as to warrant recognition as a new kind of manufacturing. Not only was it different, it was decidedly better than mass production. As they put it: "Lean production . . . is 'lean' because it uses less of everything compared with mass production—half the human effort in the factory, half the manufacturing space, half the investment in tools, half the engineering hours to develop a new product in half the time. Also, it requires keeping far less than half the needed inventory on site, results in many fewer defects, and produces a greater and ever growing variety of products."

Since the publication of that report, extraordinary attention from industry, academia, and government has focused on lean manufacturing, with much discussion of the Toyota Production System, but contributing little to the task of defining lean. Considerable confusion has resulted regarding exactly what "lean" is (what does it look like, how can we say that a given production system or site is "lean" or not?). Some assert that lean is simply another word for the Toyota Production System. Others have expended extraordinary amounts of time and effort developing related theories that essentially rehash the same concepts (agile manufacturing, re-engineering, continuous improvement, world class manufacturing), adding little of substance but much confusion to the issue.

The concepts *mass production* and *lean production* do not refer to production systems. They reflect *ways of thinking* about production—the assumptions that underlie how people and institutions formulate solutions to the problems of organizing people, equipment, material, and capital to create and deliver products for customers. Mass and lean are paradigms that reflect and inform the thinking about production within particular cultures and eras. Production systems emerge from these paradigms. The original Ford production system, and all the systems subsequently developed by auto and auto parts manufacturers and virtually all manufacturing systems in most industries around the world, have reflected the mass paradigm for most of the twentieth century. The rise of the Japanese manufacturing industry after World War II took place within constraints on effective operation in the mass paradigm, giving birth to a new approach to manufacturing, lean production, which is best exemplified by the Toyota Production System, or TPS. Thus, TPS is nothing more, or less, than a set of solutions designed to achieve the "lean" ideal.

If we have had trouble conceptually understanding lean manufacturing, we have had even more difficulty trying to implement it. Most of the concepts are actually quite simple, many are common sense, and others are counter-intuitive. Implementation, while appearing to make progress in the last couple of years, continues to proceed at an agonizingly slow pace. The Big Three U.S. automakers have each undertaken major initiatives to become lean manufacturers, though their success is still to be determined.

Most efforts focus on plant floor implementation, and that is as it should be. Many would claim to understand, more or less, how we need to change the way we run our plants, but we still struggle to make it happen. One problem is that we have only begun to deal with the issues involved in trying to tie everything together for a whole-system approach. Some of the problems that continue to confound us are the following:

- The way manufacturing works with sales makes scheduling and running the plants difficult.
- We compound the above problem by the way we order from suppliers.
- Labor and management still don't trust each other.
- The way we measure performance doesn't provide information useful to running a plant and often encourages wrong decisions.

- Much of our equipment is old and designed for the old paradigm, combined in layouts that seek economies of scale under the slogan of "bigger is better."

Lean manufacturing includes a set of techniques that comprise a system that derives from a philosophy. The tremendous benefits promised by the lean paradigm will come about only if we understand and implement accordingly. In what follows, I try to illustrate just what TPS is through the story of my own encounter and continuing learning experience with TPS over the past 15 years.

Going to Japan to Learn

I went to Japan in 1983 with an explicit purpose: to work for the biggest and "most Japanese" company I could find, so I could learn what there was to learn and bring it back to my own country. I had no natural connection with Japan; I never even met a Japanese person until I was well into my 20s. Yet, here I was, after picking up a graduate degree in Hawaii, speaking marginal Japanese, knocking on doors in Japan, and looking for a job. At that time, it wasn't easy; Japanese companies did not hire foreigners, a fact I was reminded of many times. But as luck (fate?) would have it, I found my company, or my company found me. Toyota had just signed a letter of intent with General Motors to form a joint venture in California to build Corollas. They figured they should hire an American to work with them in Toyota City to help with the process. That American was me.

More specifically, they decided that they needed an American to help with the training. They offered me a job teaching their management and production systems to the employees of the new company. This fit my plans perfectly. Before I could teach anything to anybody, they had to teach me first. Little did I know what was in store. My auto-related experience was limited to a year of overhauling big American V8s at auto mechanic school in the coal-mining hills of Kentucky, so I expected to receive some training, which I would in turn share with my California compatriots. That is indeed what happened. What I did not know, however, was that

15 years later, I would still be struggling alongside much of U.S. industry to understand what it was that I had been trained in and had also trained.

It was truly exciting for me to be working in the manufacturing world of Toyota City at that time. The idea of taking their production system overseas was not a trivial matter to the people of Toyota. For over 30 years they had built, refined, and cajoled their system to get it to work as it did. They knew it was effective, and they knew how to make it work. Then as today, you could ask a Toyota manufacturing person about any aspect of their production, and you would get an incredibly detailed explanation of philosophy, principles, and techniques. But in 1983, they had no confidence whatsoever that they could make the system work as it should outside of Japan (or even Toyota City). And certainly not in California with UAW workers.

The Toyota people were excited about the prospect of what was ahead, but they were concerned. Toyota people, though, are always "concerned"; that is one of their strengths. On January 2, 1984, I heard my first "President's New Year's Address," in which Dr. Shoichiro Toyoda expressed dread that the Korean automakers were just about to make their move, leapfrog the Japanese, and put us all out of a job—this when Toyota had solidified its dominance of the Japanese domestic market as never before, when it was poised for a major push in overseas operations, and when it had more money in the bank than any company in the world.

The excitement created a great atmosphere in which to learn. I was quickly accepted as a member of the team, contrary to some of my own concerns, having read the books claiming that the Japanese never really accept "outsiders" into the fold. Perhaps I was fortunate due to the unique circumstances. The overriding atmosphere was one of, "There is a huge task ahead and we can't do it alone." That atmosphere more than drowned out the, "There's a foreigner in our midst" mentality.

All we knew in those early days was that there was to be a joint venture with General Motors. It would build a version of the Corolla at the old GM Fremont plant (we didn't know then that the Fremont plant had been GM's worst). Neither the new company nor the product had a name. The details regarding the treatment of the former workers of GM Fremont was unclear, but we knew the work force would be organized by the UAW, and we knew that Toyota would run the plant, at GM's request, and run it under the Toyota Production System.

Lessons in the Toyota Production System

So that was our job, to enable the plant to operate under the Toyota Production System. My own first task was to learn just what this system was, and get a true grasp of the power of TPS.

Lesson One: Learn by Doing

Learn by doing translates as: build some cars. After a couple of weeks of orientation, I was put to building Corollas at the Takaoka plant, which was a great experience, though I didn't appreciate every aspect of it at the time. I was lucky. I spent a week each working on the line in stamping, body welding, paint, final assembly, and plant administration. I learned the basic process of making a car; that is, in Jim Womack's words, you stamp it, paint it, stuff it, and ship it.

Later, I learned how deceptively simple the process had appeared to me. I was, after all, working in what was probably the most efficient auto assembly plant in the world. Later, I discovered the incredible amount of detailed planning, discipline, hard work, painstaking attention to detail, and sweat that went into making it all work so smoothly on the surface. I learned about the years of trial and error, the obsessive drive for continual improvement that led to the state of the system that I was working in. And I learned about Taiichi Ohno.

Taiichi Ohno

I never had the opportunity to meet Taiichi Ohno. When I joined Toyota in 1983, he had already been "dispatched" to work for a supplier (if "work for" accurately describes the role of president). Evidently, he had not been happy about being "dispatched," and when I asked about the possibility of meeting him, it was explained to me, on several occasions, that relations between Ohno and Toyota's manufacturing people were quite strained, at least for most of the time that I was there in the 1980s. But his teachings and exploits were legend.

There is no greater badge of accomplishment for a "Toyota man" (it was only the men who received this particular badge) to carry than to be able to relate a story of how he was berated by Ohno. The louder and more public the scene, the greater the honor. There are stories of Ohno, "the Old Man," as his subordinates called him, firing and hiring people several times in the same day, or ranting for hours as the room slowly emptied, leaving only the poor soul who was the object of a particular tirade, or throwing chairs, or banishing engineers to totally uncooperative plants with the assignment to change the plant or not come back.

Ohno actually began working at the original Toyoda family company, Toyoda Spinning and Weaving, and later transferred to the Toyota Motor Company, where he was manager of machining operations. Following the end of World War II, Toyota's manufacturing organization was given an assignment by the company's top management: "Catch up with the U.S. auto industry in three years." This was a tall order, but this charge was Ohno's point of departure in developing the Toyota Production System.

Toyota's situation following the war was truly bleak. The company had no money, so it was borrowing from banks. They had figured out how to make cars (or trucks, anyway) but didn't know much about selling them. Labor-management relations were disastrous and made worse because the company often couldn't meet payroll. On top of all this, when Ohno conducted a thumbnail analysis of his productivity versus the Big Three, he found that his productivity was about one-ninth that of Detroit.

Toyota had gotten as far as they had essentially by copying Detroit. That worked to get them where they were, but it wasn't going to get them much further. Toyota's method of assembling cars was basically the same as Henry Ford's. In fact, everyone assembled cars pretty much as Henry Ford had taught. The problem for Ohno in moving forward was clear. Ford's system was created to meet the demands of his day. As Ford himself put it: "This is a big country with a big population and big needs demanding big production and big supply." But Ohno had none of that, not even a single one of those five "bigs." He had a small, but diverse, market, and he (and Nissan) had to meet all of that diversity. This was the blessing and the curse that came with the closing of the Japanese domestic car markets that the U.S. occupation forces approved at the urging of the Japanese bureaucracy. Closing the market (it remained closed for about 25 years) meant that Toyota and Nissan had to make everything that Japanese automobile consumers might need, even though the size of the market and the volumes for each vehicle type were small. In 1950, Toyota was producing about 1000 vehicles per month, or what one Ford assembly line might produce in a single day. Ohno could not compete on economies of scale.

Lesson Two: Economies of Scale

Economies of scale need not be the goal of the production system. You can attain greater overall system efficiency through concerted efforts to eliminate waste thoroughly. Ohno's efforts focused on developing the ability to survive and even thrive in low growth.

Through trial and error, Ohno developed what we now call the Toyota Production System, though not until the early 1970s were the concepts captured on paper and the TPS moniker attached. Even then, Ohno was uncomfortable with labeling and codifying it, but others convinced him that this was necessary to develop and perpetuate the system.

The system that they described in the early 1970s is little changed today. Though new techniques are added daily and the system continually evolves (well-known innovations found in the RAV-4 Line at Motomachi and in Kyushu are just evolutions, not revolutions), the principles and basic concepts are the same. The two most basic concepts are simple. One is to make what customers want when they want it, nothing more and nothing less. This sounds simple, but with 15,000 parts per car and thousands of cars per day, this goal is almost impossible to achieve. The other is to treat people with respect. This also sounds simple to the point of being mundane, but it is difficult to achieve when you are under the constant repetition demanded in coordinating the activities of 5,000 people in one factory to produce one quality car every minute. These two concepts translate into a set of guidelines and activities that are described as the Two Pillars of the Toyota Production System: jidoka and just-in-time.

Jidoka

One of the first things that Ohno noticed (I imagine and as I have heard) when he looked at his new machine shop was people standing at individual machines as if they owned them, or as if they were tied to them. This "isolated island" mentality and layout was contrary to his experience at his previous company, Toyoda Spinning and Weaving, where jidoka was the overriding organizing principle. Jidoka was the creation of Sakichi Toyoda, the founder of the Toyota group of companies back in the late 1890s and early 1900s. Jidoka has been difficult to put into English, having been variously translated as: "autonomation," "built-in quality," "the quality principle," "respect for humans system," "automation with a human touch." At Toyota, we decided just to stick with "jidoka" and explain it as a new concept, since there was no exact English equivalent anyway. In fact, there was no word in Japanese that adequately contained the concept either, so jidoka is a coined term even in Japanese.

As you can glean from the above collection of translations, jidoka embodies a range of concepts. Basically, jidoka means building in quality and designing operations and equipment so that people are not tied to machines but are free to perform value-added work that is appropriate for humans. If people are stuck watching machines just to make sure that the machine is performing properly, we might ask, "Who is working for whom? Are the machines working for us, or vice versa?" With jidoka, people aren't tied to one machine, but are free to tend to machines only when they need tending and free to operate several machines within the same period.

When Ohno tried to bring this jidoka concept into his machining operations, he encountered resistance. It is human nature, it seems, to want to feel that you own your machine. Ohno's concept was to have one worker operating two or more machines. To test his ideas, Ohno would go into the plant at night after production had shut down, just to try out his ideas for himself on the equipment. He would run parts and see what worked and what didn't work. Legend has it that although his concepts worked just fine, his machining work didn't always turn out so well. He turned out defect after defect through his trial and error experimentation. Upon completion, he would dump all of his defects and scrap into a pond behind the plant, hoping to hide it and thinking that no one knew what he was doing—but they did. After a time, the pond filled up with his rejects (or so goes the legend).

Just-in-time

Toyota defines just-in-time (JIT) as "the right part at the right time in the right amount" and we could add "at the right place" to complete the requirements. JIT is one of the most well-known yet least understood buzzwords of modern manufacturing. In Detroit, it has come to mean "daily delivery" and is listed as a "competency" in almost every company brochure. For the most part, however, all we have done is to move inventories around without reducing them or shortening lead times. This brings us to lesson three.

Lesson Three: Transferring Technologies Is Easier Said Than Done

Transferring technologies around the globe is easier said (simply using the words) than done (actually using the technology as intended). JIT, more than any of the other system mechanics, visibly distinguishes TPS from conventional manufacturing. After all, manufacturing is simple in its essence; the aim is to obtain materials, transform them, and provide them to customers. The problem of achieving this proposition in the auto industry is the complexity of manufacturing a car. Here you are dealing with tremendous volumes and pace of production, combined with a huge number and variety of parts, combined with long lead times to get things through the system. At Toyota, JIT is nothing less than a solution to the nightmare of trying to coordinate all the parts and materials that go into an automobile. Often, it seems that we attempt to fight complexity with complexity. JIT, however, instructs us to learn to respond quickly and to roll with the chaos. If you can understand the following two assumptions, you can understand JIT: Production plans always change; production will never go according to plan, anyway.

The concept of JIT began at Toyota back in the 1930s when Kiichiro Toyoda (son of Sakichi and founder of Toyota Motor Company) realized that he didn't have the production volume, the space, or the supply base to hold a lot of raw material inventory. During the 1950s, when Ohno began experimenting with "supermarkets" and "kanban," JIT became the backbone of TPS.

Legend has it that Ohno went to the U.S., saw American supermarkets, and returned to Japan to develop JIT as a "supermarket system" with a kanban-based pull system. Actually, though, Ohno didn't visit the U.S. until 1956, well after he had begun experimenting with pull systems. No doubt, news of U.S. supermarkets was available to Ohno in the early 1950s, but another source of inspiration evidently came from a U.S. manufacturer in the aircraft industry, no less. A small article in a 1954 Japanese trade paper referred to savings of $250,000 per year that Lockheed had gained from installing a "supermarket system" in its production operations. Although news of American supermarkets and Lockheed's success was available and must have provided some hints, Ohno had already been experimenting with "pull systems" since the late 1940s.

Toyota's JIT is a system unto itself comprised of the *pull system*, *one-piece flow*, and *takt time*, all of which are integrated with Toyota's *heijunka* method of production scheduling.

Heijunka

Heijunka refers to *leveling* of production by both volume and variety. That means that if today I'm planning to make a batch of 8 Widget A's followed by a batch of 4 Widget B's, and tomorrow I'm planning on batches of 12 A's and 6 B's, then what I really need to do is make 2 A's followed by a B all day long each day, as I make a total of 15 each day, rather than 12 today and 18 tomorrow. This is one of the *counter-intuitive* aspects of TPS. It may jar our normal sense of what is "efficient," but production by heijunka accomplishes a steady demand of resources, shortens the lead time of individual product variation, and enables us to level work requirements throughout the production process. Without it, *muda* (waste) will build up increasingly from beginning to end; in particular, implementation of a pull system will become impractical, ineffective, and maybe even impossible.

Toyota's heijunka is another component of TPS that is widely misunderstood in general, and particularly in Detroit. It is widely believed that Toyota freezes their production schedules (for example, the sequence in which vehicle specifications run down the assembly line) far in advance, and that freezing provides the advantage of smoothly running production operations. However, while it is true that Toyota establishes heijunka production planning on a monthly basis, the setting of monthly volumes for different model variations does not lock in the actual production sequence. That sequence can be and is changed up until the last day prior to sending production instructions to the beginning of the production process (the first processes of the body welding and assembly operations).

The rest of JIT just will not work well without heijunka.

Pull system: The kanban system

The pull system is Toyota's specific answer to the dilemma presented by the axioms mentioned above: Production plans will always change; production will never go according to plan, anyway. The conventional response has been to deal with the complexities of production scheduling with equally complex forecasting and scheduling systems. TPS compels us to assign supplier-customer roles throughout the production flow. "Customers" are then responsible for obtaining what they need when they need it based upon their own "sales." As a "supplier," I am then responsible for maintaining a "store" (supermarket) of my customer's products, so I can provide them what they want when they need it. Thus, the pull system fights complexity (changing customer orders for models with thousands of variations) with simplicity (as opposed to complex computer systems that generate schedules for every process).

Kanban is the Japanese word for "sign," a very ordinary word that Toyota uses to describe its means of signaling to supplier processes what they need to do next. Kanban are usually cards (though they can be anything from flags to ping pong balls) that carry various pieces of information about the part to which they are attached: part number, quantity, location, delivery frequency, etc. They are attached to and physically travel with the actual parts, usually a small container of a predetermined number of parts. If everyone follows the handful of clear rules for proper usage, the kanban system is a foolproof way of making the right part at the right time in the right amount.

Originally, all the cards were hand-written each month (remember, the heijunka plan is set each month) by about 200 office staff at Toyota and another 2,000 or so among the suppliers. In the mid-1970s, this became a problem when Ohno issued the edict that he wanted to reduce inventories by cutting lot sizes and increasing delivery frequencies. A move from a daily delivery to every shift to hourly would mean a corresponding increase in paperwork (writing kanban), or the *cost of ordering* (one of those ill-defined costs that still are rounded up under the heading of "overhead"). As a solution, Ohno's staff introduced the printed kanban (somewhat over his initial objections, as he hated anything smelling of computerization), thus immediately freeing the 200 + 2,000 people from what was now unnecessary work so they could turn to value-added work. Kanban now contain bar codes, and scanning provides real-time information to accounting and purchasing about the flow of plant floor material on an actual-use basis.

Most importantly, the kanban system itself is a tool for kaizen. By making the entire material and information flow transparent to everyone, problems surface and improvements are easy to find, on both micro and macro levels.

One-piece flow

Once we have a customer pull, we want simply to flow everything one piece at a time. One-piece flow is the quickest way for material to get from point A to point B, with the shortest lead time and least amount of work in-process in between.

True one-piece flow would have us manufacture items with essentially no waiting time, no queuing, and no batches. Sounds

easy enough, yet the vast majority of manufacturing occurs in a traditional batch and queue mode, where items wait their turn in line
to be processed, wait, then move on to wait in queue again. This
takes time; time that has a far greater non-value added than value-
added percentage.

Ideally, we would perform all operations in one-piece flow. But,
even if we want to, technology often won't allow us; issues such as
setup times (the time required to change from running one product
to another) and equipment that is designed to produce enormous
batches often stand in our way. One-piece flow calls for "right-siz-
ing" our tooling and placing machines directly adjacent in a "product-oriented" production flow.

Perhaps the most instructive of Ohno's insights for us today is
the focus on reducing lead time. If we focus on how to reduce lead
time, all other processes and measures will come along. The path to
reducing lead time is one-piece flow. If one-piece flow isn't possible
in a given circumstance (and it's certainly often not possible), we
move to the next best thing: smaller batches, more frequent
changeovers, more frequent deliveries, whatever will get us even
one step closer to the ideal of one-piece flow. The advantages of one-
piece flow are numerous, but the most important is reduction in
lead time. So the most important question we can ask is: How can
we shorten lead times?

Takt time
The final element of JIT is takt time (*takt* is the German word for
musical meter, which came into Japan in the 1930s when the
Japanese were learning aircraft production from German aerospace engineers). Takt time is the tool to link production to the customer by matching the pace of production to the pace of actual
final sales. If blue Celica hatchbacks are selling at a rate of one
every half hour, we should build a blue Celica hatchback every half
hour. Furthermore, if half of those Celicas are air-conditioned,
every other one that comes down the line should have an air con-
ditioner installed. The way it works is you calculate actual takt
times for each product and part. Then you use the number of seconds required for each product and part to determine the number

of seconds that should be allotted to each actual process in the entire production chain. Toyota determines takt times as part of the heijunka plan, once a month.

Determining the takt time is where we usually begin in establishing a JIT system. What are the requirements? How many of a supplier's process products are required by its customer(s)? How can we then create a process that can fulfill that need with a minimum of waste and in the shortest lead time? (*Minimum waste* and *shortest lead time* should lead to the same solution.)

Putting It All Together and Making It Work

I didn't personally realize the central importance of takt time until years later when I saw American suppliers attempting to implement JIT. It seemed that the suppliers we dealt with usually had an understanding of many of the tools of lean—error proofing, quick changeover, visual control, kanban, etc.—but they were having little success putting those tools into practice, and even less success in building their own lean system. Often, there was little understanding of why they were trying to put the tools in place, of their requirements, and their problems in reaching those requirements. Producing according to takt time puts customer requirements out in front of everyone all the time.

Lesson Four: Begin from Need

People need to understand clearly the reasons for changing the way they do things. Change for the sake of change, or changing simply because this year's management fashion says so, will only result in superficial alterations in the way things are done. The fundamental shift in thinking and behavior required by lean requires much more. Ohno felt strongly that change should begin from need, and even stated that without a crisis no company would be capable of successfully making the shift to lean.

This emphasis on need underscores Toyota's daily management process. At Toyota, even now, all proposals—whether in manufacturing or any other function—are challenged to demonstrate the need that is being met by the proposal; in other words, why it is necessary.

In my experience, planning for new programs was accomplished by employees, engineers and staff, bringing proposals to their supervisors for approval. This is how all new initiatives got started. Through it all, the superiors avoided ever telling anyone exactly what to do. As my first manager and mentor at Toyota told me, "Never tell your staff what to do. Whenever you do that, you take the responsibility away from them." So, the Toyota managers, the good ones anyway, would rarely tell their people what to do; they would lay out a problem, ask for an analysis or a proposal, but always stop short of saying, "Do this." The employee, upon getting a problem to work on (actually, finding the problem to work on was usually his job, too), would develop solution options to take to the manager. The manager's first answer was, invariably, "No." The employee would return to his desk and rework his proposal—three times, five times, ten times if necessary. The manager was the "judge and jury" while the employee was the attorney with whom rested the "burden of proof" to justify his proposal by presenting and analyzing all the viable options. It took me a good three years to figure out how this worked.

Policy management, as revolutionary as TPS
This was the famous Japanese "bottom-up decision making" in action. My initial reaction was a level of disillusionment, declaring bottom-up decision making a huge lie. Wasn't "bottom-up" supposed to be some kind of enlightened form of democratic self-management whereby people essentially do what they want? It took a while for me to see that it wasn't a lie so much as it was one of the many misconceptions of how most Japanese organizations work, Toyota included. Obviously, it wasn't decision making, it was proposal generating, but it was powerful nonetheless: No one was telling anyone else what to do. What a beautiful answer to the control-flexibility dilemma that dogs all large organizations: The company gets basic adherence to the desired corporate direction, and the workers are free to explore best possible real solutions to problems that they themselves know best.

This is *policy management*, and it is a management system or decision-making process that is probably as revolutionary as TPS itself. It results in a system that is flexible and changes continually, yet does not accept change lightly and without strong justification. That's where the famous discipline of the system comes from: policy deployment on a yearly planning basis, and PDCA (plan, do, check, action) on a daily basis. PDCA assures that learning is continuous—that we are moving forward, not repeating old mistakes, not continually starting over with blank slates.

A contrasting example could be found at New United Motor Manufacturing, Inc. (NUMMI). The Toyota Maintenance people quickly recognized that the U.S. skilled workers were good at putting out fires. At NUMMI, the skilled trades group was populated by the same people who had worked at the old GM Fremont plant or at the old Ford Milpitas plant located nearby. The Toyota side remarked at how quickly the Americans could get robots back up and running after a problem had developed. As time went by, however, they noticed that the same robots kept breaking down over and over. The workers would get them running again, another Band Aid, and sure enough, they would break down again. The system was good at providing Band Aids, but not very good at preventing problems from recurring. The problem solving often didn't seem to go deep enough in those early days to identify the root cause.

Policy management is often confused with policy deployment, a relatively simple prioritization process in which the desires and objectives of senior management (the company) are "deployed" throughout the organization (the employees).

That is a good first step. But policy management Toyota-style was a much more dynamic process, with lower levels of the organization taking part in formulating policy as well as carrying it out. As lean organizations mature policy deployment should evolve into policy management.

Lesson Five: Ask the Five Whys, Not the Five Whos

We instituted an extensive training program to kick off NUMMI. We sent every person in a supervisory capacity, including hourly team leaders, to Toyota City for three weeks of training at the Takaoka plant where they produce the Corolla. The training included long hours of excruciating lectures in hot classrooms with slides on TPS, and a good two weeks of trainees working alongside their counterparts learning what was to be their job back in Fremont. Toward the end of each training tour, we asked them what they would most want to take back with them to Fremont of all they had seen in Toyota City. The answer was invariably the same: "The ability to focus on solving problems without pointing fingers and looking to place the blame on someone. Here it's 'five whys,' in the U.S. it's the 'five whos.'" Call attention to the problem to solve it, or to the behavior to change it, but not to the individual for being somehow "wrong."

"Problems," in fact, were looked on quite differently to begin with. Americans seemed to be fond of responding "no problem" to questions of how things were going. In fact, one phrase known and used with gusto by every early member of NUMMI was the Japanese word for "no problem," which, when spoken with a typical American accent, sounded pretty much like "Monday night." So when Japanese trainers (approximately 600 three-month stays at NUMMI by Toyota trainers from Japan took place over the first few years to get NUMMI off to a good start) tried to ask how certain problems were being handled, American NUMMI employees could be heard all over the plant cheerily shouting, "Monday night!" A favorite response to this by the Japanese quickly becomes, "No problem is problem." In other words, there are always problems, or issues that require some kind of "countermeasure," or better ways to accomplish a given task.

The salient word here is *responsibility*. TPS operates by placing as much responsibility as possible at as "low" a level as possible. That is what makes it possible for a Toyota worksite essentially to run itself. Given no major problems or design changes, managers are totally unnecessary to the day-to-day running of plant floor operations.

This all translates into hourly worker processes as well, forming the basis of the "standardized work and kaizen." With standardized work, best practice is assured and the current best practice becomes the baseline for further improvement, or *kaizen*. As long as current standards are as they are, no deviation is allowed. However, if someone has a better idea, that idea is easily proposed, approved, and implemented, and a reward is presented under the suggestion program. This is all so easy that Toyota workers in Japan give a suggestion—which means a change in their standardized work— every three days or so. (Actually, it had better be easy; takt times change every month with the heijunka plan, and the standardized work has to match the takt times.) The involvement (good for the company) and fulfillment of employees (good for the employee) thus occurs.

Standardized work alters roles

Many people hear the term *standardized work* and immediately see visions of human automatons tirelessly performing repetitive, endless, mindless tasks. The truth is quite different. To paint a picture of a TPS worksite as full of nothing but life-enriching activities would be misleading; in the end, auto manufacturing entails hard physical work for plant floor operators. But it would be equally incorrect to deny the opportunity for involvement and benefits for the individual presented by a lean operation. If we envision a worksite containing the features described above, we see workers continually redesigning their own jobs, worksites managing themselves except when problems arise, and engineers initiating new plans and managers approving them. The nature of all three roles is dramatically altered: workers are engineers; engineers are managers, planners, and problem solvers; and managers are psychologists.

Success at NUMMI

Prior to NUMMI, Toyota had some experience with production outside Japan, in Brazil and in Long Beach, California, in particular, but the experience was very limited. Those operations involved mostly small-scale assembly and did not demand implementation of the total system. NUMMI, however, did.

Establishing the system at NUMMI was a success but far from perfect. It's not difficult to spot aspects of NUMMI that are well off the mark of an ideal TPS system. But that is true of any Toyota worksite—it is just a matter of degree.

Lesson Six: Don't Confuse Toyota's Production System with the Toyota Production System

Not infrequently you will find Toyota doing things "wrong." There can be numerous reasons for this: individuals make mistakes; sometimes they don't understand. Yet the TPS goals are still there as an ideal to strive toward. I remember once explaining to a group of suppliers that "in TPS we don't try to do one-piece flow out of stamping" and my mentor kindly, but firmly, corrected me: "In TPS we want to flow out of stamping; it is just the realities of current technology that keep us from it. However unrealistic implementation may be in a particular instance, the ideals of TPS are still the ideals."

Let's look at the NUMMI scorecard for a moment. The old Fremont plant was GM's worst worldwide. It had the worst quality on the regular GM quality audits, absenteeism over 20 percent, and several thousand grievances on the books when GM closed the plant in 1981. Wildcat strikes occurred repeatedly. After Toyota took over plant management and brought in the Toyota Production System, absenteeism immediately subsided to 2 percent, and the new company's score on its very first crack at a GM quality audit was reportedly the highest any GM plant had ever scored. As for grievances, all problems were handled jointly by union and management as they occurred. Even 13 years after the birth of the joint venture, you were hard-pressed to find NUMMI employees who were not wholly supportive of the NUMMI system.

NUMMI is a great success story … but
NUMMI, is in my view, a remarkable success story, but most importantly, it represents clear evidence that TPS can indeed work in an American UAW environment. NUMMI had some unique enabling conditions, however, that made it particularly amenable to success, thus leaving unanswered questions about implementing TPS in traditional, completely U.S. manufacturing environments. First, NUMMI had the benefit of proven, high-quality, easy-to-

build products (the Toyota Corolla and Toyota truck) along with production processes that were robust and in control (that is, tried out and proven in Japan before being put on a boat for NUMMI). Those two factors alone gave NUMMI a significant leg-up on your average assembly plant.

Second, NUMMI created a totally new human resources system that was fully appropriate to support TPS. I am often asked what motivates Toyota's employees in Japan to "work so hard." Clearly, a powerful motivator is the concept and feeling of membership. It is important to ask ourselves, "What is the nature of our company-employee relationship?" In Toyota and NUMMI's cases, there is clear and evident commitment on the part of the company to the employees. Toyota, even in Japan and contrary to popular myth, does not guarantee lifetime employment. No employer can ever do that. What an employer can do and Toyota does, is make a policy that the last thing the company desires to do is lay off an employee. Only as a last resort will they turn to reducing the work force. Through such a policy, real trust can develop between the company and employees, along with the motivation for employees to accept responsibility and take ownership. This leads to lesson seven.

Lesson Seven: Employee Motivation Comes from Assuring Membership in the Organization

At NUMMI, this "laying off as the last resort" was put to the test in the late 1980s. NUMMI's product wasn't selling well. Production volume was down to the extent that several hundred workers were actually unneeded to run the plant. Naturally, the workers, who had experienced layoffs before, became nervous. On top of the production downturn, NUMMI management was asking the work force to cooperate with line-rebalancing activities that would show even more clearly the excess labor. To demonstrate the company's sincerity toward the employees' welfare, NUMMI wrote into the contract the commitment that before they would lay anyone off, certain steps would be taken, including reductions in plant operating hours and cuts in management bonuses. Employee motivation comes from assuring membership in the organization, more than from buying and selling time, whatever the price tag.

The above factors combine to make NUMMI's situation a bit unique, a sort of part-brownfield, part-greenfield operation. Even after NUMMI, questions remained regarding the implementation of TPS in purely traditional, American, brownfield environments.

Bringing TPS to U.S. Suppliers—TSSC

My last assignment with Toyota was to help establish the Toyota Supplier Support Center (TSSC) in Lexington, Kentucky, beginning in 1992. One of TSSC's objectives was to answer some of the questions left unanswered by NUMMI. Those questions were out in front as we discussed and debated what kind of Center to create.

Some of the debate went as follows:

TPS authority 1: "We'll focus almost entirely on the plant floor, just demonstrating how to implement. As companies implement and begin to understand, they can do their own training."

TPS authority 2: "But Americans need a rulebook. They don't like to play a game when they don't know the rules. So we have to give them the rules."

TPS authority 1: "But there is no rulebook for TPS. If there is, please give it to me; I want it, too. If you try to simplify it and carve it in stone, it will lose its essence. All we can do is teach guidelines and principles and demonstrate how to use the tools."

Another debate:

TPS authority 1: "TPS is more than just the plant floor. We have to create a Center that provides support in all the necessary functions: engineering, human resources, management…."

TPS authority 2: "TPS may be more than just the plant floor, but the plant floor is where we need to focus. That is where the most help is needed. And that is where we know *how* to help. Besides, if we include engineering, business issues will get in the way."

And another:

TPS authority 1: "Why are we doing this anyway? What are we going to get out of it?"

TPS authority 2: "First of all, we made a promise to George Bush, and we need the good will anyway. Also, Toyota will benefit from having a few stronger suppliers. Besides, we'll learn a lot as well."

The approach to implementing TPS in existing, brownfield environments was pioneered, of course, by Ohno. He put together a team in the late 1960s to help him do just that. That group, known as the Operations Management Consulting Division, or OMC, still exists today. In the late 1980s, one of the senior members came to me proclaiming that he wanted to change the English name of the group, which was then known in English as the "Production Research Office," which was a direct translation of the Japanese. That name described one of the group's functions—responsibility for monthly productivity audits of each Toyota worksite—but most of their work involved consulting on TPS implementation with suppliers. One of the junior consultants had recently studied in the U.S., where he learned that the function of managing manufacturing operations is called operations management at U.S. business schools. So together, we came up with the title of OMC. (Actually, I must accept the blame for much of the jangled English that you may find in Toyota literature about TPS.)

The group remained quite small for many years and only very recently ballooned to around 60 or so consultants. The methodologies developed have been simple enough, if quite "Japanese" in some respects, as well as very labor intensive. The difficulty for anyone trying to copy this particular piece of TPS, however, is that it demands a cadre of highly qualified consultants. The consultants typically work with a worksite (usually at a supplier, but sometimes internally as well) on a TPS project for a period of a few months or so. The OMC consultant will work alongside an internal (to the supplier, or plant) TPS specialist to develop a plan, implement it step-by-step, and follow up to ensure that it can be sustained and "kaizened" further. The plans are detailed, the implementation precise (though it may vary considerably from the plan), and the follow-up thorough. (The best reference on the TPS apprenticeship experience can be found in D. T. Suzuki's *The Training of the Zen Buddhist Monk*. Berkeley, CA: Berkeley Window Press, 1974.)

Kaizen workshop

The kaizen workshop is a related methodology to bringing TPS to the shop floor. These are events of intensive team involvement, typically of four to five days in duration, in which you try to accomplish as much actual kaizen as possible. Typically the workshops go like this:

- Day 1 involves some training and explanation of the kaizen goals (not just "kaizen for kaizen's sake," which becomes "change for change's sake").
- Day 2 you are given a detailed current state analysis and develop the kaizen plan.
- Day 3 is devoted to implementing the kaizen plan (actually moving equipment, changing operator movement, revising material and information flow).
- Day 4 is when you fix what didn't work from Day 3.
- Day 5 you report to management and have confirmation of follow-up items.

One consulting company has dubbed the exercise "Four Days and One Night." In my first experience at a Toyota plant, around 1987, though I was accustomed to working long hours by that time, I was unprepared for the rigor of that kaizen event. The event lasted only three days in that case. Day 1 literally saw no one getting any sleep at all—after all, we had to observe the night shift conditions as well as day shift. That was okay. The following day, we instituted our changes, and then had little time to put them in place and observe them in operation. So it wasn't until after midnight that we began working on the report for management. Some of us slept a couple of hours the second night; most didn't sleep at all.

The kaizen workshop has become a phenomenon in itself recently. Numerous consulting and training groups market them, and many companies are even trying to measure success based on the number of kaizen events conducted in a year. What's good about the workshops is their action focus. If nothing else, they provide an opportunity for company members to get together on the plant floor and make things happen. What's not so good is when they are not used strategically as part of a larger plan to get a company or a plant from here to there, with a vision and plan of where "there" is. (For more about this, see Chapter 8 by Jeffrey Liker and Keith Allman, and Chapter 14 by Mike Rother.) Developing that vision and plan requires management leadership. TPS, or lean, needs to be realized as a system. Isolated "improvement" events produce isolated improvements; they do not build a system. We know exactly what will happen when we use "number of events" as a measure: the numbers will be attained.

Another difference between my observations of how Toyota used kaizen workshops and how they take place at many companies is that Toyota used them first and foremost as a human development tool. Yes, they also improved the worksite and, yes, they removed waste, but you realize the real power of kaizen when all employees are applying it in their work every day. The events can help instill that kind of thinking.

Creating pilot areas
When we began TSSC in 1992, there were methodology options available to us. The methodology adopted was one of creating "Model TPS Lines" or pilot areas that could be used as a showcase from which to learn. Efforts focused on establishing as much of the system as possible within a somewhat defined area; the project company would then be responsible for disseminating it from there. (For more about the TSSC methodology, see Chapter 6 by Sean Traynor.) Kaizen workshops were considered a specific tool to be used in the right time and place. When I left the Center in 1994, the first TSSC kaizen workshop was still in the planning stages.

Lean off the Plant Floor

I've described TPS itself as a manufacturing system, but the thinking of TPS or lean applies to any function. Whether you're dealing with 15,000 parts, 15 parts, or just providing a service, lean works. It works because it is a way of thinking, a whole systems philosophy. Techniques aside, lean thinking gives you a broad perspective on providing goods and services that goes beyond the bottom line, beyond the stodgy principles of mass-producing capitalism. It is a human system—customer focused, customer driven—wherein employees within and outside the workplace are also customers.

When you undertake to develop a lean manufacturing system, you must also embark on creating a lean enterprise. Making what the customer wants when he or she wants it, treating employees with respect, building in quality, shortening the lead time, eliminating waste—these are all principles with application to any endeavor. Kanban may not always be applicable, but quick response to customer demand is appropriate in any situation. Plant floor–style visual controls may not be applicable, but transparency that allows any work situation to be easily understood at a glance is powerful in any setting. "What adds value for my customer?" is a question that can and should be asked throughout all types of organizations.

Are We Lean, Yet?

Implementation of TPS, or perhaps I should say the development of U.S. lean production systems, continues to move slower than it seems it should. Over the past decade or so, we've played around with the techniques or tools and they've helped; in some cases, they've helped a lot. Companies are now trying to put into place full-blown, lean production systems such as the Chrysler Operating System and the new Ford Production System. These seem to be steps in the right direction, and let's all be optimistic that much that is positive will come from those efforts.

But how much have we really moved in a lean direction? Yes, we've improved quality to the customer, but at what cost and how much better is our in-plant first-time-through performance? We've moved inventories around, but have we scrapped batch and queue for flow? Have we trashed our complex push scheduling systems for customer demand–based pull? We've put in visual factory and error-proofing, but are we focusing on shortening lead times through eliminating waste and its sources? We've tried "self-directed work teams," but have we built human resource systems that make people integral members of the enterprise? Have we agreed that the majority of value-added that we provide our customers comes from the plant floor? The quantum leap to lean will not come from just the tools or even the "system" until we also adopt the philosophy or the way of thinking, what Jim Womack and Dan Jones call *Lean Thinking*.

What I found in Japan was different from what I expected. I was looking, basically, for "culture." I was one of the many who read books on "Japanese management" and "Quality Circles" and the rest, and who thought that there must be mysterious cultural reasons underlying the "Japanese economic miracle." Years later I can now say that I still don't really know "the reason" for the Japanese economic miracle, but I know that the most profound business practice to be uncovered in Japan seems to have surprisingly little to do with being "Japanese." That business practice is the Toyota Production System and, although it's not strictly a cultural thing, it certainly is something that strikes to the very heart of how we think about things, specifically about how we make things, how we organize ourselves for collective activities, and how we conduct business for customers. The Toyota Production System is not "Japanese" in that very few Japanese companies use it. Aspects of it are shared with many Japanese companies, yet other aspects—in particular, just-in-time— are as foreign to the typical Japanese company as they are in the United States. It was a total coincidence that Toyota was the company that I found; I didn't specifically seek it out. I assumed that what makes Toyota tick would be the same things that make every Japanese company tick. Only over time did I discover that I had landed myself inside a very unique company that had discovered its own unique ways of doing things. To my delight, I discovered that those ways of doing things provide great lessons for all of manufacturing and, in fact, all of business. Quite by accident, I was able to fulfill my original mission of learning from "Japan" and bringing that learning back with me to my own country.

Some of this learning is indeed coming "back," as technology that traversed the Pacific once is finding its way back again (demonstrating that technology transfer can be accomplished if approached properly). For example, the central idea of flow—that everything should flow from raw material to customer—came directly from

Henry Ford. Another interesting example is that of the U.S. Training Within Industry program that was developed by top minds in U.S. industry to support the war production effort beginning in 1941. Following the war, this proven set of productivity-enhancement training modules (four modules: Job Instruction, Job Methods, Job Relations, and Project Management) was brought to Japan and spread among Japanese industry. I discovered them in a roundabout way in the process of "adapting" some Toyota training materials to make them appropriate for NUMMI. When I found myself struggling with some of the concepts of a certain training program, my Japanese colleague fetched from a back-room file a yellowed, dog-eared, coffee-stained copy of the English-language original training manual, just as they had received it (minus the coffee stains I trust) some 30 years before. To my absolute amazement, the program that Toyota was going to great expense to "transfer" to NUMMI was exactly that which the Americans had taught the Japanese decades before. Toyota still uses it to this day, yet rarely do I find a U.S. manufacturer who has even heard of it, much less still uses it here in the country of its origin. So we had to repatriate the expatriated technology.

"Are we lean yet?" The answer is no, and it seems that we should be further along the curve than we are. But if lean is a continuum and not a steady state, how do we know when we're there? This question brings us full circle to the theme of this chapter and this book. Clearly, some companies have progressed more than others, and it hasn't been easy for the companies that have achieved relative success so far. The struggles in each case are greater than what the champions involved imagined when they first began. That is where learning from the experience of others can steepen our own learning curves.

The title of this volume, *Becoming Lean*, implies a journey. We will reach our destination when we apply the philosophies underlying lean to develop our own lean systems. There's no reason not to start trying. *Lesson Eight*: There are no experts, just people with more experience. The longer we wait, the more experience our competitors will have when we start.

 **Jennifer Yukiko Orf** *is half Japanese and half American and has enjoyed a bicultural lifestyle for most of her 24 years. She has recently completed a B.S.E. in Industrial and Operations Engineering at the University of Michigan, and is currently working as a software developer for a small company in Seattle, Washington. To keep sane, she wind-surfs and consumes food and wine of as high a quality as she can afford.*

3

Japanese Education and Its Role in Kaizen

by Jennifer Yukiko Orf

Editor's prologue: Jennifer Orf, who is half Japanese and half American, had the unique experience of attending elementary and high school in both Japan and the United States. When she later studied to become an industrial engineer and learned about Japanese kaizen, she found that her Japanese education had prepared her perfectly to participate in kaizen activities. Japanese children from kindergarten on learn to work in small groups, solve problems, document their processes, improve their processes, collect and analyze data, and, most importantly, learn self-management within a peer group. Jennifer Orf writes very personally about her experiences in a "day-in-the-life" format. From this chapter, U.S. managers can better understand how intricately connected the socialization of Japanese children is with their later kaizen roles in Japanese corporations. For U.S. employees to "get it" and actively participate in continuous improvement of lean manufacturing, they will clearly need significant compensatory education that is not needed in Japan.

The concept of KAIZEN is so deeply ingrained in the minds of both managers and workers that they often do not even realize they are thinking KAIZEN.[1]

Ask a typical American how they picture a Japanese classroom, and the response is likely to be a description of rows of highly pressured and identical children mechanically performing drills under the strict eye of their teacher, who stifles each child's individuality and demands conformity from his pupils. These children, compared with their counterparts in the United States, may be able to achieve much higher scores on international comparative tests, but this is at the cost of their creativity and individuality—characteristics that we Americans strive to foster in our children.

While this stereotype may hold somewhat true for Japanese education at the middle and high school levels, where the pressures of impending university entrance examinations create the widely criticized "exam hell," it is absolutely the opposite of Japanese education at the elementary school level. A typical Japanese elementary school classroom is often boisterous. Exuberant children gleefully participate in class discussions under the gentle guidance of a teacher whose role is as facilitator rather than dictator. This stage of the Japanese education system is driven by the belief that children of this age develop best if left to follow their own curiosity. There is much spontaneous expression, and instructional approaches involve a great deal of student-to-student interaction and group activity.

Why the stark contrast between the elementary school classroom and the high school classroom? To understand this, we must keep in mind that children's education is a process that has as its goal a final product, and to judge the system, we must look at its success in reaching its goal. It would be unfair to examine and criticize a single stage of Japanese education in isolation from other stages. The system must be seen in its entirety as a 12-year process. What is being sought is totality of character, not individual excellence, and this is the product that makes its way into the Japanese workplace.

Kaizen Philosophy in the Classroom

Of particular interest is the role of education in developing the characteristics essential to the kaizen philosophy, which has under its umbrella the management and production techniques for which the Japanese have been admired. I will describe some of the most important fundamentals of the kaizen philosophy. Masaaki Imai's highly acclaimed book[2] on the subject offers the following characteristics (sorted by me) as cornerstones of the kaizen philosophy.

Characteristics of People and Philosophy
- Kaizen requires one to be able to work effectively in a group.
- Kaizen requires the participation and involvement of everyone.
- In kaizen, since everyone is involved, there is a need to understand how things will affect everyone.
- Kaizen requires the willingness to improve things for everyone.
- Kaizen requires continuous commitment and effort.
- Kaizen requires the awareness that things can always be improved upon.
- Kaizen requires the motivation to reap the small rewards associated with an incremental change and take pride in even this small improvement.
- Kaizen stresses process, not product.
- Kaizen requires the ability to think long-term.

Characteristics of Methods and Discipline
- Kaizen requires continuous assessment.
- Kaizen requires discipline.
- Kaizen uses the Deming plan-do-check-act (and standardize) cycle.
- Kaizen stresses the use of documentation.

- Kaizen requires standardization of the best solution, then improvement on the standard.
- Kaizen uses visual management.
- Kaizen requires the use of time management.

Kaizen is all about people. As James Womack and John Shook point out in their contributions to this book, it is a way of thinking, not just a set of tools and techniques. The characteristics needed to "think kaizen" effortlessly in the workplace are ingrained in the Japanese throughout their education system—though the activities that promote this way of thinking are most apparent in the elementary school stage. By middle school and high school, the values inherent in kaizen have become so ingrained that they are not obvious to the casual observer.

Learning How to Work as a Group

Japanese society is well known for its group orientation, which leads to a high degree of social order. Japanese workers have been admired for their high productivity and loyalty, which depend largely on the ability of Japanese group members to sustain a sense of common purpose. A chief feature of successful group processes is the ability of group members to identify with and contribute toward collective goals. This is one of the characteristics instilled in a Japanese child at the elementary school level. It is not simply a matter of being able to work in a group, but also the ability to work as a group.

Ideally, group effort does not entail sacrificing personal goals for the sake of the group, but rather identifying with the group to the extent that the individual sees the group's goals as being his or her own. He or she will then feel a sense of personal pride and satisfaction when these collective goals are reached. Thus, a key part of learning to work as a group is gaining a sense of collective identity so that the success of the group results in a personal feeling of achievement for each individual within that group. In order to instill this sense of collective identity, the group must play a strong emotional role in the life of the individual. Members that feel a sense of belonging and acceptance will feel a strong emotional attachment to their group. A sense of collective identity results, whereby members of a group come to define themselves in terms of their group affiliation and incorporate aspects of the group into their individual personalities. Consequently, they adopt the goals of the group as their own, and feel personal pride and achievement in the attainment of group goals. This in turn leads to the desire to work for the sake of the group. As we will see, the Japanese elementary school functions to instill this sense of collective identity and emotional attachment to the group in its children.

One of the reasons often given to explain why Japanese managers succeed in winning such a high degree of commitment from their workers is that instead of imposing their own decisions on the workers, they often leave decision making up to their workers, so that they feel a sense of participation and personal investment in the company. Decisions are reached through a lengthy process of discussion involving the whole work team, and absolute consensus is sought before any decisions are implemented. This same process characterizes how decisions are made in the classroom. In the next section, I address how *soodan* (discussion) is frequently used as a teaching tool in the Japanese elementary school classroom.

In this chapter I draw on my experiences in the Japanese school system as well as research conducted by several U.S. experts in the field of Japanese education. I address elementary, middle, and high school, but pay particular attention to the elementary school stage. It is at this stage that the Japanese worker is first exposed to the group-oriented structure found in Japanese society and the workplace. Here, the foundation of all that is to follow is laid out. Without this stage, the strict discipline demanded of the child during the years of "examination hell" could not be met.

I received my exposure to Japanese public elementary and middle schools when I spent my so-called summer vacations in Japan from age 9 to 14. During these four months, I attended Japanese public schools near my grandmother's home in Japan, the same schools I would have gone to had my mother had her way in her desire to rear me as a Japanese child in Japan. I also spent a full year in a Japanese high school the year before coming to university here in the United States. The vignettes throughout this chapter are my recollections of actual experiences during the summers in grades 4 to 6 of elementary school and grade 7 of middle school. Any of the elementary school vignettes could just as well have been from any grade. Even the scene in which students prepare the lunch could have been from first graders, though they probably would not do it as well.

Shudan Seikatsu Socialization: The Role of Elementary School in Group Socialization

It is 8:00 A.M. exactly when the doorbell signals the usual arrival of the group of girls I walk to school with every day. We have one more person to pick up on the way to school. Everyone walks to school in a group, except for the boy who lives right across the street from the school gate (by coincidence or design, he ends up being one of the delinquent group later on when we are in middle school). Though we wear no uniform, anyone can tell we are students at K-school because of our matching sky-blue school hats. Anyone who cares to take a closer look can tell from the badges on our hats that we are proud members of fourth grade—fourth kumi. As we draw nearer to the school, we join the flow of more and more groups of school children making their merry way toward the school, soon becoming one with a sea of sky-blue hats. We pass through the gates in a swarm, and make our way into the entrance of the school building. Here, we find the principal of the school and several teachers lined up as usual to greet all the students.

"*Ohayoo gozaimasu!* (Good Morning!)," we chirp in unison, and bow in greeting.

"*Ohayoo gozaimasu, genki desu ne!* (My, you are energetic and cheerful today)," they return the greeting and praise us.

We push through the throng of students to our class's set of cubby-holes, where we change our shoes from our outdoor pair to our indoor pair, being sure to line up our outdoor set neatly in our cubby-hole just as our teacher has shown us to do.

In the classroom, things are in uproar. Children are rushing around shrieking at the top of their lungs. Daisuke-kun is leaping off the desks in his best imitation of Ultraman, and there is a mock pro-wrestling tournament taking place on the teacher's platform. Chigira-kun has Tanaka-kun in what looks like an illegal headlock of some sort. There is no teacher in the room to tell us that it is all fun and games until someone loses an eye and how sorry we'll be when that happens. One of today's class monitors is neatly recording the date, day, and weather in today's class log. We put our books in careful stacks in our desks—biggest books on the bottom, just as is shown on the poster on the wall. Today is Monday, so at the sound of the chimes over the loudspeaker, we make our clamorous way out onto the school yard for the Monday morning assembly.

Once on the school yard, we know exactly how to line up. Each grade is separated into four *kumi*, or classes. First grade–first kumi is on the side of the school yard closest to the school entrance, then first grade–second kumi, first grade–third kumi, and so on until at the far end stands sixth grade–fourth kumi. There are two lines for each class, one for the boys, and one for the girls. We stand ordered by height with the shortest at the front. We don't need our teacher to call us into line, because we have heard the special set of chimes that tell us that the assembly is about to start. She is facing us, standing about 20 feet away, lined up with the other teachers along either side of the principal's podium. We stand in perfect silence, ready for the principal of the school to make his entrance. He makes his solemn way up onto the principal's platform, and when this week's sixth grade greeting-caller calls, "Attention!" we all straighten up, palms pressed to our sides, just as we have been shown to do in the first grade.

"Good Morning!" the greeter calls out to the principal. We repeat, "Good Morning!" in unison, and bow.

He bows back. The greeter calls out, "At ease!" We relax our stance, hands folded behind our backs. The principal does the same, then starts off the assembly by telling us that both the Red and White teams performed magnificently and really *gambatta* (did our very best) on Sports Day last Saturday.

After he has finished talking, we all sing the school song together, then watch in silence as this week's flag raisers hoist the school flag. It is a proud and solemn moment. The silence is broken by the sound of a march being played over the loudspeaker. Everyone knows at exactly which point in the music we all start to march in place (except me, and I always have the wrong foot raised). Starting with first grade–first kumi, each class in turn makes one round of the school yard, little legs in perfect syn-chrony, before entering the school doors back to the classrooms.

Back in the classroom, the scene is as before. It is utter bed-lam when the teacher enters the room and without a word stands on her platform at the front of the class. The class monitors call us to attention, and we all immediately go to our desks. We stand behind our chairs in silence. One class monitor calls out, "*Sensei, Onegaishimasu* (Teacher, please [teach us])." We repeat in unison and bow to her. She beams at us and returns the bow, and at the word from the other class monitor, we sit as one.

Elementary school in Japan plays two major roles in the social development of the child. The first is as a means of socializing the child into the group-oriented nature of Japanese society, and builds the willingness and ability to live and work as a group. To do this, the students must first learn to feel a sense of collective identity with the groups with which they are affiliated, and to value what this collective membership means. The ability to work in and as a group is a central feature of the kaizen philosophy. The second role of the elementary school system is to instill in Japanese children the characteristics (such as persistence, self-discipline, self-reliance, and responsibility) and nurture the special connections that will later allow them to successfully withstand the "exam hell" of high school. Note that these same characteristics are also a vital part of the kaizen philosophy.

In discussing the Japanese elementary school, I begin with some general background information. I next discuss how elementary school teaches young Japanese students to work in groups. I then discuss two other features of Japanese elementary school pertinent to the kaizen philosophy. The first of these is the stressing of process over product. The second is the awareness that things can always be improved upon and the drive to continuously improve.

Elementary School Background and Setting

The typical Japanese elementary school classroom is sparsely fur-nished in comparison to its U.S. counterpart. There is no carpeting in the classroom, no computers, and little furniture other than a small desk and chair for each pupil and a set of "cubby-holes" where students store their backpacks. There is a television set so that the regularly aired educational programs may be viewed, should the teacher decide to use these programs as part of his or her teaching. Often there is some sort of class pet that doubles as a class science project. In our fourth grade classroom we had a good dozen or so of rather disappointingly unexotic (in my view, at least) crickets. The walls are decorated with children's work; with posters illustrating the correct posture for sitting at a desk, the correct way to hold a pencil, etc., and with banners blazoned with school and class goals, such as "Let's try our hardest."

The school year begins in early April, rather than September, and continues to approximately the middle of the following March; the major vacations are a six-week summer vacation and a two-week winter vacation. Japanese children spend an estimated 195 to 240 days in school (the estimation is difficult because they continue to come to school during vacations for extracurricular activities) while U.S. children spend 180 days.[3] However, much of this time is spent on noninstructional activities that do not take place in the U.S. system. Catherine C. Lewis estimates that total instructional hours in the Japanese system equates to approximately 185 school days.[4] About 30 days of the "longer" Japanese school year can be accounted for with special activities and ceremonies designed to build a sense of community and team spirit, such as Sports Day, field trips, and festivals.

The Ministry of Education defines the curriculum in the Course of Study. Japanese teachers lack the high degree of independence that U.S. teachers enjoy. Though it presents clearly what the children must learn, the national curriculum is not so rigidly defined that everyone will be learning the exact same thing at the exact same time. Instead, it serves more as a set of guidelines, which each school must interpret to fit its own needs. The more detailed aspects of the curriculum are left up to schools and private publishers, who use the Ministry's Course of Study to create the appropriate materials for each grade. The textbook series to be used in a city or prefecture is selected by local educational authorities, not by teachers, but the teachers are free to develop their own approaches to teaching the content of the required text.

Table 3-1. Required Elementary Instructional Periods

Subject	Grade					
	1	2	3	4	5	6
Japanese	306	315	280	280	210	210
Social Studies			105	105	105	105
Mathematics	136	175	175	175	175	175
Science			105	105	105	105
Daily Living	102	105				
Music	68	70	70	70	70	70
Art & Crafts	68	70	70	70	70	70
Home Economics					70	70
Physical Education	102	105	105	105	105	105
Moral Education	34	35	35	35	35	35
Special Education	34	35	35	70	70	70
Total	850	910	980	1015	1015	1015

Table 3-1 shows the number of 45-minute classroom periods per school year required for each subject as specified by the Ministry of Education's Course of Study for elementary schools. Note that nonacademic, or what Americans would call "enrichment," subjects account for a third or more of instructional hours at all levels; the proportion of time spent on these subjects increases, rather than decreases, with the grade level.

School lasts on average five and a half days per week (Saturday is a half day). A 1993 comparative study of elementary schools in Japan and the United States[5] found that first graders in Japan spend an average of 5.6 hours a day in school—the same as their U.S. counterparts. In the fifth grade, U.S. children still spend 5.6 hours per day while Japanese children spend closer to 7 hours a day in school. Much of this extra time is spent in extracurricular activities called *kurabu* (clubs), where students participate in activities such as sports, drama, literature, music, and traditional Japanese arts.

The school day is organized around 40 to 50-minute class periods; each period is followed by a recess of 10 or 15 minutes. The study quoted above shows that Japanese children spend 15 percent of their time in recesses, while U.S. children spend less than 5 percent. In addition to recesses, the Japanese lunch hour lasts from one to one and a half hours, which includes the time spent for the whole-school cleaning, which takes place after lunch, and free-play.

Retention in a grade is not an option. The same group of children move up a grade together, and stay with the same homeroom teacher for at least two to three years. Japanese teachers, knowing that they will be with the same set of children for a while, are highly motivated to understand each child.

Japanese teachers hold a respected place in Japanese society, and their salaries reflect this high status. Their salaries are competitive with those holding university positions, or those working in business or other professions. Japanese teachers spend eight to nine hours a day in school, and teach for about four to six of these hours. The rest of the time is spent interacting with other teachers. This allows them to hold discussions and learn from each other. A Japanese teacher will remain at a single school for a maximum of seven years, after which they are offered the opportunity to encounter new schools and pupils and the challenges that these may present. The result of this policy is a continuous, widespread sharing of information between teachers.

Learning to Work in and as a Group

"Okay class, let's go to the science lab to do the experiment," Oohashi-sensei says.

We all jostle our way down the hall to the science lab. We all know that we will do the experiment in our *han*, or small group. Once in the lab we sit, grouped by han, at our stations. This week's science monitor for each han goes to the front of the class to receive, carefully, a beaker of very hot water and small containers of salt of varying coarseness from the teacher. The rest of us quickly divvy up between us the task of fetching the remaining equipment. Morita-kun, being the tallest, gets the electronic scale from its shelf in the equipment cabinet, I fetch three empty beakers, Takeuchi-san gets the glass stirring rods, and Daisuke-kun goes to fetch a thermometer.

Once we are all back at our station my group goes over each step of the experiment together and decides who will perform each step, and how. With the tasks split up, the experiment runs smoothly. Oohashi-sensei makes her way around the class, occasionally asking a group whether they think that is the best way to stir the salt solution, or whether they think that two seconds is long enough to get a good reading on the thermometer. We discuss, as a group, the observations we make, pointing out anything we see that the other members may have missed, and reaching an agreement among us on what we have seen. We carefully record our observations in our science notebooks in the special section for this. We have already filled out the section on what we expect to happen. We had discussed this as a class back in the classroom. Oohashi-sensei had asked us all for our ideas of what would happen but had not given us any hint as to what the actual outcome might be.

Once the experiment is over, we divide the clean-up with no argument. Daisuke-kun, Takeuchi-san and I wash out the beakers and containers we have used, while the others put the equipment back where it came from. Once we have inspected our workplace and agreed that it is spic-and-span, we return to the classroom and wait for the other groups to join us.

When the class is once again fully assembled in the classroom, Oohashi-sensei asks us for our opinions as to what happened in the experiment. Everybody has something to say. She acts as mediator, occasionally spurring a flagging discussion with a deeper question. We discuss our findings as a class until we feel we have all reached an understanding of why things happened the way they did. We write down our conclusions in our science books. Oohashi-sensei praises us for working so well together.

In Japan, students are taught how to work together as a group as distinct from working in a group. Teachers recognize that this ability is something that needs to be taught. Working as a group implies somehow that the group itself is an entity of its own that is more that just the sum of the individuals that comprise it. This means that not only do the children learn that they can accomplish more as a group than they could individually, but also that they feel a sense of collective identity with the group and recognize the special responsibilities that come with being part of a group, such as the ability to listen to the other members in the group and to delegate responsibility. A sense of collective identity and the value of collective membership must be taught to the students.

The groupings the children are exposed to are kumi and han. Kumi is the children's class, and they are expected to identify themselves with and are referred to according to their classroom group. Often, the children will wear badges identifying their kumi. At the elementary school that I attended, we wore color-coded pins on our hats. Han are the small groups that are the basic units of the class, with four to six pupils each. Small group activities take place in the han. New han are created every few months, and the members of each are determined at the discretion of the teacher. These are of mixed ability grouping, so that slower learners can benefit from the help of their faster-learning han members, who benefit in turn by helping them. Small group activities range from such things as science experiments to eating lunch together.

A 1992 study of 24 elementary schools in 6 districts across the United States found that 60 percent of U.S. teachers use small groups.[6] However, these groups were used to organize children by ability within a certain activity; for example, reading groups determined by reading ability. There is little student-to-student interaction within these U.S. ability-based group activities, which are usually activities such as round-robin reading. This is in stark contrast to the mixed-ability, multiple-activity groupings of the Japanese classroom, where the students in each group work together toward a common goal.

To nurture a sense of collective identity, children have to feel an emotional attachment to the group and learn to feel a sense of pride and satisfaction in knowing that "we did this together" rather than "I did this all by myself." Membership in a group does not entail the loss of individuality. Catherine C. Lewis quotes a Japanese teacher: "To nurture the group, you must nurture each individual."[7]

A sense of belonging to a group is taught by building connections among the children by drawing out the children's personal experiences and ideas. The day is often started with the daily monitors giving "one-minute speeches" on what they did the day before after school or over the weekend. The other students ask questions for about five minutes. This sort of activity leads the children to feel a sense of belonging to the class group. Similarly, the han activities lead to strong group identification. Within the closer familiarity of these smaller groups, the children are even more willing to express their ideas and feelings. Many of the more pleasurable activities of the day, such as lunch, drama and art projects, and games, take place in han groupings, thus strengthening the bonds felt between the students. Despite a certain amount of healthy competition that might arise between these groups, the reward for functioning smoothly and efficiently is usually no more than a word of praise— directed at the entire group—from the teacher. "Points" or other rewards of this type are not common in the Japanese classroom. Systems of reward based on a "winner" and "loser" are not used, as these are not conducive to a healthy group dynamic. Groups that "lose" would not be happy working together and may ostracize the less able children in the group. Furthermore, seeing other groups as adversaries would lessen the sense of classhood.

Other means of nurturing a sense of collective identity include praising individual efforts as contributions to the group. The children are taught that talent and creativity are praiseworthy because they make a meaningful contribution to the group effort. Individual projects that the children work on present the children with the opportunity for creative self-expression, but these projects are usually integrated into a whole-class project at a later point. The children learn to regard their own and other's work not as isolated individual expression, but as arising from and contributing to the group.

Self-Reliance, Responsibility, and the Creation of Bonds

The chimes over the loudspeaker signal the end of the last recess of the day. It is now last period, which is, on most days, a class meeting. Today's monitors note down on the daily check-sheet which han are gathered at their desks by the time the chime ends. Han that are sitting quietly with all members present are given a double circle, those whose members are all present but still talking get one circle, those who are missing a few members and are still talking get a triangle, and han who are mostly missing get an X. Eventually the whole class is gathered. The teacher stands at the front of the class silently. The monitors call us to attention, and we greet the teacher. The monitors start the end-of-day meeting; one of them reads from an outline if they forget what topic of discussion comes next, and the other makes a log of what we talk about. The first item of discussion is group chore performance. We are asked to reflect on whether we performed our chores well. Then, Oohashi-sensei asks each han in turn to report to the class on their chores. When the monitors call on han six, my group stands. This week we are on second-floor stair-cleaning *toban* (duty).

"Did you perform your chore well today?" Oohashi-sensei asks.

"No, we didn't finish," Takeuchi-san admits with a flush.

"Why not?"

"Because the boys were playing Ultraman on the stairs while we were trying to clean them," I pipe in. Other students start offering their own experiences with group members who have not helped with the chores.

"Class, let's think about what to do if only a few people are doing their chore while other group members are off playing," Oohashi-sensei suggests.

After a few moments of thought, people in the group start offering their suggestions.

"The people that aren't playing should do it!" someone offers.

Oohashi-sensei appears to give this some thought.

"Do you think that is the way it should be done?" she asks us. After much protesting, other suggestions are offered.

"Don't give them seconds for lunch!"

"Make them stand in the hall!"

"Make them do it ALL tomorrow!"

"Go get a teacher to make them do it!"

Oohashi-sensei asks us to think carefully about what she is going to say next.

"Do you think it is a good thing if people work because they are forced to, or because they are afraid?"

We all think about this, and agree that it is not an ideal situation. Finally someone suggests, "The people who are working should ask the other people nicely to help them with the group chore so that it will get done properly."

Oohashi-sensei asks the rest of the class how we feel about this. We all agree that it seems like a good idea. I consider the Ultramen in our group and with some American cynicism wonder whether this would actually work. Oddly enough, it does.

Self-reliance and group responsibility

Students are taught responsibility both in self- and classroom-management, and also in shaping their learning environment. Self-responsibility is taught in the form of self-reliance. Students are responsible for being on time and for keeping their own personal space neat. This is made easy by the use of school chimes and set lesson periods and by the use of charts and posters easily understood by students of a young age that demonstrate the correct way to perform certain tasks. Established routines and set procedures facilitate the smooth execution of these tasks. Making school routine predictable ensures that students have control over these routines, and allows them to manage themselves successfully. Note the striking similarity to the use of visual management and the standardization of tasks in kaizen.

In terms of classroom-management, elementary school students learn to operate under minimal adult supervision and, again, to rely heavily on a set of established routines and procedures. They are involved in the shaping and enforcement of the school norms and practices that keep the han, kumi, and school running smoothly, and thus they grow to care genuinely about the rules and regulations by which they live, and continue to uphold them, even in the absence of an adult.

Students are responsible for classroom chores such as serving lunch and cleaning, and are able to perform these tasks quickly and effectively due to their routinized nature. The serving of lunch is a sensational example of classroom management by students.

Just before the chimes at the end of the period before lunch sound, we hear the familiar rattle of our class's lunch cart as it is left outside the doors of our classroom by one of the kitchen staff. At the sound of the chimes, the monitors call on us to stand at attention. We thank Oohashi-sensei and bow, and once she has bowed back, the classroom undergoes a transformation into a dining room. The han on *kyushoku-toban* (school lunch duty) for this week is Han Three, and they rush off to don white chef hats and aprons and to fetch the lunch cart, while the rest of the class rearranges the desks from their usual straight rows to form a dining table for each han, made up of the desks of the members of that han. One of Han Three's members is going around the classroom with a milk crate, placing a bottle of milk at each person's place. The cart has been wheeled in. It is constructed so that it expands to form a long, narrow service table. Han Three set up the trays and utensils at the far end of this table, and then the stacks of empty plates and bowls. We are already starting to line up for our food. The steaming pots of rice and curry sauce, the large bowl of salad and the chocolate bread for dessert are carefully laid out on the table's surface. All preparations done, the rest of us make our way down this "cafeteria line" and are served our food by the aproned members of Han Three. Those who get served first come back to get a tray for a Han Three member and the teacher. Only when everyone has a tray of food and is sitting ready to eat do we as a class say a quick but heartfelt "thank you" to nature and the people who prepared the food, and start to eat.

In my experience, groups looked forward to being on lunch duty, and the faces on the other side of the "cafeteria counter" were more often than not beaming under the chef's hats. The students relish this responsibility. The student-management of this chore, which even first graders perform daily, is made possible because of the standardized nature of the process. Charts list the responsibilities for the different toban, so that students can check off the steps as they perform their duties.

Class meetings, even at the first-grade level, are also run by students. Charts showing the agenda for daily class meetings allow the daily monitors to lead the meetings. Discussion about the class chores is a regular topic on the class meeting agenda. Students actively discuss what worked, what didn't, and what can be done to improve the process. Though in my experience the problems that arose had invariably to do with the people involved in the process rather than the process itself, I feel confident that my fellow students would have been fully capable of making improvements to the process. Here we see a clear indication of the plan-do-check-act (PDCA) cycle used so widely in the Japanese workplace, and the dedication to continuous improvement as a way of thinking.

I'd like to point out here that the position of daily monitor, as its name implies, changes from day to day. There are usually two monitors per day, one girl and one boy, who split up the duties of this position between them as they see fit. They are responsible for quieting the class before each lesson, for evaluating han and class performance, and for leading class meetings. Every student in the class is given the chance to be the class leader, and the privilege is usually passed down through the class in "alphabetical" order, independent of behavior or popular vote. Each child has his or her opportunity to fill this position simply because he or she is a member of the class. Being in this position gives the children a chance to experience leadership, with all its responsibilities, and serves also to build a sense of empathy with authority.

The students also play an active role in shaping the direction and content of their lessons and learning environment. Rote learning and memorization are strongly de-emphasized in Japanese education in elementary school. A teacher is more likely to introduce a topic for discussion and to elicit as many ideas and opinions as possible from the class, giving no indication of whether their responses are right or not. She or he will encourage the class to debate among themselves, occasionally fueling the discussion with a question designed to provoke further thought. It is the students' own contributions and ideas that drive the lessons.

Participation in the whole-class and small-group discussion is treated as a responsibility, rather than a choice. For instance, students may be called on in turn by the teacher to offer their own opinions, or each student who offers an opinion might be asked to ask another student to give theirs. Students are also taught to consider the conditions that support healthy class participation. At the end of a lesson or day, the students are often asked to reflect on matters to do with classroom participation: Did I volunteer my ideas? Did I listen to others' ideas? Did I think of others' feelings before I spoke?

The absence of rewards based on academic achievement ensures that the motivation to learn comes primarily from the interaction of students with the subject matter and not from rewards or incentives offered by the teacher. This is in contrast to the common practice of giving out "points" or stickers in the U.S. classroom. The emphasis here is on the process that the students use to learn, a subject that I discuss in more detail below.

Considerable emphasis is placed on the value of *gambaru* (persistence, trying one's hardest). Japanese pupils are taught that effort, rather than natural ability, is the most important part of academic achievement. When faced with a difficult problem, a Japanese child is less likely to give up on it by dismissing it as beyond his or her ability. A part of persistence is identifying the goal one is striving to attain. Daily and weekly class meetings often include the setting of goals for the class, or the individual personal goals of each child, and the success toward goals is often evaluated in part by how hard everyone *gambatta* (tried their very best) toward them. In this way, students are taught the need for continuous self-improvement. An important part of this is the setting of goals and reflection on how they have performed in relation to those goals. They spend considerable time in *hansei* (self-evaluating reflection) to focus on their shortcomings, and are aware that there is always room for improvement. This parallels the use of targets and evaluation against those targets that is central to kaizen, as well as the need for continuously asking how we could have done better.

Creation of bonds

The social development of Japanese elementary school children is focused on long-term bond-building to the groups with which the child is affiliated (school, kumi, and han) as well as to individual friends and the teacher. I have discussed already in some detail the close nature of the Japanese groups, and this is aided by the entire class moving up a grade together, along with their teacher. (Note that a common practice in Japanese factories that run multiple shifts is for the whole group, along with the group leader, to rotate across shifts.)

Another means of strengthening and maintaining these bonds, especially with the teacher and other students, is the way discipline is handled in the Japanese classroom. Often a teacher will single out a misbehaving child for praise. The rationale here is that the misbehavior itself is not the root of the problem, but rather, the child is misbehaving because his bonds with his classmates need to be strengthened. Singling out the child for punishment will most likely harm these bonds, and by finding some opportunity to praise him instead, it reminds the other children of that child's merits.

Discipline often makes an appeal to the bonds that already exist, or to feelings. The teacher may ask, "How would your mother feel if you break that?" or "If you do that, everyone will laugh at me." By making an appeal to the child's emotions rather than giving a direct order, the conflict between teacher and student is hidden, and the teacher is not seen as an adversary.

Because much of the classroom management is undertaken by the students themselves, the teacher is able to keep a low profile as a figure of authority. The daily monitors are responsible for bringing the class under control, and because this is a position that each of the students has already held, or will hold in the future, they empathize with and respond to their requests. The teacher is saved from having to enforce discipline on the students, and confrontational and adversarial feelings are avoided. Nor do teachers reward especially good behavior in the way often found in the U.S. classroom, with stickers and motivators. These rewards, or the withholding of them, is more a means of immediate behavioral control, the long-term effect of which is to create a sense of competition between students, which may be detrimental to the bonds between them.

Furthermore, the style of teaching employed by the teachers, discussed above, creates a sense of common struggle and unites teacher and students in a search for answers. This strengthens the student-to-student and student-to-teacher bonds.

Stressing Process, Not Product

Some of the teaching techniques that Japanese teachers use in the classroom, such as whole-class and small-group discussion and the use of the students' natural interest and ideas on the subject to drive the lesson, I have already discussed above. Japanese teachers encourage class participation by frequently telling them to remember that there are many ways to solve a problem, and the best way to find these solutions is to think up as many possible ones as they can. They are reminded not to worry about getting the right answer. In this way, Japanese elementary school teachers place emphasis on thinking about the problem (the process) instead of getting the right answer (the product). This leads to better conceptual understanding of the topic under discussion.

Students keep ongoing notebooks for each subject, so that all their notes for a subject are bound together in one place. Because of the standardization of the textbook materials, teachers do not have to rely on their own handouts, and students do not have to keep track of loose sheets of paper. The notebooks are also available at the local bookstores where the students purchase their textbooks, and the style of these notebooks varies from subject to subject, though there is relatively little variation between different manufacturers. The notebooks are used to keep track not only of the final points from each lesson, but the entire flow of thought that leads up to those conclusions, such as the initial thinking, activities, and a summary of the group and class discussion. The entire process of learning, including the brainstorming and initial predictions, are available as a permanent record for the student to review. Often in the United States, these steps in the learning process are recorded on bits of scrap paper, if at all, and discarded by the end of the lesson.

The Japanese elementary school class still does its fair share of seat-work, or drill-type exercises. These are primarily used by the teacher as a check after each step, rather than assigned as a lump at the end of the class to provide a break for the teacher.

Errors on homework and drill exercises are not seen as an indication of failure, but as evidence of what the children do not know and what the teacher needs to clarify. Response to errors is nonjudgmental in terms of the children's abilities, and they are attributed to lack of study, not lack of ability. Errors are viewed as a good opportunity for discussing and correcting misinterpretations. The teacher will rarely provide the correct answer, but will circle the error and tell the student to think about his or her answer some more.

Middle School: Transition to Exam Hell

Summer vacation is drawing to a close, and the last of the local summer festivals is full of students from my middle school. You'd think from our schoolgirl squeals at running into classmates that we haven't seen each other at least three times a week at the school during vacation for regularly held *kurabu* (club) meetings. There are teachers from the school patrolling between the colorful *tako-yaki* and goldfish-dipping stands, and my friends and I discreetly try to avoid them, fearful but thrilled at the enormity of our misbehavior. We are chewing gum.

I have already been jostled by that group of *senpai* (senior, superior) girls that hate me for not bowing to them whenever I see them, and my friends and I keep a wary eye out for them, as well as for the teachers. This summer has been unreal for me. It is my first experience in a Japanese middle school, and my largely Western background may play some part in this culture shock. Still, this time last year I was in a Japanese elementary school for the summer, and I certainly don't remember things being quite like this. It's not that the faces are different. Many of the kids from my elementary school are in my grade here now, though the kumi from elementary school have been broken up. Oogaya-san and Daisuke-kun went on to some posh private school, but the rest of my core group of friends from elementary school are in my grade, though we are now in different kumi.

The first shock was learning that I had to bow to the girls in the grade above me whenever I saw them, be it in school or out. Put it down to my being American, but I was simply not about to do this. The concept of paying homage to someone simply because they are my senior, and only by a year or two at that, was completely alien to me. Thus the harassment from that one group of senpai girls. Of course, most of the senpai don't treat me that way, and I have seen how they help out and support my friends, acting as mentors and guides.

The other shock was how involved the school is in what I see as being my personal life. Every day, I fill out a page in my *seikatsu* (lifestyle) diary for my teacher to read. She wants to know what I eat and when I eat it, when I study and for how long, when I sleep, what I do in my free time, everything. She says that I need to learn to manage my time better, and set personal goals for myself so that I am always improving. Improving at what?! She said I should talk to some of the people in my han about these things. So I talked with Ueno-san about it, and my goals aren't anything like his. His were all about lame stuff like studying harder, and not letting his family down, and working really hard at his Aikido skills so that he can perform better in his Aikido kurabu. I think I study plenty hard enough to get through each term and besides, the classes here move too fast for me to do more than keep up, since my Japanese isn't as good as theirs. My family, well! I won't even go into what a pain my parents are being. And as for kurabu, if Ueno-san had picked something he already knew about, like I did—I picked English, so I know everything already—then he wouldn't have to work so hard to get better, would he? My goal is to collect Coke cans in every language. When I get back to my regular school, my friends and I are going to have a good laugh at how immature these Japanese kids are.

Middle school serves as a transitional period between elementary school and high school, and develops in the students the intellectual characteristics necessary to move successfully through the "exam hell" of high school. At the end of middle school, the students will take entrance exams leading to hierarchically ranked high schools, then to even more extensively ranked universities. It is here that the reality of stratification through exams confronts virtually all students and their parents. Future income, prestige, and job security ride on the results. Academic demands on the child are increased, and the group-centered, experimental approach to learning of elementary school is replaced by a text-centered, lecture-style format designed to transmit vast amounts of information quickly and efficiently to students.

Students are expected to face up to the importance of exams and learn to consider such weighty issues as their ambitions and their future. They are expected to develop the motivation and self-discipline needed to fulfill these ambitions. Thus, there is also much emphasis placed on the personal development of students through *seikatsu shido* (life-guidance) via the use of *kurabu* (extracurricular clubs), a range of nonacademic classes, and close monitoring of their private lives. Perhaps it is here that the distinction between the private life and work life become blurred for the Japanese worker.

Entry into middle school also marks the student's abrupt introduction to the world of *senpai-kohai* (senior-junior) relations. The basics of being able to work in a group have been established in elementary school, and now the students are exposed to the role of hierarchy and organization within groups. There is still considerable emphasis placed on group activities, but these interactions take place during the more socially rather than academically oriented class periods and during kurabu activities.

Background and Setting: Big Changes in Instructional Technique

A Japanese middle school classroom looks much like an elementary school classroom but with bigger desks and chairs. In middle school, for the first time the students have different teachers for each of their subjects, and these teachers are subject specialists. The curriculum still focuses on the whole person, stressing social and personal development as well as intellectual development. Guidance, counseling, and self-discipline are considered to be a part of daily education. Most of the school week (roughly 27 of the 32 weekly instructional hours)[8] is spent on academic instruction, including enrichment subjects such as music, arts, sports, and homeroom time. The other 15 percent or so is spent on health, moral, educational, and occupational guidance. Furthermore, there are still special days, such as Sports Day, class trips, and ceremonies.

There is little or none of the small-group and student-driven learning that is emphasized in elementary school. Lessons are intense, fast-paced, fact-filled, text-centered, and routinized lectures, with little time for student opinions and ideas, hands-on learning, or student-to-student interaction. Teachers, adhering closely to the text because there is no time to deviate and because the texts are based on what will be on the entrance exams, enjoy little to no control over their instruction. Time and discipline are of the utmost importance, and the motivation to keep up must come from the student. There is little, if any, provision for individual differences either in interests or abilities.

Students are examined on academic subjects two times each semester. Methods for evaluation stress individual proficiency of material in the texts, and the examination questions are overwhelmingly short-answer, fill in the blank, and multiple choice. As with university entrance examinations, the student's performance on these examinations is nearly the sole method of evaluation; other activities and abilities play little or no part.

As in elementary school, there is no ability grouping of students in middle school. The pressures of impending examinations and this lack of a differentiating mechanism have led to the rise of *juku* (cram schools) of every type, from "remedial" juku designed for the slower learner who is having trouble keeping up with the fast pace of classes, to "express" juku, which provides more specialized knowledge and faster learning. Most middle school students attend juku several times during the week and weekend.

Though this seems a dreary and uninspiring picture, especially considering that these children are roughly 11 to 14 years of age, there are benefits to the system. First of all, Japanese middle school students still spend proportionately more time on nonacademic lessons and activities than do their U.S. counterparts. Not only do they enjoy more of the enrichment subjects such as art and music, but they participate in activities such as field trips, ceremonies, special events, and preparation for special events on an almost weekly basis. Indeed, there are few weeks in which classes are not cut to accommodate some special activity. Second, given that the lecture style of the academic classes is at least an efficient means of transferring massive quantities of information to the students, it would be difficult to combine nonacademic content (such as the group and personal development activities) into these lessons without some loss of their effectiveness. Instead, the Japanese have chosen to split the social and intellectual development of the student into separate types of classes and activities, rather than trying to incorporate both aspects into all activities all day long as in elementary school.

Character and Social Development

Much focus in middle school is placed on the cultivation of character. In terms of group socialization, the lessons in mutuality and communality are replaced by the introduction to social hierarchy and learning to function as part of a chain of command. The students are still largely responsible for the management of nonacademic classroom and other activities and for the upkeep of their school and its daily processes. Their personal lives come under intense scrutiny, and through feedback from their seniors and teachers, they learn to manage their lives and develop the characteristics needed to ensure their successful passage through "exam hell"—which are also characteristics necessary for success in the workplace. Lessons in character and social development include the following:

- Further socialization to the group
- Student responsibility
- Constant effort in order to attain goals
- Integration of work and personal life
- Peer-to-peer discipline

1. *Further socialization to the group.* The most striking difference between the group interactions in elementary school and middle school is the introduction of social hierarchy and the senpai-kohai, or junior-senior, relationship. Perhaps the most important tool used to socialize students into stratified society is the kurabu, or clubs. Each student selects the kurabu of his or her choice upon entering middle school and normally stays with this group until graduation. Though a faculty member heads each club, most of the club activities are organized by the members, and the senior members are responsible for teaching the more junior members. Junior members of the group are expected to listen to and respect the senior members. Being able to learn and participate in this social context is important later on, when the students join the work force. Students within a class still form the small han groups found in elementary school, but these han interact little in the academic learning environment, and this grouping is used mainly for nonacademic activities and classroom chores. Their purpose is mainly to foster bonds among the students and to ensure that all students are part of a grouping within their class. They are also expected to listen to and respect their seniors.

2. *Student responsibility*. Similar to the elementary school toban system, middle school students take on responsibility for day-to-day tasks as *kakari* (person in charge), such as taking attendance, keeping the daily log of activities and evaluations, and calling the class to order. These positions of responsibility usually change on a daily basis, and each student fills each responsibility in turn. In addition to kakari are the school and class committees, such as the student council, health committee, and various festival committees, which tend to be longer term and are elected or rotated positions. These serve practical needs, but also are activities in guidance, whereby students learn techniques for self- and peer-management.

3. *Constant effort in order to attain goals*. As with elementary school, effort and dedication are emphasized over ability, and students regularly set goals for themselves.

4. *Integration of work and personal life*. Japanese middle schools closely monitor the lifestyles of their students to ensure that students lead lives conducive to their studies and development into responsible adults. This is accomplished by the requirement that all students keep a *seikatsu* (lifestyle) diary that they fill out every day. The students fill out information on how they spent their time, and record their feelings in a special section. There is a section for *hansei*, or reflection, wherein students evaluate themselves relative to their goals. These diaries are periodically reviewed by the teachers, who check for any personal or disciplinary problems that might arise and offer suggestions for improvement. In addition, each han keeps a more detailed daily diary in which han members take turns writing a page or two on anything they choose, which the teacher and other han members regularly read. This constant communication between han members and the teacher helps to fortify the bonds between them.

5. *Peer-to-peer discipline*. Han are responsible for the behavior of their members, and class representatives are responsible for class misbehavior. Minor disciplinary problems are handled by students, who spot and solve the problems. Problems of a more major sort are handled by the teachers. Discipline usually consists of a scolding followed by the students' reflecting on what they have done until they understand why what they have done is the "wrong" thing to do. I found that what I viewed as being minor rule-transgressions were treated with utmost gravity. For example, at my middle school, chewing gum whether in school or out was a sign of impending delinquency. I was told many times to reflect on why this was a bad thing to do.

High School: Examination Hell

The most prestigious jobs in industry and government go almost exclusively to graduates of a few elite universities. Entrance into universities depends almost solely on university entrance examinations. Grades and written recommendations play a minor role in college admission. The exams require the rote-memorization of a massive body of information, which is often outdated and of dubious applicability. By high school, the sole purpose of school is to pass the entrance examinations. The lectures are entirely teacher-centered, and there is intense pressure on the students. Critics of the system question the point of this practice, as it seemingly ignores the talents of individual students, causes extreme tension (sometimes resulting in tragedy), and perpetuates one-sided intellectual development.

Perhaps this criticism is missing the point, though. The examinations are highly predictable so that schools, students, and their parents know how to prepare. They measure acquired knowledge on the assumption that success depends not on innate ability, but on the effort one is willing to expend on disciplined study. This expenditure of effort is independent of the student's natural abilities and serves to put everyone on equal footing. Furthermore, the student is not subject to arbitrary evaluation, such as teacher recommendations (though these may play a role in marginal cases). In this respect, the examination process serves as an equalizer of opportunity.

The years leading up to this point have prepared the students for the intense pressure they now face. Students have by now learned self-discipline and the need for continuous effort. They have formed strong bonds with the "teacher," and since the teacher's authority in judging the student is irrelevant, the teacher becomes an ally. As in middle school, teachers tend to take responsibility in the students' private as well as classroom lives, and offer tremendous support to the students. The students are also dependent on their families to support them through this period. This all maintains a solidarity among student, school, and family.

The small group discussions, management of self and peers, communal chores, and hansei (reflective self-evaluation) are still found in high school clubs, university clubs, and, later, company training programs. Though these qualities still characterize the fundamental habits of the students, they have by now mastered these routines and little attention is paid to their development, as the focus shifts entirely to the effort of study. The values developed in the students during the previous nine years have been fully internalized, making them less visible to the casual observer. Although the last stage in the student's development may seem wholly one-sided, the educational process should be viewed in its entirety as a twelve-year process.

Conclusions: Japanese Education and Its Relation to Kaizen in the Workplace

If we accept the kaizen (continuous improvement) philosophy as being one of the keys to Japan's competitive success, we can see how the education system serves to internalize the characteristics needed to apply this philosophy successfully.

The final product of the Japanese educational system is an individual who is extremely group-oriented and who has the means to be able to work effectively in a group and as a group member. Being able to identify with the group to the extent that the goals of the group become their own, individuals strive for these goals and take personal pleasure at drawing incrementally nearer to them. They are able to participate actively in group discussions with the purpose of reaching a consensus, and are sensitive to others' feelings.

The Japanese graduate who enters the work force is able to think in the long term and to set long-term goals. He or she is naturally trained to continually evaluate and improve the progress toward those goals, and is willing to expend monumental, continuous effort to move forward. He or she is self-disciplined and able to manage himself or herself and others in a group effectively.

As we attempt to implement Japanese production methods in U.S. workplaces, we should keep in mind the differences between the schooling of Japanese and American students. Lean manufacturing is a way of thinking, not just a set of procedures and practices.

It is a system that depends on people. Without continuous improvement, the system will stagnate and ultimately degrade. I hope it is clear from this chapter that the Japanese worker has an almost ideal educational background to participate actively in kaizen. Stepping into a Japanese-run factory using lean manufacturing is almost a seamless extension of what the Japanese worker has been learning and doing since kindergarten. Even many of the names are the same, for example, the basic work group on the shopfloor is the *han*.

For Americans who have not been intensively socialized through most of their lives in this way, the concepts necessary for kaizen are neither deeply ingrained nor easily understood, particularly if they have worked for some years in a traditional company managed by top-down management. This is not to say that the differences in the two cultures pose insurmountable barriers to lean manufacturing, but it does mean, and this is very important, that U.S. managers will need to compensate for their employees' lack of socialization by providing intensive training and continual on-the-job reinforcement of kaizen principles. These principles will not come as quickly or naturally to U.S. employees, but with the proper leadership and the requisite education, they can "get it."

Notes

1. Imai, Masaaki. *Kaizen: The Key to Japan's Competitive Success*. New York: McGraw-Hill, 1986. p. xxix.

2. Imai, Masaaki. *Kaizen: The Key to Japan's Competitive Success*. New York: McGraw-Hill, 1986.

3. U.S. Study of Education, 1987.

4. Lewis, Catherine C. *Educating Hearts and Minds: Reflections on Japanese Preschool and Elementary Education*. Cambridge: Cambridge University Press, 1995. p. 62.

5. From a 1993 comparative study by Shin-Ying Lee, Theresa Graham, and Harold W. Stevenson of 10 Japanese and 20 Chicago schools.

6. Developmental Studies Center, 1992.

7. Lewis, Catherine C. *Educating Hearts and Minds: Reflections on Japanese Preschool and Elementary Education*. Cambridge: Cambridge University Press, 1995. p. 87.

8. Fukuzawa, Rebecca Erwin. *The Path to Adulthood According to Japanese Middle Schools*. Cambridge: Cambridge University Press, 1996. p. 297.

Additional References

Cummings, William K. *Education and Equality in Japan*. Princeton: Princeton University Press, 1979.

Feinburg, Walter. *Japan and the Pursuit of a New American Identity: Work and Education in a Multicultural Age*. New York: Routledge, 1993.

Rohlen, Thomas P. *For Harmony and Strength*. Berkeley: University of California Press, 1974.

———. *Japan's High Schools*. Berkeley: University of California Press, 1983.

Thomas, J. E. *Making Japan Work: The Origins, Education, and Training of the Japanese Salaryman*. Kent: Japan Library, 1993.

Vogel, Ezra F. *Japan as Number One: Lessons for America*. Cambridge, Mass.: Harvard University Press, 1979.

Steven F. Rasch *is president of the Ann Arbor Consulting Group, Inc. and an adjunct faculty member at the University of Michigan. He teaches courses in production, economics, and organizational theory. Before starting the Ann Arbor Consulting Group in 1991, he worked for two nationally recognized management consulting firms. He has served over 50 companies during his 17 years of consulting experience. His clients have included firms in the automotive, electronics, and utility industries, as well as federal and state governmental agencies. His areas of specialization include production management, budgeting and cost management processes, and organizational development and restructuring. Mr. Rasch has also served as an expert witness on behalf of several utility clients involved in multi-billion dollar rate case proceedings.*

Mr. Rasch has a B.S. and an M.S. from the University of Michigan and an M.B.A. from the University of Chicago. He is currently completing requirements for a Ph.D. in Industrial and Operations Engineering at the University of Michigan. His dissertation is entitled, World-Class Manufacturing Practice—Do they Work in American Companies? *His research focuses on measuring the productivity and quality improvements that U.S. companies have realized through the implementation of lean engineering and manufacturing practices.*

4

Lean Manufacturing Practices at Small and Medium-Sized U.S. Parts Suppliers–Does It Work?

by Steven F. Rasch

Editor's prologue: Steven Rasch presents a statistical analysis of data from 249 small suppliers of automotive component parts in the Midwest and looks in the aggregate at the relationship among various facets of lean manufacturing and performance outcomes. His results show convincingly that each of the major aspects of lean is associated with improvements in performance. These lean manufacturing practices include built-in quality systems, just-in-time (JIT) production, high-involvement team-based organization, and lean supply systems. Moreover, Steven finds a significant interaction between production worker involvement and authority on the one hand and the use of JIT and preventative maintenance (PM) on the other. That is, the technical features of JIT and PM lead to improvement, and the social features of employee involvement and influence lead to improvement; but in combination, these technical and social features have a multiplier effect that is more than the sum of the parts.

The Japanese form of management, typically referred to as lean manufacturing, world class manufacturing, or total quality management (TQM), is currently viewed as the most efficient and economical way to design and manufacture high-quality products and the most effective way to increase productivity and worker satisfaction. Today, these lean manufacturing concepts are widely accepted by U.S. companies. Embracing these practices has required American companies to make considerable changes in how they conduct business and organize their work forces. While many U.S. companies have adopted some form of lean manufacturing or implemented a TQM program, the actual benefits and significance derived from such programs has been greatly left to ad hoc justification or specialized case studies designed to investigate a specific aspect of lean manufacturing.

This chapter is an empirical study that statistically analyzes the relationship between lean manufacturing characteristics and company performance. The question is: Do the core practices of lean manufacturing really make a difference in bottom-line performance measures? I address this question through evaluating the data of 249 small suppliers of automotive component parts (plastics, stampings, and machined parts). The results demonstrate that built-in quality systems, just-in-time (JIT) production, high-involvement team-based organization, and lean supply systems all have strong effects on performance.

As demonstrated by John Shook and others in this book, lean manufacturing is a system of production, not just a collection of separate practices. As a system, one would expect the parts to interact. To test this, the analysis went further than looking only at individual practices and, not surprisingly, found a strong interaction between the technical features of lean manufacturing (JIT production and preventative maintenance) and the involvement of production workers. This analysis proves once again that lean manufacturing is a system wherein the whole is greater than the sum of its parts.

A Systems Model of Lean Manufacturing

The Japanese system of lean manufacturing is based on cooperation among all participants involved in the production sequence. This system of cooperation extends from the smallest parts supplier in the supply chain to the original equipment manufacturer (OEM), and finally to the customer. Within every step of manufacturing, you can view the production sequence as a system of these three major participants:

1. Supplier system
2. Core production system
3. Customer

Within this context, you can break down the core production system into these three components:

1. Human organization
2. Quality system
3. Material handling system

Figure 4-1 represents the lean manufacturing process.

This book presents many representations of the Toyota Production System (TPS). Figure 4-1 offers another representation of TPS from a systems perspective. In Figure 4-1, the double arrows connecting high involvement organization, built-in quality system, and JIT and enabling systems suggest an interaction among the parts of the system. To test this model, these general constructs were broken down into a more specific set of observable and measurable practices to create more detailed "submodels." Each of these submodels is described in the following sections.

Lean Supplier System Submodel

In order for lean manufacturing to work efficiently, first-, second-, and third-tier suppliers must participate on an equal footing with OEM operations in the production flow. Much of the traditional

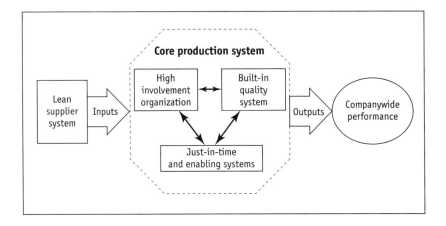

Figure 4-1. Lean Manufacturing System

oversight role of the OEM is transferred to the suppliers, and a system of mutual trust and respect is established. Typically, the OEM will single-source orders and select suppliers on quality rather than cost criteria. They establish long-term contracts to ensure supplier dedication and commitment. Finally, suppliers are expected to maintain high quality standards commensurate with the OEM and inspect components before delivery. Consequently, you can evaluate supplier performance in a lean production system by decreased order lead times and low reject rates. Figure 4-2 represents such a lean supplier system.

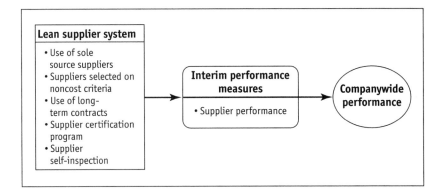

Figure 4-2. Lean Supplier System Submodel

Core Production System Submodel

The core production practices of any manufacturing system usually consist of these three components:

1. Human organization
2. Quality system
3. Material handling system

In lean manufacturing, the people who do the value-added work are highly involved in the production process. Typically, workers are cross-trained to perform many different jobs. They work in teams and rotate job responsibilities on a regular basis. Workers make suggestions and have the authority to modify or stop a production line when quality problems occur. In some cases, companies award pay incentives to workers for high quality and productivity as well as reaching high production quotas.

The quality system of lean manufacturing focuses on "building-in" quality rather than "inspecting-in" quality. Workers check the conformance standards throughout the production process. They also thoroughly understand and use standardized quality programs and procedures. Companies employ statistical process control practices to monitor and chart quality variations and to modify machine settings during production. In a lean system, product quality is set as the number one priority.

The material handling system of lean manufacturing is based on JIT production. Companies produce parts in small lot sizes as they are needed rather than mass produced and inventoried for future use. To facilitate this type of production, companies keep setup times to a minimum and in-process inventories as low as possible. JIT production is based on the concept of pulling rather than pushing parts through the manufacturing process. In an ideal JIT world, the customer triggers production when ordering a finished product. There are immediate benefits of JIT through lowered inventory. However, the biggest benefit of JIT is product quality. By producing parts in small quantities, companies can detect and quickly correct quality problems before they produce large inventories of defective parts.

In order for a company to operate efficiently in a JIT mode of production, they must keep their machinery in top working order at all times. This means they must have an effective preventative maintenance program, such as having well-trained maintenance teams carry out a well-documented program of scheduled (for example, weekly) preventative and rehabilitative maintenance. Additionally, companies must keep workplaces on the factory floor well organized by keeping machinery clean and painted, shelves and storage bins visible and organized, and factory walls and floors degreased and clear of debris.

There are several ways you can measure the impact of these core lean manufacturing practices on production performance. For this study I used three: shopfloor efficiency, product quality, and employee grievances and machine uptime.

> 1. *Shopfloor efficiency.* You determine shopfloor efficiency by shop utilization of machinery, the number of units produced per worker, and the manufacturing lead time for a typical order.
>
> 2. *Product quality.* You measure product quality by the percentage of raw materials scrapped in defective products, the percentage of workers' time spent on preshipment rework or warranty repair, and the percentage of units reworked due to quality problems.
>
> 3. *Employee grievances and machine uptime.* You measure employee grievances on a per worker basis and machine uptime as a percentage of total worked shift time.

These core production system practices are summarized in Figure 4-3.

Interaction Between Production Worker Influence and Production Strategies

You can think of the interaction effect between any two practices as the added benefit gained from having the two practices working together. In other words, the total benefit obtained from having two practices working together is greater than the sum of the benefits of the practices working individually. The whole is greater than the sum of the individual parts. This is the concept that tests lean manufacturing as a system.

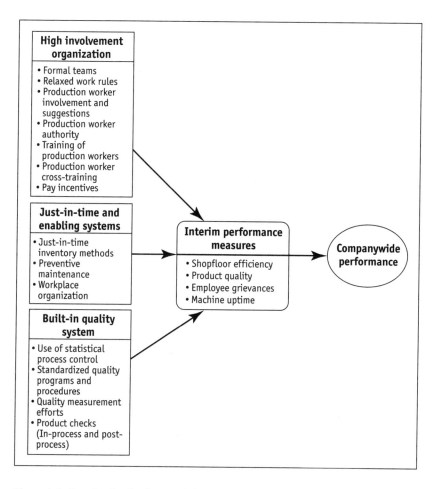

Figure 4-3. Core Production System Submodel

The interaction between production worker influence and production strategies is of particular interest in that it illustrates the synergy that exists between human involvement and technology. The number of possible interactions among all of the lean practices described above is far in excess of forty billion. The practices considered here measure the influence that production workers have in making decisions regarding production and the key production strategies that they follow. Figure 4-4 highlights these interactions.

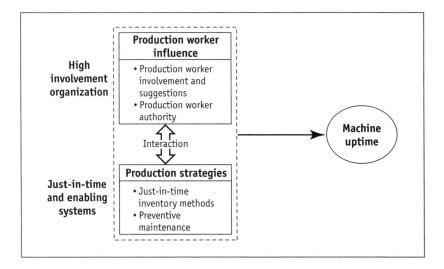

Figure 4-4. Model of Interactions Between Production Worker Influence and
    Production Strategies

The Midwest Manufacturing
Technology Center (MMTC) Survey

The empirical data used to test the effects of lean manufacturing practices on performance measures were collected through a comprehensive survey conducted in 1992. This study was performed by the Midwest Manufacturing Technology Center (MMTC) at the Industrial Technology Institute (ITI) located in Ann Arbor, Michigan. The purpose was to benchmark industrial practices of small firms and track changes in these industrial practices over time. MMTC was established by ITI as part of a federal grant given to ITI to help small manufacturing firms become more competitive.

Participating in the study were 249 small manufacturing firms from three industries. The three industries represented were metal forming, plastics processing, and tooling and machining. The study further broke the tooling and machining industry into two categories: low-volume and high-volume. This was done to separate firms that produced larger and somewhat unique machined parts and tools from those that produced smaller high-volume machined parts and tools. The companies manufactured and sold products for several different markets. Considering all 249 firms taken as a whole, 28 percent of sales were to the automobile industry, 15 percent were to the aerospace, defense, and communications industry, 3 percent were to the furniture industry, and the remainder of sales were to other, unidentified markets.

The survey questionnaire contained more than 500 questions divided into six sections that addressed

- General business issues
- Design practices
- Procurement practices
- Shop scheduling
- Manufacturing practices
- Quality management

The survey participants were solicited from a variety of sources, which included the Harris Directory, Dun & Bradstreet, the Precision Metalforming Association (PMA), the Society for the Plastics Industry (SPI), and the National Tooling & Machining Association (NTMA). All responses to the questionnaires were self-reported by the participant firms.

The companies ranged in size from 5 employees to 425 employees with an average size of 70. They were primarily suppliers located in the midwestern United States. Although companies were fairly evenly distributed across the four industry categories, the tooling and machining industry, taken as a whole, had by far the greatest number of participants. Table 4-1 highlights the breakdown of participant firms by state and industry.

Performance Impacts of the Lean Manufacturing System

Using the data gathered from the MMTC survey, a series of linear regression models was developed to determine the causal relationships, if any, between the lean manufacturing practices and the performance measures discussed above. Conceptually, a simple linear regression analysis between one independent variable (practice measure) and one dependent variable (performance measure)

Table 4-1. The MMTC Survey: Distribution of Companies by State and Industry

State	Metal forming	Plastics processing	Tooling and machining Low-volume	High-volume	Total
Alabama	1		1		2
Arizona			1	5	6
California	4	3		3	10
Colorado	1	1			2
Connecticut	3	2	1	2	8
Florida	3			1	4
Illinois	9	1	2	2	14
Indiana	2	4	3	3	12
Iowa			1		1
Kansas		1			1
Kentucky	1				1
Maine				1	1
Massachusetts	5	2	1	1	9
Michigan	20	23	19	11	73
Minnesota	2		5	8	15
Missouri	1	3	4		8
Nebraska	1				1
New Jersey	3		1		4
New York	4	2	2	4	12
North Carolina	2				2
Ohio	11	4	12	6	33
Oregon			1		1
Pennsylvania	2	1	2	3	8
South Carolina	3			1	4
South Dakota				1	1
Tennessee		1		1	2
Texas		1	2	1	4
Virginia		1		1	2
Washington				2	2
Wisconsin	3	1	2		6
Total	**81**	**51**	**60**	**57**	**249**

involves fitting the best possible straight line through a set of data points. Because the submodels and interaction models have multiple independent variables affecting a dependent variable, multiple regression analysis was employed. A major benefit of using multiple regression analysis is that you can determine the effect of a single lean manufacturing practice on a performance measure while controlling the effects or impact of other lean manufacturing practices and control variables. The control variables rule out the possibility of extraneous results due to factors such as company size and manufacturing process (for example, plastics, stamping, machine parts). This type of analysis provides the purest measure of the significance of each lean manufacturing practice without doing a controlled experiment, which would prove to be impossible in the real world.

The following sections present a simplified version of the results of these regression models. The key symbols used to describe these relationships are up or down arrows and a series of dots. An up arrow (↑) indicates that the lean manufacturing practice increases the value of the performance measure; conversely, a down arrow (↓) indicates that the lean manufacturing practice decreases the value of the performance measure. The corresponding series of dots next to each arrow designates the reliability or significance of the relationship. One dot (•) indicates a relatively low yet statistically valid level of significance, whereas three dots (•••) indicate a very high level of significance. The following tables show only relationships with some statistically valid level of significance. If a relationship was not significant (could not be reliably distinguished from zero), it was left blank.

Relationship Between Lean Supplier Practices and Supplier Performance

Table 4-2 shows that using sole source suppliers, granting long-term contracts, and selecting suppliers on noncost criteria such as quality and delivery increased supplier performance. In other words, such suppliers have low order lead times and low reject rates of parts by OEMs. This system is in stark contrast to the philosophies used by

Table 4-2. Relationship Between Lean Supplier Practices and Supplier Performance

Practice measure	Supplier performance	
Use of sole source suppliers	↑	•••
Suppliers selected on noncost criteria	↑	••
Use of long-term contracts	↑	••
Supplier certification program		
Supplier self-inspection		
Relationship level: • Significant •• Very significant ••• Extremely significant		

mass production manufacturers of Henry Ford's era. These mass production manufacturers used many different suppliers to produce the same part and each supplier had a very short-term contract and was selected solely on a lowest bid basis.

Relationship Between Lean Manufacturing Practices and Performance Measures

Table 4-3 shows the relationship between the core production system practices and four performance measures reflecting shopfloor efficiency, product quality, employee grievances (as an indicator of quality of work life), and machine uptime. Employee grievances were addressed in such a way that even if a plant was non-unionized, managers could provide data based on whatever system they had to gather formal employee complaints. The most striking result shown in the Table is the large number of relationships that are significant and the fact that almost all of the relationships are in the direction one would expect from the theories of lean manufacturing. A closer look shows that different practices have stronger impacts on different performance measures. For example, each of the aspects of built-in quality system had a very significant effect on product quality but no measurable effect on shopfloor efficiency, employee grievances, or machine uptime. On the other hand, employee involvement influenced three of the four performance measures, though surprisingly not machine uptime.

Summarizing the results on a performance measure basis, the use of formal teams, production involvement and suggestions, pay incentives, and JIT inventory methods increased shopfloor efficiency.

Product quality was increased by the use of formal teams, production worker involvement and suggestions, preventative maintenance, the use of statistical process control, standardized quality programs and procedures, and quality measurement efforts. However, product quality was decreased by production worker cross-training. One possible explanation for this contradictory result is that at the time of the survey, the workers were in the process of being cross-trained and had not yet mastered the new skills.

Table 4-3. Relationship Between Core Production System Practices and Performance Measures

Practice Measure	Performance Measure			
	Shopfloor efficiency	Product quality	Employee grievances	Machine uptime
High involvement organization				
Formal teams	← ●	← ●●	→ ●●	- - -
Relaxed work rules	← ●●●	← ●	→ ●	- - -
Production worker involvement and suggestions			← → ●●●	- - -
Production worker authority				- - -
Training of production workers				- - -
Production worker cross-training				- - -
Pay incentives	← ●●	← ●		- - -
Just-in-time and enabling systems				
Just-in-time inventory methods	← ●●	← ●	- - -	- - -
Preventative maintenance			- - -	← ●●
Workplace organization			- - -	← ●●
Built-in quality system				
Use of statistical process control		← ●●●		
Standardized quality programs and procedures		← ●●	- - -	- - -
Quality measurement efforts		← ●●	- - -	- - -
Product check (In-process and post-process)			- - -	- - -

Relationship level: ● Significant ●●Very significant ●●●Extremely significant - - - None

Employee grievances were decreased by relaxed work rules, production worker authority, and pay incentives. Conversely, employee grievances were increased by production worker cross-training. One possible explanation for this result is the existence of union rules and regulations regarding cross-training. Since this is central to most union contracts, it is a prime area for grievance.

Finally, preventative maintenance and workplace organization increased machine uptime.

Interaction Between Production Worker Influence and Production Strategies

One of the most exciting things about this study is the evaluation of interaction effects. Far too many studies stop when they find individual practices that influence performance. Table 4-3 points out the results of the tests of interactions between production worker influence and production strategies. Again, only a few of the most salient interaction effects were examined, as testing the billions of mathematically possible interactions would be impractical.

Table 4-4 shows which combinations of the two production strategies and the two measures of worker involvement and authority improve machine uptime. Strikingly, all four combinations have significant positive effects. For example, production worker involvement and suggestions implemented with JIT inventory methods shows that there is a positive effect of having these two practices working in combination. This effect goes beyond the benefits of each of these practices working independently. In total, there is clearly an important synergy between human involvement

Table 4-4. Interaction Between Production Worker Influence and Production Strategies

Interaction effect on machine uptime	Production worker involvement and suggestions		Production worker authority	
Just-in-time inventory methods	↑	•	↑	••
Preventative maintenance	↑	•••	↑	•••
Relationship level: • Significant •• Very significant ••• Extremely significant				

and the use of lean technical systems, thus bearing out the lean model predictions.

Relationship Between Performance Measures and Companywide Performance

Some managers may question the importance of measures such as shopfloor efficiency and product quality. These measures, termed *interim performance measures*, measure how well core processes directly perform. However, on a companywide basis, manufacturers are in business to make money. The question is: Do these shopfloor processes influence the bottom line at a companywide level?

To answer this question, the effect of shopfloor efficiency, product quality, and supplier performance on companywide performance was measured. The effect of employee grievances and machine uptime on companywide performance was not tested because these interim performance measures were not tested with all of the practice measures of the core production system submodel. Companywide performance was measured in two ways: (1) by the percentage of sales increase over the last two years, and (2) by the direct profit margin per unit during the year in which the survey was conducted.

Table 4-5 shows the results of testing the interim performance measures. All three of the interim performance measures tested contributed to the bottom line of the companies in the survey. In other words, they all significantly increased companywide performance and therefore are clearly worth attention.

Table 4-5. Relationship Between Performance Measures and Companywide
          Performance

Interim performance measure	Companywide performance	
Shopfloor efficiency	↑	••
Product quality	↑	•••
Supplier performance	↑	•
Relationship level: • Significant •• Very significant ••• Extremely significant		

Final Results

For this chapter I used a large database and rigorous statistical analysis methods to test the benefits of lean manufacturing. In general, the results of the models are consistent with expectations: lean manufacturing practices do lead to high performance. The results show conclusively that by implementing a lean supplier system, a high involvement organization, a built-in quality system, and a JIT system, both manufacturing performance and companywide performance increase significantly.

In addition, the results indicate that giving workers decision-making power and authority coupled with implementing JIT techniques will increase productivity by increasing machine uptime. In other words, U.S. manufacturers need lean manufacturing strategies as well as employee involvement to achieve world class results.

PART TWO

Case Studies of Implementing Lean

Daniel Woolson *is currently enrolled in the Engineering Global Leadership Honors Program through the Tauber Manufacturing Institute at the University of Michigan. Previously, Daniel resided for eight years on the island nation of Bahrain, an island in the Persian Gulf off the coast of Saudi Arabia. During the summer of 1996, he worked as an inspection supervisor at Delphi Saginaw Steering Systems Plant 6. Daniel intends to pursue a career in automotive manufacturing.*

Mike A. Husar's *business experience includes manufacturing and engineering assignments at Fisher-Body Division, Delphi operations staff, and NUMMI assembly plant. Currently, he is Director of Manufacturing Engineering for Delphi Saginaw Steering Systems Worldwide. Some of Mike's major contributions include division-wide introduction and implementation of key production system components including standardized work, customer focused cells, lean tooling and equipment concepts, error proofing, quality andon systems, 5S processes, cellular manufacturing, and work teams. Mike is a graduate of GMI and has an M.S. from Case Institute of Technology and an M.B.A. from Baldwin-Wallace College.*

Transforming a Plant to Lean in a Large, Traditional Company: Delphi Saginaw Steering Systems, GM

by Daniel Woolson and Mike A. Husar

5

Editor's prologue: Most of what we have heard about General Motors managers going to NUMMI for training and returning to GM to implement the system suggests not a lot of transfer of the Toyota Production System. But Mike Husar proves us wrong, at least in plant 6 of Delphi Saginaw Steering Systems. Mike went into a traditional, existing UAW plant staffed with highly senior employees (half the plant had over 25 years at that plant) and over a five-year period made substantial progress in most of the plant toward lean manufacturing. Customer rejects went from almost 2,000 parts per million in 1993 to 75 ppm in 1997. Cost reductions have ranged from 6 to 11 percent most years. Productivity has improved almost 8 percent per year. Whereas in 1991 less than half the employees made improvement suggestions, by 1997 the number increased to 90 percent. OSHA reportable accidents have declined significantly. Mike Husar's cellular manufacturing moved Delphi from near mass-producing extinction to winning Toyota's highest possible award—the full quality award for meeting quality requirements and deliveries 100 percent of the time for assembling the steering column for Toyota Avalon. Delphi is an example of the potential power of the employee waiting to be tapped in U.S. manufacturing, a power that is available when management and the union use lean principles to hammer out a contract.

21

With lean, everyone wins—management wins with greater employee involvement and higher profits, the union by delivering on worker security, and the employees by becoming better trained, more engaged with the manufacturing process, and happier.

From my perspective, QNMS and the teamwork and employee empowerment it created have made all the difference. [This difference] shows what can happen when an organization acts as a team—hourly work force, management, union leadership—and everyone is turned loose and can help in running the business.

Dan Crishon[1]

In the early 1990s, Delphi Saginaw Steering Systems (DSSS) Plant 6 was a captive supplier facing poor product quality, high costs, and an adversarial union relationship. These problems made the plant's product line an excellent candidate to be outsourced by General Motors (GM). To combat this situation, management and labor mutually decided they needed to get together to make some major changes if they hoped to keep the business alive. The change came in the form of the Quality Network Manufacturing System (QNMS), which was incorporated into the 1993 UAW Local 699 contract. The QNMS agreement paved the way for the implementation of lean manufacturing techniques, including work teams, pull system, and manufacturing cells into a traditional mass-production environment. Management had the vision to realize that these new manufacturing methods, even if they designed the technical aspects to perfection, would not be successful in the shopfloor environment without acceptance by the work force, so management made a concerted effort to work with labor to foster an improved relationship. This new partnership contributed significantly to improvements in productivity and quality and removed the threat of GM outsourcing Plant 6's products. Now all six plants at the Saginaw site have implemented QNMS to varying degrees. This chapter focuses on Plant 6, where Mike Husar, former plant manager, helped pioneer efforts to turn this traditional company into a lean one, thus making Plant 6 the most successful among the six plants.

History of Delphi Saginaw Steering Systems

Delphi Saginaw Steering Systems was founded in Saginaw, Michigan in 1906 as a small partnership among three owners: Jackson, Church, and Wilcox. This small business grew very rapidly. It supplied a revolutionary steering gear[2] to Buick, located in Flint, Michigan. In 1910, Buick Motor Company purchased the partnership, which then became a part of General Motors Corporation.[3] With the onset of World War I, the plant continued to grow rapidly in size, and produced trench mortar shells while maintaining production of steering components. The plant became recognized as one of the most modern manufacturing facilities in the world due to its high output.

The high rate of growth continued after the conclusion of World War I. In 1926, a completely new steering gear, the "Worm and Worm Wheel Gear," was developed. The company briefly became known as Saginaw Products Company and then changed its name to Saginaw Steering Gear in 1928. At this time, Saginaw Steering Gear became the sole supplier of steering gears to General Motors. In 1934, Saginaw Steering Gear was producing over a million gears per year. With the entry of the United States into World War II in the early 1940s, the company manufactured machine guns, armor-piercing projectiles, rapid-fire carbines, and gear units for the U.S. military. They built an additional plant to satisfy the high demand. The company received virtually every award the U.S. government could bestow as a result of its impressive volume of output.

In 1950, Saginaw began production of the first power steering system. The 1950s and 1960s were characterized by a series of successful innovations by Saginaw engineers such as the adjustable steering wheel and the energy-absorbing column. They constructed five additional plants during this period. In 1977, sales for the fiscal year reached one billion dollars for the first time in Saginaw's history. In 1984, Saginaw Steering Gear changed its name to Saginaw Division. In the early 1990s, more innovations resulted in the introduction of power-assist and variable-effort steering systems. In 1995, General Motors organized its Automotive Components Group (ACG) into Delphi Automotive Systems,[4] and Saginaw Division changed its name to Delphi Saginaw Steering Systems (DSSS). There are currently six plants located at the Saginaw site.[5]

Overview of Plant 6 at DSSS

Plant 6 opened in August 1966, specializing in manufacturing steering columns for General Motors. The factory floor currently occupies 747,980 square feet; the entire plant has an area of 1,790,730 square feet. There are approximately 1,900 salaried, hourly, and contract employees in the plant. The plant's current customer base includes all GM models, the Chrysler L/H platform, and the Toyota Avalon. The demands of the customer base are quite varied: 307 products exist for the 1997 model year. The plant produces approximately 24,000 steering columns daily; since its beginnings, it has assembled a cumulative total exceeding 180,000,000 steering columns. The plant formally received QS-9000 certification on September 26, 1996.

The plant is divided into two main areas: assembly and components. Approximately half of the employees work on the assembly side, while 39 percent work on the component side; the remaining employees are involved with service operations. The primary components manufactured in the plant are the jacket subassembly, the shaft, the upper yokes, and many different plastic components. Of the 607 machines in the plant, nearly 25 percent are plastic injection molding machines. A further 60 percent of the machines are devoted to welding, forming, and machining operations in the component subplant. The assembly side of the plant is responsible for building up the steering column with components produced internally in the plant and parts purchased from outside vendors. Assembly equipment comprises only 3 percent of the total machines in the plant. There is significant variation between steering column models in terms of production volume and the complexity of the product. For example, the Toyota Avalon steering column is a low-complexity, low-volume product. By contrast, the W-car line assembles a high-complexity, high-volume product.

1990–1993: Trouble at DSSS

In the early 1990s, poor economic times and inefficient mass production methods at DSSS prompted General Motors to consider outsourcing steering components. These shortcomings were compounded by the fact that the unionized work force received an average of $45 an hour in wages and benefits, while many other first-tier automotive suppliers did not have a unionized work force (Raynal & Phillips, 1996). Vlasic (1996, p. 78) describes the situation at Plant 6:

> Back in the early 1990s, General Motors Corp.'s steering-column plant in Saginaw, Michigan was a typical GM dinosaur. It used decades-old mass-production techniques in which each worker added parts to every column that rolled by. They complained of the numbing, repetitive nature of their jobs. Productivity growth was flat, reject levels were high. Most of the plant's output went to GM assembly plants, a captive market that put little pressure on Saginaw to improve.

Trouble was everywhere. Members were pressuring the UAW to ensure job security.[6] General Motors was pressuring management to run a more profitable and higher quality operation. Management and the UAW were at an impasse—the old adversarial way of doing business was as obsolete as the mass-producing mentality that helped create it. It was time they acted together and implemented significant changes and improvements on the shop floor, changes that would immediately translate into greater profits and a better quality product. It was the only way to ensure the future success of DSSS.

But there was that old U.S. manufacturing dilemma and stumbling block: How do you go about implementing new ideas or improvements on the shop floor with a traditional UAW contract and a bureaucratic management structure like GM? Either of these powerful entities can easily shuffle a good idea into oblivion, or with one word give it a quick, painless death. The UAW and management recognized this danger. They also recognized that implementing marginal improvements and changes to improve the work environment under the current structure would not give them what they really needed—to become more competitive. The nature of the crossroads was clear: Either initiate real change at DSSS or go the way of the dinosaurs.

Enter Mike Husar and Synchronous Manufacturing Methods

In an effort to educate the union about synchronous manufacturing methods, the then plant manager, Mike Husar, accompanied various UAW Local 699 representatives on visits to the New United Motor Manufacturing, Inc. (NUMMI) facility. Before his transfer to Saginaw, Husar had spent two years as a coordinator at the NUMMI facility, a General Motors–Toyota joint venture located in Fremont, California. NUMMI is one of the best opportunities for an American to learn the Toyota Production System (TPS). GM has sent many of its managers to NUMMI to gain the knowledge and experience to apply lean techniques in their traditional production facilities.

Visiting NUMMI was an opportunity for the union hierarchy to witness "lean production in action." Prior to the NUMMI venture, the GM-run Fremont plant was known for its very low productivity and quality, high absenteeism, militant union, and rampant drug and alcohol abuse, all of which ultimately led to the closing of the plant in February 1982 (P. Adler, 1993, p. 98). Many of the same workers were rehired once the NUMMI plant commenced production in 1984. Any negative preconceptions held by the union representatives about lean manufacturing were minimized once they had an opportunity to talk to the team members of a work group at NUMMI. During the meeting, the NUMMI team members expressed their satisfaction with their work, saying that they actually looked forward to coming to the plant each day. The union began to acknowledge that the changes in the attitudes of the NUMMI workers were largely attributable to a new management philosophy and a new production system.

These visits helped to convince the union representatives that synchronous manufacturing was a viable alternative to the mass production methods at DSSS. In 1993, the UAW Local 699 negotiated a completely revamped contract with management that created a new manufacturing system—the Quality Network Manufacturing System (QNMS). The QNMS techniques were first applied at Plant 6, under the guidance of plant manager Mike Husar.

QNMS—Going Beyond the Traditional UAW Contract

The QNMS agreement was a complete turnaround from DSSS's traditional mass production techniques. It was described in *Challenge*, March 1995, as follows:

> QNMS is the integration of people, methods, equipment, and material that together create a production system focused on achieving the highest quality products at the lowest possible cost. It enables employees to work in teams, to set goals specific to their respective operations, to plan the activities for achieving these goals, and to track the results. It acknowledges workers as the number one resource in achieving customer enthusiasm and provides tools to support their attainment of the division's QUALITY, COST, and DELIVERY objectives.

The formal introduction to the QNMS agreement in the UAW contract reads as follows (QNMS, 1993, p. 1-Q):

> UAW Local 699 and Management both share a common vision to have Saginaw Division be the World Quality leader in the design and manufacturing of steering system and driveline components that surpass customer expectations while providing our people with a superior work environment and job security, as well as maintaining an acceptable return on investment.

The contract stipulated a three-year window allowing for the implementation of QNMS at all six plants located at the Saginaw site. The traditional 1993 UAW contract would remain applicable to a department until it completed QNMS training, at which time the QNMS contract became binding. The QNMS is founded on four key principles:

1. Customer satisfaction
2. People
3. Synchronize the organization
4. Continuous improvement

The contract reflects the importance of customer satisfaction, stating that it is "our ultimate objective . . . resulting in profits and job security" (QNMS, 1993, p. 1-Q). The attainment of customer satisfaction has dual aspects: Management views it as leading to improved employee efficiency, better quality, and greater profits; labor views it as bringing job security and a happier work force. As for the "people" aspect of QNMS, the contract states the following (QNMS, 1993, p. 2-Q):

> The team structure is the vehicle we choose to effectively and efficiently manage our operations, product introductions, and continuous improvement process. Support for the worker is the focus of our manufacturing support systems and service operations.

Figure 5-1 illustrates the underlying principle of the QNMS: to provide support for the worker.

The final two foundations of the QNMS are to synchronize the organization and maintain continuous improvement. These two factors are interrelated as both aim to eliminate non-value-adding waste and to improve the responsiveness and problem solving in the work environment. Together, these four pillars form the base of the new leaner manufacturing system.

Management and labor share a common vision
Following is an excerpt of the introduction to the traditional UAW contract with Delphi Saginaw, also negotiated in 1993 (Traditional Contract, p. 20):

> Saginaw Division Management recognizes that it cannot get along without Labor any more than Labor can get along without the Management. Both are in the same business and the success of that business is vital to all concerned. This requires that both Management and the employees work together to the end that the quality and cost of the product will prove increasingly satisfactory and attractive, so that the business will be continuously successful.

This passage implies a strained relationship of conflict between management and labor. It also suggests that a great deal of animosity

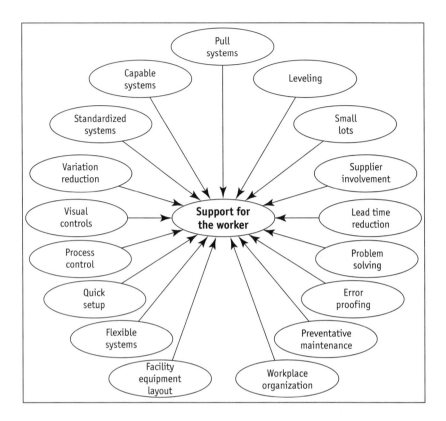

Figure 5-1. The Quality Network Manufacturing System

had plagued the relationship such that the two parties coexisted only out of necessity.

By contrast, a foundation of the QNMS agreement is increasing trust between management and the work force. The QNMS introduction states that "management and labor share a common vision." The importance of this departure cannot be overstated. Rather than drawing a line in the sand and emphasizing the sharp distinction between management and labor, QNMS helps management and labor focus on their similarities and commonalties, thus allowing for a true partnership to evolve.

The Need for Employee Training

To implement new manufacturing strategies, a company must provide a great deal of employee training. This is especially true in introducing lean principles. To address this initial challenge, the contract outlines a three-stage training process. The first phase provides a pre-orientation program for the workers that focuses on the underlying principles of the QNMS, principally the function of work teams. The second phase provides the orientation process for each department. This stage covers several aspects of the new manufacturing system, such as the following:

- Work unit–based health and safety
- Interpersonal skills (e.g., communication, problem solving, change methodology, etc.)
- Team building
- Quality Network beliefs and values
- Quality Network Manufacturing System elements (e.g., customer focus, starter strategies, pull systems, visual controls, lead time, error proofing, etc.)

The final phase of worker training is an ongoing process focusing on continuous improvement and the further development of the methods outlined in the second phase. The QNMS training is 40 hours per employee, and each employee is required to attend the training along with their entire work group.

The Work Team and Team Coordinator

The most immediate effect of the QNMS agreement was the reduction in job classifications and the creation of the role of the team coordinator, an hourly representative who assumes many of the duties normally associated with the supervisor. In the traditional contract there were 160 job classifications, now there are 12. This new structure eases the formation of work teams because workers can, with the assistance of the team coordinator, assume several roles in the plant. This structure is in great contrast to the traditional mass-producing structure wherein workers are limited to their particular job classification.

As currently designed, the QNMS agreement allows each work team to engage in job rotation at a frequency determined by the individual team. A "pay for knowledge" system determines wage rates. New hires or transfers to a department are classified as Level

1 when they become proficient at one job in the work team. Once workers are able to perform 50% of the jobs in the team, they become a Level 3 and receive a pay increase. Workers attain Level 5 classification when they are able to perform successfully all jobs in the team as well as all off-line duties such as material handling, housekeeping, and repair/rework/scrap. Level 5 employees have the highest wage rate in the work team. The team coordinator is responsible for organizing the training of new workers. The work team collectively decides when an employee demonstrates proficiency at the specified number of jobs needed to ascend to a Level 3 or a Level 5 classification.

The team coordinator's responsibilities include a number of critical issues related to the success of the work team, such as the following (QNMS, 1993, p. 26-Q):

- Schedule material flow
- Schedule overtime
- Maintain and update records
- Institutionalize housekeeping procedures
- Schedule vacations
- Facilitate team meetings
- Interact with other work units
- Maintain and improve quality control systems
- Organize daily inventories
- Coordinate manpower
- Train employees

In spite of the large scope of duties performed by the team coordinators, they do not have the formal responsibility to correct behavior or performance problems; this function remains a duty of salaried personnel.

Selection and importance of the team coordinator
The QNMS agreement sets out an objective procedure for selecting the team coordinators. Whenever a vacancy for a coordinator's position opens, management posts the job in the plant. The candidates are graded out of a possible 100 points and the worker with the highest score is awarded the position. The points are awarded based

on seniority, attendance, the employee's infraction record, a quiz on QNMS techniques, and a preselection class that all potential team coordinators must complete successfully. Management and labor jointly designed the selection process to provide a fair and equal opportunity for all team members to become coordinators. This system helped improve trust between the work force and management, a key factor in the establishment of future QNMS teams. The critical aspects of the success of the selection process are its objectivity and lack of union or management bias.

Team coordinators are of utmost importance to the success of the teams. Because they are responsible for many of the day-to-day operations of the manufacturing cell, it is important that they are properly selected. If team members feel the team coordinator is acting as a liaison between management and the individual work team, the team members may view the coordinator as a "junior foreman" or "straw boss," a condition that could inhibit the functionality of the work team. The primary mechanism to resolve problems[7] in the work team is peer pressure. If the coordinator takes an overly powerful role in the resolution of problems, he or she may not be perceived as "one of the team" but as a managerial figure. The possibility of this occurring under QNMS is somewhat limited, because the team coordinators do not have disciplinary authority or license to impose their opinions on the team.

Initial Employee Resistance to Implementing QNMS

Work teams are a radical departure from the days of mass production, when each laborer was isolated from the decision-making process. Workers simply came to work, did their job, and received their paycheck. In the traditional factory, the worker was needed primarily for the physical ability to perform the work task. The synchronous manufacturing initiative and QNMS teams are a complete turnaround from the working environment in which employees have been socialized for most of their careers. The QNMS allows the employee to take a proactive role in improving and shaping the work environment by utilizing both physical and mental abilities.

This change in work culture created some initial resistance from employees, especially among those who had been doing the same thing the same way for a very long time. Over 50 percent of the work force at Plant 6 has at least 25 years of experience with General Motors. As a result, a portion of the older work force resisted some of the changes brought by QNMS. As one quality inspector with over 30 years of work experience stated: "It [QNMS] won't work here." Old habits die hard.

The salary work force also showed resistance to QNMS implementation. The QNMS contract called for the team coordinator to assume many of the functions previously held by supervisors. Despite this apparent loss of direct control, the supervisors are still held accountable for the performance of the work teams. This changing role from supervisor to facilitator made many managers feel uncomfortable.

Several factors about QNMS (or lean production) can disenchant an employee. First, U.S. society rewards and respects people for their individual accomplishments. Besser (p. 82) notes that Americans may be reluctant to work in teams due to a fear of unequal contributions from members because everyone in the team will receive the same pay and recognition, regardless of individual performance. Also, in a mass production environment, many workers have a great deal of free time during the work day. By contrast, a lean production environment drastically reduces or eliminates this free time, creating a perception on the part of the employee of having to work harder.

These may be some of the reasons U.S. manufacturers have had some difficulty rallying their workers (and management) around the team concept. The teams often fall short of their promised results because of the lack of "buy-in" to the team concept. Work teams are built on interpersonal relationships, thus making them fragile to negative attitudes and deep suspicions. Even a single person (an employee or management) with a sharply negative attitude can destroy the cohesion and the functionality of a team. This is why training and educating employees in their new roles is so important. DSSS met this challenge head-on by training QNMS teams. For example, much of the supervisors' anxiety about the new manufacturing system was alleviated when they attended a two-day training session designed to help them adjust to their new roles as team facilitators. As related elsewhere in this book, it usually takes lots of time and training for the U.S. worker to learn kaizen and team-based efforts—but once they do, watch out!

Early QNMS Implementation Successes at Plant 6

Soon after Mike Husar's arrival in 1991 at Plant 6, experimentation with synchronous manufacturing and cellular manufacturing concepts began. It started in 1991 with a pilot cell supplying the Saturn line, based on only four machines. Previously, these four machines were remote operations, so that each unit needed a buffer inventory in front of it. The new cellular arrangement of the machines dramatically reduced the amount of work-in-process (WIP) inventory. Furthermore, this pilot cell greatly improved efficiency and yielded significant cost reductions over the traditional manufacturing methods. These advantages caused management to experiment with more cells of this type. At the time, employee acceptance and the traditional work contract were major stumbling blocks to a plantwide initiative of synchronous manufacturing. Mike Husar's successful experiment with the Saturn line provided a significant impetus to management and labor's approving the QNMS contract in 1993.

In 1991, the senior management of the plant also drafted a five-year plan detailing the proposed transformation process for material flow in the plant. They completed a cost analysis for all departments, allowing management to prioritize improvement initiatives to areas that would give the biggest "bang for the buck." Using these criteria, they constructed a migration plan to determine the progression of QNMS implementation. Another factor that guided the implementation of synchronous manufacturing was customer-driven changes, such as a major overhaul of a current product model or the production of an entirely new model. The substantial new business and model changeover in Plant 6 meant a budget for developing new production lines designed by lean principles. A major reason for the success of the five-year plan was its rigidity. The mapped-out transformation process did not "roll over" on a yearly basis. Rather, the timetable, the deliverables, and the migration plan all remained intact throughout the five-year implementation.

The 5S program — Becoming customer-focused

Although a strategic vision is extremely important, Mike Husar realized that it was equally necessary to harvest short-term gains to demonstrate that productive change was actually occurring at the plant. His first initiatives were to stress general housekeeping (the 5S's), quality, and problem solving on the plant floor. He selected these areas because he considered them nonthreatening from the standpoint of employees' beliefs and values. Moreover, these initiatives had a high probability of success and could result in some significant bottom-line improvement. Husar implemented the initiatives with a customer-focused approach wherein each employee was taught to consider the next operation or worker as the customer. This philosophy proved successful at inducing change in an environment that had been insulated from change for the 30 previous years.

The 5S program is geared toward improving workplace organization and general housekeeping in work areas. DSSS defines the 5S's as Sort, Straighten, Sanitize, Sweep, and Sustain (sometimes referred to as Sort, Set in Order, Shine, Standardize, and Sustain). According to Toyota, workplace organization is essential to implementing and maintaining robust processes because well-ordered work areas are necessary for standardizing procedures. If a customer came into the plant and saw a filthy work area with material lying in unlabeled positions and workers not engaging in standardized processes, what would be their impression of this work environment and of this business? From this customer-focused perspective, the employees came to realize the importance of a clean and well-organized working environment for attaining the organizational goal of customer satisfaction. "You never have a second chance to make a first impression" became a plant motto.

Quality improvements — Using checklists and error proofing

The second initiative focused on quality improvements on the plant floor. The DSSS Quality Policy is: "We are committed to achieving customer enthusiasm. Our first priority is to provide high quality products and services!" No matter where one is located in the plant, this statement is visible. Anyone can create a vision for the Quality Policy, but it is quite a different matter to actively follow this policy. The management of Plant 6 truly viewed quality as their number one priority. This dedication percolated down the chain of command and throughout the work force.

Plant 6 also realized quality improvements by creating work standards. Workers may take a stance against standardized work because they feel that it will stifle their creativity. Yet this argument has no basis if the issue is approached with the customer in focus. A prime example is that of an airplane copilot going through the preflight checklist. Passengers on the airplane expect the copilot to follow each step in the prescribed order on the checklist. They surely would not like to give the copilot the freedom to create his or her own operating procedure for each flight. Examples like this were used to teach team members to view their own work environments with the customer in mind. In addition to standardized work, error-proofing devices were installed on many machines throughout the plant. For example, in Department 39, fixtures were designed to prevent parts from being located incorrectly on the jacket press-up machines.

Employee training—No-blame environment
The third initiative was to improve the problem-solving skills of the work force on the plant floor—both management and the hourly employees. The hourly employees received a substantial amount of training in root cause analysis, continuous improvement techniques, and problem-solving strategies in the QNMS training. The most critical issue for management was to recognize problems as opportunities for improvement rather than as the basis for chastising an employee. A standard process was created for dealing with quality problems. After a supervisor is informed of a quality issue, he or she must first go to the worksite and see the situation personally before discussing the circumstances with other people. The supervisor then contacts the quality department. Together, they begin to collect facts about the issue rather than looking for

someone to blame. Emphasis is placed on asking the Five Whys[8] at this stage of the procedure. Once all the information is collected, the supervisor and a quality representative formulate a solution to the problem. By defining a resolution process, the root cause of many problems have been quickly determined, thus resulting in significant quality improvements.

Employees see changes as positive
Mike Husar's first initiatives met little resistance from the unionized work force. As a result, the labor force felt more comfortable with some of the changes underway in Plant 6. This gradual buy-in to the new system greatly facilitated implementation of other lean techniques as the employees realized that the changes could improve the working environment. The transformation in people's attitudes to accept change as positive was a major step in progressing to lean production, since for many years employees had been habituated to unchanging mass production techniques.

Delphi Saginaw Steering Systems Communication Model

The DSSS communication model effectively illustrates how to induce change successfully throughout an organization (see Figure 5-2). The communication process spans from providing information to the worker to realizing the corresponding action. In many organizations, a common reason for the breakdown in implementation efforts of new policies is the assumption that information translates directly into action. The DSSS communication model includes two intermediate steps in this process: the understanding stage and the commitment stage.

The information stage pertains to any sort of knowledge that is to be distributed in the organization. It is imperative that the exchange of information is three-way—up, down, and laterally in the organization—to ensure that everyone is included in the issue. The critical step of the understanding stage is linking the distributed information to organizational goals and the listeners' personal values. The employee must understand how the new information applies to the job and how it can be used to further organizational goals. Fostering a trusting relationship between management and

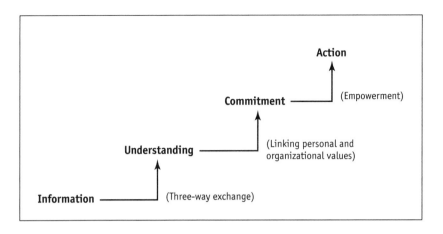

Figure 5-2. Delphi Saginaw Steering Systems Communication Model

labor can establish connections between personal and organizational goals as the employee comes to realize that "what's good for the company is also good for me." The understanding of information tends to cultivate a sense of commitment, the next stage of the model. The committed employee then becomes empowered to take action in changing the working environment. The final stage in the model is the action stage, when the information initially exchanged is applied on the plant floor. The use of this communication model was crucial to introducing successful change in Plant 6.

The Transformation of Plant 6: 1991–1997

In 1991, there were only eight assembly lines in the plant, each with approximately 100 employees.[9] Each worker on the line added only a marginal value to the product, and quality problems went virtually unnoticed until the final inspection station. Furthermore, it was common for some workers to sit idle when the line would run different models of steering columns. This situation arose because some employees had job assignments that only pertained to a specific type of a steering column. Nearly all of the assembly lines were located in the center of the plant and were surrounded by the component departments (see Figure 5-3).

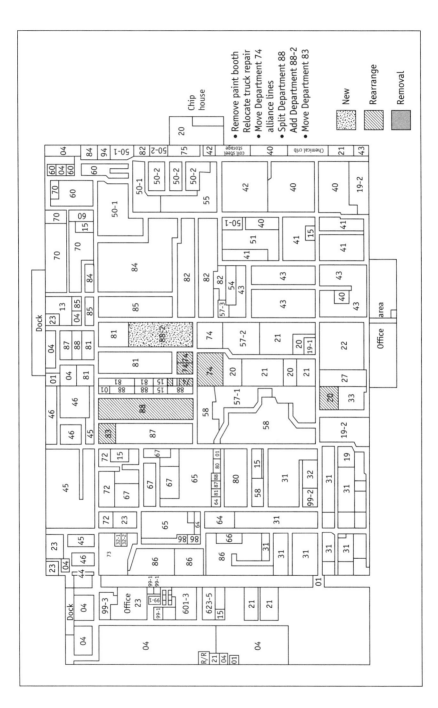

Figure 5-3. Plant 6 Layout in Base Year, 1991

For example, Departments 43 and 41 were responsible for supplying jackets[10] to all the assembly lines. This arrangement was
unsatisfactory in Mike Husar's view because there was too much
unnecessary transportation of material. The vision at the end of the
five-year plan was to streamline production by having components
flow from one side of the plant to the assembly lines, and then to
ship the finished product. By 1991 very little physical change had
begun, so it is treated as the base year. There were a few small
changes, however. The Saturn cell described above was created in
1991, and one of the products in a large, multiproduct assembly line
in Department 88 was split off into a smaller single-product assembly line, Department 88-2.

1994 Status—Creating Efficient Assembly Lines

Figure 5-4 shows the significant changes that had taken place in the
layout of the plant by 1994. The most notable addition to the plant
was a group of new, more efficient assembly lines that produce the
Component Set Strategy (CSS) steering column[11] (Departments 63,
35, 36, 38, and 52). Each line has a maximum of 25 team members.
The large gain in productivity of these lines was partially enabled
by a design that included fewer parts. A set of jacket cells,
Department 39, was added to supply jackets to the new CSS lines,
thus significantly shortening the distance that the component needs
to travel to the line, and improving the efficiency and quality of
jacket production. The completed jackets were placed on a movable
carrier in Department 39. When jackets were needed on the assembly line, an employee would roll the cart across the aisle to the CSS
line. The movement of the jackets to a line acted as a signal to
Department 39 to produce more jackets. If no carriers were moved,
no jackets would be produced in Department 39; thus, a pull system
was created. Previously, the jackets were manufactured in
Department 41 and a truck transported the material to the line.
Another effect of the new cell was improved communication
between the assembly line and the component department, and
these changes in product flow and communication resulted in dramatic improvements in quality.

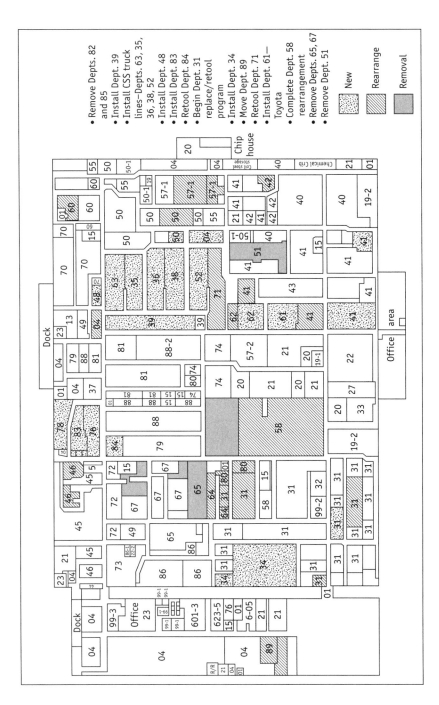

Figure 5-4. Plant 6 Layout After Three Years Implementation, 1994

Operators given power to stop the line

The new assembly lines include andon cords, which allow an operator to stop the line if a quality issue arises. A cord is located close to each worker. Boards, located above each assembly line, display the rate of production, the count for the shift, and the build goal for the shift. If an operator pulls the cord, a musical tune emanates from the board. This signal notifies the workers on the line that the line will stop due to an unresolved quality issue. The smaller assembly lines reaped great cost savings because the work was divided more equally among employees, non-value-added work was reduced, idle time minimized, and quality improved immensely over the traditional lines. Similar assembly lines were set up to produce the Chrysler L/H steering column, the J-car platform, and the N-car platform (Departments 76, 78, 83, and 84) although the jackets continued to be produced in Department 41 for these lines until new cells could be established for them.

Near the entrance to the factory floor is a board displaying the department numbers of each assembly line in green, yellow, or red to signify how well the department is keeping up with its scheduled build for that day. If an operator has pulled an andon cord and the line is currently stopped, the department number will flash on this board. The andon system was effective in improving quality-related downtime by locating the areas most in need of improvement.

DSSS made further realignments to the machinery in Department 58, which machines upper yokes, to promote a continuous flow of material. This change significantly reduced the levels of work-in-process inventory in the department. A totally new, completely cellular Department 61 commenced production of the Toyota Avalon steering column in 1994.

Creation of a commodity cell

A *commodity cell* produces a part that is similar across all models. This is in contrast to a customer-focused cell, which produces a part for a specific model. An effort to reduce setup times on commodity machines throughout the plant proved highly successful in some areas, such as Department 31, where the setup times on the plastic injection-molding machines were reduced by 75 percent.

DSSS created a commodity cell for shaft production in Department 50 in 1991. Shafts are produced in reasonably large batches because there is not enough difference in the initial shape among various shafts to justify running a separate cell for each model.[12] Once the initial shape is complete, the shaft is transferred to a customer-focused cell, where the features unique to that model are machined. Prior to Mike Husar's arrival, shaft production was split into two separate processes—a warm form press and a 10-station transfer process. These two processes were separated by 1000 feet, so each operation had a significant buffer inventory. Mike Husar approved the coupling of the two operations in an effort to reduce this unnecessary inventory. At this time, Plant 6 had 2.5 weeks of finished shafts inventory on hand, so the employees had to complete the task of moving major equipment and getting the line back up in this time frame, otherwise GM assembly plants would begin to shut down. At the beginning, most employees felt that it was nearly impossible to complete the task in the 2.5 weeks. Through much hard work, the coupling effort proved successful and demonstrated to the work force that anything is possible when employees really commit themselves.

A kanban system is designed

DSSS uses a kanban system to control the production of the commodity cell. A small buffer inventory is present between Department 50 and each of the assembly lines. When the line uses material from the buffer, its kanban card is returned to Department 50. Each kanban card is placed in one of the two color-coded areas in the kanban dispenser (see Photo 5-1). The two colors are red and green. If the card is placed in the red section, priority is given to this part because there is a very small buffer between the department and the assembly line. Lesser priority is given to those cards in the green section, because the buffer inventory is at a sufficient level.

DSSS also designed a kanban system to signal the transfer of purchase parts to the assembly line. Furthermore, they created an electronic pull system to relay the daily needs to suppliers based on the amount of material used that particular day. In the 1980s, some

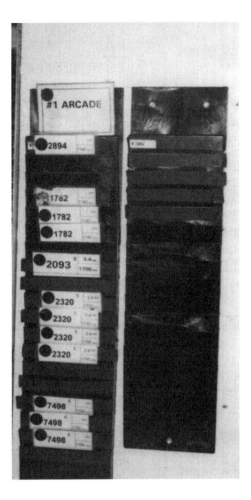

Photo 5-1. Kanban Dispenser in Department 50

departments attempted to use a kanban system, but the effort did not prove successful because employees often misplaced or lost the cards. As a result of this experience, Mike Husar placed an emphasis on creating continuous flow processes to minimize the need for a kanban system.

1997 Status—The Five-year Vision Approaches Reality

Figure 5-5 illustrates that nearly all departments are either new or have been rearranged since 1991. The number of assembly lines in

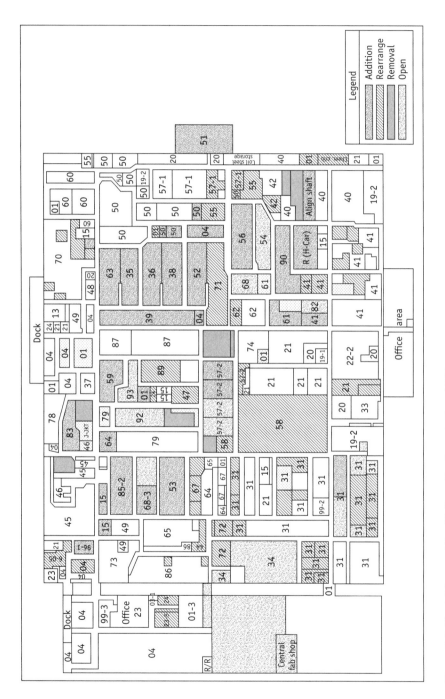

Figure 5-5. Plant 6 Layout After Six Years Implementation, 1997

the plant now total 27 compared to the 8 lines present in 1991. Moreover, the inventory space in the plant has been cut in half (area near Department 04 on Figure 5-5), even though a greater volume of steering columns are now assembled daily. The new assembly lines (Departments 56 and 54) are similar in design to the CSS lines. A new jacket cell, Department 68-1, supplies these lines, following the pattern of Department 39 and the CSS lines.

Department 59, the P-90 cell, is one of the newest assembly lines in Plant 6. It is unique because the jacket assembly cell is directly attached to the assembly line. By coupling these two processes, the plant has eliminated the need for moveable carriers, as the line pulls material directly from the jacket subassembly cell.

To reduce the amount of non-value-added work, the plant uses electronic guided carts (EGC) to transport a kit of parts to Department 85-2. This kit includes the upper and lower shroud (plastic covering) to the steering columns, the SIR coil (airbag activator), and the electronic wiring for the column. Previously, a separate driver would have delivered each of these components to the line. Once the EGC arrives at the department, workers empty the kits onto a staging area near the assembly line. The EGC then returns to the sorting area (Department 96) with a set of empty kits. Here, the workers assemble the kits and send the EGC back to the line. The four EGC's each hold 30 kits. The material from a single EGC will supply the assembly line for only 15 minutes. This arrangement represents the next wave of efforts to achieve productivity gains and inventory reduction in the plant.

A Case Study: The Toyota Cell

The QNMS agreement and the experiments with cellular manufacturing were two of the main reasons Plant 6 won a contract in 1994 to assemble steering columns for the Toyota Avalon. During the contract negotiations, the price of the steering column was the primary determining factor. Toyota considered quality a given with its suppliers. The provisions of the contract required Plant 6 to meet all of Toyota's quality standards.

The First QNMS Work Area

The Toyota cell, Department 61, was the first official QNMS work area created in Plant 6. Management and the union essentially hand-picked the team coordinator for the cell, since the cell was the pilot area for the plant and its success would be a major determinant of success for future QNMS groups. They selected the coordinator because he had very strong people skills and he had experience dealing with other automotive companies.[13] The nine other team members were made up of volunteers to work in the cell and eventually were selected through the traditional bidding process based on seniority. Since its inception in 1994, only one team member has transferred out of the cell and there has only been one grievance filed.[14] Toyota sets very high quality levels for each of its suppliers; Toyota Motor Manufacturing Kentucky (TMMK) requires a maximum of 10 defects per year (80 ppm) from Department 61. This demanded level of quality is world class. In its first year of production, 8 defective columns were returned to Plant 6. Department 61 received a certificate from Toyota for meeting the quality requirements, the highest award a supplier can receive in its first year with Toyota. In its second year of full production, TMMK returned only 6 defective columns. Department 61 once again garnered the highest award possible from Toyota, the Full Quality award for meeting quality requirements and meeting deliveries 100 percent of the time.[15] The team feels a great deal of pride for their collective accomplishments in Department 61. This success has led to additional business for Plant 6, which was awarded the contract to produce the steering column for two additional Toyota lines: the Merridian, a minivan, and the T-100, a heavy-duty truck. As a result of this notoriety, many visitors have toured the cell, including Jack Smith (CEO of GM), high-ranking executives of Toyota, and many representatives from the media such as the *Wall Street Journal* and *Business Week*.

An ominous beginning—Anti-Japanese sentiment

Despite its great success, the Toyota cell had a rather ominous introduction to the plant. Simply put, many of the workers in the plant did not like the idea of producing parts for Toyota. Much of the anti-Japanese sentiment probably originated from the cutbacks in the Big Three labor force during the 1980s due to the enhanced competition from Japan. An inspection supervisor recalled that "a lot of people wanted it [the Toyota cell] to fail." Management was able to sell the Toyota contract as *new business*[16] to the work force. Management stressed the point that DSSS had contracts with Chrysler and Ford (at that time), so supplying to Toyota should be no different. Most of all, management stressed that new business translated into corporate growth, which would lead to increased job security for the employees. During the first few months of operation, the team coordinator recalled a few cases of "pilferage" from the department. In one case, a welding machine had broken down in another department. Rather than going to maintenance to get a new welding tip, an employee simply "borrowed" the one from the welding machine in the Toyota cell.[17] However, no serious damage has been reported to the cell as a result of vandalism or theft since its inception. There have been no malicious acts, and most workers now feel some admiration of the cell for its many accomplishments in bringing notoriety and new business to Plant 6.

Daily Operations of the Cell

The working day begins for the team at 6:00 A.M. with a meeting in the team information area. The mission statement, as defined by the team, is posted in the area: "Department 61 will make a quality column with 0 (zero) defects to keep our customer satisfied and strive for continuous improvement." Other postings include meeting minutes, current issues, the business goals, the health and safety goals, and a proficiency matrix that outlines the cross training of each worker in the cell. A layout of the machinery in the cell is posted on a bulletin board. Each machine is represented by a piece of paper attached to the board with a thumbtack. The employees experiment with different machine alignments in a preliminary effort to redesign the cell once the new models (the Merridian and the T-100) commence production.

There is no supervisor for the department, as the coordinator reports directly to a plant superintendent. The superintendent meets with the workers during the morning meeting and it is unlikely that he will return to the cell again that day, unless there is

a major problem. During these morning meetings, the superintendent gives the team the production quantity for the day and the
team addresses any unresolved or quality issues from the previous
day. Each morning, a truck picks up the finished columns from the
previous day for delivery to TMMK. Upon arriving at Plant 6, the
truck drops off kanban cards that state the daily demand by
TMMK. According to the coordinator, the daily build fluctuates by
10% (ranging between 340–420 pieces per day), in accordance with
Toyota's philosophy of leveling production.

The T-shaped cell is comprised of 16 machines, equipped with
a total of 34 error-proofing devices. The machines are aligned to
promote a continuous, one-piece-flow process. DSSS has not perfected this layout yet, as there is a small work-in-process (WIP)
inventory attributable to differences in cycle time between
machines. However, this WIP inventory is significantly less than
under the former push system. The cell has an uptime of approximately 95 percent. The cell produces two steering column models
for the Avalon: a column shift model and a floor shift model.
Changeover time between the two models is nearly instantaneous.
The pace of the work, or takt time,[18] is constant at all times, regardless of the build requirements per day. The tasks are highly standardized; it seems as though the operator has no wasted motions.
Everything has a purpose. The Toyota team opts to rotate jobs each
hour. The work team used to rotate every two hours but decided
that two hours was too long to spend on a single job and that anything less than an hour wouldn't allow the team member to get into
"the feel" of the task.

The cell runs until the daily demand is produced. If the cell
meets the goal before the end of the shift, the team members will
attend to other tasks such as problem solving or housekeeping (the
5S's). The condition of the cell is immaculate. The coordinator
explains that when the department was in the prebuild stage, he
thought it was crazy that everything had to be outlined with yellow tape, including the wastebasket. Now, he understands this
attention to detail because everything in the cell has a purpose:
Everything is part of the system. The coordinator explains with
great enthusiasm why he prefers his job to his previous work on

some of the old assembly lines: "Everyone here is involved and everyone knows all of the jobs." A great benefit of job rotation is that the team members truly understand the product they are manufacturing. The coordinator recalls his old days on the assembly line when everyone did one simple task but had no understanding of the other jobs along the line or how the employee's particular task fit into the overall assembly.

The coordinator says that the cell has a high level of quality because "people notice a bad part right away." He attributes this benefit to the one-piece-flow concept and to the team members' understanding of the process so that they can recognize immediately if something is wrong. If a team member discovers nonconforming material, they notify the coordinator. If the problem is not major, the coordinator will resolve the issue; otherwise, he will work with the plant superintendent to solve the problem.

A team member waves to the coordinator who then goes over to his or her workstation. They have a few words and then the coordinator takes over the work while the employee does a quality check. A few minutes later, the employee returns and the coordinator comes back to the team meeting area. He says that the most important part of being a coordinator is that one must respect the team members and one must ask them to do things; one can't order the team members. Most of all, coordinators must consider themselves part of the team. As an example, if someone falls behind, the coordinator will work during the next break to help the person catch up with the rest of the cell.

The coordinator of Department 61 is responsible for all of the duties outlined in the QNMS contract for the team leader. He characterizes his job as "a challenge. I learned a lot here versus the old assembly process, but I only get 50 cents more an hour for doing all these things! . . . Yeah, but I like this job." Many of the team members agree that the "jobs are harder" and that "you can't sit down on the job" in this cell versus their previous work assignments. However, they also say that they "like this job a lot better than the old assembly lines" because "on the assembly line, you didn't do anything."[19] Hence, the team members feel that the benefits of job empowerment outweigh the more demanding working environment.

Measurable Results of Synchronous Manufacturing

Employee participation

Employees must be able to shape the working environment for the benefits of QNMS to be fully realized. A primary mechanism through which this is accomplished is the Employee Suggestion Program, which provides a monetary award to people whose suggestions are implemented in the plant. The participation rate is the percentage of employees who submitted at least one suggestion in the last calendar year. Table 5-1 details the results of General Motors' Suggestion Plan in 1995 (*Challenge*, March 1996).

The average participation rate at DSSS in 1995 was more than double that of GM's North American Operations (NAO) and Delphi Automotive Systems. In 1992, prior to the QNMS contract, the participation rate was already above the GM average at 39 percent. Although the adoption rate at DSSS is below the GM average, the participation rate is more telling. Its high percentage implies that the labor force is taking the initiative to improve their competitiveness and working environment. Moreover, a suggestion currently takes 120 days to be processed at DSSS, an improvement of 45 percent over 1992, when the average was 220 days. Figure 5-6 illustrates that the participation rate by Plant 6 employees in the suggestion program has increased steadily since the approval of the QNMS contract in 1993. In 1995, the participation

Table 5-1. Vital Statistics from GM's Suggestion Plan in 1995

	Net savings ($ million)	Participation rate (%)	Adoption rate (%)
North American Operations	167.1	29.2	34.1
Powertrain	60.1	26.3	41.5
Service Parts	22.6	17.7	29.3
Other	32.8	14.5	24.6
Delphi Automotive	118.3	29.9	28.1
Delphi Steering	22.8	60.9	25.1
GM Total	**$400.9**	**27.1**	**32.8**

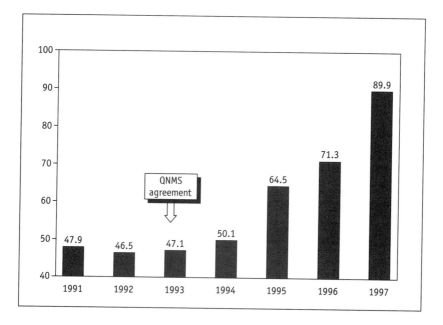

Figure 5-6. Participation Rates of Plant 6 Employees in Suggestion Program, 1991-97

rate was 64.5 percent, slightly above the mean rate of 60.9 percent for DSSS. The rate for Plant 6 is projected to reach 89.9 percent by the end of 1997. DSSS has not quite reached world class status, but it is certainly one of the more progressive suggestion programs within General Motors.[20]

Quality
The quality improvements at Plant 6 are significant. Figure 5-7 illustrates the exponential decline in Customer Return/Rejected Parts per Million (RPPM) since the approval of the QNMS contract. From 1993 to 1995, the RPPM declined from 1917 to 93, a 95 percent reduction. Plant 6 realized further quality improvements during the years 1995–1997, although the marginal improvement was a much smaller percentage. The great leap in quality at the beginning is because the system possessed very little error proofing or standardization.

The great improvement in quality has led to an almost equal reduction in scrap. Scrap, as measured by the percentage of cost of

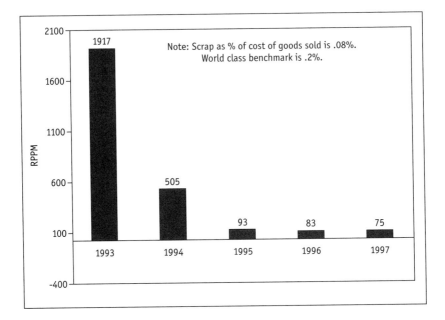

Figure 5-7. Customer Return/Rejected Parts per Million at Plant 6, 1991-97

goods sold, has followed an exponential decline similar to the reduction in RPPMs. Plant 6 has a scrap rate equal to 0.08 percent; DSSS benchmarked the world class level to be 0.2 percent. Hence, the QNMS system has contributed to a remarkable improvements in quality and scrap.

Productivity
Productivity, as measured by columns per employee per day, has increased in a linear fashion over the last few years. Figure 5-8 illustrates the productivity per worker on a yearly basis and the percentage increase in productivity from the previous year. Since 1991, Plant 6 has averaged roughly a 7 percent productivity improvement per year. In recent history, 1995 saw the greatest leap in productivity, an increase of 14 percent. What these results clearly show is that the productivity of the work force has risen accordingly as Plant 6 has implemented each of the synchronous manufacturing methods on the plant floor.

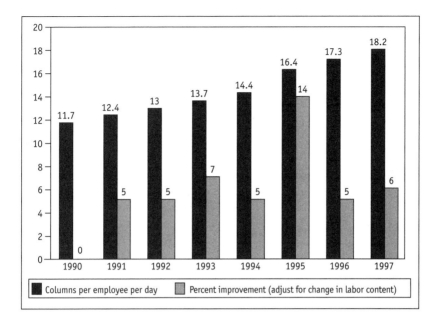

Figure 5-8. Employee Productivity at Plant 6, 1990-97

Conclusion: Moving from Adversarial Dysfunction to a Common Vision

To return to Dan Crishon's statement at the beginning of the chapter: "QNMS and the teamwork and employee empowerment. . . . [show] what can happen when an organization acts as a team." This is a lesson every manager and every union leader should take to heart. One of the primary reasons for the remarkable improvements in quality and productivity that were achieved at Plant 6 is that DSSS tapped into the potential of every employee to establish a working environment—one in which "everyone . . . can help in running the business." To unleash the power of the work force and implement real change, management, union leaders, and the work force must move together toward a common vision.

DSSS's new lean managerial philosophy was realized only when union leaders and top management broke away from their traditional adversarial relationship and made contractual a common goal: the synchronous manufacturing system. The result was the Quality Network Manufacturing System and the teamwork environment in which it could evolve and flourish. The pillars of this new, leaner manufacturing system share a common foundation: to provide support for the worker and the work team. A result of this support is greater employee involvement in the success of the plant, reflected in rising participation rates in the suggestion program. Employees are taking an active role in improving their work environment. This activism, in turn, is vital to maintaining continuous improvement efforts.

The transformation of Plant 6 to synchronous manufacturing was neither easy nor quick. Upon Mike Husar's arrival at the plant, DSSS created a five-year plan that detailed the migration of lean methods throughout the plant. To management's credit, they never strayed from this vision; all of the tactical decisions were based on the strategic plan. In order to meet the five-year vision, they needed to change the underlying culture of the unionized work force to realize short-term gains. The gradual buy-in of the work force to the new methods came with an initial emphasis on improving general housekeeping, quality, and problem solving. With this solid foundation, change permeated more easily throughout the plant. Moreover, the success of the first official QNMS area, the Toyota cell, helped to quell resistance to subsequent implementation efforts.

The other plants at the Saginaw site have since implemented QNMS, although some not as successfully as Plant 6. Plant 6 is generally recognized as the leader in QNMS, partly, of course, because it was the main proponent of the agreement during contract negotiations. The subsequent success of QNMS at Delphi Saginaw Steering Systems contributed to the creation of the Delphi Manufacturing System, a manufacturing system common to all Delphi Automotive divisions.

Although Plant 6 has become a much leaner, more efficient producer, the transformation is not complete. Indeed, the transformation will never be complete because lean production means continuous improvement, so satisfaction with the current state of affairs at Plant 6 is not a viable option. The QNMS has provided the work force with a means to reshape and improve their working environment constantly to increase the competitiveness of the plant. QNMS has enabled Plant 6 to make great strides in the past few years, thus establishing a solid foundation for tomorrow's achievements.

Acknowledgments: We would like to thank all of the personnel in Plant 6 who have helped to make this paper possible. In particular, we would like to thank Steve Gaut, Jeff McInerney, Gene Bishop, Dick Deitlein, Jerry Peterson, Jim Galm, Bob Farrand, John Casey, and Dave Reidel.

Notes

1. Dan Crishon, the former plant manager, describing the success of QNMS at Plant 6, in *Challenge*, February 1996 (a Delphi internal publication). Mike Husar preceded Dan Crishon as plant manager at Plant 6.

2. This steering gear was known as the JACOX, named after the three founders.

3. General Motors Corporation purchased the Buick Motor Company in 1908.

4. Six divisions comprise Delphi Automotive: Saginaw Steering, Interior and Lighting, Packard Electric, Chassis, Energy and Engine Management, and Harrison Thermal.

5. The original plant at the Saginaw site was permanently closed in 1984.

6. There are 10,300 UAW-represented employees of DSSS.

7. For instance, some team members may feel that an employee is not pulling his own weight or not contributing as much as everyone else to the cell's performance.

8. The Five Whys can be used to identify the root cause of a problem quickly. The principle is to ask five questions about a particular problem; each question builds on the previous one.

9. In Figure 5-3, the major assembly lines are Departments 81, 82, 84, 85, 87, 88, and 88-2.

10. The jackets cover the shaft and are designed to collapse in case of a head-on collision.

11. CSS stands for Component Set Strategy, a program initiated by GM to increase the commonality of parts across platforms. This new product allowed Plant 6 to redesign and even create new assembly lines for this product.

12. Since the plant produces 24,000 steering columns per day, it would not be economically feasible to run a customer-focused cell to machine the entire shaft for each type of steering column.

13. The coordinator previously worked on the Chrysler L/H assembly line.

14. The employee transferred out of the cell because of manpower reductions stemming from continuous improvement efforts. The only grievance concerned overtime.

15. The employees were disappointed because they expected to receive the Pinnacle award, the highest quality award given by Toyota. However, the employees were told that they had to have at least a three-year relationship with Toyota to be eligible for this award.

16. Delphi Automotive Systems has set a goal of 50 percent non-GM North American Operations (NAO) business by the year 2002. DSSS has been quite successful in diversifying their customer base, as currently 43 percent of total sales comes from non-GM NAO business, a substantial improvement from 15 percent in 1988. Moreover, management stressed the fact that American employees at TMMK assemble the columns.

17. The Toyota cell is a one-shift operation; much of the vandalism occurred on the off-shifts (second and third shifts) when there was no one in the Toyota cell.

18. The *takt time* is the cycle time of the assembly line required to meet customer demand. It is calculated as the daily demand divided by the number of working hours per day.

19. Quotes are taken from interviews with team members of Department 61 on April 8, 1997.

20. The NUMMI plant has a participation rate of 90 percent and an acceptance rate of 70 percent; this is considered world class status (*Challenge*, March 1996).

References

Adler, Alan L. *Delphi Profits Unveiled*, http: www.auto.com/makers/qgm13.htm, Mar. 13, 1997.

Adler, Paul S. "Time-and-Motion Regained," *Harvard Business Review* 71: 97–108, Jan./Feb. 1993.

Babson, Steve. "Lean or Mean: The MIT Model and Lean Production at Mazda," *Labor Studies Journal* 18: 3–24, 1993.

Besser, Terry. *Team Toyota: Transplanting the Toyota Culture to the Camry Plant in Kentucky*, NewYork: University of New York Press, 1996.

Howes, Daniel and Phillips, Dave. "Big 3 Foes Tip the Scale," *The Detroit News*, Dec. 29, 1996. http://www.detnews.com/96/biz.9612/30/12290016.htm

Krafcik, J.F. "Triumph of the Lean Production System," *Sloan Management Review* 30(1): 41–52, 1988.

Lienert, Anita and Lienert, Paul. "The Danger of Being Too American," *The Detroit News*, Sept. 18, 1996. http://www.detnews.com/1996/menu/stories/65527.htm

Muller, Joann. "A New Fear for Workers," *The Detroit Free Press*, July 2, 1993.

Phillips, Dave. "UAW 1996 Auto Talks: Tough-talking Union Changes Tune for Jobs," *The Detroit News*, April 3, 1996. http://www.detnews.com/1996/menu/stories/42484.htm

Raynal, Wes, and Phillips, Dave. "'Our Work Is not yet Done,' Chief of Delphi Empire says," *The Detroit News*, March 24, 1996. http://www.detnews.com/menu/stories.41129.htm

Shadur, Mark A., Rodwell, John J., and Bamber, Greg J. "Factors Predicting Employees' Approval of Lean Production," *Human Relations* 48: 1403–1425, Dec. 1995.

Sickman, Philip. "The Yankee Flavor of Japan's U.S. Factories," *Fortune*, 116[C]–116[P], Dec. 9, 1996.

Vlasic, Bill. "The Saginaw Solution," *Business Week*, 78–79; July 15, 1996.

Womack, James P., Jones, Daniel T., and Roos, Daniel. *The Machine that Changed the World*, New York: Harper Perennial, 1991.

Delphi Saginaw Steering Systems Publications

Local Agreements and Statements Between Saginaw Division Saginaw Site General Motors Corporation and Local Union #699 UAW, October 13, 1993 (traditional contract).

Quality Network Manufacturing System Agreement Between Saginaw Division Saginaw Site General Motors Corporation and Local Union #699 UAW, October 13, 1993 (QNMS contract).

"Behind the Wheel—Information for and About Delphi Saginaw Steering Systems Employees." *Sign of the Times: Our Site's History*, Vol. 2, No. 14, July 24, 1996.

The following articles were taken from the publication, *Challenge—News For and About Delphi Saginaw Steering Systems & Its Employees*:

"Toyota Cell Exemplifies Lean, Agile Manufacturing. Demonstrates Future of US Production: Operators Determine Speed, Quality," January 1995.

"Plant 6 Leads QNMS Implementation," March 1995.

"Plant 6: Toyota Team Recognized for Outstanding Performance," December 1995.

"QNMS Guides Plant 6 to Leadership in Quality, Cost, Delivery Award," February 1996.

"Suggestion Plan, Today: Best in General Motors; Tomorrow: World Class Status," March 1996.

Sean G. Traynor *was educated at Trinity College, Dublin where he received a Ph.D. in chemistry. He began his professional career as a research chemist with SCM Glidco Organics in Jacksonville, Florida, where he became vice president of sales and marketing. He became chairman and CEO of Garden State Tanning in 1992. Garden State Tanning is one of the largest global suppliers of leather to the automotive industry. Dr. Traynor is holder of 12 U.S. patents and author of over 30 articles in chemistry journals.*

6

Making Leather Leaner:
The Garden State Tanning Story

by Sean G. Traynor

Editor's prologue: In Chapter 2, John Shook gave his perspective on implementation issues associated with the Toyota Production System (TPS), much of which came from his experiences helping to establish the Toyota Supplier Support Center. TSSC was set up to help U.S. manufacturers implement TPS. One of the first companies they worked with was Garden State Tanning (GST). Sean Traynor was executive sponsor for the transformation to lean at GST. He tells us about the fascinating process of making tanned leather from cow hides. Quality is critical, as this is a product purchased exclusively for its esthetic quality. Each hide is unique and contains some defects. When GST was fortunate enough to get a large order from Lexus in 1991, they quickly found that they could not keep up with the order quantity. Before long, they were several months behind in fulfilling orders. Within Toyota's JIT system, this was devastating. The result was expensive air freight deliveries overseas to Japan and an unhappy customer. Rather than drop GST as a supplier, Toyota helped teach and implement TPS, at first through their purchasing department and later through TSSC. Although it seemed to Sean Traynor initially that hides were a large batch operation that could not be made into a continuous flow operation, once again a doubter was proved wrong. A shift was made from a process-oriented approach to cells including cutters, packers, inspectors, etc. The workload was balanced. The result was a reduction in lead time of cutting and packing tanned leather for shipment from 10 days to two hours. Through this and other changes to lean manufacturing over two years, inventories were cut in half, and despite the reduced inventory, better scheduling through kanban resulted in virtual elimination of emergency air freight. Also, quality defects were cut from 1 percent to .05 percent (one-twentieth of the former level), cutting productivity was improved by almost two-thirds, and lost-time accidents dropped from 242 to 2 per year.

The leather industry is one of the oldest known to humankind. From the time primitive peoples used animal hides up to today's use of leather, often as a luxury item for handbags and car seats, leather has played a unique role as a protective, utilitarian, and decorative material. Even with today's array of human-made fibers and materials, leather stands unique in its strength and tactile and breathing characteristics.

Automotive Leather

In the past 20 years, leather has made a major resurgence as the seat covering of choice in the automotive industry. In 1995, the proportion of cars with leather seat covers in the USA had reached over 20 percent, and the industry worldwide has reached over $1 billion in revenues per year. Leather is a unique product in the automotive industry for the following reasons:

- Leather is one of the few components of an automobile that is purchased solely because of its esthetic and luxury appeal, not its functionality. There are considerably cheaper seat covering materials available, such as cloth and vinyl, that have most of leather's functionality.
- Each hide is unique and has defects as a result of scratch and pit marks arising from the life experiences of the cow or steer that was the raw material source. These marks occur in different places and to greatly differing extents on each hide. Thus, each hide must be uniquely processed in order to maximize the yield and generate as much defect-free area as possible.
- The manufacture of leather is an extremely labor intensive process, since each hide must be individually handled and inspected many times to determine its acceptability for use in particular automotive applications.
- Hides are typically bought by the truckload from slaughter houses throughout the country. The industry practice is that the buyer

must accept all of the hides of a particular load without "cherry picking" the best.

Usually a hide contains healed or open scratches from barbed wire or trees as well as pits caused by flies, such as the warble fly. (These flies burrow beneath the skin to lay eggs.) In addition, when bovine animals are kept in pens during the fattening period prior to slaughter, serious damage to the hide occurs from the animals having to lie in their own excrement. Particularly in winter, when dung adheres to the animal's hair, the result is a bacterial infection of the skin called *mange*. Raw material defects such as these are commonly dealt with in the tanning business, and it is the skill of the tanner as well as the finisher that converts this substance into a product of commercial value.

The Production of Leather

The leather production process has remained largely unchanged for decades. It typically involves the following steps:

1. Removal of hair from the hide.
2. Tanning (chrome) of the rawhide to prevent decay.
3. Splitting of the hide horizontally to provide a "top grain" and a "split" hide.
4. Shaving the hide to the correct thickness (usually 0.9–1.4 mm).
5. Retanning of the top grain hide to color the hide substance as well as provide a soft malleable product.
6. Finishing (painting) of the top surface of the hide.
7. Cutting of the hide into pieces to be sewn into seat covers.

Most tanneries also employ other unit operations such as staking and milling, which stretch and soften the hide, as well as embossing of the hides at various stages of production (see Photo 6-1).

The challenge then is to recover the maximum value possible from the hide without the inclusion of pits or scars into the visible seating areas where consumers might find them objectionable. Paradoxically, many consumers realize that the presence of small healed scars in leather is a mark of genuine leather. They do not like heavily "finished" leathers that as a result of excessive paint begin to

Photo 6-1. Tannery Machinery

look like vinyl. Thus the skill of the leather cutter is to cut around the many natural markings to provide a product suitable for the auto consumer.

The tanning of leather today, although greatly mechanized compared to past methods, still requires considerable labor and multiple handling steps, which in the tanning industry has led to much inefficiency and high costs.

Garden State Tannery—Getting to Lean

To overcome these problems and remain cost competitive, Garden State Tanning (GST) implemented lean manufacturing methods based on the Toyota Production System (see Figure 6-1). The goal of this system at GST is to provide a framework that produces

- The highest quality leather
- At the lowest possible cost
- By just-in-time principles
- Within a safe work environment

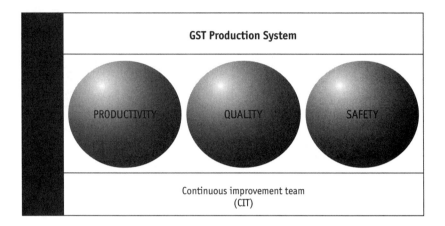

Figure 6-1. GST Production System

Getting to lean was not the result of enlightened management at GST but simply the result of necessity. In 1991, GST began to benefit from the spectacular success of the recently introduced Lexus line of luxury vehicles from Toyota. As these new vehicles increased in popularity, GST's order book for leather seat sets grew dramatically. Since we had worked with Toyota to develop a special line of durable and luxurious leather that met their specific standards, it was imperative that GST be able to deliver to meet the new demand. In 1992, our manufacturing capability became sorely tested. We ended up several months behind in fulfilling orders. The result was expensive air shipments of leather cut-sets to Japan instead of the planned ocean freight.

Standard Tanning Industry Operations

GST's production process for leather was fairly standard for the tanning industry. The process was characterized as follows:

- *Scheduling*. The push system was based on sales forecasts/ customer releases, which are generally inaccurate.
- *Cutting*. Each leather cutter cut complete seat sets which, we learned later, reduced cutting productivity by as much as 25 percent.

- *Inspection*. Excessive reliance on inspection of cut parts by dedicated inspectors reduced the cutter's responsibility for quality and resulted in inventory accumulation and widespread delays of up to 10 days.
- *Process flow*. Flow was generally poor, winding throughout the shop.
- *Flexible paths*. Products generally were processed on the equipment available at the time instead of by use of fixed path production methods.
- *Inventory*. Excessive inventory in all areas was seen to be the solution for customer's schedule and product changes.

GST's behind-schedule situation quickly became apparent to our customer, Toyota. Instead of "taking GST to the woodshed" and threatening the re-sourcing of our business, Toyota took the unprecedented step (in our view) of offering to help overcome our production difficulties. It was not without some skepticism that the offer was accepted; after all, Toyota was a car company and our problems were leather-tanning related.

Learning a New Way of Thinking— The Toyota Production System

GST was the first supplier company in the U.S. that Toyota worked with to teach the Japanese lean manufacturing concepts that are embedded in the TPS. The key to the success of the project was the acceptance by top management of the need to change. Essential management and operations personnel at a variety of levels within the company visited Toyota plants and suppliers in Japan. Toyota sent three process engineers from Japan to work at a GST plant initially for one month. They evaluated the processes and procedures and studied the plant inventories and scheduling processes. A team from the cutting department visited the sewing plant in Japan that received our product. They held discussions with the quality personnel at the sewing plant to ensure that both sides understood the cutting quality criteria and issues such as the importance of natural markings on the leather.

Teams Are Formed and New Process Flows Are Tried

GST's plant formed teams in each department to review work flow and procedures. New process flows were tried, thus creating an atmosphere of experimentation. Some ideas worked, others did not, and still others were revised. Toyota engineers helped develop goals for the various teams, but essential to the improvements was the development of realistic goals by the teams themselves and, in particular, the achievement of some early successes. One of these successes was the change in the setup time for finishing spray machines. In the new process, paint was prepared ahead of time and planning boards were provided beside each machine so that the operators could see, at all times, their progress against the daily plan. The teams, consisting of operating and supervisory personnel, worked together for one- or two-week periods to analyze various processes and to reach agreement on what might be achieved. The Toyota engineers then returned home, leaving the GST teams to work in their kaizen teams to implement and improve on the various ideas. Approximately one month later, the support staff returned to discuss the progress of the various teams.

Introduction to Kaizen (Continuous Improvement)

GST was introduced to the concept of kaizen or continuous improvement along with the following key steps to improving the process:

- Formation of kaizen teams
- Involvement of shopfloor employees
- Top management buy-in
- Fixed path production flow
- Reevaluation of all existing processes
- Using established cutting teams
- Balanced work loads
- Standardized work—takt time (keeping pace with customer demand for product)
- Kanbans introduced to regulate production and inventory
- Heijunka: Levelized schedules
- Reduction or elimination of in-process inventories

The concept of kaizen was one of the most instrumental in affecting change. As simple as it may sound, it represents a major cultural gap between Western and Japanese thinking. More specifically, in the U.S. we give great credence to individual contributions; in particular, we look for big breakthroughs in thinking—intellectual "home runs." The Japanese, on the other hand, see team activities as more productive and, in particular, put great emphasis on the concept of incremental and continuous improvements. This powerful concept of kaizen places greater emphasis on shopfloor participation rather than the undue reliance by Western managers on management and engineering as the major sources for new ideas.

It is a natural psychological trap to accept our latest improvements in productivity as the best possible and to pat ourselves on the back for a job well done. We usually then proceed to some other project, believing that our last improvements are the best that can be done. The Japanese, however, see improvement as only the beginning of constant change—the relentless pursuit of small but meaningful changes. One of the great teachers of the Toyota Production System concepts, Mr. Fuchio Cho (former president of Toyota Manufacturing, Kentucky), used to say, "Don't tell me how much you intend to improve, show me how you will measure it"—the point being that we are all filled with good intentions for process improvements but sometimes we use flexible rulers. Having a good clear methodology to measure improvements is the key to progress.

One of the keys to the success of this process is that Toyota did not come to GST to make radical changes of their own but instead guided the teams to successful answers through the use of questions. The Toyota Five Whys are now famous as one of the major techniques for identifying root causes to problems. The idea is that in addressing any problematic issue, the answer first presented is rarely the real root cause of the problem. For example:

Problem:	The machine broke down during operation.
Why?	The shaft broke.
Why?	The machine was running too fast.
Why?	The RPM gauge has been broken for one month.
Why?	Maintenance didn't fix it.

Why?   It was scheduled to be fixed next week.
Conclusion: We had a communication problem that, left unre-
            solved, resulted in serious equipment failure.

Similar questions by experienced technical personnel in process areas, such as "Why are you doing this operation that way?" usually elicit the response, "That's the way we've always done it!" Subsequent questioning, using the Toyota Five Whys, usually results in the team's discovering a new answer themselves. This answer is rarely the same as the first answer given.

Improvements in Cutting Leather

In the area of cutting leather, our mentors did introduce a radical new concept: Cutters worked in teams rather than working as individuals who completed whole sets. The teams or cells consisted of approximately 10 people whose jobs were redefined as cutters, packers, inspectors, etc. This raised some difficult issues in the area of compensation, since the cutters were previously paid as individuals, not as members of teams. In the new cutting process, the teams of cutters were arranged in a linear arrangement on each side of a conveyor. Each team member cut 10 specific pieces for a particular car set and placed the pieces on a tray that moved down the line (see Figures 6-2 and 6-3).

The workload was balanced so that each cutter had adequate time to cut large or small pieces as required. It was important to balance the workload so that each member was able to complete their tasks in a similar takt time. This way, no member was ahead or behind schedule in completing their portion of the ten complete car-seat sets. The balancing of the line was laid out diagramatically so that the members of the cell could see the individual workloads. When the tray traversed the length of the cutting line, there were 10 complete sets of leather seats ready for shipment. Inspectors were added at strategic locations on the line to check cut pieces for natural markings that could not be detected by the cutters when they cut the leather in the horizontal position. Then the completed, inspected seat sets were packed into boxes ready

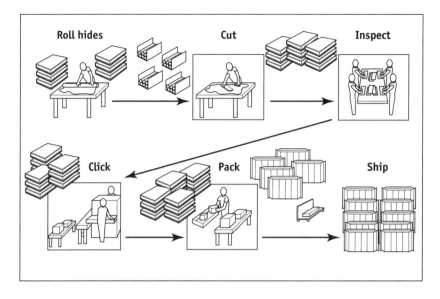

Figure 6-2. Cutting Before Kaizen

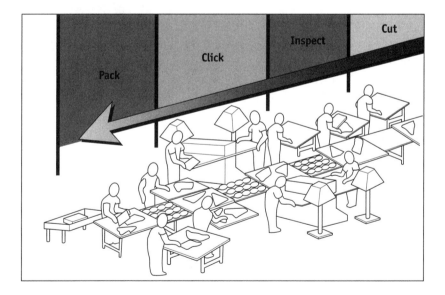

Figure 6-3. Cutting After Kaizen

for shipment. The results were amazing. Whereas before it typically took leather up to 10 days to complete the journey through cutting, inspecting, and packing, the leather was now ready for shipment in less than two hours.

Fixed Path Method and Standard Lot Size Versus Flexibility

In the leather finishing (painting) department, GST traditionally prided itself on having the flexibility of using any one of several spray machines to spray any of the four or five spray coats needed to provide the color and protection that modern-day automotive leather requires. In the minds of the schedulers, this allowed the flexibility to use whatever machine would next become available and to accommodate varying lot sizes. The Toyota engineers provided the radical thought that since we produced product mostly for Toyota on these machines, why not adopt a fixed path method and a standard lot size? The adoption of standard lot sizes allowed the synchronizing of each machine to accommodate the processing of each lot. This was in contrast to the idea that maintaining maximum flexibility in lot size and machine use improved efficiency. Adopting a standard lot size and fixed path flow improved the operating efficiency of the machines by reducing downtime and setup time. Metal tracks were bolted to the floor in front of some processes that did not permit batches of leather to be pulled out of line or otherwise delayed. This meant that each batch was processed as first in–first out, which improved overall quality by ensuring that all batches followed the same path.

Kanban Quantums

Another key element to this improved production flow was the adoption of the kanban (pull) system of lot making and processing. This system allowed for automatic in-process inventory control. The scheduling department initially had a great deal of difficulty with this concept, since it appeared to take away their flexibility and decision making. They quickly learned that the system actually freed them up to complete more important planning tasks, as they could control the number of kanban cards. One of the immediate effects of these changes was the reduction or elimination of in-process inventory.

One of the cornerstones of the Toyota Production System is the concept of *heijunka* or levelized schedules. This means that customers and suppliers work together to produce forward schedules that have a reasonable degree of accuracy. Obviously, any customer will have some fluctuations within their own production schedules, as dictated by the marketplace, but the difference in the Japanese philosophy is that they do not expect a supplier to cover schedule fluctuations by forcing suppliers to carry excess inventory. Unfortunately, one of the biggest "lies" in the automotive industry today is the concept of just-in-time (JIT). Usually this is wielded as an excuse for an OEM or system supplier to force lower tier suppliers to carry excess inventory to cover the OEM's inefficiencies and poor planning. Toyota does an excellent job of leveling production schedules by frequently balancing out variety and changeovers.

The Toyota Supplier Support Center

After approximately six months of partnership in working with Toyota on these changes, GST was fortunate that Toyota decided to establish the Toyota Supplier Support Center (TSSC) in Kentucky. Under the leadership of Mr. H. Ohba, GST was selected to be one of the immediate beneficiaries of this new center, a center set up solely to assist suppliers. One of the surprising benefits was that the TSSC engineers helped GST not only on Toyota-related production processes but also on other OEM processes and products. At first glance we were surprised how willing our mentors were to help us on problems not related to their own business. It soon became apparent that this attitude was one further example of our inhibited thinking. TSSC personnel believed that it is important to work on the "whole patient," not just to Band-Aid selected areas. As a result, a company is more likely to adopt the lean manufacturing philosophy and apply it to all of its business, as well as reduce costs and make the supplier more competitive overall. TSSC supplied these services without charge to suppliers and without any implied quick pay-back (price reductions) to Toyota. Rather, the philosophy was that making suppliers more cost competitive would allow Toyota to reach its goals on future programs.

Overall Results of Becoming Lean

The overall results of becoming lean were extremely impressive, resulting in a drop in hide inventories of more than 50 percent over an almost two-year period from 1992 to 1993. In addition, better scheduling from using the kanban system resulted in a quick departure from air freight and a return to scheduled ocean shipments. The reduction in inventories actually improved on-time deliveries, since it made scheduling easier and forced GST to fix current problems instead of assigning them to dead inventory (see Figure 6-4).

The productivity in the cutting department also rose dramatically. The labor-hours required to complete one carton of seat sets

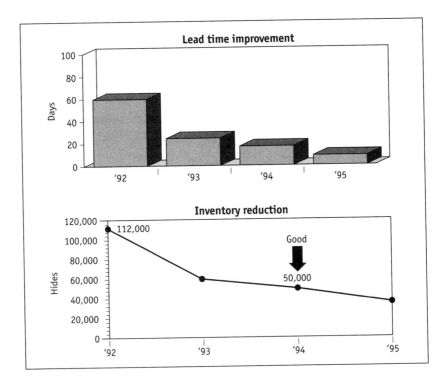

Figure 6-4. Lean Manufacturing Results I

was reduced from 43 hours to less than 17 hours. Furthermore, as mentioned above, the average time for leather to be processed through the cutting area dropped from 10 days (by the time that each piece was cut, inspected, and packaged) to less than 2 hours (see Figure 6-5).

Perhaps the most impressive feature of this progress is that we achieved these results over a two-year period without the need to spend any capital. GST's facilities are quite old and operate in a multifloor environment that is not readily conducive to a smooth flow of goods. The philosophy was to bring about these changes by modifying existing processes and use of floor-space, not by capital expenditures and computerization—that is, work with what you have to make it as efficient as possible before making capital improvements. Table 6-1 summarizes the overall results:

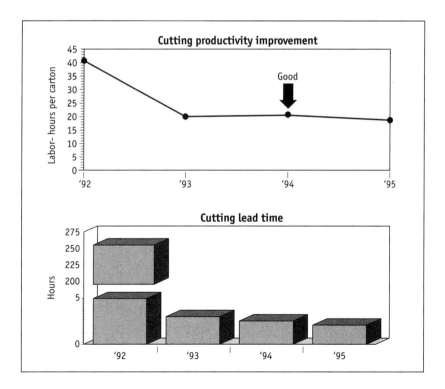

Figure 6-5. Lean Manufacturing Results II

Table 6-1. Overall Results

Category	Was	Now
Quality Defects	> 1.0%	< 0.05%
Process Inventory	112,000	36,000
Production Lead Time	60 days	9 days
Cutting Lead Time	264 hrs	2 hrs
Cutting Productivity per Carton	43 hrs	17 hrs
Lost Time Accidents	242	2

Lessons and Pitfalls of Becoming Lean

Garden State Tanning was the fortunate beneficiary of the best lean manufacturing schooling in the world—the Toyota Production System. The following are some of the lessons learned and pitfalls you can avoid in your own effort to become lean.

- Evolutionary change is the key—batting singles
- Revolutionary change is less frequent—don't wait for home runs
- Commitment by top management is vital
- Continuous improvement team projects—quality not quantity
- It's a continuous process—not "program of the month"
- Toyota "Five Whys" is great discipline
- The kanban system works best with level schedules
- Local ownership on the shopfloor is critical to success
- Fear of layoffs is a serious obstacle to progress and must be realistically addressed
- Productivity improvements do not necessarily require capital expenditures

The impact of lean thinking and its implementation at GST has been a dramatic reduction of inventories, accurate scheduling, and efficient shopfloor operations. Such changes do not come without difficulty and organizational stress, but the results are well worth the journey. The next step for GST is to institutionalize these changes and make the process of seeking further change (lean thinking) part of the corporate culture.

Note: The author is extremely grateful to Toyota Motor Corporation, Toyota Supplier Support Center, and in particular to Mr. H. Ohba, Mr. Saito, Mr. J. Maruchin, and the many other employees of Toyota and the employees of Garden State Tanning who worked long hours to bring about change.

 **Joseph C. Day** *has served as Freudenberg-NOK's CEO since its formation in 1989, after having been selected in 1988 to help establish the North American partnership between Freudenberg & Co. of Germany and NOK Corporation of Japan. Day is a proponent of lean systems in the automotive supply business and assists other companies in the application and practice of lean systems. Day has served as keynote speaker on lean systems to Harvard University's Manufacturing Leadership Summit, the American Supplier Institute, the American Railroad Association, the Philip B. Hofmann Senior Executive Program, and the Chrysler Corporation. In recognition of his "leadership abilities and ongoing success" at Freudenberg-NOK, Day was named 1994 Executive of the Year by* Rubber & Plastics News. *Day also is president of Freudenberg-NOK and sits on the board of directors. He is a director of ASC Inc. of Southgate, Michigan, director of Rubber Manufacturers Association, a member of the CEO exchange, and chairman of the board of the Wiremold Company.*

Day was formerly president of the Specialty Materials & Engineered Plastics Group for the Dexter Corporation, president of Dexter Corporation's C.H. Dexter Division, and has held numerous management, marketing, and sales positions with General Electric's Plastics Business Group.

Day earned a bachelor of science degree in plastics engineering from Lowell Technological Institute in 1966 and completed General Electric's Executive Development Course. Born in Lowell, MA, Day is married and resides in the greater Detroit area.

7

Learning About Lean Systems at Freudenberg-NOK: Where Continuous Improvement Is a Way of Life

by Joseph C. Day

Editor's prologue: Freudenberg-NOK, the largest manufacturer of sealing components in the world, is by now quite well known for their impressive continuous improvement process led by Joseph Day, CEO, who has also become a much sought after motivational speaker on the benefits of kaizen. As Joe Day says in this chapter: "I feel I've spent a lifetime over the past four years involved in the Toyota Production System. The level of immersion . . . has given me the most satisfaction of any business endeavor in my career."

Joe Day took a struggling company and after some false starts began religiously applying repeated kaizen events to part after part of plant after plant, eventually transforming much of the company. In 1992, Freudenberg-NOK launched its new lean production program called GROWTTH®, an acronym for Get Rid of Waste Through Team Harmony. By 1996, with dramatic improvements in quality, delivery times, and cost reductions, sales grew from $200 million to $600 million with unprecedented profit levels. Joe Day attributes these dramatic improvements to the use of 2,500 kaizen events in 15 manufacturing plants involving 90 percent of their 3,500 employees. Another key success factor of GROWTTH is the personal involvement of Joe Day and all of his top executives as members of kaizen teams. For the first two years of GROWTTH, Joe Day spent 35 percent of his work week on nothing but kaizen implementation. His story shows how total commitment and buy-in by top management (learning the "religion"), the need for lots of kaizen training for everyone (the lesson of Chapter 3), and total dedication of one's time in thoroughly applying lean systems can dramatically transform and continuously improve your company.

L ean systems are the best competitive tool available in business today. If manufacturers and suppliers are to meet
customer demands and contain costs, we all must address
cost and quality issues with long-term solutions that work. And
lean systems—as our company has seen over the past four years—
positively work.

Our savings on everything from productivity and cycle time to
travel distance and work-in-process inventory have been dramatic.
It all started with the workers on the shop floor, who have answers
to production problems and ways to make improvements. Tapping
the workers' knowledge and creativity through lean systems at
Freudenberg-NOK has been the most powerful resource our company has ever known.

I feel as though I've spent a lifetime over the past four years
involved in the Toyota Production System (TPS). The level
of immersion that I've had to take in order to implement this
program successfully in my own company has given me the most
satisfaction of any business endeavor in my career. Before I get
into the details, let me give you a little background information on
the company.

Freudenberg-NOK is a member of the Freudenberg and NOK
Group Companies, spanning 24 countries worldwide, with combined vehicle industry sales of $4 billion and total sales of $6 billion.
As the largest manufacturer of sealing components in the world
(with headquarters in Tokyo, Japan; Weinheim, Germany; and
Plymouth, Michigan), the group is well known for technically
advanced seal designs that significantly reduce warranty claims for
OE vehicle manufacturers. This group services the vehicle and general industries with complete sealing packages for engines and
transmissions, sophisticated noise, vibration, and harshness (NVH)
packages, and a variety of precision-molded rubber and plastic
components for steering, brake, and fuel systems.

Freudenberg-NOK's GROWTTH® Program

In September of 1992, Freudenberg-NOK launched its new lean production program called GROWTTH®. The program is rooted in the concepts of the Toyota Production System and emphasizes employee teamwork and communication in an effort to eliminate inefficiencies in the use of time, labor, materials, and space—all while continuously improving performance.

GROWTTH is a companywide program and involves every employee in continuous improvement projects called kaizen. These shift the company's manufacturing approach from mass manufacturing (in which employees generally perform one task and have little interaction with others), to lean production (in which a worker performs multiple tasks from molding to shipping while constantly supervising quality).

Since Freudenberg-NOK launched the GROWTTH Program in 1992, all of the company's 3,600 employees have had ongoing training in lean systems and more than two-thirds have participated on numerous kaizen teams. In addition, nearly 500 customers, noncompeting manufacturer executives, and suppliers have also teamed up with Freudenberg-NOK employees on kaizen teams.

Freudenberg-NOK's GROWTTH Program has won public acclaim as a benchmark in lean systems for the North American automotive industry. However, when our employees first heard the term "lean," they thought of corporate cutbacks, including reduced employment. This was one of our concerns, so my management team developed a strategy that would launch a complete culture change by educating employees on how lean systems could create opportunities for increased business while also enhancing job opportunities.

Freudenberg-NOK combated employee fears with ongoing communication, extensive training, and careful listening. I advised my managers and supervisors to explain to employees why they were working in a different way rather than telling them to make changes on short notice with no explanation. GROWTTH provides the environment to cultivate employees' ideas, giving them a sense of ownership of the processes in which they work. In today's competitive environment, we need the use of workers' minds as well as their hands.

How We Began the Journey to Lean

Back in 1989 when the Freudenberg-NOK joint-venture company was organized, we were making oil seals and lots of other rubber and plastic parts via classic batch production using press rooms, injection-molding rooms, painting facilities, etc. Parts were molded in one building, inventoried, and moved to another building or area for secondary operations like trimming and springing. Parts were inspected, put into inventory again, processed, and then stored again. Parts finally went to quality control (QC) and then to a warehouse, where they were packed and placed into finished goods.

In 1991, after two years with Freudenberg-NOK, I began to feel the necessity to find some new and better ways to get things done. In 1989, when the company was formed, our annual sales were about $200 million, and we had large losses on a pre-tax basis. I had a serious problem, so I did what anyone would expect in a classic manufacturing environment. In what we called by the kindest of terms—*rationalization*—we laid off people, we cut back overtime, we did everything that we possibly could. By 1991, the business had grown to perhaps $280 to $300 million, and we were only approaching break-even.

It became obvious that classic manufacturing methods were not the solution to the cost problems that we had. The notion of creating a lean systems program at Freudenberg-NOK developed in 1992 when I attended a board meeting at the Wiremold Company in West Hartford, Connecticut, which manufactures housing for electrical lines and multiple outlet units.

The board had just hired Art Byrne as Wiremold's new president. At his former company, Byrne had been a great proponent of lean production. One of his first priorities at Wiremold was to launch his own lean production program. I paid close attention, learning from Byrne how to convert not only a manufacturing plant from mass manufacturing to lean manufacturing, but also how to educate employees so they can contribute and understand the conversion.

Within four short months, Byrne improved labor productivity by reducing the work force by 26 percent, with a layoff and an early retirement package. Although one of the key components of lean production is the boast that no one will lose their job as the result of a kaizen project, many companies have a one-time layoff to eliminate unnecessary overhead at the onset and to protect the remaining work force in the long term. In these four months, Byrne also freed up 30 percent of Wiremold's floor space and improved gross profit margins by 3 percent.

I was amazed at Byrne's quick results. So I made the commitment in 1992 to create the GROWTTH program and make it the company's top priority. Our corporate goal remains quite simple. We are committed to improving cost, quality, and delivery for our customers through the elimination of waste. We will continue to make specific improvements in productivity by cutting unnecessary movement, inventory, and lead time, enhancing customer relationships, and giving the company a competitive edge that very few companies in North America have.

This commitment meant that my top managers and I would participate in training and kaizen projects together with the workers on the shop floor. It meant we would walk the floors and become coequals, demonstrating that senior management is involved, and that we are all on the same team. It meant that we had to help workers understand the benefits of lean production, which we discovered was not an easy task. Like management, many workers were too used to the old ways. Nonetheless, we began the process.

Getting Senior Management on Board

Despite the proven benefits, some business executives see the conversion from mass to lean as a luxury they simply cannot afford in terms of money, time, and cultural change. As someone who wrestled with these same issues, I found that converting to lean systems was actually the one thing our company had to do to ensure our future.

Because most of my senior managers had been schooled in the theory and practices of mass production, they first had to be convinced that one-piece flow and continuous improvement could actually work. I had to convince all of my staff members to want to do this. There is a big difference between being told to do something and wanting to do it. I wanted my staff to understand fully the savings and benefits of a lean systems program, because if they did, they would turn into great teachers, participants, and proponents of the program.

To begin their education, we sent staff members to Wiremold in groups of three to participate on kaizen teams and to "get religion." Here they learned firsthand the rapid rate at which improvements can be made. As staff members returned from their four-day experiences, we asked them to talk to their own management about what they had learned. I also asked my staff to "buy in."

Leadership and Getting Middle Management Buy-In

Leadership is not about managing. Leadership is about providing guidance and vision, and taking people where they do not think they can go. Your biggest obstacle will be converting all employees to lean thinking. You will find middle management the least equipped to respond to the changes because of the autocratic style that pervades mass manufacturing systems. I can remember six years ago when I asked my manufacturing organization, "Is it cheaper to make one part at a time or 10,000 at a time?" Nobody in the room concluded that making one part at a time was cheaper, but I guarantee that for every single part you study, when you look at the cost in a batch environment compared to the cost in a lean environment, you will not find a case where batch manufacturing is cheaper than lean manufacturing.

I had manufacturing guys who were working for 15, 20, 30 years in my plants. How easy do you think it was for them to turn that corner? Practically impossible. My conclusion was the only way I could convert them was through lots of training. My guess is that it will take each of you who are plant managers, manufacturing executives, or people responsible for plants, about 30 percent of your work week, minimum, for the first year to be educated in the ways of lean thinking—30 percent. I spent 35 percent of my work week for two years on nothing but kaizen implementation. But what did I get for it? Immeasurable gains.

Case in point: My corporate sales have grown from $200 million to over $600 million with unprecedented record profit levels. These are the kinds of gains that are available to you if you go after this with a vengeance. On the flip side, if you give it a half-hearted effort, you'll get nothing back.

What Are the Results of Becoming Lean?

Over the course of the past four years, my company has been practicing the Toyota Production System with no deviation and with only standardized processes. One of the beauties of one-piece flow is *constant product evaluation*. Our operators are tracking product performance each step of the way, every minute, every shift, every day. In four years, we have completed about 2,500 kaizen projects across 15 manufacturing plants. About 90 percent of our 3,500 employees have participated in numerous kaizen projects.

We audit 100 percent of our projects to verify that we capture the cost reductions projected by the kaizen teams. These audits occur 90 days after project completion to ensure that the gains are sustainable. We report all financial results to division financial managers. The average controllable variable cost savings is approximately $40,000 per project, representing 3.2 percent of sales and 18–25 percent of controllable variable costs.

The softer savings such as lower inventory, additional available capacity, and fixed cost absorption are additive to our controllable variable cost savings. Worker's compensation costs have fallen drastically—over 50 percent since 1991. These savings go directly to the bottom line. In addition, OSHA-reportable accidents have dropped by 55 percent. Since implementing lean systems, labor productivity per employee has doubled, and value added per employee has more than doubled. Accidents per employee have also been reduced (see Figure 7-1).

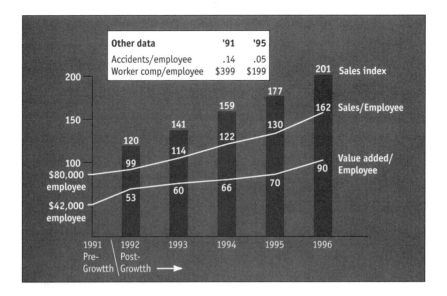

Figure 7-1. Employee Productivity under Lean

Much of this improvement in employee statistics has to do with the absence of injuries associated with the movement of product in big quantities. In 1991, our system used 55,000 green plastic tubs to move product. For example, we'd put 10,000 oil seals in one of these tubs, or 25 engine mounts. They were the standard for the movement of product. Today we have about 500 green tubs in the system. With the decline in the number of tubs has come a decline in back injuries, falling injuries, and all kinds of other problems associated with the movement of heavy product. The cost-saving opportunities for soft-side savings are substantial. Table 7-1 shows the company-wide kaizen results for 1996 on about 700 projects.

What Happens When You Practice One-Piece Flow?

With Freudenberg-NOK's GROWTTH program, one employee can perform everything from molding, trimming, assembling, inspecting, and packing to shipping, one piece at a time. To encourage communication and to enhance comfort and efficiency, we placed machines and operators in a U-shaped cell. Now workers move from machine to machine in an area where mental and

Table 7-1. 1996 GROWTTH Program Results for Freudenberg-NOK

Measure	Before	After	% Improvement
Setup time (min.)	14,141	9,207	35%
Lead time (days)	110.48	57.86	47%
Cycle time (sec.)	206,921	87,153	58%
Down time (min.)	522.6	297.4	43%
Productivity (pcs./labor hr.)	45,614	65,496	44%
WIP (pieces)	523,550	351,296	33%
Floor space (sq. ft.)	48,098	32,613	32%
Scrap (%)	86.23	47.01	45%
Travel distance (ft.)	245,083	44,895	82%

physical skills can work together. Once you begin practicing one-piece flow, factory floor space and inventories typically decrease, while sales continue to increase (see Figure 7-2). The dedicated U-shaped cells also eliminate the need for work-in-process inventory.

Take a look at the third phase of the oil-seal study shown in Figure 7-3. In early 1993, we entered phase III of this project by reconfiguring the cell into a true one-piece-flow operation. The product flows through prep, into the press, into the trimming and

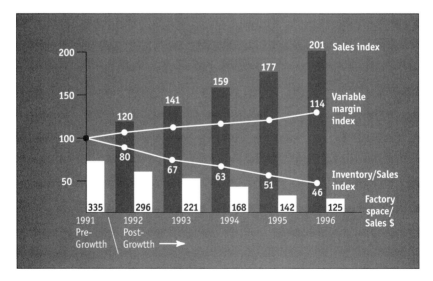

Figure 7-2. Savings from Practicing One-Piece Flow

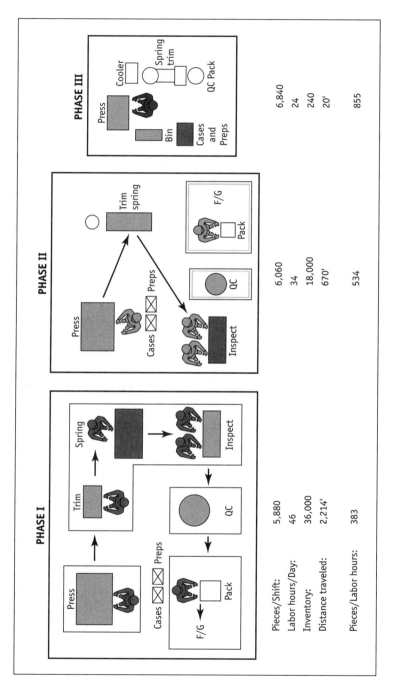

Figure 7-3. Oil-Seal Study

finishing machine, and into quality control (QC) and pack. We have only one person per shift operating the cell, 24 hours a day, and we increased productivity to 855 pieces per hour. Inventory went down to 240 pieces—precisely the number that was moving through the cell in molding, cooling, trimming, and packing—and we reduced travel distance to 20 feet. We have subsequently run two more kaizens on this particular cell and the labor productivity is now up over 1,200 pieces per labor hour. This kaizen will never end. The question is whether it will get to 1,500–1,600 over time.

One part of this cell, however, works against the principles of the Toyota Production System. This cell operates in a clockwise motion. According to TPS, most people are right handed and therefore their pick-and-place process works best in a counter-clockwise fashion. Although this clockwise motion is an inefficiency in this cell, we are limited with the equipment that we have. One of the basic principles of kaizen is "Creativity Over Capital!"

In a U-shaped cell, operators balance takt time (the rate at which a customer consumes product) with cycle time on all operations to achieve a flow. This is hard to do when you have 450-ton presses. The Japanese would tell us that, ideally, we ought to be making parts on 60-ton presses—but we are not going to throw the presses we have away, and you are not going to throw your equipment away either. The challenge then becomes figuring out how to balance what you have with what you need to do.

To reconfigure this entire cell cost us only $3,500 in incremental capital equipment. This is not expensive stuff. Those of you that are running 1,200-ton molding machines or big stamping presses should not be intimidated by the prospect of tying high-speed equipment into slow takt times. The point here is that you cannot just assume that you can dedicate the machine to the production of one part—not the way we run our businesses. In fact, what you need to do is tie together rapid setup changes, which in turn will allow you to make tool changes quickly and to use those big presses for other things.

We understand the customer's takt time. When we have the opportunity to make new investments, we typically invest to marry up with the customer's takt time, but with equipment that already sits in the plant, we have to obtain maximum utilization. This means maximum up time. We also have to produce quantities of product that are consistent with the customer's requirement while avoiding building lots of inventory. This means we have a lot of tool changeovers.

Setups and Tool Changes

Among our first realizations during our conversion to lean manufacturing was the total inefficiency of downtime and setup time. It is impossible to improve productivity without maximum utilization of equipment. That means you need fast die changes—with all the necessary tools in order and personnel ready to move when the time is ready. It is clock time, not labor content, that you must consider when changing production line setups.

At Freudenberg-NOK, tool changes are to be no longer than *three times the average cycle time*. If we're making parts on a 120-second cycle, we're committed to a complete changeover of that manufacturing cell in roughly six minutes. Now, we are also dealing with that in terms of large presses, small presses, die changes, and metal-stamping presses. The whole theory here is that three times the cycle time gives us the flexibility to deal with the customer's takt time on almost a daily, but certainly a weekly, basis. We would never be more than one week out in front of our customer's daily requirements. That is the trade-off that we make—setup time versus cycle time versus takt time.

Chassis Component Study

On one particular chassis component, we've gone through three phases of development (see Figure 7-4). In phase I, molding and assembly operations were completely separate. As a matter of fact, they were on opposite ends of the manufacturing floor. This kaizen team broke down the automated assembly equipment and created a small hand assembly operation next to the molding presses. Phase II shows these two operations side by side. Already, work-in-process inventory had been reduced from 4,950 pieces to 700, and the distance each part traveled dropped from 520 feet to 16 feet. However, at this point different operators were still performing the press and assembly operations.

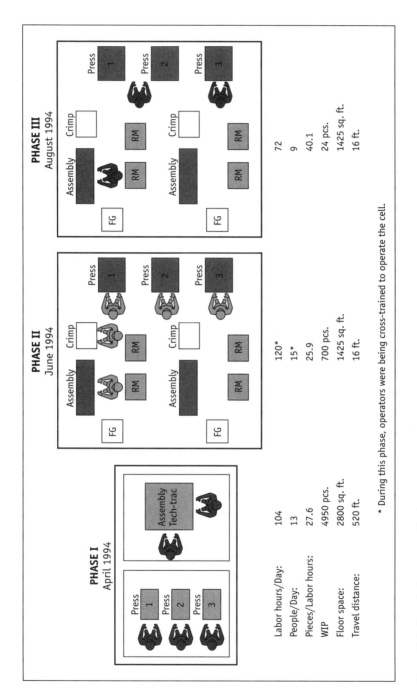

	PHASE I	PHASE II	PHASE III
	April 1994	June 1994	August 1994
Labor hours/Day:	104	120*	72
People/Day:	13	15*	9
Pieces/Labor hours:	27.6	25.9	40.1
WIP	4950 pcs.	700 pcs.	24 pcs.
Floor space:	2800 sq. ft.	1425 sq. ft.	1425 sq. ft.
Travel distance:	520 ft.	16 ft.	16 ft.

* During this phase, operators were being cross-trained to operate the cell.

Figure 7-4. Chassis Component Study

Eventually, the press operators became trained in assembly and were able to take on the assembly duties in conjunction with molding. The result is a one-piece-flow operation where the part is molded, assembled, and packed by one associate—freeing six associates from the process for reassignment, reducing floor space by 1,375 feet, reducing travel distance from 520 feet to 16 feet, and achieving an outstanding reduction in work-in-process (WIP) inventory of 4,926 pieces. Also, with one-piece-flow production in place, dramatic increases in product volume can actually yield decreases in cost of quality and parts per million (ppm), because the per part inspection is built into the one-piece-flow process (see Figure 7-5).

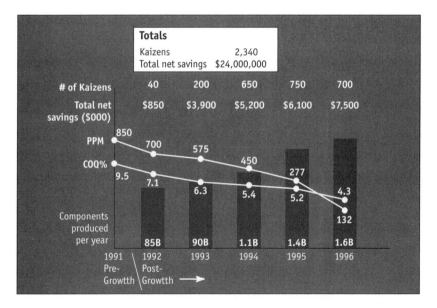

Figure 7-5. Impact on Quality Measures

Multiple Kaizens Are Proof of Continuous Improvement

It is not unusual in batch production to assign more people to a process in an attempt to increase productivity. In fact, before our GROWTTH program began, we had a perfect example of this in our Ligonier, Indiana plant, where it took 21 people and 2,300 square feet of floor space to produce one part number.

Automotive Component Assembly						
	February 1992	April 1992	May 1992	November 1992	January 1993	January 1993	TOTAL
# of associates	21	18	15	12	6	3	
Pieces/Person	55	86	112	140	225	450	
Space, square foot	2,300	2,000	1,850	1,662	1,360	1,200	
Variable cost savings (Annualized)(VCS)		367,829	147,319	93,927	126,648	116,894	852,617
VCS as % of sales		6.63%	2.65%	1.69%	2.28%	2.11%	15.36%
Space reduced 48%, inventory down 50%, production up 700%						

Figure 7-6. Repeat Kaizens on Automotive Component — Ligonier, Indiana Factory

The proof that kaizen is a virtually endless, continuous improvement process is illustrated in Figure 7-6. The chart tracks five kaizen events on the same process and shows that each consecutive kaizen continues to produce significant productivity gains and additional cost savings. Variable cost savings on this project are over $800,000, which is about 15 percent of the total cost of sales on the variable line. These are the kinds of savings that you can find time after time. The process of waste elimination is never ending—it is the process of *continuous improvement*.

Freeing Floor Space

This is what we do when we cut out floor space. This is an example of perhaps 400 or 500 square feet of space that we saved in one of our molding plants in Indiana. We rope it off. We paint the floor. We clean it up. And we put up a sign that reads, "Created for Growth by GROWTTH." The objective here is to present a visual manifestation of the successes that we achieved with the kaizen process. As you go through your own implementation plan, you'll find that you continually have things that employees can point to and say, "Look what I did!"

Once we save floor space we make a commitment to our work force that we will not use the space for anything except new equipment to accommodate new business, to increase production, and to create more jobs.

Another interesting little trick we use is called a story board. It is very simple. At our plant in Georgia, we ran a kaizen with Bosch on a fuel-injector o-ring that we supply them. Bosch's standards are extremely tight. They are even in our plants on a regular basis to ensure that our process provides the reliability of their product. In this particular case, we decided to look at all the waste in the o-ring system. Keep in mind, this was the first story board we ever put together. We told Bosch, "There are 18 steps in the process," some of which were non-value-added. The Bosch people said, "No, it can't possibly be true that there are only 18 steps in this process. Let's get a camera and go to the receiving dock. We'll take a picture of every single step that occurs from the receipt of raw material to the shipment of finished goods." When we were done we had found 83 steps.

We proceeded to mount the 83 photos on a board and post the board right in the middle of the production center. Every time we make a commitment to do a kaizen in that production area, we go straight to the board and decide where we want to focus our attention. We use a color code to identify visually the value step of each photograph. As we complete a kaizen project and eliminate a non-value-added step, we simply draw a big yellow crisscross through the photo to indicate that it has been eliminated. Again, this is another one of those simple visual tools to keep in front of the workers' eyes. It shows them the never-ending opportunity for continuous improvement, and therefore the elimination of cost, in the process.

Value Analysis/Value Engineering (VA/VE)

The typical batch-manufacturing organization flipping to lean production is capable of reducing their variable costs by between 18 and 25 percent, excluding material. This 18 to 25 percent might translate into 34 percent of your selling price, which won't get you where you need to be when your customer is asking for a 20 percent reduction in price over four or five years. Lean manufacturing is an important foundation for waste elimination, but there are other levels of lean manufacturing where you can uncover huge cost savings. Value Analysis/Value Engineering (VA/VE) is one example. VA/VE is a systematic, cross-functional team approach to maximize product/process value by identifying functions and their related costs. Value Analysis examines *current products* in an effort to detect and correct value problems and reduce costs. Value Engineering focuses on *new products* in an effort to identify and prevent value problems before production. A VA/VE team is structured very similarly to a kaizen team. Both are cross-functional, involving key players from every aspect of the part process—this includes involving your customer! Since Freudenberg-NOK's VA/VE program inception in 1995, we have uncovered over $7.6 million of annual savings opportunity for Freudenberg-NOK and its customers.

Standardizing the Process

The foundation of the GROWTTH program is based on the techniques and tools of the Toyota Production System, a standardized process of waste elimination and continuous improvement. There are both standard operations and standard operation tools that kaizen activity should follow at all times. The objectives of standard operations include establishing and clarifying the guidelines for manufacturing (quality, quantity, cost, inventory, safety, etc.) and providing a tool for kaizen. Remember—where there is no standard, there can be no kaizen.

I encountered a problem early on after I had my staff and the top 100 people in the company trained in lean systems: They all proceeded to interpret the training information in a different way. Six months into the program, I had 15 different kaizen processes in motion. Some managers said, "The standard forms that you use, like work combination sheets, don't work in my plant. My plant is different." Well, there is only one way to execute a lean systems program, and that's by the book. There is no room for interpretation.

This is, in some respects, no different from QS9000 in the standardization of that process.

You Have a Responsibility to Dedicate Your Time

Now a few tricks about how to devote 35 percent of your time to this process and still do your job. Let's assume you have responsibility for more than one plant. For the first two years, I planned my schedule so that I was at a plant either on a Tuesday or a Friday. Typically, I'd try to catch at least two plants per week, one on Tuesday and one on Friday. To demonstrate my level of commitment to the work force, I would routinely attend the training program on Tuesday morning. I would then come back on Thursday night and spend it with the kaizen teams at their dinner celebrations. (Note: Always try to run at least two to four kaizens at any one time in a plant. When you only run one, you don't get *synergy*, and you don't get enough utilization of the facilitators and the trainers.)

On Friday morning when the kaizen presentations were made, I'd sit through the entire wrap-up, and absorb all the information. I learned more about my business in that two-year period than I ever wanted to know. Machine operators, factory-floor people, secretaries, managers, and engineers, all participate as coequals on these teams, and they reveal the inefficient processes that have gone on for years. That this communication takes place frequently is terribly important. What you learn from the information flow from these employees is invaluable. You may have 50 or 55 people at these kaizen presentations, including plant management. Again, it's an opportunity for you to reinforce the importance of the program, and your presence is crucial.

With Lean Systems, Your Cost of Quality Will Drop

Let me give you some statistics. Freudenberg-NOK has two relatively new plants in Georgia that were designed and built by NOK. In one plant we have 95 manufacturing cells and in the second we have about 14. We have held kaizen presentations at these cells over and over since their installation. In 1992, the cost of quality by a classic Deming measurement across the company was about 12 percent of sales, which I thought was reasonably good (the average in the industry was about 15–16 percent). The two plants in Georgia that were operating at 100 percent one-piece flow had a cost of quality in 1992 of about 6.4 percent. Today, these two plants operate at about 4.8 and 5.1 percent.

Today, my cost of quality across the company is 7.5 percent. I've picked up almost five points of margin. With a one-piece-flow process, every single part is inspected. I can't tell you how happy it makes me to receive letters from customers saying, "Congratulations, and thank you for sending us the 15-millionth oil seal without a reject."

Let the Process Work for You

Lean systems have worked for Freudenberg-NOK and they can work for you. Implementation requires total commitment from senior management, a considerable amount of training and reinforcement, and a significant investment in the process. In 1997, Freudenberg-NOK will conduct another 600 kaizen projects. How successful we continue to be has everything to do with empowering our workers and encouraging them to make contributions and to be good creative thinkers. Senior management's role will be to stay involved, actively support projects, and train, communicate, motivate, and sponsor. I hope that one day you can see the benefits of lean systems in your organization. Good luck!

Jeffrey K. Liker *is Associate Professor of Industrial and Operations Engineering at the University of Michigan, Ann Arbor. He has been on the faculty since 1982 and has been studying Japanese design and manufacturing methods. In 1991 he cofounded the Japan Technology Management Program at the University of Michigan. Dr. Liker has authored or co-authored 50 articles and book chapters, and four books. He has received three Shingo Prizes for Excellence in Manufacturing Research in 1995, 1996, and 1997—one for a* book he lead edited titled Engineered in Japan: Japanese Technology Management Practices. *Other books about to be released by Dr. Liker are* Remade in America: Transplanting and Transforming Japanese Production Systems *(with Mark Fruin and Paul Adler) and* Concurrent Engineering Effectiveness: Integrating Product Development Across Organizations *(with Mitch Fleischer). Professor Liker has consulted on Japanese design and manufacturing methods for companies such as Whirlpool, Chrysler, Ford, LTV Steel, Renault, Peugeot, Mack Truck, Solar Turbine, and the Industrial Technology Institute.*

Keith Allman *is the General Manager for Donnelly Corporation's Exterior Mirror and Hardware Operations. After spending the first 13 years of his career with General Motors in a variety of manufacturing, engineering and quality positions, Keith has been in leadership positions in the automotive OEM supply base. Keith has a Mechanical Engineering Degree from General Motors Institute and an MBA from the University of Michigan.*

8

The Donnelly Production System: Lean at Grand Haven

by Jeffrey K. Liker and Keith Allman

Editor's prologue: Donnelly is the word's leading manufacturer of automotive mirrors and is known as a pioneer in human relations. They have no time clocks, a no-layoff policy (as much as they can guarantee, depending on business), job sharing, a wellness program (including paying for membership at an outside fitness center), and a childcare service. Hourly associates meet each year to decide how big their pay raises will be. They were recently named among the "Top Ten" in the book *The 100 Best Companies to Work for in America*. Donnelly also shows, however, that strong employee involvement does not necessarily equate to high quality and efficiency.

Donnelly launched the Grand Haven plant in 1988 to provide exterior mirrors to Honda. From the start, it had difficulty in meeting Honda's high quality expectations. The plant struggled over the years, trying one quality program after another and experiencing some good years and some bad years. By 1995, the plant was in a crisis. Because of late shipments and poor quality, the message from Honda was to either shape up or lose their business. In less than two years, Grand Haven shifted from a batch and queue process to a comparatively lean operation, reducing customer shipped defects by 80 percent, cutting internal scrap rates in half, almost eliminating premium freight, reducing inventory on hand by a factor of 5, and improving productivity by 29 percent. This was a rocky road with slips and falls, including employee morale at an all-time low in 1995 and subsequent unionization attempts. Ultimately, the plant developed an exemplary people-centered, continuous improvement process. I worked with Keith Allman, the plant manager of Grand Haven, to tell this compelling story of the transformation of this plant—rocky road and all.

*This is a story about four people named Everybody,
Somebody, Anybody, and Nobody. There was an important
job to be done and Everybody was sure that Somebody
would do it. Anybody could have done it, but Nobody did it.
Somebody got angry about that because it was Everybody's
job. Everybody thought Anybody could do it, but Nobody
realized that Everybody wouldn't do it. It ended up that
Everybody blamed Somebody when Nobody did what
Anybody could have.*

(EXCERPT FROM *DONNELLY KAIZEN EVENT GUIDE*)

D onnelly Mirror is a family-owned business founded in 1905
in Holland, Michigan by Bernard Donnelly and has grown
to become the world's largest supplier of automotive mirrors. It has long been known as a pioneer in human relations. For
example, in December 1972, at a national conference in Chicago on
"The Changing Work Ethic," Donnelly was billed as "the country's
outstanding example of worker participation in job decisions.
Workers, who are all on salary, decide how fast to run the production
line, when to shut it down, and the size of their own pay increases."

Much of their progressive management style is attributed to
John Donnelly, who, prior to becoming president in 1932, was in a
seminary preparing for the priesthood. Under the Donnelly family,
the company has been run in a very paternalistic manner. John
Donnelly was a humanist and an experimenter, and frequently
brought in the University of Michigan's Institute for Social
Research for the latest in management methods. Donnelly was
written up in a Harvard case study in 1973 as a model for application of the Scanlon plan (*Harvard Business Review* Case 9-473-088).
The Scanlon plan combines a monthly bonus based on the productivity of the plant and the corporation with employee participation

in improvement. A committee of hourly associates in the plant meets each year to decide how big their pay raise will be, and the committee's recommendation is almost always followed.

Donnelly's business has been growing in the last ten years, from $100 million annual sales to $700 million, and today operates from 25 locations in the U.S., Mexico, Europe, and Asia. Donnelly is now the world's largest producer of exterior mirrors. Despite their exceptional reputation for progressive management of people, as the company grew and auto companies began putting extreme pressure on suppliers to reduce their prices, Donnelly discovered that they did not have an efficient production system. After experimenting with a number of methods, ultimately Donnelly turned to lean manufacturing as their core manufacturing strategy.

The Grand Haven Story[1]

This is the story of one of Donnelly's plants, in Grand Haven, Michigan, which they launched on a handshake in 1988 to serve Honda of America. This was Donnelly's first plant to make painted mirrors. As of early 1997, the time of this writing, the plant was making a wide variety (1,000 part numbers) of side-view mirrors (left, right, heated, electric power, different colors): 60 percent Honda, 15 percent Ford, and smaller quantities for other customers. The plant has 150,000 square feet of factory space. Sales have grown rapidly from $20 million in 1984 to about $50 million annually in 1996. The 235-person work force is relatively young with an average of less than five years seniority. The plant is mostly vertically integrated with its own molding, painting, and assembly (the plant brings in resin, springs, small motors, mirrors, fasteners, etc.). The process is straightforward. Plastic housings are molded in the plant. They are then sent unpainted to assembly, or they are painted and then sent to assembly. All other parts are purchased and go to assembly. The plant molds housings, paints them, and assembles the side-view mirrors.

Grand Haven is a microcosm of the transformations that have occurred more broadly at Donnelly as the company has moved toward lean manufacturing. In 1995, the plant was in a crisis. Late deliveries, relatively high defect rates, and high costs led Honda to threaten to withdraw their business from Grand Haven. The plant responded with an aggressive, short-term program of externally led kaizen events to shift toward continuous flow production. This effort led to marked improvements on all key plant measures in just one year but also led to strong employee resistance and reduced morale, as people felt change was being imposed on them from outside. Largely because of the negative effects on employee morale, Grand Haven then shifted gears and focused on a more gradual and internally led movement to the Donnelly Production System, modeled after the Toyota Production System with a high degree of employee involvement. With these further shifts toward lean manufacturing, performance has continued to improve dramatically. For example, in 1995 Grand Haven increased productivity by 18 percent and then improved it an additional 11 percent in 1996. They have cut scrap rates in half and reduced customer shipped defects by 80 percent between 1994 to 1997. Premium freight was reduced from $234,000 in 1995 to $6500 in 1996.

All employees in the plant, hourly and salaried, have benefited in a very direct way from Grand Haven's improved performance. Thanks to Donnelly's progressive Scanlon plan, employees share in profits. Every year, 40 percent of profits in excess of a baseline go to employees based on a formula combining corporate and plant profits. If the corporation hits its target, all employees get 2.2 percent; if Grand Haven hits its target, all employees get another 2.2 percent of their wages. If the company and/or plant exceeds the plan, the bonus percentage goes up exponentially. On top of this, there is an annual bonus based on hitting plant targets for key measurables. Because performance was so bad in 1994–1995, there was very little in bonus for employees. But since the dramatic improvements noted above, the Grand Haven plant has been exceeding the plan, as has the corporation, so Grand Haven employees received a 10–12 percent monthly bonus in 1996. This bonus appears in their paycheck each month based on performance for the previous month. Each year, employees at Grand Haven, hourly and salaried, have an offsite meeting to develop the plan and targets for the next year. About 60 people are involved in the planning process during the two-day offsite meeting. They divide into six groups, each focused on a different area, and develop the plans based on policy deployment. Because employees decide on their own pay raises for the coming year, associates are as likely as management to demand that any new programs show bottom-line performance results.

Clearly, Grand Haven's experience to date has been a success story for lean manufacturing combined with intensive employee involvement. Major improvements were seen in less than one year; dramatic improvements occurred the following year. The plant continues to improve month by month. This is not to say the transformation was smooth, linear, or conflict-free. We begin by providing some historical background to the Grand Haven plant and then describe its path to transformation from 1995 to early 1997.

Grand Haven—The Rocky Road to Transformation

The Holland, Michigan area was settled by Dutch immigrants in the early nineteenth century and has strong religious traditions grounded in the Dutch Reform church. The city has a reputation for a strong work ethic and progressive employers. The progressive management policies, no-layoff commitment, and loyal work force of Donnelly were characteristics that reminded Honda of their plants back home, characteristics Honda hoped to encourage in all their suppliers. But Donnelly was not a "lean producer." Their success was a result of using mass production methods with progressive and paternalistic employee relations.

Donnelly had an interest in winning transplant business. They had even actively sought Honda's business in the mid-1980s. They knew about Japanese production methods and were more than willing to learn more about them. They assigned a newly hired junior manager, who had studied in Japan and worked for Nissan in Tokyo, to work on getting Honda's business. After several approaches, Donnelly was invited to submit a bid. Honda decided to keep its long-time supplier in Japan, Matsuyama, as the manufacturer of rear-view mirrors but ultimately gave business for exterior side-view mirrors to Donnelly. At first, Grand Haven based their products on Matsuyama designs and tooling to minimize variation.

Honda never overtly asked Donnelly to build a new plant especially for them, but dropped enough hints that Donnelly knew this was what they wanted. Without a written contract in hand, Donnelly built a new plant. They chose Grand Haven, about a half-hour's drive from Holland, where the local wages were about 28 percent lower. Donnelly was able to build the plant in what was a record time for them of nine months. When they launched the plant in 1988 they made only unpainted sideview door mirrors. They had some plastic injection molding machines, but were using mostly purchased components from Matsuyama, so they were mainly an assembly shop. The management focus was on trying to "control" the employees: How can we make sure they hit their individual production rates? In 1989, Honda gave a small amount of business to Donnelly to make painted mirrors for Honda's Gold Wing motorcycle. They used a couple of painters and a manual, batch operation.

From the beginning, Honda was not happy with the quality and delivery record of the Grand Haven plant. They rejected many batches of product and frequently sent people to Grand Haven to investigate the cause of the problems. The introduction of painting, the first time ever for Donnelly, caused even more quality problems. By late 1989, Honda was considering an alternative source for the Civic door mirror.

When Donnelly learned of this they began to negotiate hard for the business. After all, they had invested in an entire manufacturing facility to win Honda's business. Ultimately, Honda agreed to give the Civic business to Donnelly but suggested that Donnelly invest in a fully automated paint shop to the tune of $5 million. Again this was without a written contract, but Donnelly agreed and installed the paint booth in 1990. There were exacting specifications for the paint, which had to match the exterior paint on the rest of the vehicle precisely and hold up under a wide range of environmental conditions. For some years, the paint booth became a major bottleneck and Donnelly's biggest source of problems and complaints from Honda.

Table 8-1 shows the performance history over time for the Grand Haven plant and specifically for 1991 when the paint booth was in operation for its first full year. Only about 70 percent of the

Table 8-1. Donnelly Grand Haven Performance over Time

Major events	Limited manual paint		Install automatic paint booth	Improve paint yield		1st union drive	Delta program	Externally led kaizen events	Donnelly Production System	
								2nd union drive		
	1988	1989	1990	1991	1992	1993	1994	1995	1996	1997
Defects to customer (ppm)			5059	1015	444	662	5357	3593	1187	424
Labor productivity improvement								18%	11%	3%
% scrap (internal)						5.5%	6.1%	5.8%	2.6%	2.4% YTD
Paint yield	no paint	manual	manual	71.7%	79.7%	82.8%	82.9%	76.0%*	88.4%	89.7%
Premium freight								240,000	6,576	4,305 YTD
Inventory days in hand										
Work-in-process							5.6	4.1	3.1	1.3
Raw materials							8.6	8.0	8.1	6.2
Finished goods							2.4	2.1	2.7	1.8
Total							16.6	14.2	13.9	9.3
Annual sales (million $)	4.6	9.7	16	26.7	31	30.8	45.4	55.1	49.2	49.9 projected
# of employees	50	88	170	239	258	302	321	253	280	257

NOTE: Data shown where available. Blank cells are missing data. *Paint yield declined due to tighter quality standards to meet customer requirements.

parts that came out of the booth were usable. Nonetheless, the defects shipped to Honda dropped dramatically from over 5,000 ppm to 1,000 ppm, largely the result of much more careful inspection. Sales rose dramatically as Honda gave new business to Grand Haven, and by 1991 the plant had responsibility for nearly all the painted mirrors for the Accord and all the unpainted mirrors for the Civic. By this point Donnelly had invested almost $12 million.

The main focus in 1991 and 1992 was on improving paint yield, as well as improving quality and productivity through traditional engineering. As can be seen in Table 8-1, there was a good deal of success, as paint yield rose from 72 percent in 1991 to 83 percent in 1993. Defects dropped to a low of 442 in 1992. Sales almost doubled from $16 million in 1990 to $31 million in 1992. By 1992, the plant was winning productivity awards from Honda and getting attention from other car companies like Ford and Toyota because of its growing reputation as a model producer of painted door mirrors.

Crisis at Grand Haven

If we stopped looking at Grand Haven in 1992, this would have been a clear success story. It was a model plant in a company with model employee relations, which faced the challenge of highly demanding delivery and quality standards by Honda and won. Honda had selected Grand Haven as the first American plant to go through their Best Practice (BP) process. Honda personnel were in the plant constantly, and clearly Donnelly learned a great deal as a result of their demanding performance requirements and suggestions for process improvement. There is some disagreement as to how much of the improvement at Grand Haven was a result of Honda's BP program and how much was simply the company working hard internally to meet Honda's standards successfully. What is clear is that the plant did improve, but it did so within the context of a traditional mass production system. There were some successes in reducing off-line buffers and extra handling of parts, thus leading to a leaner flow, but by and large, Grand Haven continued to use a traditional "batch and queue" process.

One indication that all was not well in 1993 was the first attempt to unionize by employees at Grand Haven. This was almost unheard of at the paternalistic Donnelly Corporation, a company that prided itself on its exemplary employee relations. The main issues involved the pay differential with Holland and the major hiring at Donnelly. The plant added 42 people, 16 percent of the work force, from 1992 to 1993, and the hiring was done without a consistent job posting system or hiring policy. Employees felt that their voices were not being heard, that management was focusing on dominance and control and was inconsistent in its decision making. The union promoting the drive was the United Pottery Workers, who launched a poorly organized campaign with the result that the employees voted down the union.

The plant continued to grow quickly in sales and employment, often hiring temporary employees with little training to pick up the rapidly growing workload in the plant. Between 1993 and 1994 there was a 50 percent sales increase and the plant was launching two major new products—one for Honda and one for a second-tier supplier. There were too many people in the plant and no systems in place to train the temporary work force. By late 1994 the plant was operating in a crisis mode and defects increased dramatically. Overall quality performance in 1994 was dismal with defects increasing by a factor of eight compared to 1993. Paint yields remained high at about 83 percent, but this was largely because the quality standards applied to inspecting the paint had degraded; in fact, Honda rejected many of the batches because of paint problems.

The Delta program fiasco

Donnelly management's reaction to the obvious plant inefficiencies at Grand Haven and other facilities was to start a new program called Delta in 1993, which they based on General Motors' synchronous manufacturing program. Synchronous manufacturing was GM's original version of the Toyota Production System, a version that emphasized continuous flow and balanced flow of material through the plant. Donnelly also built in ideas from Honda's Best Practice program and General Motors' PICOS program. The Delta program started out of Donnelly headquarters in Holland, where they created a small staff organization to lead Delta without outside consulting help. The focus was on creating U-shaped assembly cells and combining/balancing work within the cells. It was a cookie-cutter approach, and they only used ideas that fit their predetermined direction for a specific solution—that is, put assembly into U-shaped cells.

Delta came to Grand Haven at the beginning of 1994. From the employees' point of view at Grand Haven, Delta was a staff program done to them, not with them. Delta staff came in, took their straight line assembly process, bent it into a U-shape for no good reason, measured the best person on the line, and then tried to whipsaw other workers into working that fast. The staff then said, "Now you should be working at this new production output standard we have set." But creating U-shaped assembly cells did not fix the underlying problems of overall material flow through the plant, the poor equipment up-time, or the low reliability of the paint booth. Those leading the exercises from staff did not have a lot of experience leading improvement events and did very little pre-work. There was minimal, if any, follow-through after they left, and there was no buy-in from the people because nothing improved. It was basically the same production line, but curved, and the Delta staff expected this magically to increase output. Also at the time, there was a lot of turnover among plant management, which added to what was already a chaotic environment.

By the fall of 1994, a second union drive started, this time a well-organized drive by the United Auto Workers. Also about this time Honda was becoming very vocal about their dissatisfaction with Grand Haven, calling them a "high maintenance supplier." Grand Haven shipped over 5,000 ppm defects, was launching new products late, and had reoccurring quality problems. Honda said, "Improve quickly or we will find another supplier." Losing Honda's business would have shut down the plant, since the majority of their sales were still to Honda.

"Stop the Bleeding"

It became clear to the top management of Donnelly that Delta was not working. Late in 1994, they brought in outside consultants who were experts on running kaizen events. This is a reputable consulting firm (which shall remain nameless here) with consultants formerly from Toyota. But unlike the Toyota Supplier Support Center in Kentucky, which uses a systems approach, this firm used radical kaizen events. Between Monday and Friday, a kaizen team was first trained; it then analyzed a production area, designed improvements, moved right into changing the line, evaluated the changes, and then reported their results to management. The philosophy was that the team would go through a complete plan-do-check-act cycle (PDCA) in a few days.

In October–November of 1994, the Kaizen Promotion Office was formed. About four Donnelly employees, mainly those involved in Delta, were sent for training to participate in external events that the consultants were leading in other companies. Led by the outside consultants, they then began to run kaizen events in Donnelly plants. A number of plants held events, but the main focus was on the Grand Haven plant because of Honda's threat to shut them down.

Around the same time, there was a management shakeout at the Grand Haven plant and new managers were brought in, including Keith Allman as the new plant manager (called the general manager of operations at Donnelly). The new managers were selected because they were young, forward thinking, and had some previous experience with lean manufacturing. Keith's experience came from his 12 years at General Motors in a variety of manufacturing, engineering, and quality positions, as well as his involvement with the automotive original equipment manufacturer (OEM) supply base.

The main purpose of bringing in the outside consultants and working on radical kaizen events was to "stop the bleeding." The stakes were high—fix the problems quickly or shut down. In February 1995 they held their first kaizen event. It was a public kaizen event with 60 people participating from other companies. Six events were going on simultaneously in different parts of the plant. In 1995, Grand Haven ran 29 externally led kaizen events, each four days long. The focus was on solving small problems quickly. The focus of the 29 events was as follows:

- Setup reduction: 8 events
- Paint yield: 8 events in 4 months
- One-piece flow: 7 events in Honda assembly cells
- Other: 6 events

Like Delta, these kaizen events were problem-focused rather than focused on a total production system, but they were focused on the right problems and the outside consultants knew what they were doing. The problems were poor paint yield, building in large batches, and the batch and queue manufacturing process that built up lots of work-in-process (WIP).

A number of the early events focused on reducing setup time for injection molding. They quickly managed to reduce setups from 2 hours to 20 minutes, though at first they did not reduce the lot size or increase the frequency of changeover so there were no inventory or flow benefits.

Paint yields were another major focus. As you saw earlier in Table 8-1, paint yields actually went down in 1995 from 83 percent to 76 percent. This was because they began by tightening the inspection standards to better match the requirements of their customer. This led to more defects spotted in-house and far less spotted by their customers in bad shipments. Also shown in Table 8-1, defects in ppm went down one-third from over 5,300 to about 3,600.

The outside consultants noticed that there were pockets of subassemblies done in batches with automated equipment. Figure 8-1 shows a large mass production index table feeding the whole shop, but there were actually a number of smaller subassembly stations. For example, an actuator machine cranked out actuators every 6 seconds even though the consultants figured out that the takt time was 35 seconds. This led to piling up subassembly inventory, thus leading to moving large batches of material to individual build stations where each person built up a complete product. The products were dropped onto a conveyor, and finished products were inspected by separate inspectors.

This batch and queue process struck the Toyota-trained outside consultants as tremendously wasteful. Why couldn't assembly be done as a continuous flow? Why are final inspectors needed? They got rid of the subassembly operations; this meant junking equip-

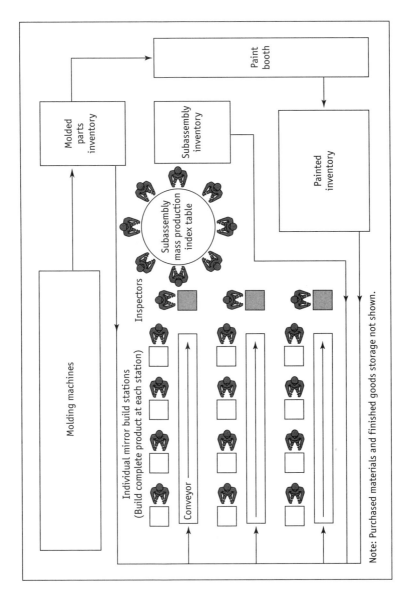

Figure 8-1. 1993 Production Flow of Donnelly, Grand Haven

ment like the large index table (literally selling it for scrap metal). The cells were designed based on takt time. Standardized work instructions were developed for each station in the cell. The required staffing was computed based on the takt time and the standardized work. For example, if a mirror should come out of the cell every 35 seconds and it should take 350 seconds to build mirrors, then 10 people should be able to do the job. Of course, there probably were 13 or 14 people doing the job, but they would balance the line as best they could and through repeated kaizen events work toward getting down to 10 people.

Employees are still skeptical
The kaizen philosophy was "just do it!" Most changes were made on the spot during the four days. Between events management tried to schedule 30-day homework periods to implement anything the kaizen team could not get done in the four days; for example, if it required ordering equipment. Every Friday they held a management review of outstanding homework, because the homework often was not done and follow-up was generally weak.

To Grand Haven employees, this looked an awful lot like the Delta program in new clothing. In fact, the events were being orchestrated by the same people from headquarters who had led Delta. Employees had already suffered through ineffective kaizen events, events that led to pain and suffering without improvement. There was already an ongoing unionization drive as a reaction to Delta and a general feeling by employees that they did not have influence and that management did not have the plant under control. Because of poor plant and company performance, they had gotten almost no profit-sharing bonus, something they had come to expect to supplement salaries already much below Holland levels. There was nothing about this new kaizen effort that convinced them to drop the union drive and kick in with management.

There was some hourly "associate" participation on the teams, but the events were being driven hard by the outside consultants. From the employees' perspective, kaizen was something being done to them by outsiders. For example, before kaizen was implemented, employees sat at individual assembly workstations and followed an established subassembly process. The kaizen team came in and videotaped the process. When the employees came to work two days later, they found the subassembly stations were gone, their chairs were gone, and everyone was now expected to work standing up in new work cells, doing jobs designed by the kaizen team. Along with the new tasks and new layout, they were told that, in order to meet takt time, they must work at a predetermined pace that seemed faster than they could handle.

There was a lot of unionization activity between December and February, and it continued to heat up in the spring in response to the kaizen events. A total of 90 percent of employees signed union cards, and a vote on whether to unionize was scheduled.

Kaizen results begin to change the tide
The performance benefits of the kaizen events were clear. Paint yields were improving over the year even with the new, more stringent inspection requirements. Internal scrap in the plant did not change much, because of the more careful inspection procedures, but scrap shipped to customers went down by one-third. All categories of inventory went down substantially, particularly work-in-process, which was reduced from 5.6 to 4.1 days, a reduction of over 25 percent. Labor productivity improved by 18 percent, mainly because of the changes in assembly, and the plant was operating with a higher sales volume and substantially fewer employees. Sales per employee went from $140,000 in 1994 to $217, 800 in 1995—an increase of over 50 percent. As the year progressed, the employees began to see that there were real benefits and that the outside consultants knew what they were doing. Following Donnelly's corporate policy, no regular employees were let go because of the performance improvements. They handled reductions through attrition and by reducing the number of part-time, contract employees. With every major improvement, the chances of the plant being closed went down.

By the end of 1995, the production flow at Grand Haven looked more like Figure 8-2. Molding machines were producing to an organized marketplace, though a kanban system was still not yet in place (this was added in 1996, as discussed below). They

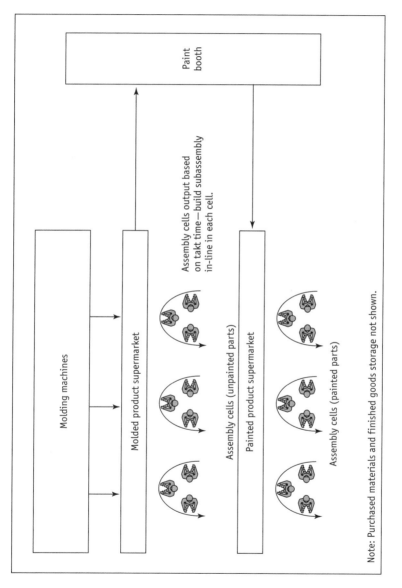

Note: Purchased materials and finished goods storage not shown.

Figure 8-2. 1997 Production Flow of Donnelly, Grand Haven

greatly reduced changeover times in molding through the kaizens, though this capability was not yet being utilized and changeovers were not more frequent. There were major changes in assembly with the mass production index table junked and all assembly incorporated into assembly cells set up for each product. The overall flow of product through the plant had been greatly improved, with significant improvements in assembly productivity, but the parts of the system were not yet tied together by a visual pull system.

Top management was pleased by the improvements in performance, but not with the negative impact on employee relations. Donnelly was a model for participative practices and high employee satisfaction, and management was very disturbed that employees were demoralized and threatening to unionize. In the summer of 1995, they stopped the externally led kaizen events and brought in a new vice president of manufacturing, Russ Scafade, who had years of experience at Toyota and a strong people orientation.

From Event Focus to System Focus

The shift was from an externally led kaizen event focus to an internally led system focus. Management and hourly associates agree that some good things came out of the kaizen events, but the approach had a high price in employee morale and was not necessarily as efficient or effective as it could have been.

The main problem was that the kaizen team did not utilize the expertise of people in the plant. We spoke to hourly associates who are now on a full-time continuous improvement team (discussed below) and who were involved in some of the externally led events. A number of the hourly associates had been more than willing to participate in the kaizen events and looked forward to contributing, but they felt that the outside consultants were not interested in their input. They came in as experts and knew what they wanted to do. Although they had asked for input from the floor, the consultants seemed to ignore it and implement what they wanted. According to the associates:

We did need to bring people in to get us going, but the outside consultants should have approached it in a different way. They made us feel like we had a say. In actuality the next day they told us what their decision was. "Here is how we will do it." That's when things started getting bad. People were open to change when they first came in, but when they didn't listen to input, people started to back off.

Many of the suggestions that the consultants made were the same ones made by employees under the old "IDEAS" program (a suggestion program before Delta), which had never been implemented. The improvements to the paint operation were mainly changes that the paint engineers already knew needed to be done. It was very frustrating to the people that they had been suggesting these ideas to deaf ears, and consultants, who spent very little time on the floor, were able to get these changes implemented and take credit for them. One associate explained:

How can someone Japanese who doesn't even know our language understand our process in a few hours? They would throw out riddles like: "I wouldn't want to cook in a dirty kitchen." We didn't need riddles. We knew the place needed to be cleaned up, but management wouldn't listen to us. They didn't want to spend the money.

Another problem was the lack of preparation in advance for the kaizen events. They started on Monday. This meant that anything that needed fabrication and took more than one day could not be done in that week. This led to generating what are now seen as the infamous "30-day homework lists." These were lists of things that could not be done during the week of the kaizen event but needed to be completed in 30 days. According to the associates: "Anything they couldn't do that week was on the 30-day list and would never be accomplished. It was like a joke to people on the floor."

There was also a question about the efficiency of the time spent during the kaizen event itself. Compared to kaizen events as they are run now, the externally led events seemed like more paperwork than action. According to the associates:

Monday was training and paperwork to prepare for the change and document the current state of the process. Tuesday was planning the changes. Wednesday the changes were made. Thursday was more paperwork to document the changes and prepare a presentation to management. And Friday morning was the presentation to management. The outside consultants were so focused on the paperwork—make sure this all gets done correctly. We would make changes one day and then just leave the floor to do paperwork.

The data in Table 8-1 show that there were significant improvements from 1994 to 1995, mainly in reduced defects (due to improvements in the paint booth) and increased productivity as a result of the shift to assembly cells. Kaizen events were eliminating a lot of waste but the event focus was not getting to the underlying causes of the waste in the system. In four months the consultants had done 29 kaizen events in various parts of the plant, whereas the Toyota Supplier Support Center will focus all their effort in four months on creating a model pilot line that embraces as much of the complete Toyota Production System as possible.

The DPS Manufacturing Philosophy for Continuous Improvement

The phasing out of the externally led kaizen events did not happen overnight, but occurred gradually over the summer and fall of 1995. This development overlapped with the hiring of Russ Scafade in the fall. Russ was hired to bring his first-hand experience with TPS to Donnelly. He gained this knowledge directly from Toyota, where he worked for years in power train, ultimately heading the power train division of Toyota in Georgetown. He left Toyota to do consulting on implementing TPS and then came to Donnelly as vice president of manufacturing. One of the first things Russ did at Donnelly was to create the Donnelly Production System (DPS) office out of the old Kaizen Promotion Office. He then set out to recruit someone to lead this office with direct experience working within the Toyota Production System. He found an old friend and associate, Art Smally, who had spent 10 years working for Russ in the power train division in Georgetown as their top manufacturing engineer. In the interim, he had also worked for a consulting firm on implementing the Toyota Production System in traditional U.S. firms. Russ and Art developed the Donnelly Production System and began training and implementation.

The DPS manufacturing philosophy drives all improvement efforts in Grand Haven (see Figure 8-3). It bears a striking resemblance to the Toyota Production System described in Chapter 2, so

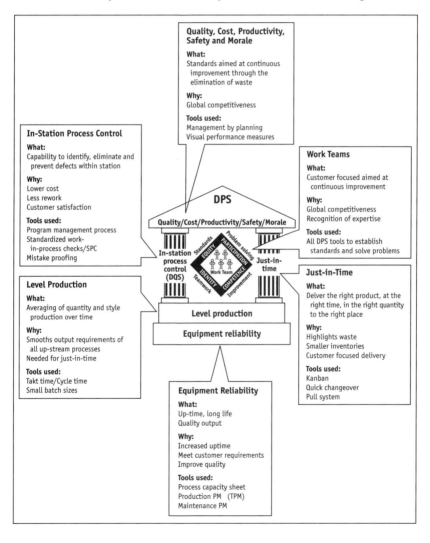

Figure 8-3. DPS Manufacturing Philosophy for Continuous Improvement

we will not go into detail discussing the DPS model. Because it was developed by former Toyota Manufacturing Corporation managers, it is no surprise it looks like TPS. For all practical purposes, DPS and TPS are one and the same. Much of the early efforts of the DPS office were focused on developing the specific model in Figure 8-3, getting top management behind it, and training plant leadership.

Training executives and managers

Getting top management on board was not a problem. After the synchronous manufacturing, Delta, and Kaizen Promotion Office initiatives, the CEO and COO already understood many of the concepts and were firmly behind the shift to lean manufacturing. The CEO hired Russ Scafade specifically to implement Toyota's manufacturing philosophy. Russ's message to the plant managers was to focus on the early steps of the Toyota Production System in a pilot area and to stop focusing on "kaizening out workers" in the first year. All improvement activities should focus initially on the following four areas:

1. *Cascading goals*. Ten corporate goals existed as a starting point. These needed to be cascaded down to the shop floor level (through a form of *hoshin management*).[2]
2. *Adjusting lines to takt time*. Focus on managing takt time. Grand Haven has a monthly meeting to adjust takt time.
3. *Material flow*. Look at the overall flow of product through the plant and develop a plant layout that creates as close to a continuous flow as possible. Grand Haven assigned the task to a newly created continuous improvement team to develop a one-year vision for plant layout.
4. *Standardized work*. The goal was to institutionalize standard work as a manufacturing tool. Grand Haven went through this process cell by cell in 1996.

Russ and Art trained executives and managers by using a DPS simulation game, presentations, and monthly meetings with all plant managers (called operations managers) to combine training and action. Operations managers at first met monthly for training in DPS and to discuss their plant activities related to DPS. In addition to formal training sessions, Russ and Art visited the plants and made suggestions for improvement projects. Two former Toyota executives were brought in to give specific training on the philosophies and methods of just-in-time and standardized work.

First Step Toward a Pull System: Triangle Kanban System for Molding

While DPS was being created, Grand Haven did not stand still. Keith Allman had been hired as operations manager (plant manager) of Grand Haven in March 1995, when the externally led kaizen events were in full swing. Keith had prior experience implementing lean manufacturing in union and nonunion environments. One of his first and most ambitious initiatives in 1996 after the phase-out of the external consultants was to implement a kanban system to pull molded plastic parts from molding to the assembly cells. This was modeled after Toyota's approach to batch manufacturing operations via a "triangle" (or "signal") kanban system. This system is a not as widely known in U.S. plants as the card system, and therefore we discuss it more fully here.

Grand Haven had tried kanban systems in the past, but the effort had failed. In early 1995, before the kaizen events started and before Keith was hired, Grand Haven tried a kanban system as part of Delta. It focused on pulling product from molding to paint and from molding to assembly (the same place triangle kanban is currently used). Individual cards were used for each bin of parts. It quickly became apparent that the system was not working. Cards were lost and shortages of molded parts were occurring. Why did the effort fail?

1. *It was too complicated and poorly designed.* There were no designated, visible storage areas for the molded parts. There were different approaches to the kanban depending on the quantities of molded parts produced. In some cases there was a kanban for each box of parts, in others a kanban for a layer of a skid, and in still other cases a kanban for an entire skid. Each part number had a set of kanbans on a rod—for some, three cards triggered a production run; others required 15 cards. When a trigger point was reached, someone put a red card on the rod. No molds were dedicated to presses, so where the next batch was to be run was unclear.

2. *It was implemented without involvement of the people who used it.* Employees resisted using it and had no commitment to the system.

3. *There was insufficient training.* Associates did not understand how to use this highly complicated system.

4. *There were no clear responsibilities for running the system.* Cards were lost and there were multiple triggers and no way to prioritize. The setup person for the press might have five cards triggered and have no rules or work standards for setting priorities. "Everyone and her brother" were moving kanban cards around.

Grand Haven tried a second kanban system in early 1995 but it also failed. This was a "single loop" system sending information directly from assembly to plastic molding. When assembly used a component, whether it was a painted part or not, they would pass the cards back to molding. A critical number of cards accumulating would trigger a setup in molding. The mold operator would run a lot and designate a paint color for that lot. Enough cards of a specific color accumulating would notify the painters to run that color. This system also failed badly. Cards were lost, people were confused, and the procedure was not followed. The system was shut down, but Keith did not give up on the idea and immediately regrouped for another attempt.

In July 1996, the manufacturing manager was assigned to lead a cross-functional team to implement a new, third version: a kanban system for molded parts. He had prior experience implementing kanban in other Donnelly plants. The team included *heijunka* associates (see sidebar), one paint associate, one molding setup person, a team leader, and a production scheduling manager. With the failed experience behind them, the focus was on making the system as simple as possible, going slowly by implementing small chunks, and providing on-the-job training in the new system. It was also apparent that too many people touching the kanban would lead to confusion. The goal was to keep the number of kanban down and the number of people physically touching kanban to a minimum. They began with one press and one consuming area (an assembly cell) to develop one success story before changing over the whole system.

What Is Heijunka?

In discussing the triangle kanban system we refer to the *heijunka person*. This is a term used by Donnelly to refer to the material mover. In the Toyota Production System, *heijunka* refers to the leveling of production. Toyota does not build to the actual flow of customer orders, which can be quite erratic. For example, if by chance there is a rash of orders for red cars with painted side-view mirrors one week, Toyota will not suddenly make a large batch of red cars. This would make life very difficult for a company like Donnelly, which would suddenly have to produce a lot of red mirrors or keep a large safety stock of each color mirror. Rather, Toyota takes their forecasted orders for the month and creates a leveled schedule with a preset sequence that spreads out red cars over the scheduling period. Inside their own plants, suppliers also do not produce directly to what Toyota is assembling every hour. Rather, they take their leveled schedule from Toyota and from that develop an internal leveled schedule and build to a marketplace. One goal of leveling is to avoid making large batches of any one item (such as all rights and all lefts, or all reds then all blacks) and mix up production to have a smooth flow and minimize inventory. As we discuss below, Grand Haven installed a *heijunka box* at the end of the Ford Econoline cell as a pilot to level the production sequence for mirrors coming out of that cell.

Because molding is a batch operation, the team chose a triangle kanban. Changeovers at that time took about 20 minutes, so it was not economical to run small lots. For example, lot sizes of 20 minutes would mean that the press was producing parts only 50 percent of the time. The triangle kanban is shown in Photo 8-1. It indicates standard kanban information, including the lot size. Note that for the Econoline part shown, a lot size is a large, 26.4-hour production run that produces 144 totes. The kanban are crafted out of metal and have a lip so they can be hung.

If we begin the process at the marketplace and work back, we start with Photo 8-2, which shows the marketplace for molded plastic parts. A fixed number of parts are placed in a reusable, plastic

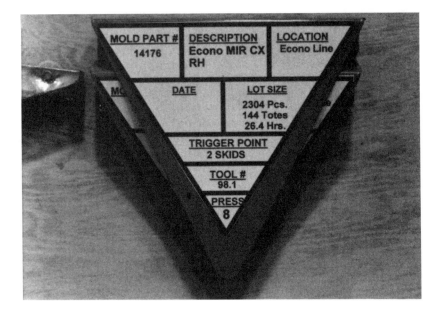

Photo 8-1. Triangle Kanban

bin. The marketplace is made up of gravity-fed roller conveyors. Each lane corresponds to a specific part number, which is marked with a sign hanging over the lane. When assembly or paint needs parts, the material handler takes the number of totes they need from the marketplace. Painted onto each lane, right on the conveyor, are yellow lines corresponding to the trigger point for signaling the need to mold more. Triggers started at about four days and over the year moved to two days. As long as there are enough totes so that the yellow line is not exposed, there is no need to make more parts. Photo 8-3 shows the signs marking right-hand and left-hand mirror housings for the Econoline vans. These are not painted parts, so they are taken directly to the Econoline assembly cell. The triangles for these parts are hanging on the lines, meaning that there is a sufficient buffer of parts available for assembly.

When the Econoline cell takes away enough totes to expose the yellow line, the heijunka person will notice this, take the triangle off the line, and bring it back to molding to schedule another batch of parts. The heijunka person rotates through every 30 minutes, checking for exposed yellow lines, and takes the triangles to the hei-

Photo 8-2. Molded Plastic Parts Marketplace Using Gravity Feed Roller Conveyors

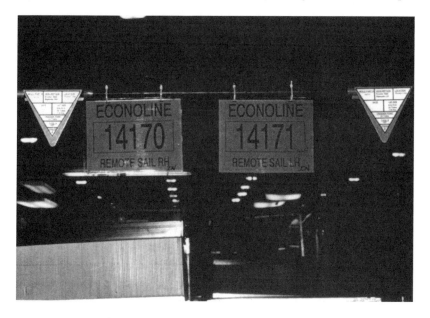

Photo 8-3. Triangle Kanban at Plastic Parts Marketplace Indicating Sufficient
Parts in Stock

junka board shown in Photo 8-4. Each mini-conveyor corresponds to a different press. The placement of the triangle kanban will then signify which press will make the part and when it will be made. If for some reason the heijunka person determines that there is a rush on a part, he or she can push that triangle ahead of others waiting for the press. The triangles in the active slots signify what the press is currently running. This visual system makes it clear what is running and what will be run next. In the case of a family of tools, for right-hand and left-hand parts, if one hits the trigger first the other triangle is automatically pulled as well. By looking at the run times for each lot of parts, one can see when a particular batch will be run (for example, if it is the third triangle for that press, one can see how long the other two triangles will take for their batches to be run).

When a press is being set up to run a new batch, the heijunka person brings to the press empty totes and a set of tags for the totes. The molded parts tote tags are shown in Photo 8-5. They are bundled with a rubber band, and the number corresponds to the number of totes that make up a batch (as signified by the triangle

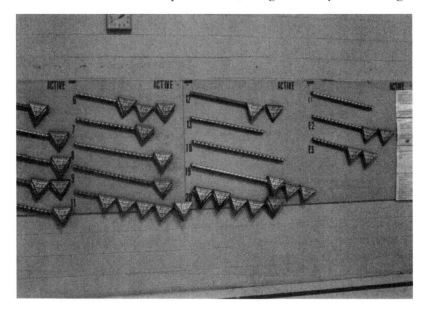

Photo 8-4. Triangle Kanban on Heijunka Board Setting the Schedule for Each Molding Machine

kanban). As the press operator makes parts, the labels are placed in slots on the totes. At some point the operator will come to a blank yellow card in the pile of labels. This was placed there by the heijunka person to be triggered 1 and 1/2 hours before the end of the run and *signifies* that setup should begin the external setup procedures for the next batch of parts to be run on that press. When the operator reaches that yellow card, he or she flips a switch to set off an on-light that contacts the heijunka person. The heijunka person will respond to this signal and check the heijunka board to see whether another job is scheduled for that press. If so, he or she will set off a red flashing light to indicate that a setup person is needed.

When the operator places the last label on a bin, thus completing the batch (a full skid), he or she flips a switch that triggers a red flashing light and a small yellow light, which call the material handler to take the batch of parts to the marketplace. The

Photo 8-5. Molded Parts Tote Tags Help Hold Operator Know How Many Totes of Each Part to Make

cycle is complete. Via a pull system, the plastic molding department has replenished what was taken away from the marketplace. The plan is eventually to eliminate the skids, reduce the lot sizes, and have more frequent deliveries of small lots of totes to the marketplace. The goal for 1996–1997 was to reduce molded parts inventory by 30 percent. As of March, this was already reduced by 32 percent, exceeding the goal. For most parts, they were at this point down to only two days of molded parts inventory. By June, a new target was set by the plant manager to reduce overall inventory in the plant by an additional 15 percent.

Improvements have been made over time to this system through additional kaizen events. When the system was first in operation, one bottleneck was die readiness. Most of the die maintenance work was being done outside, thus introducing a time delay, so Grand Haven brought most die repair work in-house and created a new die maintenance shop for this purpose. Even with this change, however, the maintenance department did not have a system for prioritizing work that matched the needs of production. For example, when a setup was requested that required a particular tool, it might be waiting for repair in-house or even at an outside shop. A triangle kanban/pull system was set up to schedule die repairs. The mold repair priority board is shown in Photo 8-6.

Problems that require some sort of die repair are usually discovered when the tool is being used to run parts. Then either setup or a quality technician "red tags" the tool. One tag is put on the tool and another tag is put on a red triangle that is placed on the mold repair priority board (not yet prioritized for repair). It is then prioritized by moving it to the "molds to be repaired" gravity-fed section. The heijunka person or team leader periodically looks at the mold repair board and manipulates the order to match the needs of production. Color-coded magnetic dots put on the triangle production kanban on the heijunka board in Photo 8-6 (also Photo 8-4) signify the state of the die needed for that run. A blue dot means that it is out of house for repair, a green dot that it is being repaired in the shop, and a red dot that it needs an emergency repair as it will be needed soon for production. The heijunka person and team leader can easily figure out how soon a particular die is needed by

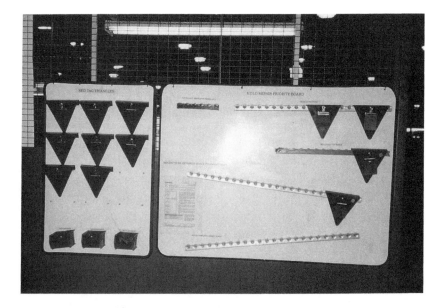

Photo 8-6. Triangle Kanban for Each Mold Setting the Priorities for Mold Repairs

looking at where the current production is in a press and what is scheduled on the heijunka board.

Many other significant improvements have been created over time in molding; for example, the use of visual management. The kanban itself is a visual system. The laminated labels that are put on totes and the yellow card signaling 1.5 hours more of production for that lot are other examples, as is the use of color-coded dots on the triangles, mentioned above. Other improvements include the following:

1. The heijunka board has color-coded areas. A white section is for scheduling production. A blue section is for running sample parts. A green section is for running parts that will be shipped to Grand Haven's sister plant in Newaygo, Michigan. An orange section is for service parts.
2. If a press is down for repairs, a red clip is attached to the triangle kanban scheduled to run on that press.
3. Cards on the side of the press itself signify whether the press is hitting its rated cycle time. Green means "yes"; if the card is flipped over to the orange side, setup should make an adjustment.

4. Andons signal material handlers, heijunka, quality technicians, and setups.
5. There is a standardized display board at a desk by each
   press with a process control sheet and a standardized work
   combination table. When the press is changed over to a new
   product, the appropriate forms are hung on the board.

This system has been very effective in controlling inventory, maintaining the proper priority for scheduling the presses, and maintaining the priority for scheduling die repairs. It is very simple. Unlike the older card system, the triangles do not get misplaced. They are big and bulky and harder to misplace; also, only the heijunka person and material handlers need to touch the kanban.

Timeline for Implementing Triangle Kanban

The timeline for implementing the triangle kanban is shown in Figure 8-4. From formation of the team to full implementation took just over four months. Kaizen event 1 was the pilot effort using one press and one assembly cell. Kaizen event 2 was the implementation of the full system. A good deal of planning prior to the first kaizen event, including conference room simulations, focused on making the system as simple as possible. After the first kaizen event the kaizen team was responsible for writing standard work instructions for using the system and training. Once the pilot was set up and functioning, it was used to train all associates on the system.

Implementation was driven by target dates for implementation and inventory reduction. All targets were met or exceeded. The most visible and immediate impact of the system was the space reductions when inventory was reduced (Photo 8-7), but this was only a small part of the benefit that has come from the pull system. Once the kanban system was in operation and molding was operating on a pull system, manufacturing issues that prevented just-in-time production were exposed. These included setups that took too long, dies that were not ready when needed, and lack of level scheduling of production, which created large spikes in demand. Kaizen teams then began to focus systematically on these issues.

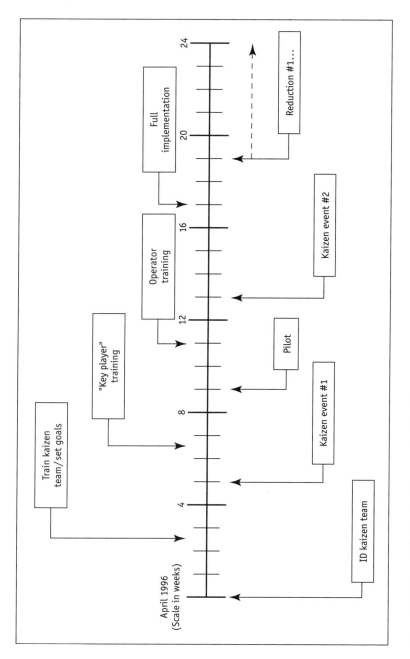

Figure 8-4. Triangle Kanban Implementation Timeline

Photo 8-7. The Triangle Kanban System for Molded Parts Leading to Major Space Reductions.

Focus on People and Material Flow

In 1996, the focus at Grand Haven was on creating the people systems needed for continuous improvement and on material flow to support a pull system and drive toward batch-of-one capability. We first discuss the people systems, then discuss other material flow initiatives beyond the triangle kanban.

People and Continuous Improvement Team (CIT)

Although in 1995 Donnelly succeeded in stopping the bleeding, it saw a near disaster in employee relations. A major goal for 1996 was to bring back the employee involvement that Donnelly has been known for and to make continuous improvement by and from the people instead of something done to the people. The vehicles for doing this were as follows:

- A plant continuous improvement team (CIT)—four full-time hourly associates (called CI technicians).
- Problem solving teams—task forces set up for specific problems.

- Work teams—to meet weekly in each area for 10 minutes at the start of each shift.
- 15-minute monthly meetings on overtime.
- Associates are always involved in kaizen events and activities.

Keith Allman established the CIT in January 1996. These were posted positions; from the dozen interviewed, four were selected as the first cohort. Several had been heavily involved in the previous kaizen process. They reported to the manufacturing manager. The first group was originally appointed for one year and then were reappointed for a second year to keep the momentum going. Associates join this team on a six-month rotation to aid in transferring knowledge throughout the plant.

The CIT has gone farther than anyone thought possible and is now seen as a model for other Donnelly plants. Although it was originally expected only to work on small projects and to lead kaizen events, in their words, "We own that plant." They have developed a layout looking one year out for the entire plant. They have played a central role in planning new product launches. Keith made it clear to the engineers that nothing new will be implemented on the shop floor without first going through the CIT.

CIT members knew that they had to prove themselves to people after the negative experience with outside consultants. At first other associates thought they were "just another kaizen team—flavor of the month." But when the CIT had some successes in making changes, other associates began to ask, "When are you coming to our area?" This is when they knew they were over the main hurdle.

The CIT leads events that are different from the old externally led events. 1. They involve more people and everyone's ideas are taken seriously. 2. There is much more prework. Generally, the preparation starts several months in advance. For example, a long lead-time item may be designed and fabricated in advance. 3. The 30-day list comes back to the CIT and gets done. 4. The events are chosen very selectively; about one such major event takes place per quarter. Most improvement is ongoing.

Like most things at Grand Haven, there is a standardized procedure for continuous improvement events and a manual documenting the procedure. The manual includes a timetable for planning and running the event, preparation work that needs to be done, guidelines for running the event itself, and follow-up activities. It also includes standardized training materials in the form of presentation materials.

The manual has a particularly strong emphasis on preparation and follow-up. The implementation timetable starts four weeks in advance of the event, but planning often begins even earlier. Table 8-2, the Kaizen Preparation Checklist, shows the level of detail necessary to prepare adequately for an effective event. Each of the items in the checklist is spelled out in detail in the manual. There are detailed checklists and forms for all phases. For example, there is a standard list of supplies for a team kit for the event, including such things as pencils for each team member, calculators, stopwatches, and a full set of forms like a standard work combination sheet, cycle time/takt time bar chart, and a kaizen 30-day-goals form. There is even a sample "kaizen training menu," which includes suggested lunches, dinners, and snacks from Tuesday to Friday. Detailed statistics on the kaizen area are also collected and included in a packet of information given to participants one week in advance of the event. Often preparation for the event includes fabrication of long-lead-time items. For example if the focus is on quick die changeover, a quick die changeover table may need to be fabricated in advance.

The keys to effective kaizen are preparation and follow-up. Often, many ideas are generated in the event, but there is not time to implement them all. When the events were externally led, there was little commitment to follow up and the 30-day homework lists were typically never done. Now it is the responsibility of the CIT to ensure that all tasks are completed. There are guidelines for follow-up at +1, +2, +3, and +4 weeks after the event, along with who is responsible for specific items and when they will complete them. A weekly status meeting is held after the event.

The keys to success of the CI events are threefold. 1. They are driven by a broader systems vision for the operation of the plant as

Table 8-2. Kaizen Preparation Checklist

Kaizen Event — 4 Weeks	Who responsible	When	Complete
Area selected			
Begin plans to run inventory if need be			
Objectives developed			
Informal notification communicated			
Maintenance prepared			
Staffing			
Supplies/Tools/Equipment			
Maintenance personnel			
Kaizen team work area			
Kaizen Event—2 Weeks			
Team/Team leader/Subleader identified			
Selected team members begin soliciting improvement ideas from their shift team (w/Pre-Kaizen Team Input Newspaper)			
Rooms/Equipment reserved			
Large room (trg./summary pres.)			
Small breakout room (each team)			
Team work space in target area			
Camcorder/Tapes/VCR/TV			
Training notebooks			
Separate break room for shingijutsu consultant (lunch as well)			
Daily team leader meeting room reserved			
Food arranged			
Invitation memos published			
Team participants			
Summary presentation participants			
Kaizen summary/objectives sheet completed			
Resource personnel list compiled			
Team kits assembled			
Take pictures and videos of targeted area (capture the existing flow, function of equipment)			
Develop list of resource personnel with responsibilities and phone numbers			
Kaizen Event — 1 Week			
Project area statistics information			
Have "completed" Pre-Kaizen Team Input Newspaper form from each shift			
Publish into kaizen teams			
Mail to outside participants			
Kaizen workshop notebooks for each participant			
One set of overheads for instructor(s)			

a whole, with a focus on overall flow of the product throughout the plant. This vision is the Donnelly Production System. 2. Associates have responsibility for running the events and implementing the solutions. 3. There is a carefully thought through standardized process for running the events that begins with careful planning and continues through follow-up after the event.

Material Flow—Extending the Pull System Further Upstream

The triangle kanban was Grand Haven's first major success in implementing a pull system. In 1996 and early 1997, they went much farther than molding. As discussed above, the approach to implementation shifted from running many kaizen events all over the plant to trying to implement core features of DPS on a pilot line and then migrating that to other parts of the plant. After establishing a kanban system for molded parts, the next step was to extend the pull system further upstream to assembly and from there back to purchased parts. To simplify this process, an assembly operation was chosen that used unpainted parts, thus avoiding having to tie-in the paint operation with its long lead times and somewhat unpredictable yields.

Ford Econoline exterior mirrors pilot

The product chosen to pilot a fully integrated process was the Ford Econoline exterior mirrors. One assembly cell makes manual mirrors, left and right, and a second cell makes left and right automatic mirrors. Consistent with the new systems-oriented philosophy, an overall systems vision was created for the Econoline model line, shown in Figure 8-5. The model calls for a complete pull system based on a leveled production schedule that replenishes what is taken away by the customer from finished goods storage. When the system is fully implemented, there will be no scheduling of production per se. Production is to be based on replenishing what is taken away and building to takt time.

If we start with the customer and work backwards through the pull system, takt time is adjusted each month based on forecasted orders for the month. Based on the takt time, a leveled pace of production is set. Based on historical fluctuation in demand and the

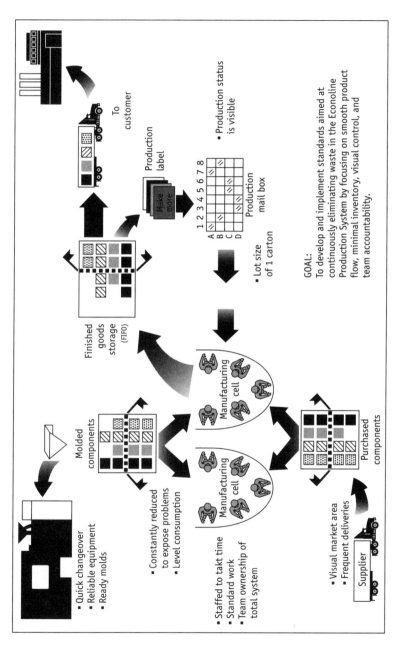

Figure 8-5. Donnelly Production System—Grand Haven Econoline Model

frequency of deliveries to the customer, the level of finished goods inventory is set. Shipping scans the shipping skids when they are loaded onto the trucks. A computer system automatically generates a master label for production scheduling. Every 24 hours, the production labels are sorted by the heijunka person into a production mailbox (a heijunka box), in which the assorted products are listed in vertical columns and the times of day (based on a 24-hour clock) are listed horizontally (see Figure 8-5). If there are still some cards left over from the day before, they are put into a past due slot, and they will get first priority. The material handler prints labels and inserts them into the slots to level production across product types. So instead of making all of product A, then switching to make all of product B, then all of product C, and then all of product D, the configuration in Figure 8-5 shows A, then B, then two batches of D, then two batches of C, then A, and then B.

As of March 1997, when we started writing this chapter, the material handler made rounds every 30 minutes. One hour's worth of components are staged at the assembly cell. He takes the parts to shipping and puts the label in the side slot of the bin. The material handler also pulls cards from the production mailbox for the next production run. After the first draft of this chapter was written, Grand Haven progressed to six-minute withdrawals from the heijunka box. So every six minutes, the material handler makes the rounds and schedules what the cell will make for the next six minutes. This leads to an extremely level flow of work.

Supporting batch-of-one capability
In order to build to a leveled sequence from the production mailbox, the Econoline assembly cells needed to develop "batch-of-one" capability. This would mean building one carton of material, changing over, building another carton of another material (if called for by the leveled sequence), etc. This requires very rapid changeover capability. The Econoline cell already had some of the elements of quick changeover, but the main bottleneck was shifting from right-hand to left-hand fixtures. A clever solution was found. The fixtures had been set up to make two parts per fixture, either

two lefts or two rights. The solution was to break the fixtures in half and rebuild them so that there was one right and one left leading to a zero setup time. Also needed for batch-of-one capability was to have all the parts needed for all the different product types (four types) line-side at all times. These changes were made in a kaizen activity in February 1997, which included adding in the production mailbox. The event was supported by the CIT but was led by production and inventory control, whose manager had prior experience with a similar system.

Even though in principle batch-of-one capability was developed in the cell, it was not being used at first. The material handlers were still moving complete skids of parts from assembly to shipping. Since the cells were building to skids anyway, they decided to build a complete skid-worth of one part before changing over to a different part. The takt time for manual mirrors is 31 seconds; a skid holds 81 parts, so it takes about 42 minutes to build one skid. This is an improvement over the past, when they were running 3 skids in a row before changing over. When they shifted to the six-minute withdrawal cycle, the process was changed significantly so that all parts were available line-side and batch-of-one capability was now possible. At any point, either a left-hand or right-hand mirror could be built without a changeover.

Other characteristics of the cell are necessary to support batch-of-one processing. The cells must be staffed to takt time. It is impossible to know whether the cell is staffed to takt time unless there are standard times and standard work to support these standardized times. There are several standard work sheets available for different numbers of people to support different takt times. If the takt time goes up, they might put away the four-person standard work sheet and pull out the five-person standard work sheet, add another person, and they are ready to go. Associates in the cell are cross-trained so they can adapt to changes in takt time, unexpected absences, breaks, etc. Much of this had already been developed through the externally led kaizen events. The main challenge was to transfer ownership of the cell to the teams to maintain the discipline needed to use the systems in place and to see that the cell is continuously improved.

The supplied parts are on a pull-signal loop that replenishes the purchased components store. This system goes beyond Econoline; all suppliers deliver on a kanban system, replenishing what is used. There is a visual market area for purchased components. Purchasing makes a daily review of what purchased components were consumed and generates a fax to suppliers ordering parts for the next day. Plastic resins for molding have been on a system like this for some time. The production/inventory control department was in the process of developing standard milk runs (called "lean lanes") to pick up parts from several suppliers once or twice per day. As of March 1997, three lean lanes were being developed.

With low inventory buffers and frequent changeovers to level production, it will be critical for all equipment to operate at very high levels of reliability. Much work has been done on preventive maintenance already, including standardized procedures and preventive maintenance checklists for each machine. In 1998, the focus will be to get more deeply into total productive maintenance (TPM). For example, in some cases it may make sense to run a tool to failure intentionally but have such a quick change capability that it does not matter. Injection molding press setups used to take 2 hours; the goal is to get to 5 minutes (now at 20 minutes). The goal will be to do changeovers with no bolts and no cranes—just slide the equipment in on a channel and use hydraulic clamping.

Lessons Learned from Grand Haven

We have told a story of a plant with a solid history of strong employee involvement on a journey to lean manufacturing filled with ups and downs. With the vision of the Donnelly Production System, Grand Haven seems to be headed on a solid course. While writing this chapter, we noted in several instances that what we described at the first writing had already changed by the next month's reviewing of the chapter. Because Grand Haven is continually improving, we cannot pin down this moving target. This suggests that it would not make sense for a company to blindly copy any of the specific techniques used at Grand Haven such as the triangle kanban scheduling board. If you were trying to emulate

Grand Haven, by the time you copied something it would probably already have changed. The point is to learn from the philosophy and general approach but develop and improve your own system of production.

Grand Haven is an interesting and important case study, as it is a transformation of an existing mass production operation into a lean system. Clearly, Grand Haven had many factors in its favor to help ease this transition. These include a young, motivated work force, a history of employee involvement, the Scanlon plan, which rewards all employees for improvement, a knowledgeable plant manager, some excellent engineers, a relatively new plant and equipment, and sales growth over this period. Despite all these favorable characteristics, the improvements did not happen overnight or without struggle and mistakes along the way.

A number of lessons can be learned by reflecting on the experiences of Grand Haven. Since this is one case and we do not know "what would have happened if," we cannot prove that we have identified the right factors, but the following seem to be important lessons:

1. *A compelling need for change will accelerate the process*. It is hard to imagine that Grand Haven would have made the dramatic changes they did without a compelling need for change. The threatened loss of business by Honda, their major customer, was the shock to the system needed to drive change. This is not to say proactive change is impossible, but it is likely to be slower.

2. *Just do it! (then check it and improve it.)* This has become a phrase used often at Donnelly. There is a clear bias for action on the shop floor. Yet changes need to be planned, and the kaizen process led by the CIT is much more systematically planned than were the earlier, externally led events. But planning and doing and checking and acting must all be done for effective continuous improvement. Creating models like the Donnelly Production System are important as overarching visions, but each plant must learn how to implement the abstract concepts of DPS on the shop floor. Grand Haven did not go through a six-month training program to communicate abstract concepts to all employees prior to implementation. Most of the important training on lean concepts that occurred at Grand Haven came from on-the-job training through kaizen events and living with the system. The training that has been done at Grand Haven, whether in kaizen events or standardized work training,

has been followed immediately by implementation. The Toyota Production System was created on the shop floor of Toyota factories, and its implementation must be a process of learning on the shop floor of each plant.

3. *Getting buy-in is a slow process . . . sometimes too slow.* To get everyone involved to the critical mass needed to achieve buy-in to major change is clearly important, but it can take as much time as you are willing to spend to communicate, sell, and involve people. In 1995, when Grand Haven had to stop the bleeding or possibly go out of business, time was a luxury that could not be afforded. In retrospect, it is not clear whether running 29 externally led kaizen events was the right or wrong thing to do. It upset and alienated a lot of people. There is agreement that some type of outside help was needed to accelerate the change process, but there may have been ways to combine a sense of urgency and radical change with more genuine employee involvement. The reality is that no one knows what would have happened if a more people-sensitive, involving approach were used. Would the change have occurred fast enough to satisfy Honda? This remains an unanswered question. One thing is clear: The most important sales vehicle for selling lean manufacturing at Donnelly has been successful implementation leading to measurable results. When associates have seen results, for example by the CIT, they have quickly been won over and now ask to have the CIT come to their area.

4. *Changes should be system-driven focusing on product flow, not event-driven.* The externally led kaizen events focused on fixing isolated problems. There was no overarching vision for what the product flow in the plant should look like after the series of events. Although the consultants may have had a vision based on their experience with TPS, this vision was not specifically applied to the Grand Haven plant or shared with anyone inside Grand Haven. The result was a lot of islands of specific lean practices that were not tied together. For example, changeover times were reduced but there was nothing driving the need to change over quickly except a little time saved here and there. The Donnelly Production System provided a broad vision and even that needed to be cascaded to an overall vision for the flow of Grand Haven and even the flow of the Econoline product. The issue may not actually be one versus the other but a matter of timing. In retrospect, it is not clear at Grand Haven whether the radical kaizen events set the process back because they alienated employees or whether these events were just the thing needed to shake up the culture and force some badly needed changes. Perhaps without these kaizen events a systems vision would have led to no action or only to

small, incremental steps. Ultimately, once the system became unstuck, DPS provided a vision to guide a rational step-by-step approach toward a production system.

5. *Most big changes occur in short bursts*. Even after the CIT was formed and the DPS vision guided change toward a system vision, a place remains for the four-day kaizen event. For example, the major system changes to the Econoline cell (production mailbox for leveling the schedule and batch-of-one capability) were made in a kaizen event. There was planning, but the event served as a focus for the activity. It provided a deadline by which to do the planning and preparations, and it provided an opportunity for a cross-functional team to focus intensively on the details and implementation during the event itself. Many little changes occur during the normal work week, but the big system changes that have transformed Grand Haven have occurred in focused events.

6. *The transition to lean must be driven by knowledgeable and committed managers who understand it in their gut*. That top management support is needed for any major change has become axiomatic. At Donnelly, the chief operating officer was firmly behind the shift to lean manufacturing, but the next levels of management must also be committed and have a deep understanding. In Donnelly's case, this was the vice president of manufacturing and the plant operations managers. Not only were they committed to a change to something that sounded good in concept, they had experienced the system and understood it in their gut. So they were leading toward a vision that was detailed and real to them—one they had lived firsthand. The transformation to lean at Grand Haven could hardly have been effectively led by managers whose understanding of lean came only from a book or short courses.

Notes

1. Much of the historical background on Grand Haven was based on John Paul MacDuffie and Sue Helper, "Creating Lean Suppliers: Diffusing Lean Production Through the Supply Chain," to appear in *America: Transplanting and Transforming Japanese Production Systems*, edited by J. K. Liker, M. Fruin, P. Adler. Oxford University Press, Forthcoming.

2. *Hoshin* is a Japanese term referring to a broad policy statement with an associated statement of the means by which the policy will be actualized. In *hoshin management*, top management creates the policy and means for the organization, and this is elaborated further, with increasing specificity, at each management level in the various departments. For more on hoshin management, see Yoji Akao, ed., *Hoshin Kanri: Policy Deployment for Successful TQM* (Portland, Ore.: Productivity Press, 1991).

Matthew J. Zayko *is Manufacturing Engineer at Gelman Sciences, Inc. in Ann Arbor, Michigan. He received his B.S. in Physics from Alma College in Alma, Michigan and his M.S. in Industrial and Operations Engineering from the University of Michigan, Ann Arbor. Mr. Zayko is a member of IIE and SME.*

Walton M. Hancock *is Professor Emeritus of Industrial and Operations Engineering at the University of Michigan in Ann Arbor. He received his B.E., M.S., and D. Eng. degrees in Industrial Engineering from Johns Hopkins University. Professor Hancock's current teaching, research, and professional interests focus on implementing lean production by improving processes in stamping, injection molding, casting, medical devices, and more. Professor Hancock is an IIE Fellow and has written over 72 journal articles, 15 book chapters, and 90 technical reports.*

Douglas J. Broughman *is Plant Manager at Gelman Sciences, Inc. in Ann Arbor, Michigan. He received his B.A. in Business from Eastern Michigan University in Ypsilanti. Mr. Broughman has been with Gelman Sciences since 1988. For the past three years, as plant manager, he has been leading the transformation from traditional manufacturing concepts to lean manufacturing and employee empowerment.*

9

Implementing Lean Manufacturing at Gelman Sciences, Inc.

by Matthew J. Zayko, Walton M. Hancock, and Douglas J. Broughman

Editor's prologue: Gelman Sciences is a small company that has grown rapidly. It was performing reasonably well as a business before embarking on the journey to lean manufacturing. In February 1997, Gelman merged with Pall Corporation, a world leader in microfiltration and separations with sales of over $1 billion. The shift from mass production to lean production was internally initiated without an external crisis. In retrospect, after beginning the shift to lean production, the company realized how much waste existed in the way they were running the operation.

The story of Gelman Sciences' major change to lean is told by two employees who were very active in the transformation, and Walt Hancock, the key outside consultant in this process. They describe how, in just six months at one of Gelman's plants, they cut the lead manufacturing cell inventory by almost two-thirds and lead times in half while increasing inventory turns by 185 percent. The results have been major improvements in on-time deliveries, increased productivity, and improved quality. This plant quickly became a model for manufacturing practice within the rest of Gelman and indeed for all of Pall Corporation. When this chapter was written, Gelman's lead plant was still in the early stages of transformation to lean. From forming a steering committee, creating experimental teams, to cell training and implementation, the authors give a detailed description of the process of change, the resistance they faced, and the results they were able to achieve along the way to becoming lean.

Gelman Sciences is a wholly owned and recently acquired subsidiary of Pall Corporation. Pall Corporation is the world leader in the rapidly expanding field of microfiltration and separations, with sales of more than $1 billion in fiscal year 1996. Like many entrepreneurial companies, Gelman Sciences (Gelman) started in 1959 with an idea of doing something better than was then done. In Gelman's case, the impetus was the founder's frustration with the time and effort required to collect air samples by hand. Charles Gelman developed a machine that took precise samples at automatic intervals. Sales in the first year totaled about $65,000. Gelman's initial years focused on instrumentation. Not until the company began experiencing quality and delivery problems with its filter supplier did it look internally to meet this need by producing its own membrane filters.

By the 1990s, Gelman Sciences, based in Ann Arbor, Michigan, was recognized for developing and manufacturing more kinds of membranes, in more types of devices, than any other company in the world. Gelman's products for filtration and membrane separation are used in laboratory research, high technology manufacturing, and critical medical applications, including patient care. It has an array of thousands of products ranging from cartridges, capsules, and filter housings to syringe, ophthalmic, and intravenous filters. Gelman also sells its membranes to original equipment manufacturer (OEM) producers for incorporation into their devices. Gelman's annual sales had grown to $112 million (40 percent of which were international sales) before it merged with Pall Corporation in February 1997.

Gelman manufactures its products in three manufacturing facilities in the United States. Each plant is responsible for an exclusive group of products. The two Ann Arbor plants depend on the Pensacola, Florida plant for supplying most of the membrane they use to incorporate into the devices they make. Prior to the introduction of some lean manufacturing techniques in 1993, each of the plants built products utilizing a make-to-order, make-to-stock, engineered-to-order, or some other hybrid method of scheduling with the traditional mass production, batch-and-queue mentality—a mentality resulting from long setup times or other operational inefficiencies. The manufacturing facilities and technologies employed ranged from new, state-of-the-art, and high-volume to old, labor intensive, and low volume. The hourly work force was nonunion, with an average age of 38 years and 6 years of seniority, made up primarily of non-degreed females.

Pre-1997 Process for Manufacturing of Cartridge and Capsule Filters

The manufacturing of cartridge and capsule filters in Plant One begins with the production of membrane. Gelman's plant in Pensacola, Florida supplies the majority of their membranes. These membranes are slit with cutters to specified lengths and widths and are then shipped to Ann Arbor for use in Plant One, where they are integrated into the building of cartridges and capsules.

Figure 9-1 shows the production flow (from a pre-1997 viewpoint) once materials arrive in Plant One. The first step for filters is pleating or corrugating of the membrane in order to give a higher effective filtration area (EFA). Rolls of membrane are put on a rack and fed into a pleating machine. The membrane is protected from damage by blades within the pleater by sandwiching nonwoven fabrics around it. These multiple layers of material enter the pleater machine at a pulled set pressure and specified height on the blades. A repeating folding-over action creates an accordion-type pleat on the material. Warming lamps or heated platens may also be used within the pleating machine to yield higher quality and more definitive pleats. The material is then cut perpendicular to its flow through the machine at a specified number of pleats by an operator and placed in an outer tube to form a pack. It is put in queue.

The next process done on the *pack* is seaming. (A filter is called a "pack" until it is endcapped, at which time it becomes a "module." After customization to a customer spec, it is called a cartridge or capsule "filter.") The majority of products use heat-seaming

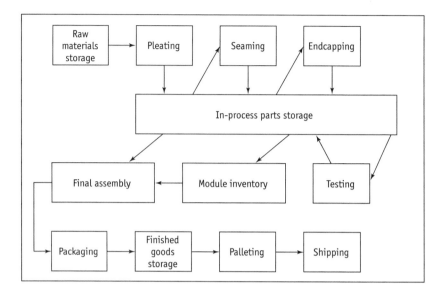

Figure 9-1. Process-Based, Functional Layout, Pre-1997

technology. A seaming operator takes the pack from the outer tube and aligns the two ends into a jaw guide on a seaming machine. These two ends are pushed together by a pressure control and heated. Because the nonwoven material is on the outside of the pack, the inner microporous membrane pores are penetrated by the molten outer layers, giving a transparent, sealed area.

After heat seaming, the operator inserts a center tube and outer tube on the pack. The next operator heats the ends of the seamed pack and two caps in an endcapping machine that forces the components together at a specified pressure. This transforms the pack into a module. The module is then wetted and tested for integrity in various sample sizes. The drying of a wetted module may take up to two days. After drying, the module is taken to inventory for future use or taken directly to final assembly for final build to a customer's specifications.

This is a highly customized process. One-piece orders are frequent, and new part numbers enter the system every week. Each piece is labeled according to the customer requirement and is then bagged before entering into the packaging area. Since the manufacturing area is in a clean-room environment, packaging must occur in a separate room because of the high particulate levels from the cardboard.

Beginning of Culture Change—Vision of Future System

The vision for the plant was to achieve greater than 95 percent on-time customer delivery performance, to reduce lead times, and to eliminate virtually all scrap while improving quality across the board. The introduction of a culture change in Plant One started in February 1993 with the hiring of Gregory Scheessele (Greg) as the associate director of manufacturing. Prior to 1993, the plant's culture was typical of many manufacturers—management was paid to think and the hourly workers were paid to do. Upper management was insulated from the hourly ranks by several layers of managers (see Figure 9-2). They typically focused on short-term results, such as quarter-end targets, labor utilization, and micro-managing day-to-day activities, while doing little long-term planning and directing.

Although comparing the filter industry to the automotive industry was like comparing apples to oranges, Greg saw many similarities between Gelman's situation and the decade-long slide of the American automotive manufacturers. Gelman's manufacturing was characterized by

- Extended lead times
- Redundant inspections
- High scrap and inventories
- Large batch runs
- Long setup times
- Inaccurate product costing

This system did not aid the already lengthy product development times. Gelman was also seeing its major competitors continue to grow faster and much larger, thus making the competitive pressures that much greater. At the same time smaller companies were entering niche markets, putting pressure on prices, and turning some products into commodities.

With an understanding of where the opportunities were in the plant, Greg, now the vice president of operations, proceeded to pro-

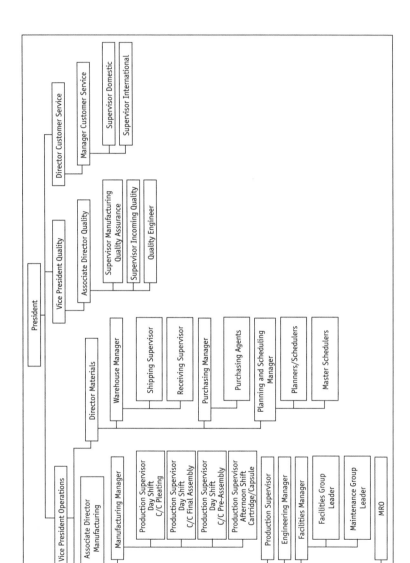

Figure 9-2. Operations Organization Chart, 1993

vide his vision and direction for where he wanted the plant to go. One tool that the plant needed for direction was to be able to measure key performance indicators. Former measures focused strictly on cost issues, such as capacity utilization or productivity per hour. These indicators hindered the switch to lean concepts because improvements in efficiency would not necessarily correlate to improvements in the capacity measures. Baseline measures were needed to quantify change objectively and to decide how to proceed with it. The plant needed more nonfinancial performance targets. They selected three measures in the areas of throughput, quality, and delivery that satisfied the goals of the plant.

Early Continuous Improvement Teams

One of Greg's first actions was to organize a continuous improvement (CI) initiative with the aid of an outside consultant, Susan Heathfield (Susan). Greg recognized that if the plant was going to reach its full potential, the culture within it was going to have to change, and that was going to take the contributions of everyone through empowerment. This approach ran against the plant's typical manufacturing culture whereby the hourly people were expected to work, not think. This had to change, but first Susan and Greg needed to convince the management group that empowering their people was good and that management would not lose control.

Core Training for Supervisors and Managers

Initial CI training began in May 1993. The supervisors and managers went through six months of training, led by Susan. Bringing management on board to support this effort 100 percent was imperative before exposing the hourly work force to the concept. Gelman had a reputation of trying "program of the week" initiatives. Each had met with some success, but all ultimately failed. Greg's steadfast vision and commitment to CI was aided by the hiring of a new manufacturing manager, Douglas Broughman (Doug), in June 1993. With the top two managers in the plant now fully behind CI, there were no acceptable excuses for the others' refusing to come on board. As the training ensued over the following months, most of the management group did come on board. Those who did not either left on their own or were asked to leave.

The training for the supervisors and managers included the following topics:

- Continuous improvement process
- The ten things you must do to implement CI successfully through teams
- Team formation
- Leadership for change
- Employee recognition
- The changing role of the manager/supervisor
- Motivation for leaders

As the core training for the supervisors and managers was winding down, the management group had three major questions to answer:

1. What is the best way to roll out the CI team concept to the hourly work force?
2. How should the teams be set up and who should be on them?
3. How will the training be conducted?

Unfortunately, there were no easy answers or a manual to follow. From each of these questions several ideas and a great deal of discussion took place in order to reach a consensus.

For question 1 it was decided that the CI team concept would be rolled out at a plantwide meeting attended by all the shifts. Gelman was on the verge of a paradigm shift. The significance of the change had to be communicated to all employees, and shutting down production for the meeting was the best way to do this. Everyone would hear the same message, the same comments, and the same questions. Everyone in the management group, including Greg, participated in the meeting. This reflected the top-down commitment to CI teams.

Question 2 regarding team structure was answered by setting up 15 teams around the primary operations of the plant. For example, all the operators who worked in packaging became a team and all the people in testing became another team. Team sizes ranged from three people to 15 people, most teams having seven or eight members. The larger operations had two teams in order to keep the team sizes manageable.

The teams were centered around common operations rather than product lines because management was still focused on optimizing individual operations versus an entire process. Some of the teams had representatives from upstream and downstream operations with the thought that these people would be able to give the "supplier and customer" perspectives. These people were in the minority, however, and management's focus was operation optimization, thus causing the supplier and customer viewpoints to be squashed by the teams in most instances.

Question 3, dealing with training, was the most difficult to answer. To emphasize the long-term commitment to the CI program, they scheduled the core training for the hourly workers to take place two hours per week every month for twelve months, facilitated by Susan. This format provided many benefits, such as minimizing downtime, increasing flexibility in scheduling around the business needs, and avoiding the retention problems of a one-week crash course.

Monthly Training Schedule for CI Teams

The monthly training schedule allowed for specific concepts to be taught, tried in practice for a month, and then followed-up on and fine-tuned at the next class. The specific concepts that were covered during the monthly training were as follows:

I.   Creating the team
    A. Class 1:   Building the team
    B. Class 2:   Facilitating team meetings
II. Establishing problem solving and process improvement methods
    A. Class 3:   Plan-do-study-act (PDSA) cycle of continuous improvement
    B. Class 4:   Problem solving
    C. Class 5:   Continuous process improvement
    D. Class 6:   Problem solving tools

E. Class 7:   Practice problem solving
F. Class 8:   Eliminating waste
III. Becoming effective with people
   A. Class 9:   Interpersonal skills
   B. Class 10:   Building trust and feedback
   C. Class 11:   Conflict resolution and decision making
   D. Class 12:   Skill review

Specific training in advanced skills, such as statistical process control (SPC), motion economy, and filling out request forms, was provided as the team members progressed and the needs were identified.

As the CI team training was underway, there was a broad range of support: 10 percent of the people were openly skeptical; 10 percent were fully supportive; the middle 80 percent were the "wait and see" type, many of whom saw this as the "program of the week." Typical comments included the following:

- Why do we have to do this if the other plants do not have to?
- Why do we have to go to all these meetings and classes if we are working overtime?
- Sure, I will do it. It is not going to last very long (program of the week), but I am going to get all the support and help out of it while it is alive.

Management reacted to these comments by restating the long-term goal and maintaining that short-term sacrifices and expenses were needed to get there.

Early in the first year, the teams worked on small projects that typically improved the quality of their working environments and usually did not result in tangible improvements in bottom line profit. Projects centered around improving shift communication, simplifying paperwork and operating procedures, and making sure sufficient and proper production supplies were always available. These projects allowed the teams to become cohesive and reinforced the training. As the year progressed, the teams started to tackle the more complex problems such as setup reduction, scrap minimization, and uptime improvement.

Results of CI Training

The CI training produced mixed results. It helped in changing the attitudes of those involved by causing them to reflect on and discuss operational procedures or practices pertinent to their individual processes. Unfortunately, as discussed below, many of the major problems of the plant, such as high scrap rates, were occurring from the interaction between processes, an issue not effectively addressed by the CI teams. The result was that the success rate of the teams in improving manufacturing quality was marginal. The functional, process-based team structure that the operations group had organized was limiting the ability of the workers to interact with other processes that were affecting their work.

Another reason the CI teams produced marginal root-cause results was because the manufacturing engineers, who were resources for the teams, did not have a high level of technical expertise in the processes. Their main effort had been the development of new processes, and they were not required to do in-depth analyses of existing processes. Thus, when the CI teams met, practically no one on the team had the requisite knowledge to provide leadership on how to improve setup times, whether or not the process specifications were correct, or whether the equipment needed specific repairs.

Introducing Lean Manufacturing Concepts

Parallel to the CI program, plant management brought in a lean manufacturing and quality assurance consultant, Professor Walton Hancock (Walt), from the University of Michigan Industrial and Operations Engineering Department, to look into the high scrap rates.

The main support for the work came from Greg Scheessele, the vice president of operations. From his earlier endeavors in the automotive industry, Greg had intensive experience in manufacturing operations in a fast-paced environment. Greg knew they could improve the operations with the use of modern quality control and manufacturing methods, but he did not have the personal time to get involved, so he engaged Walt to do the teaching and provide the main support.

Initial Sources of Resistance

Resistance to the efforts came from two primary sources. The first source was the quality control department, which had a large staff involved in auditing, checking, and reporting on the quality of the products at many stages in the production process. These procedures were the result of interpretations of the FDA requirements for medical products. Walt's class instruction emphasized that modern quality control is only effective if it is actively involved in the solution and correction of production problems. This approach would require the quality control personnel not only to report problems but also to provide the leadership in correcting them. This additional requirement was not met with enthusiasm by the quality control personnel.

The second source of resistance came from the manufacturing engineering group, which placed the highest priority on the development of new processes. They perceived the solution of root-cause quality and production problems as being of secondary importance, which would result in insufficient problem-solving capability for present products and processes. In the class sessions, it was repeatedly emphasized that the solution of root-cause problems was a necessary requirement of both manufacturing engineering and quality control. This emphasis required the manufacturing engineering supervision to re-evaluate their priorities, a task that also elicited little enthusiasm.

Results of Initial Investigating

After much investigation, Walt verified that scrap was occurring in batches due to the manufacturing system. Root-cause analysis was difficult because of the weeks of work-in-process (WIP) sitting between machines. Thus, the vision for the plant could only be realized by putting in a lean manufacturing system that, among other things, allowed for little WIP. Walt was now responsible for teaching these lean methods to all the engineers and management staff in the facility.

Lean Manufacturing Classes are Set Up

Walt proposed that the most efficient way to improve overall quality was to teach modern quality control and lean manufacturing in classes where the concepts were presented and reinforced by examples and homework from the plant. The format for the class was two hours per week with homework assigned each week for 14 weeks. These short sessions allowed the class more time to work on homework with fewer disruptions of their regular duties.

The lean manufacturing class was made up of representatives from quality, engineering, and operations. The heads of these various functions through the entry-level personnel attended. Walt made sure that the highest ranking managers and engineers set the example for subordinates by regularly attending the classes and doing the homework. Some felt they were too busy for the exercises, but most of these individuals have since left the company.

Curriculum and Projects

To foster implementation of lean manufacturing most effectively, the format of the class had to be designed to sensitize the students to major areas of waste in the plant. The wastes that were focused on were a modification of Suzaki's seven wastes and included the following (Suzaki, 1987: 12):

- Overproduction
- Lack of standardized work
- Queue (waiting) time
- Transportation (handling)
- Inventory
- Unnecessary motions
- Defective products
- Underutilized skills

Once there was a clear understanding of the importance of attacking these examples of waste, homework was assigned that focused on actual plant problems.

Frequently, the homework was too difficult to do in a week without outside expertise. For example, if the homework assignment was to work with the operators and develop a standardized setup procedure for a machine, specialized tools had to be designed and constructed and the operators taught how to use them. In cases like these, Walt would work with members in groups outside the class to implement the projects, who would then report back to the class on the results.

Focusing on Scrap

One waste that was very high in the plant was scrap. High quality of shipped product was attained only after 100 percent testing of many of the finished products. This was a time-consuming but important part of the process because the average scrap rate ranged from 8 to 22 percent.

The manufacturing equipment was arranged in a process-oriented layout. All orders went through the various processes in a batch, and testing was one of the last steps in the process. The amount of rejected product was unknown until the product was virtually in a finished condition. If a product failed an integrity test due to a seam leak, for example, the filters could not be repaired and, in most cases, the reason for the leak could not be specifically determined. Since an entire order was processed as a batch with throughput times of approximately one month, it was very difficult, if not impossible, to determine the condition of a particular machine during the time the defects were produced. The result was that the scrap rate was high, and only minor improvements could be made because the root cause could not be easily determined.

The testing cost, which represented approximately 50 percent of the labor, was also waste. If the products could be manufactured with little scrap and 100 percent quality, two major sources of waste could be greatly reduced. The lean manufacturing class analyzed the scrap reports to determine the percentage of scrap that was being generated by each process and by suppliers. The results showed that the suppliers were contributing approximately 5 percent of the scrap because parts were contaminated with foreign particles. The remaining 95 percent stemmed from the manufacturing processes within the plant. The class concluded that if the company reduced the time it took a product to be produced and tested, they would have a much better chance of determining the root cause of the defects. They could only accomplish this by reducing the WIP between each process.

Before they could reduce WIP, the lean manufacturing class needed to address two items: setup standardization/time reduction and wasted motions. The techniques used to standardize setups included identifying all setup steps as external or internal elements, transferring internal elements to external elements, and repeating the process over again. Machine speeds were established with their resultant cycle times. This was done to give floor workers a target of what they were expected to produce.

They reviewed the principles of motion economy, emphasizing body, position, and eye motions because of their high time consumption and potential for improvement. They also analyzed any occurrences of double handling, complex positions, and walking motions. Tools were located closer to the point of usage and modified for more efficient handling.

Supplier Scrap

The lean manufacturing class then focused on the suppliers who were contributing to the scrap because of foreign particles in the supplied product. Historically at Gelman Sciences, the primary contact between the company and its suppliers was through the materials purchasing department. The prevailing opinion was that Gelman was such a small purchaser of supplied parts that complaints concerning supplier quality would be ignored by suppliers. Moreover, the specifications given to suppliers concerning foreign particles permitted, in most cases, an average quality level (AQL) of 2.5% defects. This policy reflected quality control practices dating back to the Military Standard 105 of World War II. Gelman's incoming quality procedure was to sample the supplied products. If a lot was found to have excessive defects, a report was issued to the supplier, but the material was almost always used anyway due to the lack of time to obtain a new lot.

Lots of material from suppliers were received by truck and offloaded into the warehouse. Receiving inspection would sample the product within the lot and then place the lot in storage. Whenever a product was scheduled, the appropriate quantities of material would be withdrawn from the lot and "staged" with other necessary materials for a production run. The staged material was then trucked to the plant (approximately 1000 feet) and off-loaded on the plant's incoming material dock.

All of the supplier products were received in cardboard boxes with double-bagging to keep contamination from the product. The parts were removed from the boxes and the outer bag just prior to entering the manufacturing area, which was in a clean room-type environment. The lean manufacturing class's homework was to chart the flow of incoming materials to determine where contamination might occur and to attempt to minimize the double handling of supplies. Further, the class examined the incoming quality control procedures and product specifications.

The class found that the major source of contamination came primarily from two suppliers. A contingent of the managers and engineers visited the supplier plants to determine if the suppliers could do a better job of reducing the contamination. These visits and subsequent visits by the suppliers served to sensitize the class to the need for a systematic method of communicating the specific needs of the plant. The contingent found that although each supplier did not have a good understanding of the quality needs, they were very interested in helping to fulfill these needs, and a few simple steps would attain this.

The class completely evaluated the incoming material system and proposed the eventual elimination of the warehouse. Their accomplishments included improving supplier quality and reducing double handling of incoming materials. The lean manufacturing class understood that their current system involved unnecessary redundancies and inefficiencies that were a cost to the company.

Process Control Procedures

Most of the engineering staff of the plant attended the lean manufacturing classes. Their responses and questions revealed that their level of understanding of the plant processes was, in most cases, superficial. Their emphasis had been on new processes, which did not require them to be knowledgeable about existing processes. The existing processes had been developed by the research and development (R&D) department and then "handed-over" to manufacturing. Unfortunately, knowledge of how to run the processes to produce high quality and productivity was not transferred very well, partly because of the manufacturing engineers' antagonism toward R&D. There were various reasons for this, including the transfer of poorly developed processes.

A well-known concept in process control is that if you standardize the operational procedures and run the process within pre-specified limits, a good product will be produced. Walt proposed that this method be followed. There were five "generic" processes in the plant at this time:

1. Slitting (later moved to Pensacola)
2. Pleating
3. Seaming
4. Endcapping
5. Testing

Walt proposed designating an engineer as the primary technical person for each of these processes, and giving them the primary assignment of determining the most appropriate operational procedures. They chose slitting as the first generic area, and Sarah Neill (Sarah), a manufacturing/industrial engineer, as the expert. Sarah and Walt established the following procedures:

1. Obtain and read all of the R&D reports and experiments regarding slitting and the impact of slitting on quality.
2. Revise the measurement methods to minimize measurement errors.
3. Establish standardized setup procedures. This work required equipment rebuilds, new slitter wheels, and slitter spacers.
4. Teach operators the new procedures.
5. Establish cleanliness standards.
6. Perform process capability studies and revise the slit width specifications.

The result of this effort was a 400 percent reduction in slit width variability, greatly reduced setup time, and less contamination.

A secondary result was that Gelman Sciences could modify the specifications of material slit at suppliers with confidence that the new specifications could be achieved.

Pleating was the next operation chosen, and the same procedure was used. Sarah was the lead engineer again because she had learned how to do the work and because the establishment of pleating procedures required an intimate knowledge of slitting. The other manufacturing engineers were assigned specific tasks to assist Sarah.

Sarah and Walt's involvement in all of the successive processes made them realize the interdependencies among the processes. For example, the endcaps would not seal properly if there were problems with the slit width. This realization led to a series of design of experiments (DOEs) in which the independent variables were the slit widths, the amount of overlap of materials, material thickness, pleater temperature, seam temperature, and seam overlap. The dependent variables were percentage of defects and location of defect.

The exercise of designing, running, and analyzing the DOE provided tremendous insight into how to make a filter that was defect-free. Walt and Sarah further modified specifications and standard operating procedures to reflect this knowledge. An important benefit of this work was that visual standards now existed to tell a good product from a bad product. For example, if the end seam exhibited a dislocation of more than 1/32 inch, the defect rate would be high. Sarah and Walt's systematic examination of the generic processes led to a number of engineering projects. This type of knowledge was needed for future manufacturing progress.

Supply Chain Management

In 1993, Gelman started a plastic parts ship-to-stock program. They put together a team consisting of quality, manufacturing, engineering, and purchasing to begin the process of evaluating what was needed to improve plastic part quality. It was at this time that quality introduced first "article inspection," process capability requirements, and mold flow analysis. These documents called for more stringent requirements and process control from suppliers.

Also, the team began auditing larger molders as potential partners. Prior to this, Gelman Sciences had eleven molders, all small shops, none of which understood process capability analysis or had proper measurement equipment. They chose one new supplier and kept three old suppliers to consolidate the molding. They told the old suppliers that they had to respond to the new requirements, but that doing so would result in further business. The mold engineer was purposely kept out of the selection process because of bias toward certain molders. The entire process was long and painful but successful.

While the operations group was focusing on adding value to its activities, the materials procurement group was beginning to do the same based on the lean concepts they were learning. Prior to 1994, supplier management consisted of placing an order, followed by screaming matches to determine the delivery and cheapest price. The production manager stated that he never wanted to run out of component parts. Therefore, the material handlers kept months of component inventory stashed away on the production floor. Customer management consisted of making the customer wait for an unknown time for special requests until their components arrived.

In the fall of 1994, the materials manager and buyer positions were modified to start reporting directly to the plants. This was the first step in moving many corporate resources into the product or value stream. Bryon Marks (Bryon) was appointed senior purchasing agent and tasked by upper management to draft and implement a strategy for the procurement of Gelman Sciences membranes used in its products for Plant One. This strategy focused on value and was based on developing partnerships and sharing the savings that resulted. Bryon ordered product to minimize the handling required by Gelman Sciences after it hit the dock. Raw membrane material was purchased already slit to specified widths. This shortened the product lead times and lowered the inventory level by eliminating the membrane bulk width stock completely. A certified supplier system was implemented that cut down on rework of incoming parts. Incoming inspections were eliminated when suppliers were able to demonstrate that they were meeting specifications all of the time. As with the molders, the number of suppliers was consolidated.

Results of Lean Education

Bryon knew that Greg Scheessele, the vice president of operations, had a goal of one-day lead times and perfect customer delivery performance, but with the current batch-and-queue production, any improvements were minor. The lean manufacturing education introduced everyone involved to the techniques pioneered by Toyota Motor Company. They knew that to achieve the envisioned goals, the whole production system, including the supply chain would have to be converted to lean manufacturing, and that this would involve the introduction of just-in-time (JIT) parts delivery and production.

Formation of the CI Steering Committee

One year into the CI team process, the CI team consultant, Susan Heathfield, encouraged the company to hire a full-time person to monitor the progress of the teams in late 1994. The teams were getting stalled on issues and having trouble communicating their goals. Gelman searched for an internal candidate but could not agree on one person, feeling most candidates would favor one plant over another. Susan suggested a cross-functional steering committee including finance, engineering, quality, planning, and operations.

In July 1995, the company started the continuous improvement steering committee for Plant One. The group decided to meet with each of the 15 CI teams at least once per year (and more often with troubled teams). The committee would look at the projects, team minutes, mission statements, and objectives of the teams. They broke up larger teams (more than 20 members) to increase everyone's involvement. A team's presentation to the steering committee was expected to be very informal, with a limited amount of handout material, but the teams started preparing elaborate presentations up to two months before their meeting. The result was an attractive-looking handout that lacked weight because the team meetings were used as practice for the "firing squad." The committee knew that something had to change, but they were not sure what.

At this point in late 1995, most of the CI teams were process-based or a mixture of process- and product-based. For example, the Seam Team was made up of eight members who represented the various seaming methods across all the product-lines. The Polypure Team was the lone, purely product-based team. The operations staff was looking into cellular manufacturing on the plant floor and considering a product-based setup with cell concepts for the Polypure Team to see whether any improvements would be possible.

Cellular Manufacturing Experiment and Education

Before anyone had a true understanding of cellular manufacturing, the plant operations staff went ahead and set up a test cell on a line consisting of three operations and two workers—pleating of the membrane, seaming of the pleated material, and endcapping of the tubed material (this was a non-integrity-tested product). Prior to this, large quantities of WIP would build up between seaming and endcapping (one operator was already running both pleating and seaming with one-piece flow between). One supervisor recalled having 120 tubs of WIP between seaming and endcapping prior to the experiment, each with 35 pieces. Hence, 4,200 pieces were sitting in queue. This equated to about seven standard shifts of in-process inventory between the successive operations.

Experimental Polypure Cell

Plant One organized a lean manufacturing group made up of individuals from the operations staff (maintenance, engineering, production) in January 1996 to help focus on constrained areas and to lay out the Polypure Cell (see Photo 9-1). The group met every two weeks and focused on improving bottleneck processes by assigning projects to certain individuals. The goals were to decrease downtime and improve responsiveness to floor problems.

In early 1996, they moved the endcapping station closer to the other two operations to put the cell concept in place. The operations staff believed that simply by moving the machines closer (but still 16 feet apart) and setting WIP limits of three tubs while using conveyors to move the tubs, a cell would be born. It soon discovered,

Photo 9-1. Polypure Cell

however, that the conveyor was a bad idea ("moving warehouses") because it was constantly filled to its maximum length and did not allow immediate root-cause analysis. But since the machines were not close enough for part hand-offs or chutes, little could be done but reduce the maximum number of tubs of WIP.

Even with this imperfect solution, the results of simply controlling WIP levels on the Polypure Cell were encouraging. Table 9-1 sums up the progression of the Polypure Cell through an eight-month period (March to November 1996) achieved by further tightening WIP limits prior to a final cell configuration. Inventory turns

Table 9-1. Polypure Cell Results

Cell #2	March 1996	June 1996	November 1996
Inventory turns	20	30	57
Inventory value	$86,000	$67,000	$33,000
Normal lead times	3–4 weeks	1–3 days	1–3 days
Expedited lead times	1–3 days	Same day	Same day

increased 185 percent, inventory levels decreased 62 percent, and lead times were reduced over 86 percent.

Society of Manufacturing Engineers Seminar Training

By seeing the positive results from the Polypure Cell from simplified, but still far from optimal, manufacturing, the plant operations staff was now committed to switching the entire facility to cellular methods. But first the plant manager, Doug Broughman, sent four individuals—supervisors Luanne Ignasiak and Doug Fett and manufacturing/industrial engineers Sarah Neill and Matt Zayko—to a seminar on planning manufacturing cells that was sponsored by the Society of Manufacturing Engineers (SME). The purpose was to learn what tools could be applied in the plant to switch over to cells and subsequently to teach the entire operations staff.

The cell planning seminar focused on organizing similarly produced parts into families and arranging the equipment around their process flows. The attendees charted a mock product from its initial to final operations on a process flow chart while classifying all steps as one of five elements (operation, transport/handling, storage, inspection, delay). Other tools that were stressed included calculating takt time (keeping up with the demand at which a customer orders a product), designing various shaped cells (L, U, straight line), forming self-directed work teams, developing long-term and short-term planning, and more.

Reorganization of CI Teams to Cell Teams

Realizing that they could not efficiently plan the cells without including floor personnel in the critical aspects of planning, management decided to educate the entire floor staff on cellular manufacturing concepts. First, a drastic change had to take place—all CI teams had to be realigned into product-based cell teams. For the cells to work, the cell teams had to organize people around machines specific to a product line.

Management organized the former 15 plant teams into eight cell teams—five pre-assembly, two final assembly, and one flexible cell (midnight shift). Eight training sessions were planned, in the order of cell urgency, to educate personnel in all the new cells. Each session was one week (five days); training lasted two hours per day in the afternoon to accommodate day and afternoon shifts. The midnight training was held early in the morning at the end of that shift. The supervisors and engineers who attended the SME seminar would transfer their new-found knowledge to the operations personnel.

Group Leader Issues

The group leader position presented a problem that hampered a quick switch to cell teams. Previously, a group leader oversaw the activities on a certain set of machines. For example, the pleating group leader would help schedule five pleating machines of three types. He or she would aid in setups and scrap reporting but would not run production during the shift. The group leader's knowledge was deep-rooted in the one operation but limited elsewhere. Therefore, by shifting to cells, there would now be a shift in demands on leaders—the role of the group leader would have to be replaced by that of cell facilitator. The CI steering committee would work on defining this role in the coming months.

Cell Training Program

On the first day of a cell's training period, the newly formed teams were given a list of results expected from the training, a definition of cellular manufacturing, and the difficulties and advantages in switching to cells, such as reduced material handling, higher quality, faster problem-solving, and more. Teams were also encouraged to keep a running-issues worksheet for questions that could not be answered at that time, such as how components would be brought to the cell. This material was included in a packet put together by the four cell training leaders who had attended the Society of Manufacturing Engineers seminar. This material represented the text for the week. Time was reserved at the end of this first day to make sure everyone understood the concepts of cell manufacturing and how they tied into the lean manufacturing activities already going on.

Developing a process flowchart

On the second day, the cell teams developed a process flowchart for a product in their cell. Matt Zayko led the teams in defining every step (operation, transport, etc.) that the product followed from setup of material through shipping. They tracked the steps on a dry-erase board. The cell teams learned that of the five elements used to classify the steps, only one, the operation, was a value-added element. All the other elements were non-value added and something for which the customer was unwilling to pay. Also, cell members rarely knew every operation done on products within their cell, due to the old batch-and-queue, dedicated operations.

Members were surprised to see how repetitive some steps were in their flows. No quantities were initially input for times and distances on this day. Instead, at the end of the second day, cell members were assigned homework to fill in all the blanks left on the chart, which included cycle times, machine distances, and more. Furthermore, homework was also assigned to measure the footprints of all machines, racks, trash barrels, WIP/staging areas, etc. for later use on the fourth day of training. Measurements and distances were easily estimated, since each floor tile was one square foot.

Filling in the process flowchart

Before the third training class, the trainers met with each cell member to make sure that each understood the previous days' concepts and had gathered the necessary information (for example, cycle times, machine areas). When it was confirmed that all information was collected, the third day of class began by filling in all the blanks in the process flowchart. There was some general discussion on the redundancies of handling and transporting. After all data was input, the instructors tabled the discussion until the next day to allow time to formulate a final chart and compute distances, times, etc.

Standardized work procedures

The other topics on the third day centered around the development of standardized work procedures and were presented by Sarah Neill. The procedures included cycle time analysis, capacity analysis, line balancing, takt time calculation, quality control through the establishment of standard WIP levels, visual control systems, and cell progress measurement. The group spent the largest amount of time stressing the importance of calculating takt times. This was done by showing the cell members how to calculate the necessary production rate for the cell based upon product demand for the week or month.

The cell teams were then shown how to balance their line based upon the necessary takt time. From this, they could then calculate the number of people they needed to run the cell. The intent was that the cell would use this tool to calculate expected production when they were understaffed or to get additional help from their supervisor when it was needed to meet demand.

Introducing visual control systems

Once the cell members understood these techniques, they were introduced to visual control systems, such as production boards and tool boards located at the machines. Although some people were uncomfortable with posting their daily production for all to see, they were comfortable with the reasoning behind it. It was stressed that the production board would be used as a tool by management to check on daily progress and to troubleshoot processes when production fell behind. It would also be used by engineering to monitor how well preventive maintenance (PM) programs and process improvements were working.

Also, the trainees were told up front that the main purpose of the production board was to keep people (particularly in engineering and maintenance, who would be asked to answer for lost production due to machine downtime) motivated to help on the floor. The tool boards were introduced as a form of standard housekeeping. They were constructed so that a tool could only fit in one spot. If it was not there, it was missing, and a new one needed to be ordered. Tags were also put on the board indicating the vendor and part number of purchased tools, so that replacement would be quick and easy. Photo 9-2 shows the Disposable Capsule Filter (DCF) Cell with its visual production board and tool board systems.

The purpose was to develop standard procedures for running a cell. Previous to this, operators had their own method of setting up their machines, as well as running them. Setup times, quality levels, and production rates varied widely between operators. Furthermore, certain jobs were considered so complicated that only the most

Photo 9-2. DCF Cell

talented workers could learn them. After cell training, however, when cross-training began, it was discovered that with proper training, documentation, and methods, almost any worker could master any job.

Final version of process flowchart
The fourth day of training focused on the process flowchart. Matt Zayko had prepared a final version of the process flowchart—a visual flowchart of the process showing distances and times. He also prepared a summary that computed the total travel distance, total throughput time, operating time (value-added time), and the percentage of overall time that the product had value added during processing. Typical process flowcharts were 30 steps long with four or five value-added operations and less than 2 percent value-added time while in process. Figure 9-3 shows the DCF Cell process flow summary. Travel distances were on the order of 1.5 times the length of the plant floor. After these observations and presentations were made, the group discussed ways to cut the wastes in their cell.

Members began to see how limiting WIP drastically cut throughput time. The cell team also saw how they could reduce distances by moving machines closer and flowing product in a nonlinear path. This transition led to the design of cells.

Designing cells

The manufacturing engineers and supervisors discussed the various shapes of cells and their advantages and disadvantages with the group. Cell shapes included straight-line, L-shaped, and U-shaped. Matt Zayko had the footprints of the cell machines, racks, etc., that

Operation	○
Transport	⇨
Inspection	☐
Storage	▽
Delay	D

Step	Description: DCF capsule line	Distance (feet)	Time (seconds)	○	⇨	☐	▽	D
1	Setup material on pleater #1							✕
2	Pleating process	2	35	✕				
3	Repeat step #2 99 times		3465					✕
4	Put tub in queue						✕	
5	Repeat steps 2–4 two times		7000					✕
6	Transport to seamer	25			✕			
7	Seaming process	3	61	✕				
8	Repeat step #7 49 times		2989					✕
9	Put tub in queue						✕	
10	Repeat steps 7–9 two times		6100					✕
11	Transport to endcapping	97			✕			
12	Endcapping process		53	✕				
13	Sample test 5	28			✕			
14	Repeat step #12 99 times		2623					✕
15	Put tub in queue						✕	
16	Repeat steps 12, 14, and 15 two times		5300					✕
17	Transport to test queue	15			✕			
18	Delay at test queue (two days)		172800					✕
19	9-station process		510	✕				
20	Drying process (four hours)		14400	✕				
21	Delay/Transport to release area	4			✕			✕
22	Transport to module inventory	90			✕			
23	Storage at module inventory						✕	
	Totals	264	215336	5	5	1	4	9

5 value-added elements (operations) of 24 elements
Total value-added time = 1975 sec. = 32.9 min.
Total processing time = 215,336 sec. = 59.8 hrs.
% of value-added time vs. total processing time = 0.9%

Figure 9-3. DCF Process Flowchart

were previously measured by the team. He had made paper cut-outs of each piece of equipment to scale to show a mock cell on a magnetic board. The cell team was shown its existing shape on the board, which usually extended past the boundaries. Product flow was zig-zagged without pattern, and work areas were cluttered with racks, tables, and WIP.

Next, the cell team had to devise an example for each of the three shapes while utilizing counterclockwise material flow. They instructed Matt where to lay out the equipment on the board. When it was not clear how the team wanted the layout, the team was encouraged to present their ideas individually. Some individuals were concerned about being too close to each other or too constrained, even when plenty of space existed. These critics were quieted when the benefits of reduced WIP, travel, and processing times were estimated. Each cell team decided on about three designs that satisfied cell manufacturing requirements. These designs were recorded and put on file for the future layout.

Ergonomics training and standard work procedures

The final day of training was a methods analysis and standardized work presentation by an engineering intern, Mike Smith, that focused on motion economy and ergonomics. The cell teams were taught not only the most efficient ways to unload/load machines, but also the safest. The goal was to limit idle time and reduce repetitive stress injuries (RSIs). Left- and right-hand analysis revealed that work between the hands was not equal on most of the machines, thus leading to balance fatigue. Cell teams watched a videotape of a machine running within their cell and analyzed it for inefficient motions or high-risk contributions to stress injuries.

After the training, Mike continued to work with the cells to develop standard work procedures for running machines, a process that continues today through the support of others. This part of the program seemed to meet with the most resistance. Many of the operators were long-time employees of Gelman Sciences and found it very difficult to change habits. They also found it difficult to believe that their fatigue level and productivity could be changed based upon something so simple as switching the hand they held their parts in. Some workers agreed to try the new methods for a one-week period, and soon began out-producing their peers. Furthermore, they were less tired at the end of the day. Due to peer pressure, some of the more resistant workers reluctantly began to practice the new methods. The cells agreed that all new workers would be trained in the standard methods (see Photo 9-3).

Cell cross-training

After a team completed its week of training, the first item they concentrated on was cross-training. Because cell manufacturing requires the flexibility of all team members to know the entire process, it was time to give hands-on education to everyone. This would be a difficult task, because the plant formerly operated in a batch-and-queue mode whereby operators ran their dedicated machines full-tilt every day, no matter what the upstream or downstream process was doing. If they stopped to help a fellow operator on a setup or problem, their hourly production totals would diminish and count against them in their review.

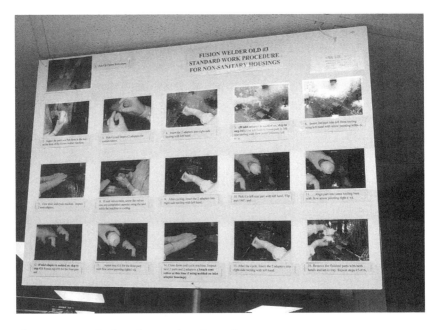

Photo 9-3. Standard Work Procedure Example

The cross-training matrix in Figure 9-4 is based on an article from Baudin in *IIE Solutions* (Baudin, 1996: 32). The matrix measures training proficiencies of up to five levels through the use of pie quarters. Prior to the cell training, no teams had any visual record of cross-training (it did not exist). The speed in which they embraced the new matrix gave encouragement to management that the concepts of cell manufacturing were sinking in.

Since a total plant re-layout would not occur for a few months, maximum WIP levels were placed between all machines that were on the order of 60 minutes' worth of inventory. Some machines were located next to one another, yet material was still passed in batches! These machines integrated chutes to aid one-piece flow and eliminate double-handling, and decreased WIP to almost nothing.

Supor Cell results
The results of the training were encouraging to all involved. Cell teams began to implement changes on their own. For example,

Associates	Seaming	Pleating	Endcapping	Testing #1	Testing #2	Tape changes
Days						
Louie	●	◔	○	◔	○	○
Mary	◔	●	◕	◔	○	○
Rosie	◔	●	●	◑	◑	●
Michael	◔	◑	○	●	●	○
Tina	●	◕	●	◔	◔	◑
Don	○	●	○	○	○	○
Afternoons						
Tim	●	◔	◑	◔	○	◔
Neal	◔	◔	◑	●	●	○
Andy	●	◕	◑	○	◑	○
Julie	◔	◑	●	◔	○	◔
Sheryl	◔	●	●	◑	●	●
●	=	Fully-trained and ability to train others in all aspects				
◕	=	Three-quarter trained and ability to setup and run machine without supervisor				
◑	=	Half-trained and ability to run machine without supervision				
◔	=	Quarter-trained and ability to run machine with some supervision required				
○	=	Still need one-on-one training while learning the process				

Figure 9-4. DCF Cell Cross-Training Matrix

before the training for the Supor Cell, the engineering staff wanted to move a seaming machine next to a pleating machine. The reasons for wanting a move were that the RSI rate was increasing alarmingly in the plant, product damage was not decreasing, cycle times were longer in the present setup, and an occasional product made it to endcapping without being seamed, mostly due to the double-handling of cartridges. The pleater would cut the pleated material, insert it into an outer tube (since the pack was springy) to form a pack, put the pack into a tub, and pass the tub to the seaming WIP area, where it would sit for hours. The seamer would then take the pack and remove the material from the outer tube, align the material into the seamer, cycle the machine, remove the seamed material, and re-insert it into the outer tube. Because of the springiness of the material, tight pinch and high force power grips were needed, thus causing tendinitis and leading to carpal-tunnel syndrome. Prior to the cell training, the engineering staff had proposed that the line do hand-offs between the pleating and seaming stations with zero WIP. The workers were opposed. They wanted plenty of space and WIP, which they thought was efficient since it was a buffer against machine breakdowns. The move of the seamer next to the pleater was unsuccessful.

After the members of this team were trained in cell concepts and methods analysis, the manufacturing engineers and supervisors walked onto the production floor to see the seaming machine moved next to the pleating machine with the pleater handing off each part to the seamer. Some cell members resisted this effort and moved the seamer back, but it was soon a permanent fixture next to the pleater. All WIP between these two operations was eliminated, RSIs have declined (zero in the last six months) due to removal of the double handling, and the two machines now work in a rhythm with each other. No one forced the cell team to move—they had become educated and motivated enough to do it themselves.

Role changes

One problem encountered with the new cell team structure was in integrating the group leader role, discussed above, into each cell. The CI steering committee wanted each cell to be led by a cell facilitator who would have a thorough understanding of the entire cell and who would be the first line of responsibility for smooth production runs. During the cell training sessions, the steering committee had to decide how to transform the group leader position and also to set new levels of pay and requirements for all cell members.

Originally, the steering committee thought that they should post the position to show that a new mindset was taking shape. The group leaders were defensive about this and believed that they deserved to be the cell facilitators because they had the best leadership abilities on the floor. But the steering committee was concerned that the group leaders, who had supervised only one machine area, lacked knowledge about the entire cell. No production personnel, however, fit this need. The steering committee wondered whether the group leaders were motivated enough to change existing attitudes and learn all processes.

The group leaders and CI steering committee met to discuss the visions that each had. The steering committee decided that the group leaders would evolve into the cell facilitator roles if they successfully provided written justification and a job description as they saw it. In other words, the steering committee wanted a guarantee that the group leaders were willing to change along with everyone else.

The group leaders developed a transition plan to detail what roles and expectations would change in their duties over time. The plant manager and supervisors changed the existing job descriptions for all production personnel to focus more on teamwork rather than individualism. In addition, a new pay level was added to take into account operators becoming more highly skilled at multiple stations.

A 90-day review period was established for comparing new cell facilitator performances versus expectations. The steering committee met with the cell facilitators as a group to discuss what progress was being made. In addition, the supervisors met one-on-one with cell facilitators to inform them of what expectations they were and were not meeting. About 90 percent of the cell facilitators accepted and embraced their new roles whereas the other 10 percent refused to change. These 10 percent were either transferred or asked to leave. Team members are taking more ownership of their cells, while others are accelerating beyond their immediate supplier operations and becoming the benchmark for companywide manufacturing.

Configuring the Plant into Cells

A small group of the plant operations staff met to decide upon a layout of the new cell locations. The layouts from the cell training sessions would be used to plan the details of the cells, but before this could happen, a general location was required for each cell that would minimize travel distances and provide smooth flows and accessibility. All of the cells had one thing in common—they each depended on either a machine or an area that was located in a corner and was very expensive to move, such as in the two testing stations and the packaging area. These types of machines are referred to as "monuments" by James Womack and Daniel Jones in their 1996 book, *Lean Thinking* (Womack & Jones, 1996: 176). Therefore, the two test stations and the packaging area were dealt with as fixed locations. Once this was decided upon, the seven cells were located in the plan next to the fixed location they depended on.

After the general plan was completed, a cross-functional group made up of the facilities, microbiology, and operations groups (with input gathered from other areas when appropriate) was formed to finalize all details such as air handling systems, utility hook-ups, construction/destruction projects, and more. The detailing of the cell flows favored one-piece flows and U-shapes with counterclockwise flow. The plans were changed in the ensuing months due to a number of conditions, including a planned building relocation, its cancellation, a merger announcement, its termination, a new merger announcement, and planned expansion of four constrained lines. The last plan called for allocating space for these future cells and drastically changing the layout.

When a final decision was made for the layout, Matt made a precedence diagram (see Figure 9-5). Because all the cells were locating machines closer, this diagram was needed to figure out which equipment had to be moved before the others or which pieces could be moved concurrently while production continued. Twenty-one sets of items were included in the diagram. The project plan was put in place, allowing roadblock objects to be moved first to enable multitasking to occur.

Resistance to New Layout

Meanwhile, the facilities group was resistant to any changes to the existing layout. This was due in part to the numerous layout changes that had occurred in the previous decade that were sup-

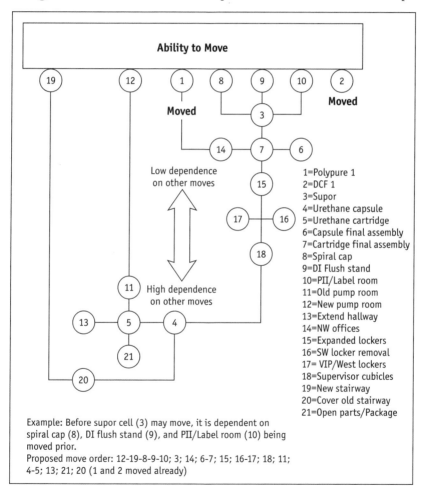

Figure 9-5. Precedence Diagram for Cell Layouts

posed to be panaceas for all constraint ills. One could understand their resistance to yet another change. The facilities group became more cooperative during the process of developing a final layout design after much prodding. Matt showed them the benefits of switching to cells by comparing measurable success indicators that the plant tracked.

DCF Cell Success

At the end of 1996, the plant manager was scheduled to give a tour to personnel from another Gelman Sciences plant that would focus on the progress achieved with product-based cell teams (before the cells were even implemented). Doug Broughman wanted to show-case all the teams on the floor but also have one team do a formal presentation on the benefits and results of cellular thinking. Teams were hesitant to volunteer because of the presentation part—many said that they were too nervous. One team, the DCF Cell, said that they would do the presentation only if they had the cell configured the way they planned during the cell training sessions.

Five days before the tour, Doug met with Matt to look at what space was available for the cell. The DCF Cell wanted to be located near the 9-station tester, which it depended on for 50 percent of its product. Fortunately, the DCF Cell could be moved without having to move any other equipment. Also, the DCF Cell Team had some of the best cell designs of various shapes to accommodate many scenarios. Therefore, the decision to go ahead and grant the cell permission to move was easy. Matt met with the cell team, went over their layout, and detailed the layout on computer. He worked with the cell team to mark the locations for the machines in masking tape. The production engineering group moved the equipment, the facilities group hooked up all lines, and the cell was set up and ready for operation in less than 24 hours. Figure 9-6 shows a before and after look at the DCF Cell move.

Table 9-2 shows the results achieved by simply moving the machines in the product-based DCF Cell closer. The table includes the batch-and-queue mentality in March 1996, the shift to cell thinking in June 1996 when maximum WIP levels were set, and the final configuration to cell manufacturing in November 1996. At

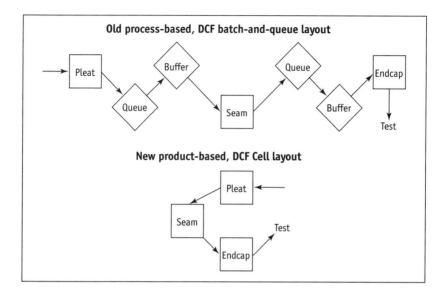

Figure 9-6. DCF Cell Before and After Progression

first, parts would be rushed through a process operation and wait, and the process would repeat twice more. Furthermore, parts would be passed between operations in tubs that held up to 200 pieces. A machine would have virtually no WIP one minute and 200 pieces the next after being flooded with a tub. After the cell was moved and machines were located next to each other, no space was available for WIP buildup (the easiest way to limit WIP) and in-process pieces were passed between operations via hand-offs or chutes. First-piece processing times, the time taken to complete the first piece of the job, were reduced almost 99 percent (6 hours to 4 minutes).

Table 9-2. DCF Cell Evolution Results

DCF cell	March 1996	June 1996	November 1996
WIP between machine in cell	1600 pieces	400 pieces	0
1st piece processing times	>3 days	6 hours	<4 minutes
Throughput time (entire 500 piece job)	>3.25 days	10 hours	5 hours
Distance traveled per part (feet)	>250	127	18

Even though no other machines had been moved at this point, the benefits of limiting WIP and working on product-based cell teams began to show. The following five plantwide performance indicators showed significant improvements the six months following the cell training sessions:

1. Customer delivery performance (CDP)
2. Inventory value
3. Inventory turns
4. Scrap and material usage variance per unit
5. Production lead time

Scrap and lead times were used as evidence that cell manufacturing was not simply another "program of the week."

Customer delivery performance
Customer delivery performance measures the percentage of on-time delivery to Gelman Sciences, Inc. customers. Typical CDP values were on the order of 75 percent in 1993, 85 percent in 1994, and 88 percent thereafter. Figure 9-7 shows the CDP over a 16-month period for

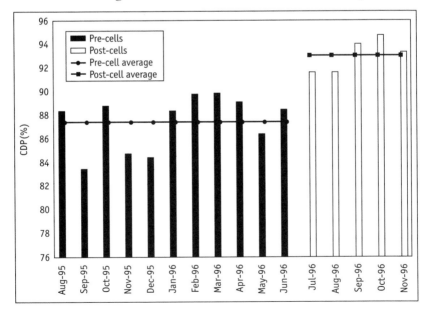

Figure 9-7. On-Time Customer Delivery Performance (CDP)

the plant, the last six months of which occurred after the formation and training of the cell team. Prior to the cell manufacturing training, the CDP had never exceeded 90 percent for a month in the plant. In the six months following, the CDP averaged 94 percent. The products were processed through the chain faster with reduced WIP between machines. Note that this was before the entire cell layout was implemented, which was still underway at the time of this writing.

Inventory value

The reduced WIP on the floor was verified by an analysis of inventory value over the same period used with CDP. Figure 9-8 shows the weekly inventory values for raw components through finished goods in the entire plant. For the period prior to cell manufacturing training, inventory values averaged $3.8 million. Post-cell training values for the following six months averaged $2.7 million. The downward slope was steepened after the training by 50 percent. By focusing on smaller job sizes and quicker processing times, management was able rapidly to cut the inventory costs on-hand.

Inventory turns

Inventory is turned over more rapidly by decreasing the WIP on the floor and shortening the amount of time that product spends on the floor. Figure 9-9 shows the weekly inventory turns over the same period for CDP and inventory value. The average inventory turns were 3.6 before the cell training and 4.7 after the training.

Scrap and material usage variance per unit

Another waste that decreased dramatically after the cell manufacturing methods were introduced was scrap and material usage variance (MUV) per unit. MUV is a measure of the deviation of returned material that is in stock from what is calculated to be in stock according to the inventory system. With the realignment of teams into product-based cells, the members were able to organize their efforts on the entire line to reduce scrap losses, not just at one machine center. Scrap levels have reached all-time record lows. Figure 9-10 shows the scrap and MUV per unit costs over a 16-month period.

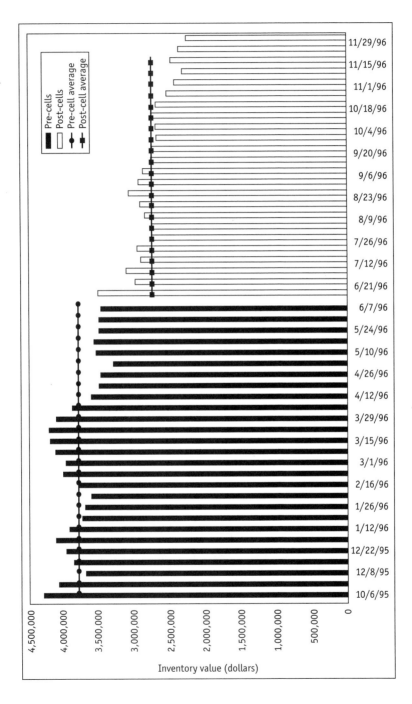

Figure 9-8. Overall Inventory Values

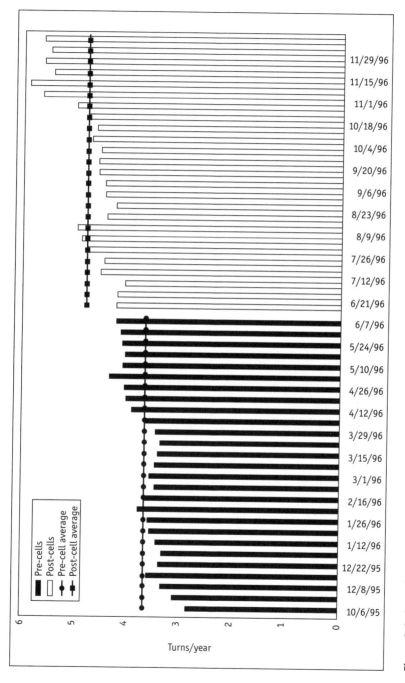

Figure 9-9. Annual Inventory Turns

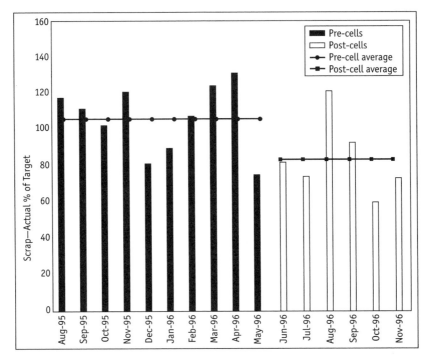

Figure 9-10. Scrap and Material Usage Variance (MUV) per Unit

Production lead times

The last major indicator observed was lead time. Lead time is the amount of time that elapses between customer order entry and shipment. The list below summarizes the progress achieved in reducing lead times. Lead times have been dropping one day for the past three quarters and will continue to drop each quarter as part of the overall plant goal. Overall, pre-assembly lead times have been reduced over 42 percent in the six months after the cell training. Pre-assembly area lead time reductions are as follows:

- Pleater No. 1 (Disposable Capsule Filter Cell) lead time reduction of 52 percent
- Pleater No. 2 (Supor Cell) lead time reduction of 49 percent
- Pleater No. 3 (Urethane Cartridge Cell) lead time reduction of 28 percent
- Pleater No. 5 (Polypure Cell) lead time reduction of 52 percent

The trends in the performance indicators provided evidence of the power of cellular manufacturing to convince any non-believers (the facilities group, for example) in the system. Even though only one cell was fully implemented, all product-based cells were showing signs of great potential by eliminating sources of waste. Customers were getting product on time more often, even though they were also having to wait less for receipt after placing their order.

Vendor improvement on DCF line
The benefits of completing entire jobs faster were immediately seen. Gelman Sciences produced most of its membrane at a facility in Florida but purchased some types from suppliers. One product's membrane, used on the DCF line, came from a new vendor with whom Gelman was working to improve their processes.

On occasion, the vendor would ship a membrane lot that was defective but that would still somehow pass both their outgoing inspection and Gelman's incoming inspection (further double-handling). Before the DCF Cell was moved, this membrane would be processed through endcapping in batches of 200–400 pieces, which took up to 12 hours to process. At endcapping, a sample test was used to reveal integrity failures, including membrane leaks. When a membrane leak was found, the entire lot of WIP (anywhere from 400–800 pieces) was scrapped.

This same scenario on the new cell layout is as follows: Only the sample size is processed through endcapping (duration less than 5 minutes); the sample size is tested for leaks, and results of integrity are known within minutes instead of hours. The sample size is scrapped instead of the entire job in the event of a leak. Gelman Sciences is able to notify the supplier immediately. Results like these transform those hesitant to embrace cell concepts into die-hard followers.

Once the DCF Cell was relocated, it was easier to arouse enthusiasm about projects among its members. One project was to eliminate time wasted looking for misplaced tooling. Working with Mike, Sarah, and Matt, the cell team designed vertical tool boards (see Photo 9-4) that allowed a "place for everything and everything in its place" (Suzaki, 1987: 25). These boards were

Photo 9-4. DCF Cell Tool Board

located at every machine. Another project standardized all work procedures within the cell. The engineering staff and assigned team members developed efficient and ergonomic ways to carry out operations. Digital pictures of each process step were put on a visual board above each machine.

Expansion of Lean Concepts
Throughout the Entire Company

The number of changes needed to implement lean production are many. Allow at least five years. Education, which is specific to the area as discussed earlier, is an important first step. In most companies like Gelman Sciences, the employees, the managers, and the engineers have had very limited exposure to other manufacturing systems. They have been asked to work hard and do the best they can under the manufacturing system as it exists. As they have worked under that system, they have become experts in its processes. This expertise generates a great source of pride, a feeling of accomplishment, and the notion that future employment is guaranteed. The concepts of lean production require the development of new skills and tend to make old ones obsolete. Everyone's goal in a lean system should be to make their role obsolete. This can be threatening to many people.

Examples of Changing Roles

Some examples of changing roles follow. With the extensive use of cell manufacturing concepts, the production supervisor no longer has to give detailed instructions to employees. Instead, he or she must respond to the requests of the cell facilitators to implement improvements developed by the teams and ensure the highest level of cooperation between shifts. The manufacturing engineer is no longer asked to lay out the workplace, but to teach the workers how to do it and then support their efforts. The quality control person, who in the past performed auditing functions, is now asked not only to do the audits but to assist actively in improving any situations that received a negative response during the audit.

Why Change When Everything Is Going Well?

An argument can be made that it is against human nature to want to change the way things are done unless there is a compelling reason to do so. If a company is likely to go out of business or if layoffs are likely due to the loss of business, organizations will attempt to change quickly to avert the pending situation. But what about a company that is prospering and whose manufacturing methods and the quality of its products are equal to or exceeding the acceptable industry levels? Why change? The answers are very obvious to the executives. A potential for a 50 percent reduction in product cost, the ability to ship on time 100 percent of the time, and a substantial improvement in product quality are convincing reasons, but they are not obvious to the floor workers.

A well-known diagram in the lean production literature shows that the only way to uncover and identify the major problems (rocks) is to lower the water level in the pond. The argument is that inventory serves to reduce the need for manufacturing organizations to focus and solve some of their major quality and production problems, so the way to cause an organization to focus and solve their problems is to reduce the inventory (water in the pond). In Gelman's case, the policy was to carry a high finished goods inventory. Yet in spite of this, the on-time delivery was less than 95 percent. The answer before lean production was to carry more finished goods inventory and to hire more expediters to "push" the product through the plant. Another prevailing feeling within the company was that it was impossible to predict how much product each of the major customers was going to order. A large amount of finished goods inventory was the only way to meet customer needs.

Spreading the Lean Concepts

At this time, the medical device division (MDD) of Gelman Sciences in Plant Two in Ann Arbor is working to switch their manufacturing setup over to a lean system. They have seen the benefits and savings that resulted from adopting lean methods in Plant One. Plant One personnel who have gone through the lean experience are serving as internal consultants to their sister facility in Ann Arbor in working with CI teams and setting up cells.

The recent merger with Pall Corporation put focus on the power of lean manufacturing. After the merger, the company planned to close down a Gelman stainless steel housing plant in California, since Pall Corporation also produced similar products at a facility in New York. But upon closer inspection, management from Pall found that Gelman had the shortest lead times in the industry for housings and decided to keep the California facility open. In the months prior to the merger, the housing plant had begun implementing lean concepts and cell manufacturing after visiting Plant One in Ann Arbor. They quickly adapted these practices to their plant and are now the benchmark for the industry. Pall Corporation recognizes the value of lean manufacturing and has invited Plant One personnel to educate other Pall facilities on the concepts.

Monthly Dinner Meetings

As part of the lean production implementation, the company established monthly dinner meetings for both Ann Arbor plants of the managers and engineers who were likely to be the most involved in leading the change. Each meeting had a pre-announced theme, which was selected by the attendees but which dealt with some aspect of lean production activities within the company. In one of the meetings, the topic was whether or not they were using the proper methods of predicting the demand of customers. Analysis of the orders of customers was presented and the weekly use rates determined. A major conclusion was that although the frequency and size of the orders had high variation, the weekly and monthly use rates were within the +/- 30 percent allowable variation of lean production systems.

After considerable discussion, the vice president of operations issued instructions that the goal was to carry no more than one week's finished goods inventory for each customer. This meant that the lot size for each product was to be one week's consumption. The time schedule to accomplish this was two months for the two plants in Ann Arbor. This decision greatly accelerated the introduction of lean production concepts because the only way to achieve the finished goods inventory levels was to have reliable production systems and suppliers. Most of the group had been through the lean production training and knew who had worked on various aspects like standardized setups, cell manufacturing, process capabilities, and JIT supplier shipments, so there was plenty of knowledge available that could be used to achieve implementation quickly. It was up to the plant managers to garner these resources and to proceed.

Supplier Production Changes

The cartridge/capsule plant is primarily an assembler of supplied parts. Thus, the suppliers must embrace the concepts of lean production so they can supply parts when needed and with no quality problems. Prior to lean production, there was so much concern over a supplier having production problems that large quantities of parts were kept in inventory in the event, for example, that a die for an injection-molded part would break. This fear was so prevalent that in certain cases 1.5 years of inventory was being carried. With the introduction of the suppliers shipping the needed quantities every week, the inventories have been reduced to reach the goal of direct shipment to the plant on a weekly basis with no parts inventory in the warehouse. Investigation of the probability of a die breaking revealed that if the supplier properly maintains the dies, the chances of major breakage are greatly reduced. As a matter of fact, a major breakage had not even occurred in the history of the company.

Lean manufacturing has created a *pull inventory system*. The new system starts with the end customer who places the order. This causes a manufacturing order to be created, which in turn causes procurement of the needed final configuration component items and the necessary module. By issuing the module for this final configuration, a "pulling" action is created to build more modules. Component items are pulled through the cell. This activity then pulls component inventory from the supplier. This is the foundation for supply chain management.

Suppliers now understand that large production runs are a thing of the past for the plant. This is mirrored in the increased number of certified suppliers. The only inventory needed is the amount to support the production schedules. Any more inventory is wasteful and costly. Not only is there a carrying cost involved, but excess inventory lends itself to damage or contamination while being stored and even becoming obsolete.

Product Design Observations

Just as the operations group is focusing on standardizing activities on the plant floor, the plant materials group, led by Bryon Marks, is standardizing component parts for greater efficiency. The group has worked with product design engineers to design products with parts that are currently used, where applicable. This leads to economies of scale. Tooling costs decrease and lead times are compressed. The capabilities and characteristics of the parts are already known. Another area that has used standardization is packaging. Suppliers now ship the product to Gelman Sciences in smaller batches, based on production run sizes. For example, a plastic supplier used to ship two component parts in separate 30 x 20 x 26-inch boxes. This box was big and awkward to handle. It also contained too many parts, now that smaller batch sizes are in use. By communicating the new requirements to the supplier, Gelman Sciences now receives the two parts "kitted" together in one box that is 10 x 20 x 13-inches in size.

Material when received is no longer being converted into a product for use. It arrives on the dock in the form that is needed for assembly. Suppliers also ship the inventory with minimal amounts of packaging. One supplier's products used to take over one hour to unpack and now take less than five minutes.

Working with Customers

Customer service personnel have been educated in lean manufacturing concepts. They understand the cost savings that result with smaller batch sizes and less inventory on-hand, both for Gelman and its customers. Customer service is working with Gelman customers to establish more frequent shipping of smaller lots instead of infrequent large lots. Other customers that are able accurately to forecast demand are on a "continuous replenishment" program whereby they receive the same quantity of product at regular delivery intervals.

Kanban vs. Materials Resource Planning Inventory Systems

Gelman Sciences is moving toward a true kanban inventory system. The goal is to have this pull system for all the cells within one year. Kanban is a visual system that differs vastly from the old materials resource planning (MRP) system of Gelman. The MRP system tended to inflate lead times and inventory levels while simulating a "push" system. Machine utilization was low yet employees worked repeated overtime shifts. If inventory counts were entered incorrectly into the MRP system, chaos would result. With a visual system in place, the right amount of inventory is always on hand ready to be utilized in the manufacturing system.

Just-in-Time Deliveries

Just-in-time (JIT) techniques are being practiced by our planner, Bill Mariouw. For a true JIT system to work it must be used throughout the entire supply chain. That is the goal. Instead of forcing the suppliers to carry inventory that we once carried, Gelman is working on reducing it. To accommodate less inventory that is ordered more frequently, "milk runs" have been set up between Gelman and certain freight companies. Product is picked up at assigned areas on designated days of the week. Then scheduled deliveries are made to the Gelman plant. This allows for firmer production schedules along the entire supply chain. Service levels have improved, delivery rates have increased, and costs for freight have decreased.

Supplier Quality Improvement

Quality issues are going to require major changes in the plant structures at Gelman. Supplier quality issues in the past have been handled by the Corporate Quality Control Department and by the Purchasing Department. This procedure has been ineffective in improving supplied parts. A new organization is evolving in which an engineer will be assigned to each supplier and will work for the plant manager of the plant using the particular part. This engineer will have the following primary responsibilities:

1. Establishing the supplier specifications.
2. Deciding on the method(s) of measurement that are to be used and the frequency of use.
3. Dealing with all complaints from manufacturing regarding the supplied product.
4. Actively participating with the supplier in resolving complaints. This includes visits to the supplier and requesting the supplier's presence in the plant to resolve problems.
5. Reviewing new and modified equipment specifications for equipment that will use the parts.
6. Participating in the acceptance criteria for new and modified equipment using the parts.
7. Reporting to plant management on results achieved.
8. Reviewing any potential new supplier of the product.
9. Reviewing and approving new products, including their specifications.

This effort is necessary to coordinate the supplied parts with manufacturing requirements, since the supplier must have current knowledge of Gelman's requirements. As Gelman becomes a global company, the product requirements, even where the same parts are used, change. These changes have to be properly coordinated with the suppliers by an individual who has intimate knowledge of the process capabilities of the suppliers and the needs of Gelman's manufacturing equipment.

Space Reductions

The plant is close to completing the shift to a cell manufacturing layout and to integrating all facets of lean manufacturing. When final, the new layout will allow an additional four constrained cells to be added on the existing floor space for a greater than 50 percent capacity improvement. Productivity per worker on existing cells has increased in the range of 10 percent to 35 percent and is expected to carry over to new cells.

Revised Plant Organization

Figure 9-11 shows the organization of the plant as a result of the focus on lean production. The plant manager now has all the staff functions working directly for him that are necessary for the production cells to receive supplier, maintenance, and quality engineering support. Since the staffs are attending the cell meetings, they know first-hand the needs of the cells for their particular specialty. The cell leadership has been instructed to inform the supervision if the staffs are not responding to their needs. Their supervision can then coordinate the staff activities so that they are more responsive. The net result of these efforts and the resulting organization is a substantial increase in the problem-solving capacity at the cell level.

Lessons Learned

The following are the main conclusions and lessons learned from this effort:

1. Classroom teaching with homework assignments that require a student to work in the plant are effective in introducing lean manufacturing and quality control concepts.

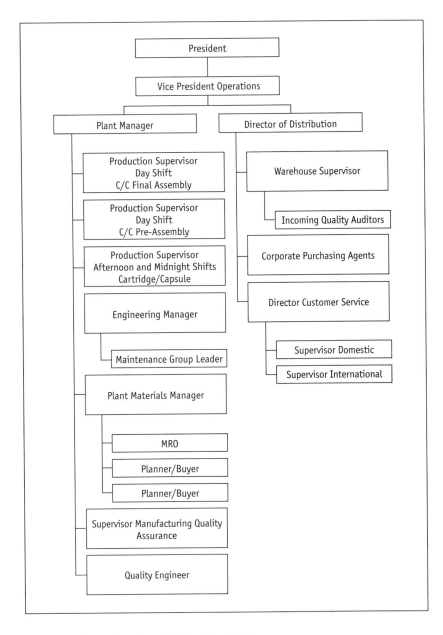

Figure 9-11. Operations Organization Chart, 1997

2. Classroom instruction has to be followed with support to continue to implement the necessary changes in the plant. Instruction without further support has little chance of succeeding.

3. Continuous improvement that focuses on individual processes is not an effective method of introducing lean production concepts. Although improvement seems to happen in short bursts (for example, physical moves), it is actually the result of concerted efforts before (training) and continuing support after the action.

4. The lean manufacturing system must be endorsed and embraced (but not necessarily started) from the top down. Anyone not willing to learn or understand lean concepts acts as a serious and costly roadblock to its implementation.

5. The manufacturing engineering function must have the technical expertise to provide leadership to the cell teams. They must be able to motivate teams to strive continually for perfection and lead by example.

6. Cell team instruction with examples from the plant is a very effective method of employee involvement. Team members must not only support the changing system but be responsible for its outcome.

7. In addition to the concepts of lean production, the cell facilitator must be taught how to lead meetings, and how to coordinate the change activities initiated by the teams and others.

8. Suppliers must be part of the total effort by delivering high-quality parts at specified times. Both suppliers and customers need to be taught the basics of lean manufacturing and the benefits and cost savings that result.

9. The quality control department must be an active partner in helping to solve root-cause problems.

10. Interviews with floor personnel indicate that lean manufacturing is preferred to and better than the old batch-and-queue method. The majority prefer to work in families or teams rather than in isolated work areas.

11. Lean manufacturing concepts greatly aid two of the main objectives in the plant—quality and delivery performance. Also, great increases in productivity and better floor space utilization lead to more space for new product cells.

Table 9-3. Gelman Sciences, Cartridge/Capsule Filter Operations

Timeline of Lean Manufacturing Progression	
Jan. 1993	Batch-and-queue mode of production in Gelman Sciences, Plant One, Cartridge and Capsule Manufacturing Operations
Feb. 1993	Greg Scheessele appointed Associate Director of Operations
Mar. 1993	Outside consultant brings in Susan Heathfield to help organize and facilitate a continuous improvement (CI) initiative
May 1993	Start of CI training to supervisors and managers (6 months)
June 1993	Doug Broughman hired as Manufacturing Manager
Nov.1993	CI team concept rolled out to hourly workforce, teams set up by process
Dec.1993	Walt Hancock of The University of Michigan brought in to look at high scrap rates
Feb. 1994	Lean manufacturing classes begin for engineers, supervisors, managers (14 weeks)
Sept. 1994	Supply chain management begins
Dec. 1994	Idea for CI steering committee
Jan. 1995	CI teams focus on improvements in their specific process areas
July 1995	CI steering committee meets for the first time
Aug. 1995	Process control investigations completed on five generic processes in plant
Jan. 1996	Experimental Polypure Cell set up with lowered work-in-process (WIP) limits
Jan. 1996	Lean manufacturing group started, consisting of maintenance, engineering, and production, with weekly meetings
Mar. 1996	Polypure Cell moved closer together (but still sixteen feet apart)
June 1996	Sarah Neill, Luanne Ignasiak, Doug Fett, and Matt Zayko attend Society of Manufacturing Engineers (SME) cell planning seminar
June 1996	Reorganization of CI teams into pure product-based, cell structure
June 1996	Weekly cell training sessions begin for the first of eight cell teams
July 1996	Group leader role examined
Sept. 1996	Cell training completed for all cell teams
Sept. 1996	Cells start working on standard work procedures, tool boards, cross-training, and more
Sept. 1996	New floor layout design starts to evolve
Oct. 1996	Disposable Capsule Filter (DCF) Cell moved
Nov. 1996	Measurable success indicators (on-time delivery, scrap, lead times, turns, inventory value) show improvement since cell thinking implemented
Dec. 1996	Manufacturing personnel job descriptions changed to advocate lean manufacturing
Jan. 1997	Final cell layout design completed
Feb. 1997	Merger completed with Pall Corporation
Feb. 1997	Polypure Cell relocated with equipment configured more tightly
Mar. 1997	Rest of floor changes begin in implementing total cell manufacturing
June 1997	Estimated completion of total facility upgrade to cell manufacturing
July 1997	Expansion of lean manufacturing throughout entire corporation

Timeline of Lean Manufacturing Progression

Lean manufacturing is not a one-time panacea or a quick fix. It is a continuous improvement process (kaizen) that is continuously applied throughout the whole organization and its supplier network. As you can see by Table 9-3, Gelman Sciences took 4.5 years before it could say it was ready to expand lean manufacturing throughout the entire corporation. There is still much work to do, with many new "rocks" to uncover. But by shifting from mass production to lean production, we are now better equipped to maintain a competitive advantage.

Note: The authors wish to make special mention of the Institute of Industrial Engineers (IIE) for publishing their article, "Lean Manufacturing Yields World Class Improvements for Small Manufacturer," in the April 1997 issue of *IIE Solutions*, 29 (4): 36-40. That publication enabled the opportunity to do a more detailed analysis of the lean manufacturing process at Gelman Sciences for this Productivity Press book.

References

Baudin, Michael. "Supporting JIT Production with the Best Wage System." *IIE Solutions* 28 (2): 30–35, 1996.

Suzaki, Kiyoshi. *The New Manufacturing Challenge*. New York: The Free Press, 1987, 255 pp.

Womack, James, and Jones. Daniel. *Lean Thinking*. New York: Simon & Schuster, 1996, 350 pp.

 **Bill Costantino** *is a lean-manufacturing specialist with RWD Technologies. He provides training, consulting services, and shopfloor implementation support to companies making the transition to lean principles. For the last three years, he has worked intimately with the development and implementation of Ford's global lean manufacturing system. Bill was one of the first 200 employees at Toyota's Georgetown plant and was heavily involved in the startup and training of team members in their plastics operations. His focus is very much shopfloor oriented, with emphasis on the transfer and development of practical lean-manufacturing skills. He has developed particular skill in the use of simulations to introduce and demonstrate the principles of lean manufacturing.*

Cedar Works: Making the Transition to Lean

by Bill Costantino

Editor's prologue: Bill Costantino worked at Toyota in Georgetown as a group leader responsible for several teams of associates and learned the Toyota Production System (TPS) firsthand. He decided to leave Toyota to help spread TPS to U.S. manufacturers. One of his clients was Cedar Works, a manufacturer of a wide variety of outdoor cedar products such as elaborate bird houses. One might imagine this to be more of a small-batch craft operation to which lean concepts do not apply, and that was the first reaction of many managers at Cedar Works. The impressive improvements in performance in this company demonstrate that the lean system indeed does work quite effectively in any manufacturing environment. Bill gives us a blow-by-blow description of selling management and the training processes that followed the plan-do-check-act (PDCA) cycle, and takes us through the stages of development. Throughout, the reader is treated to a thorough sampling of the forms and visual aids Bill used to implement lean. At the end of each stage, Bill reflects on what worked, what didn't work, and presents lessons that might help other plants progress more rapidly up the learning curve. Sit back and join Jim Obenshain, president of Cedar Works; Randy Phipps, vice president of manufacturing; Dave Meier, a fellow Toyota employee; Bill Costantino, and others as they systematically transform a grassroots company into a lean manufacturer.

This story shows us what can occur at any manufacturing plant on any scale when top management is committed to giving its full support and granting those on the shop floor the freedom and time to implement lean principles fully.

Lean manufacturing causes you to step back and actually start asking questions about why you're doing things and how you're doing things. . . . With lean, you ask the question "why are you doing what you're doing, and is it really productive?". . . down to the essence of whether what you're doing is really serving the purpose of becoming more profitable. You make the statement to the organization that it's OK to ask questions, it's OK to change, and that's your job! We're welcoming that, rather than just having you there to plug in and do what we tell you to do.

JIM OBENSHAIN, PRESIDENT

I once ranted, "Look at the incredible waste in that operation. I can't believe they are still making money and earning a profit as inefficiently as they are running out here. The productivity is so poor. People are underutilized. There is plenty of "busy-ness" but so much of the activity is wasted. Amazing! They claim they are constrained on equipment at re-saw, yet it is often down and not cutting wood for one reason or another."

Cedar Works is a small wood-processing company that makes mailboxes and bird feeders of aromatic Eastern red cedar. When I made the above observations, I had been working with this company for several months, teaching work site communication courses, and was still employed at Toyota Motor Manufacturing in Georgetown, Kentucky. I had been working with Jim Obenshain, the president of Cedar Works. The courses I was teaching were aimed at the "soft" side of the business, dealing with human relations, interpersonal skills, team building, employee discipline, coaching, and feedback. My background at Toyota opened my eyes to many problems in Cedar Works' production methods. I was struck over and over again by how inefficient many of their operations were and how much opportunity there was for improvement.

Cedar Works is a grassroots company that I have watched grow from a five-man operation working out of a Quonset hut to now more than 200 employees in two manufacturing plants. They rapidly became the largest single consumer of aromatic red cedar east of the Mississippi River. I was introduced to them in 1993, and for the previous 7 years in a row they had had record-breaking sales. They were just over $13,000,000 in net revenue with skyrocketing growth (Figure 10-1). They manufactured mailboxes, posts, decorative numbers, and an extensive line of bird feeders and accessories. The Peebles plant handled all the "rough end" processing of cutting the rough wood into dimensional component parts, as well as their mailbox products. West Union was a sister plant 14 miles away that handled final assembly of more than 25 different bird feeders (see Photo 10-1). Cedar Works was a company growing on the ingenuity of its primary founders and was struggling with phenomenal growth. They are direct suppliers to Wal-mart, Lowe's, and other large retailing chains. At this time, they were being confronted with far more demand than they could possibly supply.

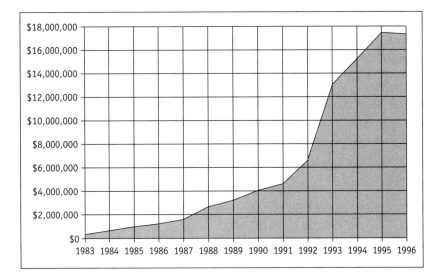

Figure 10-1. Cedar Works Net Revenue

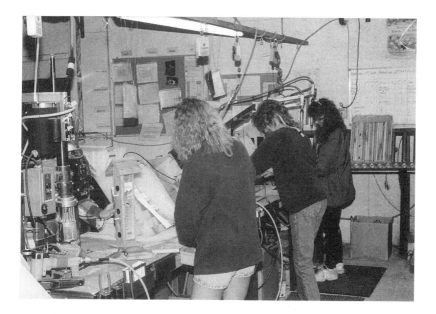

Photo 10-1. Bird Feeder Final Assembly

I had walked around the production floor many times and finally made the decision to approach Jim Obenshain about a proposal to improve his manufacturing operation. What follows is a historical account of the implementation of lean manufacturing over several years. I use a story format to describe what happened, and my main focus is on the approach we used, the key tools and disciplines we implemented, and the results we achieved.

Phase I : Attacking the Bottleneck Through Standardization

Jim and I sat in his conference room reviewing the proposal. He was uncertain whether the techniques I had been describing would really work and be of value to his company. Because Cedar Works was a small company, it did not have excess funds to waste on ineffective training. Jim had just spent a large sum of money expanding the woodworking operation and had installed a new dust collection system that used cyclone separators to accumulate chips, storing them in a huge conical hopper before they were unloaded into semi-tractor trailers. As we spoke, Jim was frequently distracted by the sound of sledge hammers banging on steel. He had turned five or six times to watch the men banging tediously on the side of the hopper to try to unload it. After the sixth time, I told Jim that the entire hopper system was a waste. If he had really thought about it, he could have designed a system to discharge directly into trucks, which would have eliminated the need for the hopper system altogether and avoided the wasted labor of banging with sledge hammers. Here was a timely illustration of what I meant by waste being non-value-added activity. Soon thereafter, Jim agreed to the first of our efforts toward implementing lean manufacturing using a 10-week program called Productivity Plus.

Productivity Plus—TPS Principles Applied

Productivity Plus was a brainstorm, a first-swing effort to see whether the principles of the Toyota Production System (TPS) actually worked outside the Georgetown plant. I launched it with the help of a friend and fellow Toyota employee, Dave Meier. We decided on a 10-week program, beginning in July 1993. Both Dave and I had an interest in training and were eager to test our ideas in the real world of production outside Toyota. We knew the most effective method would be to provide training and then allow people to apply it immediately, so our design was to meet one evening a week for 10 weeks and provide extensive homework assignments. We also realized that people learn best when they can apply the methods directly in their manufacturing areas. Because we were still employed and did not have extra vacation time, Dave and I led the training classes in the evenings from 7 to 10 P.M.

The Peebles Plant—"Re-saw Simply Can't Cut Wood Fast Enough"

After reviewing Cedar Works' production operations, we settled on the Peebles plant, which housed the "rough end" manufacturing processes. From there, we narrowed our focus to the re-saw area, which was the first manufacturing operation. Re-saw is responsible for cutting the rough wood, or *cants*, into dimensional boards. These cedar cants are the rough lumber that comes directly from local sawmills throughout the Ohio Valley. The cants can range in size from 4 inches square up to 12 inches square and can vary in length from 4 to 12 feet. The tolerance on these cants is plus or minus an eighth of an inch. After the cants are sawed into boards, they go into a drying shed for 2 to 20 days until they reach the proper moisture level. If you do not dry the wood in this manner but rush it into end product manufacturing instead, the parts tend to warp and split, making final assembly very difficult. The re-saw processes had been a production bottleneck at Cedar Works for months. "Re-saw simply can't cut wood fast enough" was the common lament of everyone at Cedar Works.

Train the trainer

The re-saw area was operating on three shifts, six days a week, when we came into the area, and it was the heaviest overtime operation in the company. We chose to work with a small group of participants in our training class, just 10 people. Jim Obenshain, the president of the company, attended 80 percent of the meetings, and demonstrated clear sponsorship and active involvement in the training. His personal investment was crucial to the overall success and was a strong endorsement of what we were doing. Randy Phipps, vice president of manufacturing, attended every meeting. He was very consistent in his support and was the champion for implementation of this process. He was closest to the actual production operations and the one directly responsible for implementation of the nitty-gritty changes on the floor. Also attending the training were Darryl Lane, the maintenance supervisor, Chris Moehlman, the traffic controller, Steve Elliott, the safety representative, Mark Moehlman, the maintenance team member, the team leaders of the re-saw area, and several assistant supervisors from Cedar Works' final assembly plant in West Union, Ohio.

Our goals and objectives for this project were very simple:

1. Provide tools, ideas, and methods to the Cedar Works team to solve problems and improve the operation.
2. Make improvements in the re-saw area as a training exercise.
3. Train the Cedar Works team to be able to implement these procedures in other areas with new team members.

Our plan was to "train the trainer" so that when Dave and I left, Cedar Works would have the capability of training others and extending the process to the rest of their organization. We felt confident that the general concepts we taught would solve their immediate problems as well as provide solutions in their long-term operations.

We met weekly from 7:00 to 10:00 P.M. We spent 50 percent of our time in classroom instruction, gaining familiarity with key principles. The other 50 percent was spent out on the floor illustrating what we were talking about and observing the processes. Both Dave and I had been through hundreds of hours of training programs at Toyota and had seen clearly that classroom lectures without practice on the production floor were doomed to failure. We took a very simple approach, giving bite-size pieces of information to people, making sure they understood it, and then asking them to apply it immediately.

A good example of this is illustrated in Figure 10-2 on identifying non-value-added activity (NVA), a homework sheet that we gave to participants following session 1. The seven forms of waste, or non-value-added activity, listed on the sheet are central to the concept of continuous improvement. After orienting the team to the seven types of waste, we asked them to identify problems out in the manufacturing area. We asked participants to keep the sheets with them during the day and make observations of their work area, jotting down notes during lunch, breaks, or other slack times. Feedback was very good. We received a diverse, large, ungainly list of problems, ranging from low morale to cold temperatures in the building. Now we needed to brainstorm, narrow the list, and focus on a few select problems.

Problem identification process
Figure 10-3 is another example of a homework work sheet given to participants to help focus our efforts. Once we narrowed the problem list, we applied a more detailed analysis by using the 4M process; that is, examining the problems from the viewpoint of Man, work Methods, Machine operations and Materials. Then we applied the Five Whys to identify root causes (Figure 10-4). As we

Identifying Non-Value-Added Activity

Instructions: For your process, identify at least one example of each type of waste. Identify as many other examples of non-value-added activity as possible, either in your area or other processes throughout the shop.

7 types of waste	Process	Example
1. Over production Producing more than is needed before it is needed.		
2. Waiting Any nonwork time waiting for tools, supplies, parts, etc.		
3. Conveyance Wasted effort to transport materials, parts, or finished goods into or out of storage or between processes.		
4. Processing Providing higher quality than is necessary, extra operations, etc.		
5. Inventory Maintaining excess inventory of raw materials, parts in process, or finished goods.		
6. Motion Any wasted motion to pick up parts or stack parts. Also wasted walking.		
7. Correction Repair or rework.		

Figure 10-2. Worksheet for Identifying Non-Value-Added Activity

went through the more detailed analyses of these problems, the root cause often turned out to be a lack of defined or consistent work procedures. This led us quite naturally into the topic of standardized work.

Standardized work was one of the cornerstones Dave and I hoped to embed in the Cedar Works organization. Along with standardized work came other fundamental tools and ideas, such as

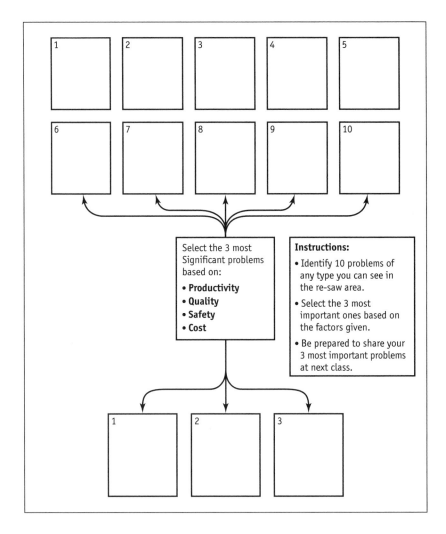

Figure 10-3. Worksheet for Identifying Problems

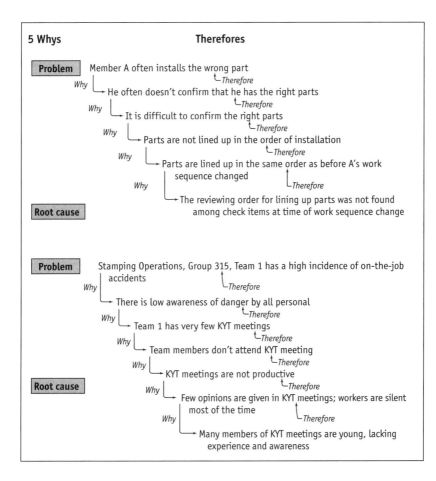

Figure 10-4. An Example of Problem Analysis

work sequence, the order and definition of tasks that make up standardized work. We provided numerous handouts that described these concepts in simple, easy-to-understand language. We also introduced the use of job analysis data sheets for collecting information directly from the production operation (Figure 10-5). A key to the effectiveness of these materials is their simplicity and clarity. Excess verbiage simply confuses people.

Identifying root causes for why blade change takes so long
Figure 10-6 is a sample summary of our problem identification process, combining the 4M and Five Whys processes on a single

Job Analysis							Your name:			J. O'Meara

Job description: _Chop Saw: Small Parts_   Date: _____

Worker name: _Ernie Burt_   Shift: _____

Work element	Repetition				:		Time in seconds				Best
	1	2	3	4	5	6	7	8	9	10	repeat
Pick lumber/square	7	6	7	9	7	8	9	7	6	7	7
Cut, inspect, stack	89/96	90/96	88/95	88/97	89/96	89/97	90/99	89/96	88/94	89/96	89/96
Tag white tub	4/100	4/100	4/99	3/100	4/100	3/100	4/103	4/100	3/97	4/100	4/100
Stack to pallet	9/109	8/108	9/108	3/113	8/108	8/108	8/111	8/108	9/106	8/108	8/108
Replace new tub	6/115	6/114	6/114	6/119	5/113	6/114	6/117	5/113	6/112	6/114	6/114
_____											
Total for one cycle	115	114	114	119	113	114	117	113	112	114	114

Figure 10-5. An Example of a Job Analysis Data Sheet

sheet. Our overall theme was that "re-saw can't cut wood fast enough." The general problem was "too much stop time." We identified and quantified the specific problem areas in terms of the amount of stop time for each process. This provided a basis for setting priorities. Using the third item under problem area in Figure 10-6 as an example, "blade change takes too long," we then looked into all the reasons. Of the 16 possible reasons for the blade change taking too long, we focused on the top three. The third one, the fact that the blades are not easily accessible, was then given expanded analysis via the Five Whys technique.

The root cause of why blades were not easily accessible was that there was no place or method to have the blades close to the saw. We spent as much as 50 percent of our effort developing analysis sheets such as these to identify root causes of the problems, rather than identifying quick fixes that would not produce long-term, lasting

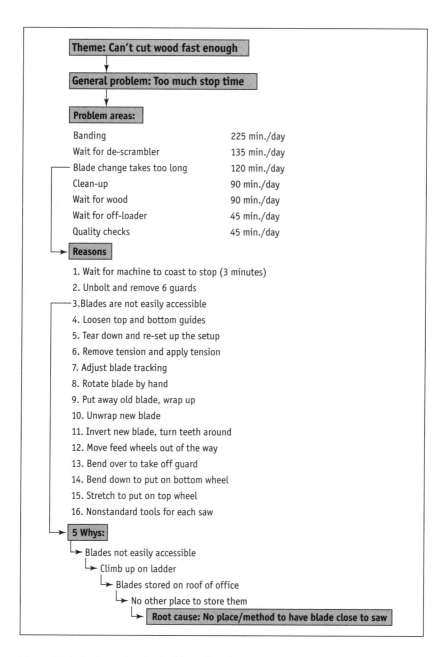

Figure 10-6. An Example of a Problem Identification Process

results. The class was often impatient with this process. They wanted to race out and "do something" or "fix something," but in going through the process, they eventually recognized that they had applied quick fixes and Band-Aids too often in the past, and that root cause analysis was indeed a more powerful tool. They recognized that once they identified the root cause, they could create effective countermeasures and implement them quite easily. Figure 10-7 shows a tool that we used to brainstorm and evaluate possible countermeasures for a given root cause. Though the class identified

Countermeasure Rating Table

Root Cause: _____
_____

Possible countermeasures	Effectiveness (Hi-Med-Low)	Feasibility (Hi-Med-Low)	Impact +/- (Hi-Med-Low)	Overall assessment
1.				
2.				
3.				
4.				
5.				
6.				
7.				
8.				
9.				
10.				
11.				
12.				
13.				
14.				
15.				

Figure 10-7. Countermeasure Rating Table Worksheet

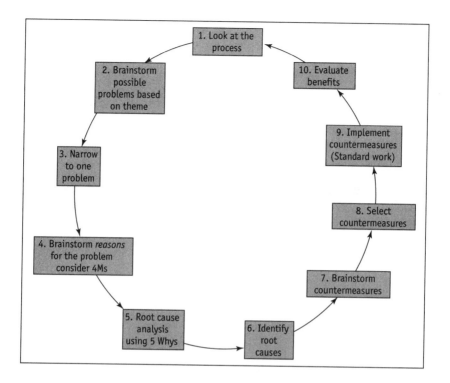

Figure 10-8. Continuous Improvement Cycle

many possible countermeasures, only the best ones were selected for implementation. Putting all these pieces together led to a continuous improvement cycle (Figure 10-8).

Introducing standardization to team members
Our whole focus during this phase of implementation was on identifying the root causes for problems and then standardizing effective countermeasures. As we started delving into the details of standardized work, we introduced another valuable concept, called the *cycle balance table*. Figure 10-9 shows an actual worksheet that we used for introducing the idea of standardization to team members in the training session. We demonstrated the power of this tool for indicating imbalance in the work load among team members by showing that some were underworked, some were overworked, and some had an appropriate level of work. We also introduced the

concept of *takt time*, which is the manufacturing time needed to match customer expectations.

The companion to the cycle balance table (Figure 10-9) is Figure 10-10a, the *cycle balance table worksheet*, a tool for collecting data directly from the operation for the purpose of creating the

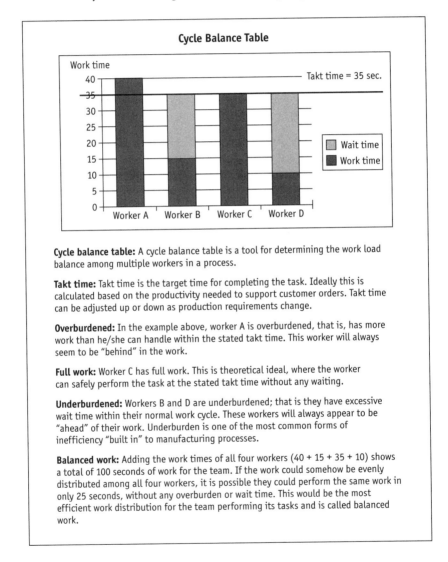

Cycle balance table: A cycle balance table is a tool for determining the work load balance among multiple workers in a process.

Takt time: Takt time is the target time for completing the task. Ideally this is calculated based on the productivity needed to support customer orders. Takt time can be adjusted up or down as production requirements change.

Overburdened: In the example above, worker A is overburdened, that is, has more work than he/she can handle within the stated takt time. This worker will always seem to be "behind" in the work.

Full work: Worker C has full work. This is theoretical ideal, where the worker can safely perform the task at the stated takt time without any waiting.

Underburdened: Workers B and D are underburdened; that is they have excessive wait time within their normal work cycle. These workers will always appear to be "ahead" of their work. Underburden is one of the most common forms of inefficiency "built in" to manufacturing processes.

Balanced work: Adding the work times of all four workers (40 + 15 + 35 + 10) shows a total of 100 seconds of work for the team. If the work could somehow be evenly distributed among all four workers, it is possible they could perform the same work in only 25 seconds, without any overburden or wait time. This would be the most efficient work distribution for the team performing its tasks and is called balanced work.

Figure 10-9. How to Use a Cycle Balance Table

Cycle Balance Table Worksheet

Trial date:

Worker A: (Description) _____   (Name) _____

Observation	1	2	3	4	5	6	7	8	9	10	Average
Work											
Wait											
Total cycle											

Worker B: (Description) _____   (Name) _____

Observation	1	2	3	4	5	6	7	8	9	10	Average
Work											
Wait											
Total cycle											

Worker C: (Description) _____   (Name) _____

Observation	1	2	3	4	5	6	7	8	9	10	Average
Work											
Wait											
Total cycle											

Worker D: (Description) _____   (Name) _____

Observation	1	2	3	4	5	6	7	8	9	10	Average
Work											
Wait											
Total cycle											

Seconds   **Cycle Balance Table**

Wait time

Work time

Worker A   Worker B   Worker C   Worker D

Figure 10-10a. An Example of a Cycle Balance Table Worksheet

cycle balance table. Figure 10-10b provides an example of how the worksheet translates into a graph for the Gazebo line. We found that constant reinforcement and practice with these tools via homework assignments was a very effective teaching method for skill development and comprehension.

Performance measure for re-saw operation

Throughout the implementation we were plagued with the questions: "How do we measure our progress; how do we know we are improving?" We had struggled with using the measurables of linear board feet per shift or board feet per minute, but there seemed to be no consistent, reliable performance measure for all the types of lumber they were processing.

Midway through the course we came to the root question, "What is the value-added activity for re-saw?" After half an hour of debate we realized that the only value-added activity in the re-saw operation was when the blade of the saw was cutting wood. Everything else was non-value-adding activity. If the saw was running but idling without cutting wood, it was non-value-adding activity. If the saw was down for maintenance, it was non-value-adding activity. If employees were cleaning their area when the saw was down, it was non-value-adding activity. Very much of what the organization considered essential and important was, in fact, non-value-adding activity.

So the question became, "How do we measure this?" The very simple answer resulted in installing a small limit switch near the blade that was activated whenever wood was being cut. This switch was hooked directly to a clock that measured the amount of time the saw was actually cutting wood. A brand new measurable arose in Cedar Works called *percentage cut time*. It was a direct measure of how often wood was being cut on each shift. Today it remains one of the key measurables in the re-saw area. Figure 10-11 is a trend graph of percentage cut time as it is used today. We also began tracking other key measurables as indicators for progress, such as blade change time (the time required to change a blade) and banding time (the time needed to bundle and secure a pallet of wood for handling).

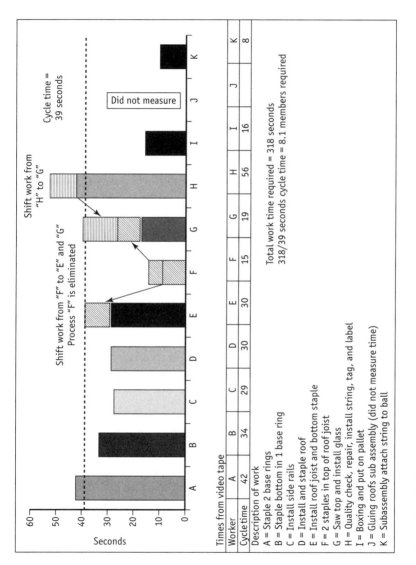

Times from video tape

Worker	A	B	C	D	E	F	G	H	I	J	K
Cycle time	42	34	29	30	30	15	19	56	16		8

Description of work
A = Staple 2 base rings
B = Staple bottom in 1 base ring
C = Install side rails
D = Install and staple roof
E = Install roof joist and bottom staple
F = 2 staples in top of roof joist
G = Saw top and install glass
H = Quality check, repair, install string, tag, and label
I = Boxing and put on pallet
J = Gluing roofs sub assembly (did not measure time)
K = Subassembly attach string to ball

Total work time required = 318 seconds
318/39 seconds cycle time = 8.1 members required

Cycle time = 39 seconds

Did not measure

Shift work from "H" to "G"

Shift work from "F" to "E" and "G"
Process "F" is eliminated

Figure 10-10b. Baseline Cycle Balance Table—Gazebo Line

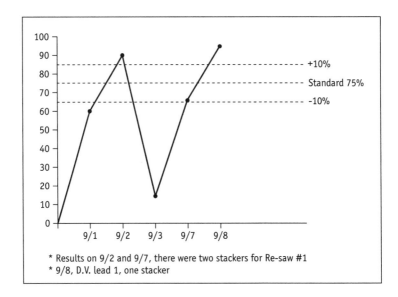

* Results on 9/2 and 9/7, there were two stackers for Re-saw #1
* 9/8, D.V. lead 1, one stacker

Figure 10-11. Percent of Cut Time in Re-saw

Testing and evaluating new methods
As we identified more root causes for problems and invented new countermeasures to solve them, we saw the need for a way to test and evaluate these new methods. We introduced another tool for systematic evaluation of changes to the process called the *process trial plan*. This trial plan provided a systematic method for the entire operation on both shifts to test and evaluate new work procedures and new work methods. It also arranged the work elements in a logical order that was compatible with a standardized work process. This became a very valuable tool for translating problem-solving activities into practical application on the manufacturing floor. Figure 10-12 is an example of a process trial plan for the re-saw area. It describes the work elements for each of the four operators in the area, and provides room to document results and observations. This plan allows everyone in the area to understand how the work steps will be divided before the actual change is made to the process.

As our 10-week project neared its end, we used a final report to management to bring the whole process to completion. This was a full two-hour presentation allowing the entire team to summarize

Re-saw Process Trial Plan   Operation: <u>Long cants into boards</u>

Date: _____   Shift: _____

Lead #1: _____

Step	Work element
1	Feed saw
2	Retrieve wood for second cut
3	Quality check
4	Stage cants for #2 while saw #1 is cutting
5	Descramble as saw is cutting
6	
7	
8	
9	

Off load #1: _____

Step	Work element
1	Return wood to lead #1
2	Stack and grade
3	Sticker once per layer
4	Help stage lead #2
5	
6	
7	
8	
9	
10	

Lead #2: _____

Step	Work element
1	Feed saw
2	Retrieve wood for second cut
3	Stack wood when saw is cutting
4	Adjust feed wheel
5	
6	
7	
8	
9	
10	

Off load #2: _____

Step	Work element
1	Receive cants and boards
2	Stack wood
3	Sticker once per layer
4	Help lead #1 stage wood:
5	• stage cants on descambler
6	• call for wood
7	• break new bundles
8	
9	
10	

Results:

1. % of cut time: [   ]
2. Prepare cycle balance table for trial
3. Comments and observations

_____
_____
_____
_____
_____

Figure 10-12. An Example of a Process Trial Plan

their activities and present their results to upper management. As they prepared, the team experienced a new level of investment and ownership in what they were doing. This session firmly consolidated their learning as they worked to capture and report on the key points. Management was curious and very supportive of this activity, and the whole process took on a quality of celebration. Members of the team received a high level of recognition from all five management leaders for the results they achieved during their 10-week effort, which are as follows:

1. Created a critical new measurable for the re-saw area called percentage cut time, which is still a standard recognized as one of the key variables in productivity (Figure 10-11).
2. Identified specific punch lists to focus team activities in areas that would lead to maximum benefit.
3. Standardized work procedures in the re-saw area that made the procedures efficient and productive.
4. Reduced banding time, a time-consuming work element necessary for all re-saw operations.
5. The re-saw area, which had been a bottleneck for months prior to this class, was no longer the limiting process. The bottleneck shifted from re-saw to the molding operation further downstream.
6. Eliminated chronic overtime in the re-saw area.

As Randy Phipps, vice president of manufacturing, stated:

Productivity Plus was valuable because it started us on the road to lean manufacturing by introducing key concepts, such as value-added activity, standardized methods, 5-Whys, root cause analysis, etc.... Productivity Plus was the beginning of the thought process of how to look at things in a logical way and eliminate waste.... You have to get over that "why change" attitude, and this was really our planting of the seed that "Yes, there really is a need to change."

Phase II: Attempting to Propagate the System

We achieved significant improvements in one key production area of re-saw. Our hope was that the tools and principles we had used during our classes would become the basis for cultural change throughout the rest of Cedar Works. Figure 10-13 shows the cascade effect we had hoped for as a means of propagating change through-

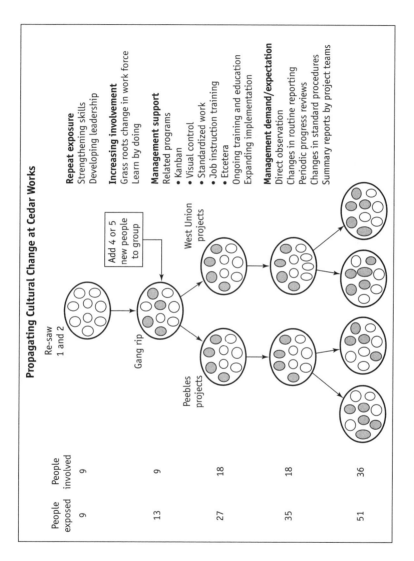

Figure 10-13. An Example of Propagating Cultural Change

out the organization. This plan assumed that the nine original members of the re-saw team would work with four or five new members on a similar project in the Gang Rip area. This larger group would then split and work with four or five new members on two other lines in the plant. Continuing in this fashion, the tools and principles we had been delivering to the original group would be spread throughout the plant.

We learned an important lesson here, because this plan for propagating change never did yield results in other parts of the plant. In retrospect, the root cause was not having a champion assigned to carry the process forward. We left the session with a general assumption that participants would somehow "transfer" what they learned to others without a solid plan for implementation or training. Instead, we observed that the training we provided, while good for the initial group, did not percolate further into the organization. We did provide a solid exposure to the principles of lean manufacturing, but this was insufficient to ensure its spread and growth in other areas.

Using 50 Percent Classroom and 50 Percent Floor Activity

The teaching method of using 50 percent classroom and 50 percent floor activity was very effective and well received by all participants. Homework assignments that required students to use the tools with immediate and practical application were an effective way to reinforce key concepts. The continuous improvement cycle (Figure 10-8) was a reliable process that combined the practicality of floor observations with the strength of continuously eliminating waste as we moved toward improvement of standardized work. Using a model area as a teaching example (re-saw in this case) was the best way for employees to gain understanding, familiarity, and real mastery of key principles. When employees could see it work in their area in actual day-to-day operations, we teachers gained credibility, trust, and the support of plant floor workers.

"If You Can't Measure It, You Can't Improve It"

Even with all the reference and effort we made toward standardized work, it was still not fully developed and did not remain a lasting tool. More work was needed. We failed to provide enough emphasis on standardized work sheets for them to become a common document with visibility and easy access in the work area. This was an oversight that diminished the effectiveness of our long-term training. You cannot expect a self-perpetuating organizational change without a solid plan and dedicated resources to support and execute it. If you can't measure the continuous improvement process, you can't improve it.

Even with these shortcomings in our training effort, Cedar Works as an organization was very pleased with the results we had obtained. They felt they had been given fundamental and powerful tools for improving their workplace. On the basis of their satisfaction, Cedar Works asked both Dave and I to continue providing ongoing consultation and support in their efforts toward standardizing and improving overall operations.

Phase III: Standardized Work and Job Instruction Training on the Gazebo Line

Due to model change activities and high demands on our time with Toyota, more than a year and a half passed before Dave and I were able to continue our efforts with Cedar Works. This time we focused our attention on the West Union operations, which were responsible for final assembly of finished goods. We followed a format similar to our first training, meeting once a week March to June 1995. This time however, the sessions were more intense. We met for five hours, 9:00 A.M. to 2:00 P.M. every Friday. Again we selected a model area in which to apply the principles directly. The area we chose was Product B118 and Cedar Works' most popular product, the Gazebo bird feeder.

"Can't Make Them Fast Enough"

The Gazebo bird feeder was the most complex product that the company produced and had the greatest number of component parts. In addition to being one of the most complicated products, the Gazebo had tight tolerances that made assembly even more challenging. We were dealing with wooden materials, which had a high obsolescence due to declining moisture content. Old parts would crack and split, resulting in another frequent problem for production. A tremendous amount of floor space was also tied up in congestion and parts storage.

This situation was further complicated by the fact Cedar Works could sell as many of these as they could make. They were always on backorder and never able to catch up, despite operating all three shifts. First shift did the final assembly, second shift made one subassembly for the base of the bird feeder, and third shift made a subassembly of the roofs. All told, 14 people were involved in the production of this finished product. There were constant conflicts over work force shortages and an excessive reliance on temporary help. It was not unusual to see a 50 percent rollover from month to month in personnel, and there were frequent training and absentee problems.

At the organizational level there were team leaders on each shift, but they were tied to a full-time assembly line position. As a result, they were unable to troubleshoot or support problem solving on the line. The subassembly operation for the roof was being done on third shift. They had a difficult time completing enough parts to support first-shift production. Poor quality was a common problem, and there was little success in discovering the root cause of problems. Not uncommonly, first shift produced only 20 percent of their expected production before shutting down for either bad quality or lack of parts. The seven or eight people on final assembly were all working at their own pace. Consequently, there were huge work-in-process (WIP) inventories between each operator (Photo 10-2).

Everyone was working very hard, but they were often frustrated and had no sense of accomplishment. This frustration had translated into significant discontent at the West Union shop and had resulted in a recent flurry of union-organizing activity. Confusion about resolving quality issues was a constant concern. What are the standards? Who should we communicate with? Who is responsible? Who has what role? These were questions that were asked on a daily basis, with no good answers.

Photo 10-2. Typical Final Assembly Line at West Union

Mirroring the Productivity Plus Training at the Peebles Plant

Our design for instruction included a small group of key people limited to 10 participants. Jim Obenshain, the president, again demonstrated clear sponsorship by attending 50 percent of the classes. His personal investment and follow-up with key people was critical. Randy Phipps, vice president of manufacturing, again attended every meeting. There is no substitute for this level of support when a company works on becoming lean. Consistent demonstration of interest and involvement from Randy and Jim sent a clear message about the priority of this program. Mike Ranly, plant manager at West Union, was also a course participant. At first, during the nine-week training program, he was skeptical of the process. Under the pressure of production he occasionally wavered and went back to the "old ways" of adding float for protection. For example, we changed the roof subassembly from operating on a separate third shift to building the roofs just-in-time as they were needed to supply the line. This reduced the in-process buffer to only three pieces. Once, when they were having trouble with the glue guns on this subassembly operation, Mike added back approximately 30 extra roofs to help keep the line running. This, of course, only helped to conceal the root problem of the trouble with the glue guns. Ultimately, though, Mike became a solid believer in the system and now recognizes the importance of solving root problems rather than hiding them with increased inventory.

Bonnie Sowards was the first-shift supervisor and a key player in this round of training. She was the person under the gun for day-to-day production and was constantly under pressure trying to balance work force fluctuations and shortages, internal and external parts shortages, poor quality, and special orders. Pam Bowling was the first-shift team leader for the Gazebo area. Pam had been a very strong force in the unionizing effort at West Union. She entered the class frustrated with current conditions but still open to new ideas. In addition, there were five other participants, ranging from assistant supervisors to team leaders and team members from the line.

Our approach mirrored earlier Productivity Plus training: weekly meetings with 50 percent classroom instruction to gain familiarity with the principles, and 50 percent time on the floor

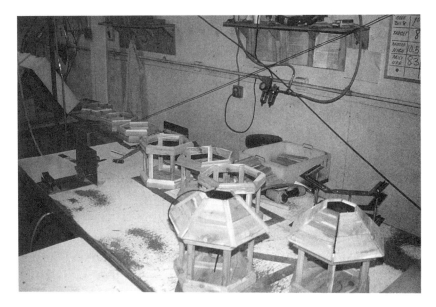

Photo 10-3. Controlling WIP on the Gazebo Line

illustrating and observing the process. Again, we made heavy use of homework assignments to reinforce key concepts. During our first training session with the team, we emphasized three main themes that would serve as our departure for implementing the system:

1. Measurables for baseline data. We would use key measurables to track progress throughout the implementation. This would also help gain an understanding of the current level of performance in the area.

2. Control of in-process stock. We told the team that we would bring all the subassembly operations from second and third shifts to work simultaneously with first shift so that the entire product would be built at one time. In addition, we were going to limit WIP from an unlimited number of parts down to three parts between stations. We used simple tape squares on the assembly table to control this. Once an operator accumulated three parts, he or she would have to wait for one of those parts to be used before building the next unit (Photo 10-3). This would require workers to build parts only when they were needed rather than working at their own rates and building up huge WIP between stations. This was the first step toward introducing the idea of a pull system rather than pushing product onto the next workstation.

3. Stabilizing the process. We would work hard to achieve stability in strategic areas. These would include production rate, quality fluctuations, frequency of defects, quantities of material on line, and employee turnover that resulted in heavy use of temporary help.

Implementing Major Change to the Process

Our implementation generally followed the above three themes. Establishing baseline measurables was important to quantify improvements and evaluate the benefit of changes to the process. We focused on controlling material flow very early in the implementation for several reasons:

1. Lack of discipline in material handling allowed large buildup of WIP between all workstations, which created tremendous clutter and confusion.
2. Approximately 50 percent of the "work" in this area was actually non-value-added material handling, stacking, unstacking, and restacking of WIP.

3. We saw a great opportunity for more efficient layout by elim-inating all the space occupied by WIP.
4. Eliminating the WIP between stations would more tightly link each process to the next. This served the dual purpose of developing teamwork and demonstrating the mechanics of a pull system.

Introducing these ideas in our first class set the stage for our sec-ond meeting, when we would implement major changes to the process. To prepare the organization for this, we gave the team a "fact package" to share with the rest of the shop. It gave the general work force information about what we were doing and what changes they could expect to see.

As described earlier in Figure 10-8, we emphasized with the team members that we would be moving through a continuous improvement cycle that would entail a consistent pattern of

- Collecting data
- Solving a problem
- Standardizing
- Implementing changes
- Observing results
- Assessing the benefits
- Repeating the process all over again

We introduced the idea of the standardized production system comprised of key principles such as just-in-time, elimination of waste, and continuous improvement, etc. We spent ample time in the early phases introducing simple concepts such as standard in-process stock and the importance of standardizing, as well as dis-cussing the benefits they could expect to see.

Looking at measurables before training

This time around Dave and I paid attention to key measurables before heading into the start of the training. Figures 10-14a and 10-14b show trend data we collected on the two subassembly processes and the final line.

These data show the typical performance of their operation before any changes were made. Because all three teams were

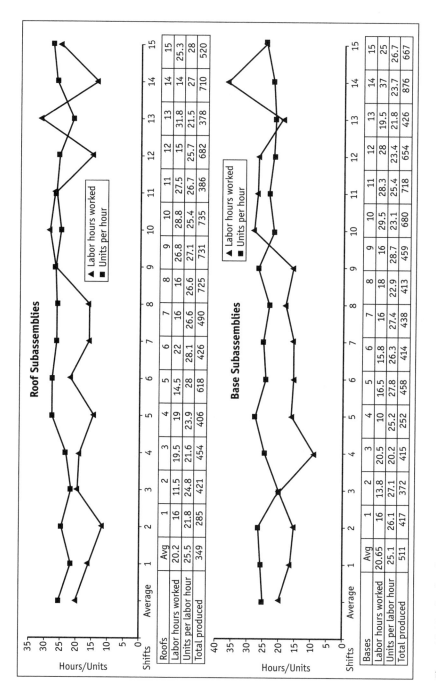

Figure 10-14a. Roof and Base Subassembly Graphs

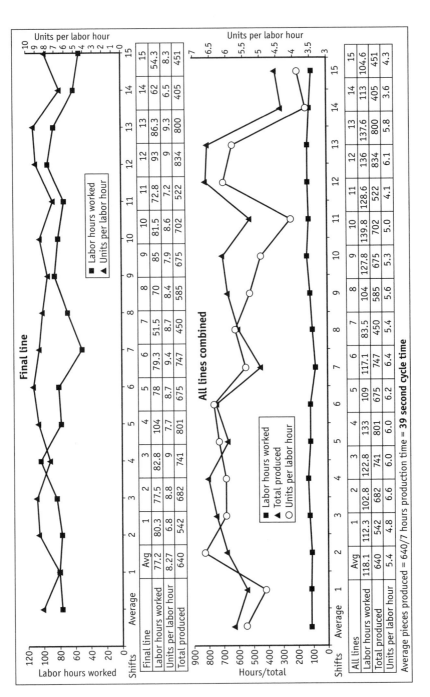

Final line

Shifts	Average	1	2	3	4	5	6	7	8	9	10	11	12	13	14	15
Final line	Avg	1	2	3	4	5	6	7	8	9	10	11	12	13	14	15
Labor hours worked	77.2	80.3	77.5	82.8	104	78	79.3	51.5	70	85	81.5	72.8	93	86.3	62	54.3
Units per labor hour	8.27	6.8	8.8	9	7.7	8.7	9.4	8.7	8.4	7.9	8.6	7.2	9.3	9.3	6.5	8.3
Total produced	640	542	682	741	801	675	747	450	585	675	702	522	834	800	405	451

All lines combined

Shifts	Average	1	2	3	4	5	6	7	8	9	10	11	12	13	14	15
All lines	Avg	1	2	3	4	5	6	7	8	9	10	11	12	13	14	15
Labor hours worked	118.1	112.3	102.2	122.8	133	109	117.1	83.5	104	127.8	139.8	128.6	136	137.6	113	104.6
Total produced	640	542	682	741	801	675	747	450	585	675	702	522	834	800	405	451
Units per labor hour	5.4	4.8	6.6	6.0	6.0	6.2	6.4	5.4	5.6	5.3	5.0	4.1	6.1	5.8	3.6	4.3

Average pieces produced = 640/7 hours production time = **39 second cycle time**

Figure 10-14b. Final Line and All Lines Assembly Graphs

running on different shifts, they were accustomed to measuring only their own shift performance. They had never examined the combined efforts for the total product across all three shifts (see Table 10-1).

As you might expect, based on the table below, roof and base subassemblies were generally overproduced compared to final assembly's needs. The Cedar Works team was surprised that their true productivity was only averaging about 5 units/labor-hour, as compared to 8 units/labor-hour for first shift's final assembly. Bringing the big picture to light demonstrated the inefficiency of off-shift production that was not coordinated and not in sync with other shifts. It also demonstrated much greater variability and fluctuation in their process than they had imagined.

Looking for solutions to problems

Once we established a firm baseline of data, we began making changes to the process, beginning with the reduction and control of WIP between processes. This elimination of in-process stock and excess inventory was the greatest shock for the production floor operators. People literally did not know what to do with themselves if they could not stay busy cranking out parts. We fully expected that when we stripped out this inventory, problems would quickly come to the surface, and they certainly did. Developing a tolerance for problems was one of the most difficult tasks the team faced. In the past, the response to problems was to work harder, make more parts. We were now asking them to stop making parts and look for solutions to the problems. This simple change in behavior was the most difficult one for the team to embrace.

Table 10-1. Average Productivity for Three Teams and Three Shifts

Component	Average Productivity
Roof Subassemblies	25 units per labor-hour
Base Subassemblies	23 units per labor-hour
Final assembly line	8 units per labor-hour
All lines combined	**5 units per labor-hour**

As mentioned above, we emphasized measurables right from the start. Figure 10-15 shows our data tracking for the Gazebo line, first operating on all three shifts, and then after consolidating to one shift. As you can see from this graph, our baseline productivity for the three separate shifts averaged about 5.4 units/labor-hour. After consolidating to one shift, we experienced a slight improvement for three to four weeks followed by a steady decline. Reasons for this will be discussed.

We also implemented a new approach for defect tracking. Prior to this class, Cedar Works collected quality data through random quality control (QC) audits. This meant that they were not collecting quality checks or defect data during daily production. Figures 10-16a and 10-16b are examples of what we tracked as we began the class. Figure 10-16a identifies defects of the most common type, for example, ridge caps that are loose, cracked, or overshot. Figure 10-16b is a Pareto chart of data that had been collected for one week. Quite typically, 89 percent of all defects were coming from only three causes. This was a real eye-opener for everyone in the class. Prior to this time everyone was convinced that they were laboring under dozens of different problems.

Perhaps the most important point to this exercise was not only that we were collecting data but that we were posting it on large data summary boards in the manufacturing area. This provided direct and meaningful feedback for the entire team on exactly how they were doing and what kind of progress they were making.

Operating as a team
Now that we were paying attention to defects, a new series of problems began to emerge. How do we handle the defects? The answer to this question led to another "first" for Cedar Works—introducing their first "off-line" team leader. Formerly, all team leaders had full-time working positions on the line. Our off-line team leader had totally different responsibilities. She became responsible for keeping the line running, dealing with defects, and making decisions. Figures 10-17a and 10-17b (pages 340–341) are documents we created to clarify how defects should be dealt with and what the decision chain would be.

Y-axis: Unit per labor hour (12, 11, 10, 9, 8, 7, 6, 5, 4, 3)

Annotations:
- Chicken line
- Start of one shift production
- Average productivity before standard work = 5.4 units/labor hour

New targets as of 5/12
- 500 units/shift
- 6.7 hrs production/shift
- 24,240 sec/shift
- 48 second takt time
- 7 team members and 1 T/L
- 54 labor-hr/shift
- 9.3 units/labor-hr

Date																3-Apr	4-Apr	5-Apr	6-Apr	7-Apr	10-Apr	11-Apr	12-Apr	24-Apr	26-Apr	27-Apr	28-Apr	1-May	2-May	3-May	8-May	9-May	10-May	11-May
Team size																—	—	—	—	—	—	—	—	8+1	8+1	8+1	8+1	8+1	8+1	8+1	8+1	7+1	7+1	7+1
Bases l-hrs	16	13.8	20.5	10	16.5	15.8	16	18	16	29.5	28.3	28	19.5	37	25																			
Roofs l-hrs	16	11.5	19.5	19	14.5	22	16	16	26.8	28.8	27.5	15	31.8	14	25.3																			
Final assembly l-hrs	80.3	77.5	82.8	104	78	79.3	51.5	70	85	81.5	72.8	93	86.3	62	54.3																			
Overall l-hrs	112.3	102.8	122.8	133	109	117.1	83.5	104	127.8	139.8	128.6	136	137.6	113	104.6	61.25	57.5	56	61	7	71.75	51	59	63	62	55.5	63	72	66	72	68	60	56	60
Units	542	682	741	801	675	747	450	585	675	702	522	834	800	405	451	405	360	369	360	90	270	234	288	225	180	216	216	270	225	279	315	324	324	279
Units/Lhr	4.8	6.6	6.0	6.0	6.2	6.4	5.4	5.6	5.3	5.0	4.1	6.1	5.8	3.6	4.3	6.6	6.3	6.6	5.9	12.9	3.8	4.6	4.9	3.6	2.9	3.9	3.4	3.8	3.4	3.9	4.6	5.4	5.8	4.7

← Average productivity before standard work = 5.4 units per labor hour → | ← Using up excess inventory → | ← Just-in-time production →

Figure 10-15. Gazebo Line Daily Productivity

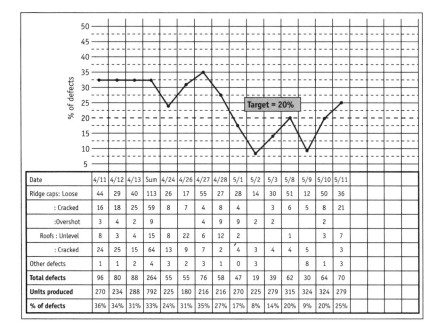

Date	4/11	4/12	4/13	Sum	4/24	4/26	4/27	4/28	5/1	5/2	5/3	5/8	5/9	5/10	5/11				
Ridge caps: Loose	44	29	40	113	26	17	55	27	28	14	30	51	12	50	36				
: Cracked	16	18	25	59	8	7	4	8	4		3	6	5	8	21				
:Overshot	3	4	2	9			4	9	9	2	2			2					
Roofs : Unlevel	8	3	4	15	8	22	6	12	2			1		3	7				
: Cracked	24	25	15	64	13	9	7	2	4	3	4	4	5		3				
Other defects	1	1	2	4	3	2	3	1	0	3			8	1	3				
Total defects	96	80	88	264	55	55	76	58	47	19	39	62	30	64	70				
Units produced	270	234	288	792	225	180	216	216	270	225	279	315	324	324	279				
% of defects	36%	34%	31%	33%	24%	31%	35%	27%	17%	8%	14%	20%	9%	20%	25%				

Figure 10-16a. Gazebo Line Defect Trend

The team was now in uncharted territory. They were uncertain how to respond and how to operate without their cushion of in-process float. They were not used to operating as a team. Whenever there was a problem, people would spend excessive amounts of time trying to solve it, inadvertently idling the entire assembly line. As instructors, we had to create simple training guides on the fundamentals of operating under a lean system. Figures 10-18a and 10-18b (pages 342–343) illustrate how to use wait time productively and how to respond to line-stop situations. Roles slowly began to be clarified. Prior to a standardized system, line workers would often solicit opinions from five or six people to get the answer they wanted. If they did not get the answer they wanted from their team leader, they would ask the assistant supervisor. If that was not good enough, they would go to the plant manager, the vice president of manufacturing, or even Jim himself. As a result, there was a constant conflict of opinions about what was good quality and how to resolve problems. As roles were clarified, this arbitrary searching for the answer came to a close, workers

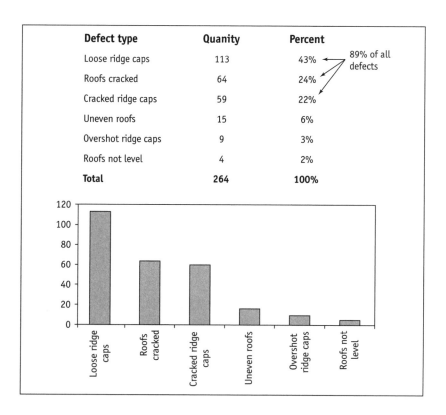

Defect type	Quanity	Percent	
Loose ridge caps	113	43%	89% of all defects
Roofs cracked	64	24%	
Cracked ridge caps	59	22%	
Uneven roofs	15	6%	
Overshot ridge caps	9	3%	
Roofs not level	4	2%	
Total	**264**	**100%**	

Figure 10-16b. Gazebo Defect Data

came to rely on their team leader to provide answers, and operations became smoother. Quality became more consistent, and the team leader eventually had much more direct control of operations in his or her area.

Hitting the targets—The fried chicken lunch approach

Before we knew it we were into the fourth and fifth week of implementation. Figure 10-15 (page 337) shows the bumpy road we followed during the various stages of implementation. April 3 was our first day of one shift production, without the off-shift production of subassemblies. April 3–12 we were using up excess subassemblies in the system that had been overproduced by the other two shifts. As this float was consumed, the shift was forced to produce with one-piece flow. This was a difficult transition that required the team to

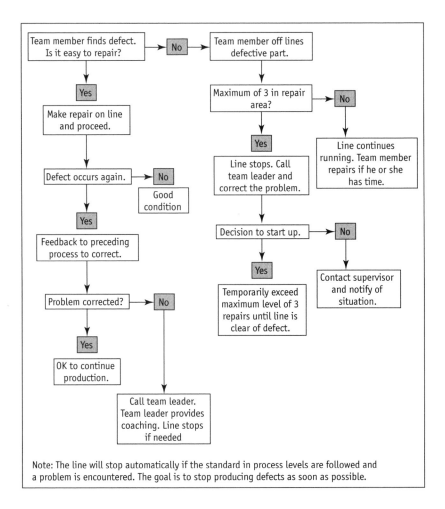

Figure 10-17a. Defect Decision Tree

work as a coordinated unit, something totally foreign to them. By April 26 we had "bottomed out," posting an all-time low in productivity for the line of 2.9 units per labor-hour, half of what it had been before we had started. At this time it took great persistence to continue coaching and reinforcing the principles of the new system. Slowly the team coordination improved, working more as a unit, getting used to one-piece flow, and adapting to their new roles. As team coordination improved, we discovered we could further reduce the number of team members on the line from eight to

Case	Conditions	Response
1	Team member finds single defect. Repair area has space. Buffer has space. Line is running	Repair defect if able to keep up *or* Set to repair if not able to keep up. Keep running.
2	Team member finds multiple defect. Repair has space. Buffer has space. Line is running.	Feedback to preceding process. Repair if able to keep up *or* Set to repair if not able to keep up. Keep running.
3	Continuing defects.	Notify team leader.
4	Team member finds single defect. Repair is full. Buffer has space. Line is running.	Repair if able to keep up. Keep running *or* Stop the line if not able to keep up. Fix all repairs.
5	Team member finds single defect. Repair has some. Buffer is full. Line is running.	Fix repairs until buffer has space.
6	Line is down for repairs.	Help fix repairs.

Figure 10-17b. Decision Table for Repairs

seven. Although this improved overall productivity, we were still far from our goal of 8 units per labor-hour.

We discovered, quite by good luck, that a successful way to motivate production is through the stomach. In an off-handed comment one day, Dave said that if the team could hit the target of 8 units per labor-hour, he would buy the team fried chicken for lunch. Not surprisingly, they asked, "Are you serious?" He said, "Yes." Within eight days the team had become well enough coordinated to achieve the 8 units per labor-hour and gained their reward of chicken box lunches. They changed the name of the target line to the "chicken line," and everyone loved it. Though this may seem like a trivial incentive, it really did the trick for coordinating the team's effort and pulling them to a higher level of performance than they had ever experienced before. Real trust began to blossom in the reliability of the new production system.

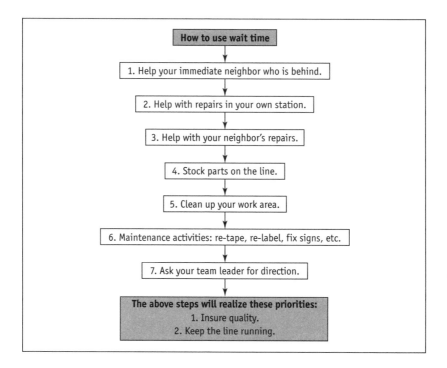

Figure 10-18a. How to Use Wait Time

Producing with consistency and predictability

Now that the team was producing with one-piece flow, the consistency and predictability of the total operation became more important. Figure 10-19 (page 344) is an example of a daily performance analysis record that was used to track production quantity throughout the day. During each two-hour segment of the day, the line should produce a predetermined number of units. If actual production varied from the plan, it was obvious to all, and corrective action could be taken immediately to address the problem. This reinforced the mentality needed to achieve daily scheduled production goals.

Other problems were being worked out along the way. For example, the fluctuations in personnel resulting from reliance on use of temporaries caused us to make a special request of Cedar Works to keep the team together and intact for this trial. The results were dramatic. A sense of teamwork emerged that

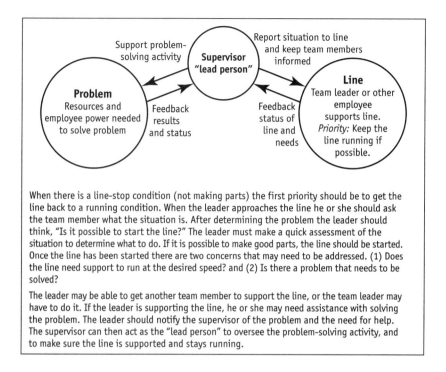

When there is a line-stop condition (not making parts) the first priority should be to get the line back to a running condition. When the leader approaches the line he or she should ask the team member what the situation is. After determining the problem the leader should think, "Is it possible to start the line?" The leader must make a quick assessment of the situation to determine what to do. If it is possible to make good parts, the line should be started. Once the line has been started there are two concerns that may need to be addressed. (1) Does the line need support to run at the desired speed? and (2) Is there a problem that needs to be solved?

The leader may be able to get another team member to support the line, or the team leader may have to do it. If the leader is supporting the line, he or she may need assistance with solving the problem. The leader should notify the supervisor of the problem and the need for help. The supervisor can then act as the "lead person" to oversee the problem-solving activity, and to make sure the line is supported and stays running.

Figure 10-18b. How to Handle a Line-Stop Situation

had not existed when the team had constantly churned with replacements.

As we began controlling inventories more tightly, we began to affect the material handling group as well. Dave and I set a preliminary guideline of two to three hours' worth of material on-line at any time. At first, operators were uncomfortable without lots of material around. In time, however, they came to enjoy the increase in open space and the improved organization of their work areas. They no longer wanted excess inventories of five or six days' worth of parts surrounding them. This created unusual demands for the material handling group, who were accustomed to making daily deliveries in large quantities to the production lines. With Randy's support, we were able to create a special two-hour material delivery schedule for the Gazebo line. Though not yet driven by kanban, this more frequent material delivery pattern clearly demonstrated that reliable production could be achieved with low inventory.

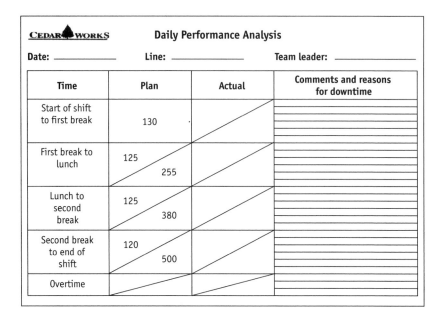

Figure 10-19. An Example of a Daily Performance Analysis Worksheet

Systematic training—Everyone is a master in their area
As the entire process began to stabilize, our next goal was to improve the overall skill level of the team through job rotation and the use of job instruction training. Figure 10-20 is an example of a job breakdown sheet that we used as a training aid for teaching workers new jobs. The goal was to introduce systematic training to allow all team members to master all jobs in the area. Figure 10-21 is a sample of a multifunction worker training table that we used to track the skill level of team members for each of the jobs in a specific area. The team already had experience rotating jobs, so this training table gave them a tool for determining their strengths and weaknesses and a way to monitor overall skill level within the group (Photo 10-4).

Review of Standard Work/Job Instruction Program

In looking back over the implementation of this most recent training, some key observations are worth noting. First, there was

Job Breakdown

CEDAR WORKS

Group: _____

Job: _____

| | T/L | T/L | 1st supervisor | 2nd supervisor |

Analyzed by: _____

Major steps	Key points	Reasons for key points
	Safety: Injury avoidance, ergonomics, danger points **Quality:** Defect avoidance, check points, standards **Technique:** Efficient movement, special method **Cost:** Proper use of materials	
#1 Install cap rail	1. Two 1" staples top and bottom 2. Bottom staples between roof staples, top in middle 3. Every other rail must be red 4. Hold guide flush 5. Hold boards together 6. Two staples per side then over to the other side 7. Keep finger from inside when stapling	1. This is the standard needed to hold 2. Best location to get best hold 3. Provide best look for customer 4. Correct angle for staple to hit roof board 5. Pulls boards together for tight fit 6. Less bending of the wrist—ergonomics 7. Staple could hit finger
#2 Repeat for other five rails	Same key points	
#3 Check	1. Cap rails tight at top of rail 2. No cracked wood 3. No over shot staples	1. So feeder doesn't come apart 2. Split wood has defect—no good for customer 3. Means staple not properly located for best hold in wood

Figure 10-20. An Example of a Job Breakdown Sheet

Multifunction Worker Training Timetable

CEDAR WORKS

Name: Pam Bowling
Section/Group: I/P Trim IR 140
Date: 1/3/95

Number	Name	Base ring assembly (6)	Bottom base assembly (5)	Corner rail assembly (7)	Roof gluing operation (5)	Roof assembly (6)	Cap rail assembly (6)	Sawing operation (5)	String, tag, label (5)	Inspect, box (5)	Capabilities Jan.	Capabilities Jun.	Capabilities Dec.	Remarks — Employee power needs / Performance needs (Work manner)
1.	Marsha Brown										9	9		6/10/95 Leave of absence
2.	Chester O'Neal										9	9		
3.	Randy Phipps										9	9		
4.	Bill Johnson										7	7		
5.	Karen Wagoner										7	7		
6.	Joe Haupert										6	7		Inadequate skills Sawing Operation
7.	Mike Ranley										6	6		
8.	Mona Johnson										2	3		
9.														
10.														

Result of training

	Base ring	Bottom base	Corner rail	Roof gluing	Roof	Cap rail	Sawing	String, tag, label	Inspect, box
Beginning of year	7	6	7	3	7	6	3	6	7
Middle of year	8	6	8	3	8	7	4	7	8
End of year									

Remarks / Job needs (Production change): 20,000 piece order July 10, 1995

Legend:
● = 100% performance
◐ = 75% performance
◓ = 50% performance
⊕ = in training

Figure 10-21. An Example of a Training Timetable

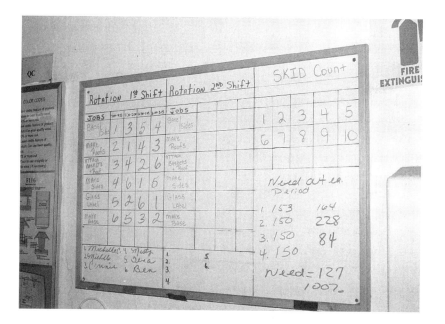

Photo 10-4. An Example of Worker Job Rotation Board

clearly a transition period during which things got worse before they got better. Line workers were not used to working as a coordinated team. They did not understand the importance of small line stops and how to respond to them, or that wasted seconds and minutes add up to tremendous impact and loss of production over the entire day. Second, simple as it was, the "chicken line" was a significant motivation for giving the team a common goal and a tangible reward.

The impact of this standard work/job instruction program was dramatic. Through the reduction of non-value-added work and the steady use of cycle balance tables, during the 10 weeks of this course we reduced labor on this assembly line from 14 line workers and one on-line team leader down to seven assemblers and one off-line team leader. Overall productivity increased from 5.4 to approximately 8 units per labor-hour.

Cedar Works reduced total production area floor space by 40 percent. Remote subassemblies that were once done on different shifts in different areas of the plant were totally coordinated and built only as needed. This helped eliminate storage areas for subassembly parts, as well as the labor needed to store and recover the parts. Cedar Works dramatically reduced excess line-side inventories and recovered warehouse space, as there was no longer a need for storage of off-shift subassemblies. Likewise, material handling no longer included the parts in and out of storage for off-shift subassemblies. They greatly increased production flexibility, because now each shift had the capacity to produce the entire product, whereas before it required the effort of all three shifts. They could now run production on all three shifts or fewer if so desired.

Word spread quickly to other areas of the plant that the Gazebo line was the place to work. Requests came pouring in from other workers who wanted a chance to work on this improved line. Prior to this project employees had been frustrated to the point of taking steps toward unionization. Worker discontent and the drive for union activity entirely vanished. Tools of visual management allowed anyone—production supervisor, plant manager or team member on the line—to see at a glance the status of production (Photo 10-5). Once again, the team's presentation to management brought focus and closure to the overall activity. As Randy Phipps stated, "You were able to see the elimination of inventories and why some people were working themselves to death. The real success from it came in the fact that as you were able to make some changes in those areas, people bought in because their jobs were easier."

Though our results in the Gazebo area had been dramatic, obviously there was still much work to be done. There was a very serious need for improved forecasting and planning to gain better schedule stability. We needed to revise personnel practices in order to stabilize the work force and begin weaning away from heavy dependence on temporary labor. This would also allow Cedar Works to develop and maintain a higher level of skill within their workers. There was also the challenge of extending this process to the 12 other assembly lines in the West Union plant.

Unlike our first Productivity Plus training session, this session did succeed in propagating change throughout the rest of the West Union lines. Why? A major difference was that we assigned a coordinator to be responsible for implementing this change. Pam Bowling, the former team leader for the Gazebo line, was given an

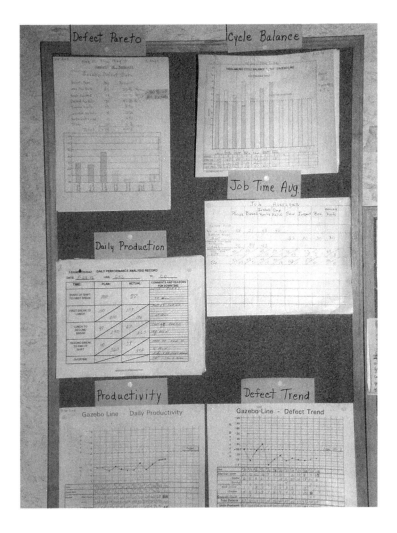

Photo 10-5. Visual Display Board for Gazebo Area

initial one-year assignment to deploy the system to the rest of West Union. Dave and I provided a six-phase standard implementation template (Figure 10-22, *a* through *f*, pages 350–355) that served as a blueprint for repeating the implementation process for the other assembly lines at the West Union plant. The teaching model of 50 percent classroom time and 50 percent on-the-floor time was extremely effective. It led to rapid internalization of the principles and genuine transfer of skills. It was particularly clear to us as we hit the "bottom of the barrel" that participants may require extensive coaching and support in the principles of the new system before they are familiar enough to generate improved results. When Cedar Works gets into a performance crunch they will face the crisis of deciding whether they are going to revert to old methods of behavior and practices or rely on the principles of the new system.

A model area is a very powerful teaching tool for the entire organization. Most production people hold the view that "I'll trust it when I see it work on the floor." A model area provides the needed "real world" proof to convince most shopfloor people. Trend data are also essential to the continuous improvement process. Having high visibility for these data where workers can see them on a daily basis is a strong motivation and reinforcement for change. Our efforts toward job instruction training were useful for

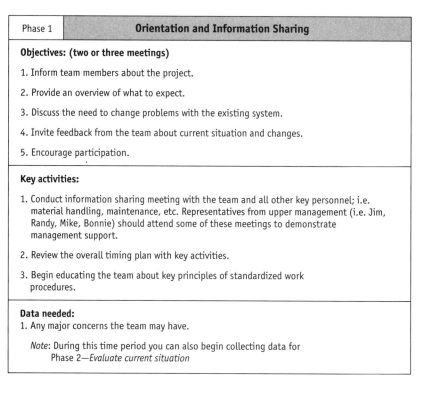

Phase 1	Orientation and Information Sharing

Objectives: (two or three meetings)

1. Inform team members about the project.

2. Provide an overview of what to expect.

3. Discuss the need to change problems with the existing system.

4. Invite feedback from the team about current situation and changes.

5. Encourage participation.

Key activities:

1. Conduct information sharing meeting with the team and all other key personnel; i.e. material handling, maintenance, etc. Representatives from upper management (i.e. Jim, Randy, Mike, Bonnie) should attend some of these meetings to demonstrate management support.

2. Review the overall timing plan with key activities.

3. Begin educating the team about key principles of standardized work procedures.

Data needed:
1. Any major concerns the team may have.

   Note: During this time period you can also begin collecting data for
   Phase 2—*Evaluate current situation*

Figure 10-22a. West Union Phase 1 Standard Work Implementation Template

Phase 2	Evaluate Current Situation

Objectives:

1. Establish trend data for the key measurable that will be used in this process; i.e. units/labor hour, scrap, defects, downtime, etc.

2. Introduce concepts of work balance, and non-value-added activity (NVA).

Key activities:

1. Create trend graphs for key measurable: units/labor hour, defects.

2. Create cycle balance table for current work situation.

3. Create an action plan to eliminate obvious NVA through simple layout changes; i.e. eliminate walking, reaching, bending, double-handling, etc.

Data needed:

1. Past performance data for the line.

2. Average work and wait time for each position.

3. Observation of current NVA activities on the floor.

Figure 10-22b. West Union Phase 2 Standard Work Implementation Template

introducing fundamental tools and concepts. More work, however, is still needed here to gain maximum benefits from work standardization and job instruction.

Phase IV : On-Going Coaching of Lean Manufacturing Principles

Following the standard work/job instruction training course we had just completed on the Gazebo line, Jim was determined to ensure that the new system was successfully deployed throughout the rest of the plant. To support this, we began a six-month period of consulting support. During this time, Dave made monthly visits to West Union to assist them in implementing the production system principles throughout the remainder of the West Union assembly lines. I, meanwhile, returned to the Peebles plant, where we initially worked in Phase I. They had been working with a kanban system for nearly two years, but it was more a parts-labeling system than a tool for actually controlling material movement and production. West Union assembly lines had also been experiencing a grow-

Phase 3	Standardize Work Procedures

Objectives: (two to three weeks)

1. Implement standard work practices at the process.

2. Consolidate any off-shift subassemblies to a single shift production.

3. Introduce key concepts:

In-process stock levels	Line side stock levels
One-piece material flow	Rules for repairs
Pull system	Role of the team leader

Key activities:

1. Re-balance work elements to achieve better load distribution.

2. Ensure that subassemblies can produce at a rate to support full production; redistribute work if necessary.

3. Define standard work steps for each work station.

4. Tape off location for two to three in-process parts between each work station.

5. Define minimum/maximum levels for all line side stock components.

6. Establish a central communication board for data tracking and documents.

7. Re-configure the process to eliminate obvious NVA.

8. Re-organize work layout so team members can help each other if needed (side by side instead of across the work table from each other).

9. Reduce worker rotation and use the temporaries in order to build team member skills.

Data needed:

1. Continue tracking key measurables:

Unit/labor hour	Downtime
Defects	Etc.

Figure 10-22c. West Union Phase 3 Standard Work Implementation Template

ing number of part shortages from the Peebles plant, which resulted in significant production losses. Based on these two facts, we began a separate initiative to correct and revitalize the kanban and material movement system at the Peebles plant.

Dave focused his efforts exclusively at West Union. For a period of six months he visited regularly in the evenings for about four hours per visit. Dave worked primarily with the West Union management team and Pam, the production system coordinator. His focus was to provide ongoing coaching and direction as they deployed the lean manufacturing system to other lines at West Union. This ongoing, though periodic, support was important for a number of reasons. First, it provided a resource for dealing with new problems. For example, one of the other assembly lines at West Union required a separate subassembly process located in another part of the plant. Dave provided the needed coaching to train the team in using kanban so that they could coordinate just-in-time production and delivery of parts between the main assembly line and the subassembly area. Second, Dave's coaching also provided continued reinforcement and support for trusting and mastering the new principles of lean manufacturing. Many times Cedar Works was tempted to slip back into old patterns of doing business. Regular reinforcement by an outside expert helped to discourage this backsliding. Third, regular contact over time allowed the

Phase 4	Reinforce Standard Procedures

Objectives:

1. Develop discipline and automatic response in team members to function correctly under the new system.

2. Deepen team members' comprehension of standard work principles.

Key activities:

1. Define and clarify rules for repairs and unusual situations.

2. Clarify roles and responsibilities for team members, team leader, supervisor, etc.

3. Hold short meetings with team members to clarify key topics about working within the standard system; i.e. handling repairs, role of the team leader, productive use of wait time, etc.

4. Create large visual aids that remind team members of correct procedures; i.e. use of wait time. Also, provide large trend graphs that show daily progesss toward goals.

Data needed:

1. Continue tracking key measurables:

    Unit/labor hour   Downtime

    Defects   Etc.

Figure 10-22d. West Union Phase 4 Standard Work Implementation Template

organization to develop confidence and ownership of the process. As of June 1997, almost two years after the standard work/job instruction training was first presented, West Union is just completing conversion of the last of their final assembly lines. Some time is needed to internalize and embrace this process as a permanent shift in the culture. Ongoing coaching also allows for continued growth and development of the system even after "the honeymoon is over." Eventually lean principles come to be seen as solid and trustworthy for everyday production life. This is what Mike Ranly, plant manager at West Union, had to say:

Phase 5	Continuous Improvement

Objectives:

1. Reduce defects.

2. Improve line up-time through better team member coordination.

3. Involve the team in finding ways to eliminate NVA.

4. Set challenge targets to productivity (Chicken Line).

5. Clarify quality issues.

Key activities:

1. Meet with the team to discuss ways to improve up-time and efficiency using cycle balance table and by eliminating NVA.

2. Review the seven types of NVA.

3. Discuss takt time and daily production targets.

4. Clarify procedures for minimizing line stops and finding productive use of wait time.

5. Get management to support and *recognize attainment of goals*; i.e. Chicken Line, Steak Line, brief recognition of the team, etc.

6. Clarify quality issues using boundary samples, go/no-go gauges, etc.

7. If possible, install some type of pacing mechanism for the line; i.e. pacing light on the boxer unit.

Data needed:

1. Continue tracking key measurables.

2. Add some type of measurable for up-time or down-time.

3. Daily production target board.

Figure 10-22e. West Union Phase 5 Standard Work Implementation Template

Phase 6	Finalizing and Extending to Other Shifts

Objectives:

1. Stabilize the process with current best practices.

2. Finalize job breakdown sheets for all jobs.

3. Train off-shifts using standard procedures.

Key activities:

1. Set up data tracking sheets for all shifts.

2. Complete job breakdown sheets for each position on the line.

3. Complete multifunction worker training chart.

4. Arrange cross rotation of team members from other shifts to begin learning the new procedures.

Data needed:

1. Performance data tracking sheets:

Units/labor hours

Defects

Downtime

Multifunction worker training chart

Etc.

Figure 10-22f. West Union Phase 6 Standard Work Implementation Template

> I think a lot of the support [for implementing lean principles] was that there were outsiders here working with us. Having someone outside the organization, like Bill and Dave, come in was a little more entertaining, new, different, and wasn't the same old people telling us something.... There's a difference.

Another critical role of ongoing coaching is clarification and reinforcement of roles and responsibilities under the new system. Very often there were questions of responsibility, orders of priority, and practical logistics that needed to be solved. What are the new roles and responsibilities of a team leader if he or she is no longer tied to production? Having an experienced coach available can clarify many of these organizational questions and avoid much confusion and chaos. Very simply, when people are in a process of dramatic change, they need a continuous resource whom they can trust to guide them through the change. Without this resource, there is a high likelihood that the process will either be abandoned or modified so that it no longer meets its original purpose.

Phase V: Introducing Kanban at Peebles

While Dave was concentrating on West Union and final assembly, I began a six-month process with the Peebles plant for implementation of kanban. The use of kanban for production scheduling and material flow at the Peebles facility was another fundamental step forward. We started the process with a full-day kanban workshop to introduce the principles and practices of the kanban system. Up to this point Peebles had been using kanban primarily as a material label but not to control material movement or patterns of production. Iveagh Leahmann, an assistant to Randy Phipps, had been working with the concept of a kanban system for well over a year, but was trying to implement it based solely on information from books. As champion for the kanban system, she had invested tremendous effort to make it work, yet was still frustrated at not being able to use it to its full potential. Figure 10-23 shows a relatively high degree of complexity in Peebles material flow involving 3 processes, 201 intermediate codes, and 55 end items.

Counting by hand—A cross between a nightmare and black magic
Our situation before implementation again showed the re-saw process as the bottleneck, but this time not simply due to throughput limitations. Now the problem was confusion about what products to produce, at what time, and in what quantities. Cedar Works was keeping large inventories of more than 200 parts at both the Peebles and West Union locations. They were processing most of these parts through multiple operations. Every day, material managers at each location would count the quantity of parts on hand, compare them to production requirements, and then decide the production schedule for more than 20 cutting, molding, and shaping operations at Peebles. This task was a cross between a nightmare and black magic. It relied heavily on the skill and experience

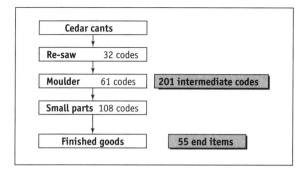

Figure 10-23. Peebles Wood Flowchart

of two key employees, Scott Sullivan and Jeff Swayne, the material managers for each shop. This process was very labor and time intensive, occupying a sizable portion of the day for these two people. Accuracy was poor and production stops due to lack of parts were commonplace. Individual operators would decide what products they were going to produce, in what order, and in what quantity. Often they were grossly overproducing parts that were easier to run while ignoring badly needed parts. They were moving material from Peebles to West Union in one large shipment per day. Any problems with this shipment usually had to be corrected the next day, always with an interruption to production.

The whole Peebles plant seemed to be in a perpetual mode of crisis management. Jeff and Scott, the material managers, were continually under pressure for part shortages and subsequent schedule interruptions. Final assembly operators at West Union were faced daily with part shortages and production shortfalls. Vendor supplies and components were also a sore spot. There were frequent stock shortages resulting in production losses. And finally, quality problems were a regular part of life, with no systems for tracking the problems back to their source. Production workers were simply asked to deal with it and live with high scrap rates.

A Six-Month Plan for Implementing Kanban

We reviewed the situation described above as part of the one-day kanban workshop. All of these major problems were clearly highlighted. We presented an ideal case of how the system might look under the disciplined practices of just-in-time production, a pull system for material movement, and systematic scheduling. A very important element was that we created a vision of what would be possible with more accurate forecasting and production scheduling, stable predictable processes, and a more responsive material handling system. We proposed a plan to implement the needed changes strategically over the next six-month period.

Our approach was to concentrate on a model area in which to apply and demonstrate the principles. We chose re-saw as the model area. The questions now were, "Are we cutting the right products in the right quantities, at the right time? Do we have enough capacity for the mix of products that we are making at any point in time?" Cedar Works' product mix varied considerably from season to season, so the demand on re-saw varied. We began by systematically evaluating machine capacity at re-saw. Figure 10-24 is an example of a capacity planning worksheet we developed for evaluating the machine loading on re-saw for a given mix of products. We also undertook a thorough understanding of other key factors that were affecting performance, like tool setup and changeover time (see Figure 10-25 for setup charts). We spent time focusing on the fundamentals of kanban, the mechanics of how it works, and how you can use it as a tool for scheduling production and managing material movement.

Figure 10-26 is a general scheme of how material flow and production would work under a kanban system:

1. The process starts when you remove materials from the finished goods store area. Kanban for these parts are dropped in a kanban post.
2. You transfer these kanban from the post to the re-saw kanban board on a regular schedule; for example, twice per shift.
3. The kanban board dictates production sequence and lot size. You use red, yellow, and green colors to indicate priority for production of each part.
4. You produce and return needed parts to the finished goods store area, tagged with the appropriate kanban card.

Re-Saw 1 and 2 : Capacity Planning Worksheet

Finished goods needed		Net quantity needed (pieces)	Description raw stock needed	Yield Units Type	Quantity raw stock (cants)	Process cycle time (sec/cant)	Item run time (minutes)	Setup time (minutes)	Combined item time (minutes)
Part #	Description								
5019	3 7/16" x 3 7/16" x 8'	0	5" x 5" cant	1 post	0	15	0	0	0
		0	6" x 6" cant	1 post	0	15	0	0	0
		800	7" x 7" cant	1 post	800	15	200	10	210
5025	4 13/16" x 11/16" x 8'	1,200	5" x 5" cant	5 boards	240	15	60	10	70
5050	4 1/2" x 11/16" x 8'	0	6" x 6" cant	6 boards	0	15	0	0	0
		420	7" x 7" cant	7 boards	60	15	15	10	25
5973	4" x 11/16" x 8'	900	4/14" x 4 1/14"	4 boards	225	15	56	10	66
5086	6 1/4" x 9/16" x 8'	780	6" x 6" cant	8 boards	98	15	24	10	34
		0	7" x 7" cant	9 boards	0	15	0	0	0
					cants =		Runtime = (cants* cycle)/60	Setup = 10 if need>0	Item time = run + setup
Part #	Description	Need	Stock description	Y boards	(Need/Y)	Cycle			

Planner does data entry in this column only. Raw stock needed and item run times are automatically calculated.

Total planned machine time (hours)   6.76

Available shift time (hours)   7.25

Can Do :)

Figure 10-24. An Example of a Capacity Planning Worksheet

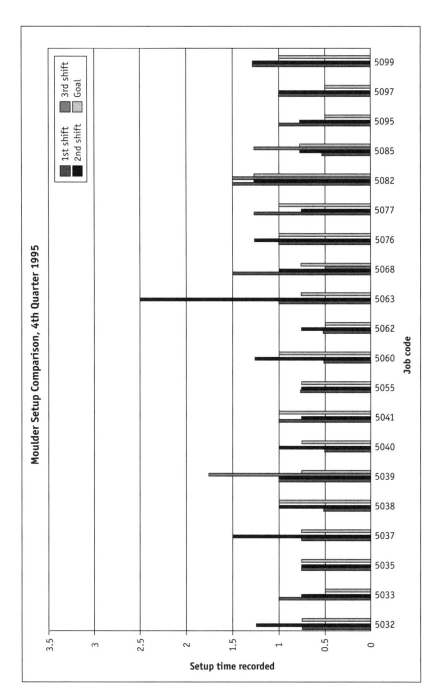

Figure 10-25. DSG Setup Time Comparison

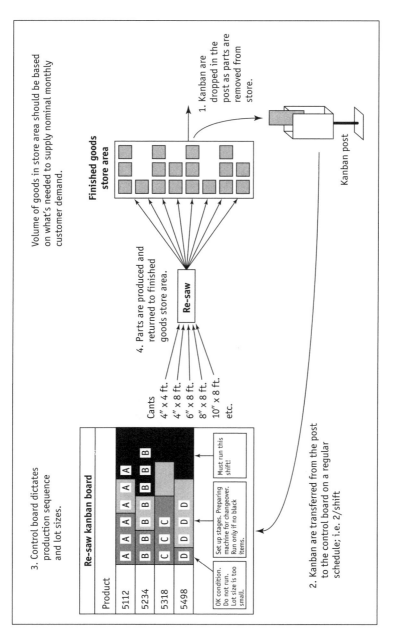

Volume of goods in store area should be based on what's needed to supply nominal monthly customer demand.

Finished goods store area

1. Kanban are dropped in the post as parts are removed from store.

Kanban post

4. Parts are produced and returned to finished goods store area.

Re-saw

Cants
4" x 4 ft.
4" x 8 ft.
6" x 8 ft.
8" x 8 ft.
10" x 8 ft.
etc.

3. Control board dictates production sequence and lot sizes.

Re-saw kanban board

Product				
5112	A	A	A	A
5234	B	B	B	B
5318	C	C		
5498	D	D	D	D

OK condition. Do not run. Lot size is too small.

Set up stages. Preparing machine for changeover. Run only if no black items.

Must run this shift!

2. Kanban are transferred from the post to the control board on a regular schedule; i.e. 2/shift

Figure 10-26. Kanban and Material Flow Around Re-Saw

We also designed the template for a generic kanban tag that could be used throughout the entire Peebles operation (Figure 10-27). Since our meetings were now on a monthly basis, homework assignments were a key vehicle for getting work done between sessions. Figure 10-28 is an example of the homework assignment from our September meeting. Randy Phipps worked with a core group of 8 to 10 people to get the work done, including two administrative assistants, his material handling supervisors, members of maintenance, and select team leaders as needed. Generally, we were able to complete all assignments, though the timing would often be extended for more complicated tasks.

Preparing for the shift to kanban
Despite the consistent effort from everyone on the team for the first three months, our progress was slow. It simply took time to get the infrastructure in place: clean out and establish a central storage area for small parts, install storage racks with clear visual aids, physically create the actual kanban tags and get them laminated, and establish drop and collection points. Slowly the stage was set to introduce the kanban as a genuine cultural shift at the Peebles plant.

Supply info	Part info	Customer info
	ID#	User processes
Raw material code	Description	Storage locations
Raw material location	Quantity	Kanban #

Supply info	Part info	Customer info
	Part # 52107	User processes Small parts DSG
Raw material code 4″ x 4 ft. cants	Description 3/8″ Board x 4′	Storage location C-12
Raw material location Shed 1 - B6	Quantity 400/skid	Kanban #/Issue date #4 - 3/18/95

Figure 10-27. Templates for Generic Kanban Tags

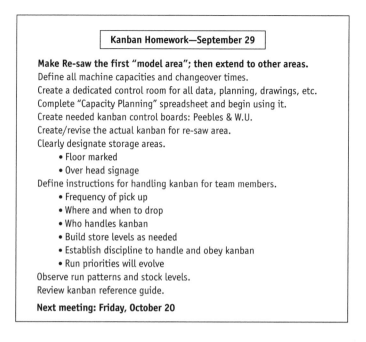

Kanban Homework—September 29

Make Re-saw the first "model area"; then extend to other areas.
Define all machine capacities and changeover times.
Create a dedicated control room for all data, planning, drawings, etc.
Complete "Capacity Planning" spreadsheet and begin using it.
Create needed kanban control boards: Peebles & W.U.
Create/revise the actual kanban for re-saw area.
Clearly designate storage areas.
- Floor marked
- Over head signage

Define instructions for handling kanban for team members.
- Frequency of pick up
- Where and when to drop
- Who handles kanban
- Build store levels as needed
- Establish discipline to handle and obey kanban
- Run priorities will evolve

Observe run patterns and stock levels.
Review kanban reference guide.

Next meeting: Friday, October 20

Figure 10-28. Example of Homework Activities

We also evaluated the ship frequency of material from Peebles to West Union. Figure 10-29a shows a comparison of the pros and cons of Peebles' original one-shipment-per-day pattern. Figure 10-29b shows the pros and cons of a proposed three-shipments-per-day pattern. You considerably reduce the amount of material needed in the system as a result of more frequent shipments—and obviously you are moving the product more quickly.

Schedule interruptions after kanban launches
About one month after the launch of the kanban effort, the issue of schedule interruptions began to surface as a major problem. Bonnie Sowards, the production supervisor at West Union, had been fighting schedule interruptions for as long as she had been in the role. Again, we used simple Pareto graphing to identify the most common causes of unexpected schedule changes. Figure 10-30 (page 366) shows a weekly tracking sheet of schedule changes at West Union. Figure 10-31 (page 367) shows a monthly summary

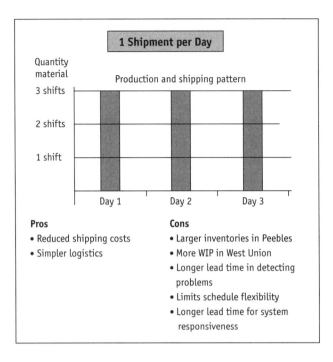

Figure 10-29a. Pros and Cons of One Shipment per Day

of schedule changes for the period of September 21 through October 8. Surprisingly, the number one cause of schedule changes was individual employee problems such as work force shortages, poor coordination, lack of training, etc. The second largest scheduling problem was vendor related, such as the lack of material, changes in shipments, short shipments, or the wrong products being delivered. These results brought Cedar Works' internal personnel policies and the question of vendor reliability to focus. In response, the company began moving more aggressively toward limiting the use of temporary labor. We used this opportunity to introduce simple reorder kanban to indicate when vendor parts had reached the reorder point. This simple technique alone nearly eliminated all vendor shortages.

Quality problems
During this time it was clear that there was no reliable way to track quality problems through the production processes. Therefore,

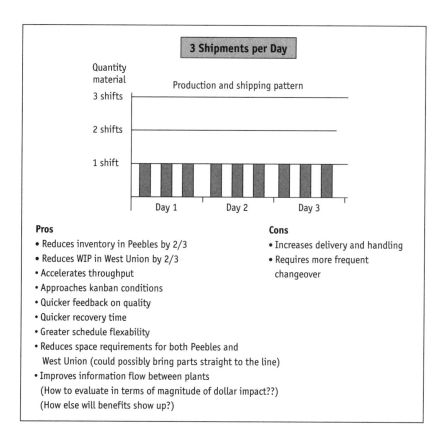

Figure 10-29b. Pros and Cons of Three Shipments per Day

we instituted a simple quality tracking card that would follow the material through all the production processes at both facilities. If a tub contained defective parts, you could trace it back to the process of origin to investigate root causes. Figure 10-32 (page 368) is a weekly trend graph that shows the number of problems with small parts for each shift. This created a sense of ownership and accountability for each shift, as well as a solid indicator of progress (see Figure 10-33, page 369).

MRP versus kanban

As we were wrestling with the whole question of production planning and material movement, we took a hard look at Cedar Works' existing material resource planning (MRP) system. They used a

Weekly schedule change—West Union **Week of** **10/12 to 10/18**

	People			Machines/ Equipment			Promotional/ Special orders			Subcontractors			Vendors			Internal part shortages			Miscellaneous		
	Date	Shift	Description	Date	Shift	Description	Date	Shift	Description	Date	Shift	Description	Date	Shift	Description	Date	Shift	Description	Date	Shift	Description
15																					
14																					
13																					
12																					
11																					
10																					
9																					
8													10/18	3rd	Drop SF due to no cartons.						
7													10/18	1st	Out of CF cartons. Switch to RF.						
6	10/17	3rd	Dropped CFBA–not enough people										10/18	1st	Out of SF cartons. Ran CFSA.						
5	10/16	1st	Ran SF. Had more people than planned										10/17	1st	Out of SF cartons. Line down at 2:00						
4	10/16	3rd	Drop SF due to people										10/16	1st	Shut down lantern line–finals too long						
3	10/13	2nd	Short 1 person on 62																10/18	2nd	Part wrong: 62 pcs. send back
2	10/13	2nd	Short on people on RF	10/13	3rd	Problems with saw CFSA							10/13	3rd	No DF cartons. Had to change schedule	10/16	3rd	Ran out of CFPC	10/13	2nd	Had to rework RF's from 10/12
1	10/13	1st	Couldn't run CF	10/12	3rd	Problems with saw CFSA							10/12	3rd	No DF Cartons. Had to change schedule	10/12	3rd	Ran out of CFPC	10/12	1st	3 people on light duty.

Figure 10-30. An Example of a Weekly Schedule Change Form

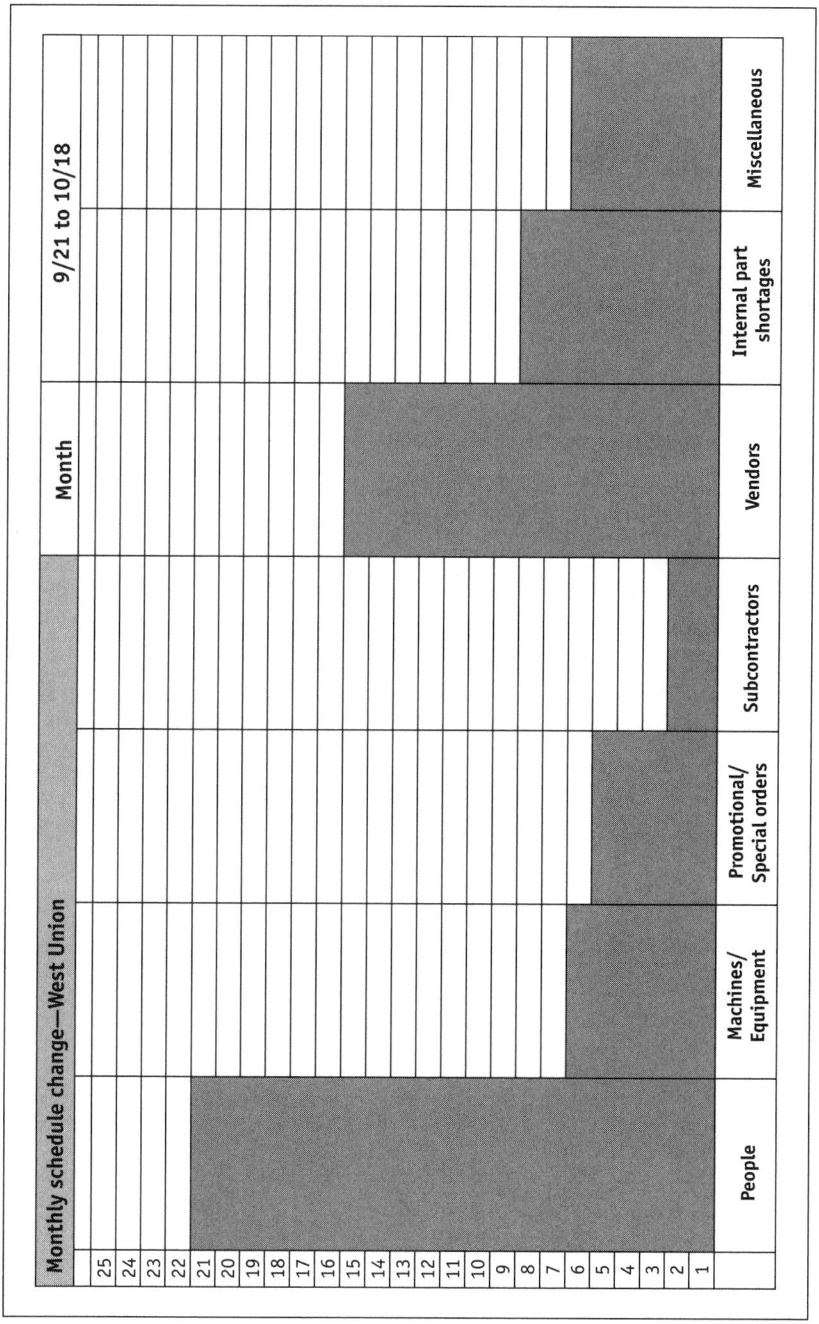

Figure 10-31. An Example of a Monthly Schedule Change Form

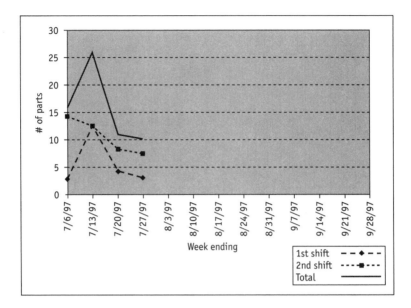

Figure 10-32. Parts Issues for Peebles, 2nd Quarter 1997

Symex system for tracking the finished goods inventory levels and reorder of materials for vendor parts. They had the capability of scheduling all component production processes, but they had not programmed and set up it up to do so. Component process scheduling, therefore, was handled exclusively by the material handling supervisor. Chaos erupted when he was absent, because no one else fully understood the connection between material inventory levels and production requirements. As we considered both systems, kanban versus MRP, the decision was made not to further automate and computerize the production planning process but rather to simplify the process to its most essential elements. Ultimately, the simple, homely kanban system became the tool for production scheduling of all component processes. This relieved the material handling supervisor of the burden of scheduling all component processes and allowed production operators to make moment-by-moment decisions based on actual consumption to support customer demand. It instituted a reliable system for managing shop floor production that was no longer dependent on the skill or expertise of one individual (see Photo 10-6).

Some Key Lessons from Implementing Kanban at Peebles

The steps described above to get the kanban system installed and functioning as a way of life took six full months. There was much infrastructure that had to be built; new habits and ways of thinking needed to be cultivated and reinforced. Once it was implemented, though, the entire organization embraced it quickly. They could see clearly that it provided a simple, objective basis for product changeovers and production scheduling. Much of the ambiguity, confusion, chaos, and unnecessary work of the past had been eliminated through a very simple, predictable kanban system. The benefits to the organization were many. Parts storage was consolidated into one location at each plant. We had eliminated the task of daily part counting for both material handling supervisors. We had eliminated production scheduling for small parts operations, as this function was now evident from the kanban scheduling boards. We had reduced lot sizes on all parts by 50 percent or more. We recovered floor space that had been used for inventory storage. We had

Batch # Original batch date: _____				Batch # Original batch date: _____			
Code	Initials	Shift	Date	Code	Initials	Shift	Date
Resaw				Re-saw			
Gang rip				Gang rip			
Moulder				Moulder			
Post line				Post line			
Parts				Parts			

Figure 10-33. Sample Problem Tracking Cards

Photo 10-6. Kanban Board for Peebles "Small Parts" Production Area

greatly reduced production interruptions due to part shortages. We had almost totally eliminated vendor part shortages. Through the use of clear, visual controls we had simplified the entire material handling process, greatly reducing cross-training time and effort.

Some of the lessons learned from the process of implementing kanban were the following:

1. Using a distinct model area to demonstrate and prove the kanban principles is a very valuable learning tool for the entire organization. Deployment of the kanban system to other production areas at Peebles went very quickly and smoothly following the initial success of the model area.

2. There is no substitute for a dedicated resource to support the effort. Iveagh Leahmann was the champion for the kanban system and provided support and continuity for the effort.

3. Use homework. It is very valuable in giving responsibility for the implementation to key people in the area, thus building ownership and understanding of the process from the very outset.

4. The kanban system lends itself well to use of many visual tools. Using kanban boards in each area presented a prominent and visual indi-

cator for what was happening with the replenishment system. Also, arrange storage areas so that they are very visible and clear for all to see. The entire organization responds well when they can see visual evidence of progress and changes.

It is noteworthy that Cedar Works never used their computerized MRP system for controlling material movement or intermediate production scheduling, whereas the kanban system served both functions even with a high level of part complexity.

Phase VI : Companywide Deployment

Our six-month coaching visits for kanban support at Peebles and lean implementation support for West Union came to an end in February 1996. It was now time for Cedar Works to assume the challenge of maintaining momentum and sustaining the system on their own. During this window, I left Toyota Motor in Georgetown to join RWD Technologies. RWD was providing consulting support to Ford Motor Company in the creation and implementation of their own lean manufacturing system, the Ford Production System. Over the months, however, Jim and I stayed in touch, comparing notes and experiences in implementing lean principles at the tiny Cedar Works and the immense Ford. During this time also, Cedar Works was laying plans for significant growth in terms of new product lines and expanding their customer base within the next 12 to 18 months. In preparation for this growth, they wanted to strengthen their understanding of and practical skill with lean principles throughout their organization.

Cedar Works made the decision to launch an extensive training program as a first step toward institutionalizing the Cedar Works Production System as a centerpiece of company culture. Table 10-2 summarizes some key points in this effort.

This training effort represented a major commitment to embrace lean manufacturing and make it a routine way of doing business. Every salaried member and all hourly leadership personnel in the manufacturing organization would receive the training at the same time. They appointed a second full-time production sys-

Table 10-2. Cedar Works Companywide Lean Manufacturing Training

Subject focus	• Standardized work
	• Job instruction training
Target audience	• Supervisors
	• Assistant supervisors
	• Team leaders
	• Assistant team leaders
	• Management team
	• Total group size 66 people
	• All three shifts
	• Peebles and West Union plants
Class size	• 12 to 17 participants
	• Four training groups
Training window	• February to mid-April, 1997
Training exposure	• Sessions held one per week for each group
	• Average three hours per session
	• All four groups trained back-to-back over two days
Objectives	• Develop working knowledge of standardized work and job instruction training through hands-on practice
	• Develop in-house training resources for Cedar Works through a "train-the-trainer" approach

tem coordinator, Evelena Durbin, to support the Peebles plant. She and Pam Bowling, from West Union, would become in-house trainers-in-training. They attended every training session four times; the first one as participants, the next two as observers, and the last as co-leaders. Developing this training resource in their own employees was a step toward weaning Cedar Works' dependence on consultants and strengthening their ability to support and extend the system on their own.

As team leader Delbert Scott at the Peebles plant said:

I feel [what helped in the transition to using lean principles] was management's overall way of bringing the team leaders into it, explaining to them, and showing them the charts, saying, "This is where we are, this is where we want to be, we feel this is the way to get there, will you help us?"…more or less asking for our help and involving us in it. By management delegating that down, the team leaders have delegated into their crews of actual team members. I feel that's the biggest thing, management's approach to involving people instead of standing back and saying, "This is the way it's gonna be or else."

The training content for these sessions was nearly identical to the material used on the Gazebo line two years earlier. Either Jim or Randy kicked off the first training session for each group, demonstrating their on-going commitment and support for the process. They emphasized the need for changing to this new production system by reviewing the challenges facing the company (Figure 10-34). Cedar Works is in a very competitive business. Their customers are consolidating suppliers who expect lower costs, rapid delivery, consistent quality, and a steady stream of new and ingenious products. As their larger customers head increasingly to single sourcing of products, it is becoming more of a "winner take all" game when supplying mega-marketing chains like Wal-Mart, Lowe's, and Home Depot. The Cedar Works Production System was presented as an integrated manufacturing system that would provide the ongoing competitive edge to keep the company both healthy and growing in the marketplace (Figure 10-35).

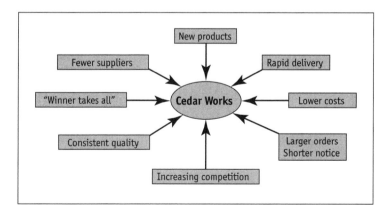

Figure 10-34. The Cedar Works Challenge

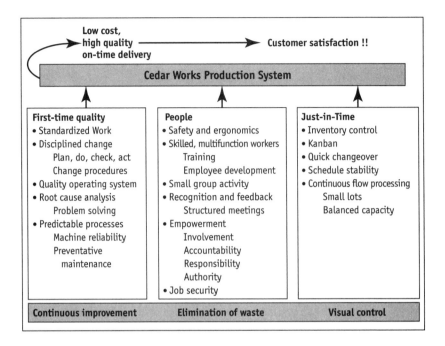

Figure 10-35. The Cedar Works Production System

The training focus was on having all participants actually practice with and apply in their areas the tools they would be learning. John O'Meara, an RWD manufacturing specialist, was the lead consultant for the effort. Another Toyota alumnus, John was ideal for his role in that he brought strength both as a classroom trainer/presenter and as a floor coach; he was able to advise and support efforts in the production areas. Each of the four training groups was assigned target lines where they would practice and apply what they were learning. This scheme served three purposes:

1. It provided all participants with hands-on practice in these new principles in existing production areas.
2. It was a step toward implementing lean tools in four more areas of the business.
3. It exposed a large percentage of production hourly people to the new ideas.

The fundamental tools and concepts for standardized work remained just as they did during the Gazebo line training:

- Identify and eliminate seven types of waste
- Standardized work sheet
- Work combination table
- Job analysis data sheet
- Cycle balance table
- Understanding of takt time versus cycle time
- Work sequence
- Standard in-process stock

The training placed very heavy emphasis on all participants' having the ability to create and use standardized work sheets. To support this end, videotapes of actual production jobs were reviewed in the classroom. Participants practiced identifying and timing work elements based on the videotapes. Once they were familiar with the classroom activities, they went directly to the floor to use these new skills with live jobs. The trainers even went into the detail of training each participant on how to use a stopwatch with split and lap functions. Again, substantial homework between sessions served to encourage practice and to reinforce key points. Simple pocket reminder cards for quick reference to key ideas were also provided (Figures 10-36a and 10-36b). According to Randy Phipps:

> I would have to say that standardized work has made the biggest impact as far as I'm concerned. We've gained better quality, less off-line repairs, the flow is actually smoother, training is not nearly the headache that it was, and as team members and team leaders write out their standardized work, they actually get to see what is total waste that they didn't see before.

Perhaps one of the most exciting and practical activities conducted during this training was the exercise of line rebalancing. As mentioned above, each of the four training groups was assigned a target line for practice in applying the tools they were learning in each session. Cedar Works' end products are seasonal, with wide variations in demand during different times of the year. The object of the line rebalance exercise was to create two additional work configurations for each line to provide greater flexibility during periods of fluctuating customer demand. Results were impressive (Figures 10-37 and 10-38, pages 378–379).

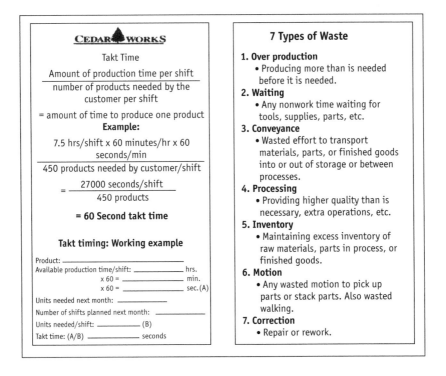

CEDAR WORKS

Takt Time

$$\frac{\text{Amount of production time per shift}}{\text{number of products needed by the customer per shift}}$$

= amount of time to produce one product

Example:

$$\frac{7.5 \text{ hrs/shift} \times 60 \text{ minutes/hr} \times 60 \text{ seconds/min}}{450 \text{ products needed by customer/shift}}$$

$$= \frac{27000 \text{ seconds/shift}}{450 \text{ products}}$$

= 60 Second takt time

Takt timing: Working example

Product: _____
Available production time/shift: _____ hrs.
x 60 = _____ min.
x 60 = _____ sec. (A)
Units needed next month: _____
Number of shifts planned next month: _____
Units needed/shift: _____ (B)
Takt time: (A/B) _____ seconds

7 Types of Waste

1. **Over production**
   • Producing more than is needed before it is needed.
2. **Waiting**
   • Any nonwork time waiting for tools, supplies, parts, etc.
3. **Conveyance**
   • Wasted effort to transport materials, parts, or finished goods into or out of storage or between processes.
4. **Processing**
   • Providing higher quality than is necessary, extra operations, etc.
5. **Inventory**
   • Maintaining excess inventory of raw materials, parts in process, or finished goods.
6. **Motion**
   • Any wasted motion to pick up parts or stack parts. Also wasted walking.
7. **Correction**
   • Repair or rework.

Figure 10-36a. Waste and Takt Time Pocket Reminder Card (2 sided)

Each line achieved two additional takt time configurations, usually with fewer workers. The groups evaluated all three takt time scenarios relative to 1996 production requirements. The manufacturing time (in terms of the number of shifts required to produce this volume of units) typically improved from 7 percent to 30 percent; that is, less time was required to produce the same volume of product. In only two cases was additional time required. In all cases, they reduced direct labor hours (DLH) to manufacture a given volume of product by 25 percent to 40 percent. This provided Cedar Works with a new level of flexibility. There were two major options for rebalancing:

Option 1. Rebalance their lines for greater production where employee power is not a priority. Applying this option to only four of their assembly lines would yield a 25 percent increase in volume at a labor savings of $78,000 per year (or 33 percent reduction in labor hours).

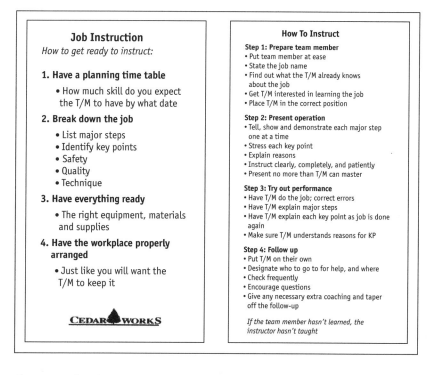

Figure 10-36b. Job Instruction Pocket Reminder Card (2 sided)

Option 2. Rebalance their lines for lower labor requirements where production rate is not a priority. Applying this option to the same four lines yielded mixed results in production rates, from –21 percent to +24 percent. Labor savings under these conditions was $74,000 per year (or 31 percent reduction in labor hours).

As important as these one-time results were, of greater importance was the fact that the course participants now had the working knowledge to apply this same type of analysis anywhere else in the plant. Broad-scale cultural change was earnestly underway. People were truly empowered with key skills of lean manufacturing.

Roles and responsibilities

As the system became more widely deployed, role clarification became increasingly important. Cedar Works prepared one-page summary documents for the roles of supervisor, team leader, and

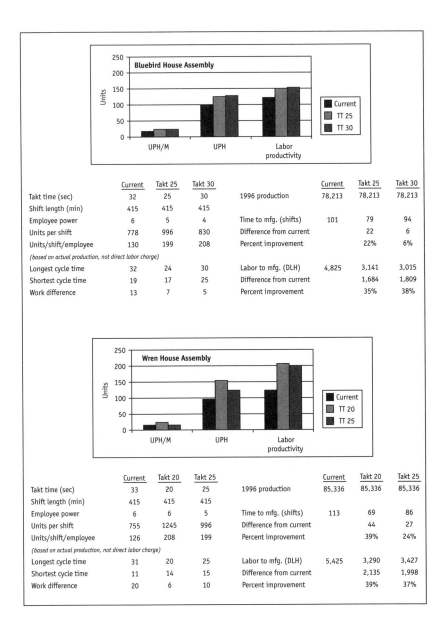

	Current	Takt 25	Takt 30		Current	Takt 25	Takt 30
Takt time (sec)	32	25	30	1996 production	78,213	78,213	78,213
Shift length (min)	415	415	415				
Employee power	6	5	4	Time to mfg. (shifts)	101	79	94
Units per shift	778	996	830	Difference from current		22	6
Units/shift/employee	130	199	208	Percent improvement		22%	6%
(based on actual production, not direct labor charge)							
Longest cycle time	32	24	30	Labor to mfg. (DLH)	4,825	3,141	3,015
Shortest cycle time	19	17	25	Difference from current		1,684	1,809
Work difference	13	7	5	Percent improvement		35%	38%

	Current	Takt 20	Takt 25		Current	Takt 20	Takt 25
Takt time (sec)	33	20	25	1996 production	85,336	85,336	85,336
Shift length (min)	415	415	415				
Employee power	6	6	5	Time to mfg. (shifts)	113	69	86
Units per shift	755	1245	996	Difference from current		44	27
Units/shift/employee	126	208	199	Percent improvement		39%	24%
(based on actual production, not direct labor charge)							
Longest cycle time	31	20	25	Labor to mfg. (DLH)	5,425	3,290	3,427
Shortest cycle time	11	14	15	Difference from current		2,135	1,998
Work difference	20	6	10	Percent improvement		39%	37%

Figure 10-37. Bluebird and Wren House Takt Time Results

team member that clearly defined their responsibilities regarding standardized work and line rebalance activity. This definition was critical to people's understanding of how to behave under the rules of the new system, and so that they would not regress to old behaviors.

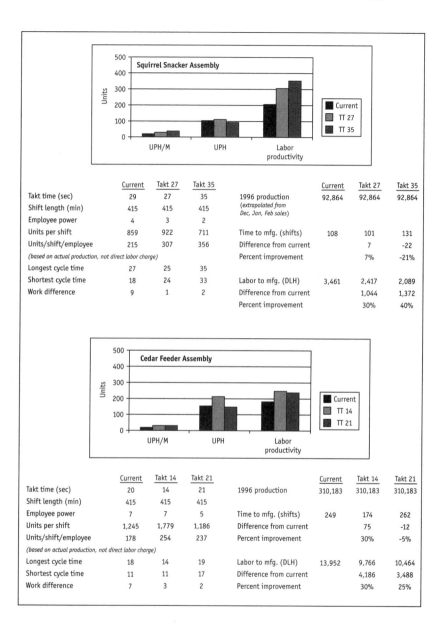

	Current	Takt 27	Takt 35		Current	Takt 27	Takt 35
Takt time (sec)	29	27	35	1996 production	92,864	92,864	92,864
Shift length (min)	415	415	415	*(extrapolated from Dec, Jan, Feb sales)*			
Employee power	4	3	2				
Units per shift	859	922	711	Time to mfg. (shifts)	108	101	131
Units/shift/employee	215	307	356	Difference from current		7	-22
(based on actual production, not direct labor charge)				Percent improvement		7%	-21%
Longest cycle time	27	25	35				
Shortest cycle time	18	24	33	Labor to mfg. (DLH)	3,461	2,417	2,089
Work difference	9	1	2	Difference from current		1,044	1,372
				Percent improvement		30%	40%

	Current	Takt 14	Takt 21		Current	Takt 14	Takt 21
Takt time (sec)	20	14	21	1996 production	310,183	310,183	310,183
Shift length (min)	415	415	415				
Employee power	7	7	5	Time to mfg. (shifts)	249	174	262
Units per shift	1,245	1,779	1,186	Difference from current		75	-12
Units/shift/employee	178	254	237	Percent improvement		30%	-5%
(based on actual production, not direct labor charge)							
Longest cycle time	18	14	19	Labor to mfg. (DLH)	13,952	9,766	10,464
Shortest cycle time	11	11	17	Difference from current		4,186	3,488
Work difference	7	3	2	Percent improvement		30%	25%

Figure 10-38. Squirrel Snack and Cedar Feeder Takt Time Results

Kanban support

In addition to the training described above, there was yet one additional objective during this period, to provide kanban implementation support for both Peebles and West Union sites. The last work I had done with Peebles about one year earlier, enabled kanban to be established and to work effectively in selected production areas. One major shortfall of that training was that it did not provide sufficiently deep understanding of the mechanics for *maintaining* the system. As production demands fluctuated and unusual circumstances developed, they were unable to adjust the system as needed. As a result, the discipline of using the kanban cards to control production eroded. "Exceptions" slowly became commonplace. The net effect was confusion and further skepticism as to whether a kanban system could really work here.

For the Peebles plant, we now had two strikes against the kanban system. To correct this problem, the trainers developed a very simple classroom simulation that involved toy ball and jack kits, 3x5 cards, and markers. The simulation was a very valuable learning tool because it allowed all members to experience the mechanics of a kanban system directly and without the pressure of production. It also gave people a sense of how to adjust the system in order to adapt to changes in production needs and provided an essential training tool for understanding how to function under the rules of a newly installed kanban system. The simulation allows the facilitator to demonstrate a wide variety of production scenarios, some of which may occur only rarely, but can cause great confusion when they do. It also allows participants via direct personal experience to really "get it in their bones" how kanban is designed to function.

The simulation was first delivered to management and class participants from both plants. We then installed a kanban system at the West Union plant to manage part delivery from their warehouse to the assembly lines. This system established a credible, working model for Peebles to follow as they undertook their third effort to establish kanban. Fortunately, on the third go around the system "stuck" and has become an established practice at both facilities.

Kanban implementation required Cedar Works to modify one of their key human resource policies. Up to this time, the company still had an incentive system based on production volume. Therefore, workers had strong motivation to produce parts even though they weren't needed. This was a tough call, but the company abandoned their production incentive program as a necessary step to support the kanban system. The message now was, "If the kanban system is not calling for parts, don't produce." As Randy Phipps observed:

> One of the earlier problems we had [with kanban] was that when you have problems, you put more kanban in [to the system]. We definitely had issues with [the low number of kanban in the system] earlier on, people feeling we can't make it with so few kanban; so we'll just add more, just a few more. That was really a very self-destructive route. Now, we have a good understanding from everybody that less is better. We're having more success, in general now, than we've ever had before.

This was a major paradigm shift for everyone involved.

In Retrospect and Today's Situation

Cedar Works has been steadily implementing their lean manufacturing system over the last four years (Table 10-3). It has been a stepwise process of demonstrating lean principles in model areas, building credibility with the work force, and then extending the process to other areas and at higher levels of finesse. And profit margins have soared, according to Randy Phipps:

> [In our early business] we had some items that we didn't make money on. In order not to upset the customer, we continued to make them and put the burden of profit on the other products we were selling. Through the work with lean manufacturing, we've been able to slowly target the ones that aren't highly profitable and put our energies to improving the profitability internally, not by changing the price but by improving the processes. For example, our biggest seller, the economy feeder, started at a 6 percent margin and it has moved up to where it is 17 or 18 percent now. The two big feeders started out with one actually losing money, and now they're up in the mid-20 percent range. The tower feeder started out at a 4 percent margin, and we have skyrocketed it up to the upper-30 percent range now. That's not to say that we've made these kinds of improvements on all the lines, but every one we do helps out.

Table 10-3. Cedar Works Implementation Summary

Date	Event	Description	Comments
7/93 to 9/93	Productivity plus	• 10 week training program • Workshop activity focused on bottleneck operation	• Introduced principles of lean manufacturing at Peebles shop • Eliminate chronic overtime in re-saw area
3/95 to 6/95	Standard work and job instruction training for Gazebo line	• 10 week training program • Kaizen workshop activity focused on final assembly line for one end item at West Union	• Introduced principles of lean manufacturing at West Union • Full time coordinator appointed to support implementation
7/95 to 1/96	Kanban implementation	• Monthly ongoing consulting to support implementation of kanban at the Peebles plant	• Good progress during coaching phase • Insufficient knowledge to maintain the system long term. Some backsliding here.
9/95 to 2/96	Standard work and job instruction follow-up	• Monthly ongoing support to deploy standard work/job instruction to other lines at West Union final assembly	• Production system extended to other final assembly lines at West Union
2/97 to 4/97	Standard work and job instruction training for supervisors and team leaders	• 8 week intensive training program for all supervisors, team leaders, and their assistants, company wide • Classroom exercises in line rebalancing	• Major improvements in line flexibility and productivity • Cedar Works production system embedded as centerpiece of manufacturing culture
	Kanban system support	• Consulting support to key personnel at both Peebles and West Union • Use of classroom simulation as a training tool	• System embraced company wide • HR policy changes required • System wide inventories are steadily reduced

The following are some of the key lessons we have learned along the way, which are applicable to any company's becoming lean:

- Top management must be committed and visibly demonstrate their support.
- Dedicated resources can greatly enhance the rate of company-wide deployment.
- Classroom training should be followed by direct hands-on practice to promote skill development.
- Target lines/model areas are valuable tools to demonstrate the process and gain credibility with production personnel.

- Classroom simulation is a valuable aid when installing a kanban system to help people understand how the system is intended to work and learn how to react to a variety of scenarios.
- Human resources policies will need adjustment to support a lean manufacturing system.

Cedar Works has made the transition to a truly lean manufacturing organization. I say this because they are able, on their own, continuously to improve their operations toward the elimination of waste; that is, non-value-added activity (Photo 10-7). Recent activities within the last six months provide the evidence:

- On-floor inventory throughout the system has been reduced by 50 percent from four shifts to two shifts.
- Float at Peebles has been entirely eliminated. Kanban cards are now being taken from the assembly operations at West Union directly to the production processes at Peebles. The intermediate parts store has been totally removed. This trans-

Photo 10-7. Typical Cedar Works Assembly Line—May 1997

Photo 10-8. Pallet Storage at West Union Prior to Lean Implementation

lates into huge savings in terms of material handling and available space; for example, an entire building that had been dedicated to small parts storage is now available for other purposes. As Randy Phipps observed, "One thing that it has done that's really shocked everybody is that, as we were going through this, I was on track looking to build another building. As we're moving along, it's going to end up that I've got space I don't know what to do with."

• Material deliveries from Peebles to West Union have been increased from one shipment per day to four shipments per day. This allows much smaller lot sizes, further reduces total inventory in the system, and provides much greater responsiveness in the overall production process.

• They are now working on reducing their unit quantity per kanban from a pallet (which contains from 9 to 18 tubs) down to a single tub. This means that as a single tub of parts is consumed by assembly, a kanban returns directly to the Peebles production process for replacement. Now that's *lean*. (For reference, at the outset of this process four years ago, a standard pallet contained 36 tubs. See Photos 10-8 and 10-9.)

Photo 10-9. Pallet Storage at Peebles—May 1997

- The small-parts processing area is also being redesigned for better material flow according to end product rather than production process. This will reduce double-handling of parts by 50 to 70 percent.

Cedar Works is a classic American success story of a tiny grass-roots company that has steadily grown and made the transition to employing world class lean manufacturing practices. The level of sophistication or size of the company is not the issue (Photo 10-10).

Willingness to experiment with and earnestly apply better methods is the key ingredient in making a successful transformation to lean. Listen to one satisfied president, Jim Obenshain:

> [Without lean manufacturing] I think we would have been hanging on by a thread. We sell to the major retailers in the U.S. who are demanding more and more and not wanting to take any price increases for it. So they're basically saying, 'You figure out how to do this. We don't want a price increase, but we want better fill rates, better quality, etc. That's your problem if you want to deal with us and grow with us, because we are going to become the dominant retailers' [for example, Wal-Mart, Lowe's, Home Depot]. So that is the incentive, survival. I'd say that [without lean] it would've become more and more difficult to satisfy those needs. We would've had more out-of-stocks, [our customers would've been] looking for other possible suppliers, our competitors definitely would've made stronger inroads. We wouldn't have been able to develop new products, which they are constantly asking for, because we just would not have had the space to set up the lines, to store the parts, to store the finished goods. It

Photo 10-10. Small Grass Roots Company

would've just become exponentially more and more difficult to deal with that. I can't say whether we wouldn't be here, but it would've been a whole different picture in terms of stress levels and the fun of doing it.

Note: Should you be interested in gaining further information, you can contact Jim Obenshain, president; or Randy Phipps, vice president of manufacturing, Cedar Works, 19 Cedar Drive, Peebles, OH 45660, telephone 937-587-2656. Also, Bill Costantino would like to hear from you. He can be reached at Kentucky Center for Experiential Education, Route 9 Box 527, Cynthiana, KY 41031, telephone 606-234-6376. Bill's e-mail address is EllenBill_KCEE@classic.msn.com.

Mark F. McGovern. *As a co-founder and consultant with the Phoenix Consulting Group, Mark helps organizations improve operational effectiveness. His focus is on implementation of progressive management techniques such as lean manufacturing, TQM, JIT, cellular manufacturing, and business process reengineering. He has in-depth experience with implementing process improvement through training, coaching, and facilitating improvement teams.*

Mark holds a B.S. in industrial engineering from Lehigh University and is a member of the American Society for Quality Control (ASQC) and the Institute of Industrial Engineers (IIE). He has also been a guest speaker for the National Association of Purchasing Managers (NAPM) and the Shingo Prize for Excellence in Manufacturing National Conference.

Brian J. Andrews *is a co-founder and consultant with the Phoenix Consulting Group. He specializes in progressive management techniques such as TQM, JIT, MRPII, business process reengineering, set-up reduction, factory redesign, supplier partnerships, statistical process control teamwork, and pull system scheduling. He has led process improvement efforts throughout the world in many industries.*

Brian is on the board of examiners for the Shingo Prize for Excellence in Manufacturing. He is an active member of the American Production and Inventory Control Society (APICS), the Association for Manufacturing Excellence (AME), the American Society for Quality Control (ASQC), and the Association for Psychological Type (APT). Brian has an M.S. in management and a B.S. in industrial management/industrial engineering from Purdue University.

Operational Excellence: A Manufacturing Metamorphosis at Western Geophysical Exploration Products

by Mark F. McGovern and Brian J. Andrews

11

Editor's prologue: This chapter describes another unusual application of lean manufacturing, in this case, in a cell within Western Geophysical Exploration Products, a manufacturer of seismic exploration equipment. Mark McGovern and Brian Andrews tell us about the successful transformation of the bay cable manufacturing cell of the land cable–focused factory. The bay cable cell manufactures cable that is 1,250 feet in length, 1.5 inches in diameter, weighing about 1,500 pounds. These cables are used by seismic data collection crews working in shallow water less than 200 feet deep. When the transformation process started, the bay cable cell manufacturing process was in desperate need of improvement. It had 50 percent more demand than it ever produced, first-run yields below 50 percent, high field failure rates, poor on-time delivery, high inventory levels, frequent material shortages, and high cable costs. Western hired Mark McGovern as a consultant to help implement lean manufacturing. By redesigning the flow from a process-oriented layout to product-oriented cells, the bay cable manufacturing area reduced the physical movement of the cable from almost one mile to 0.3 mile and reduced floor space by 30 percent. Cellular manufacturing also led to immediate quality feedback among workers on adjacent processes. Through this feedback, combined with cross-training and problem-solving training, responsibility for quality was spread throughout the cell, thus resulting in an increase in first-time yields from less than 50 percent to over 90 percent and final yields from 75 percent to almost 100 percent. Other improvements were aimed at controlling work-in-progress (WIP) through kanban, adding visual controls, and using kanban for supplied parts. Western's leadership, with the help of Mark McGovern, brought lean principles to their employees through the "spirit of excellence." By continually communicating the operating philosophy and guiding principles to the employees, Western provided its bay cable cell team members with a deep understanding of what waste elimination, teamwork, quality, simplicity, and customer-focus are all about. Now these lean habits are spreading to other parts of Western Geophysical Exploration Products.

We are what we repeatedly do. Excellence, then, is not an act, but a habit.

ARISTOTLE

Western Geophysical Exploration Products (WGEP) is the manufacturing division of Western Geophysical, a large seismic exploration company. WGEP manufactures seismic exploration equipment at two plants in the greater Houston, Texas area. Most of the manufacturing takes place at the Alvin, Texas plant. With approximately $90M in sales, the 250,000 square-foot plant employs about 500 employees. The plant produces a wide selection of seismic equipment, ranging from large vibrating vehicles and small hydrophones and geophones (microphones) to 100-meter marine streamer cables.

Historically, the plant had a very poor reputation with its customers. Problems included marginal product quality, poor on-time delivery, long manufacturing lead times, inconsistent product reliability, and high product costs. WGEP undertook a detailed assessment of the organization to understand the challenges facing the factory. The assessment helped the company leadership to understand the current situation and to identify gaps in performance. The assessment provided leadership with a comprehensive set of recommendations focusing on two major needs: restructuring and dramatically redesigning key business processes.

In keeping with the recommendations, the plant reorganized into four focused factories to respond to the unique needs of a diverse customer base. Each focused factory was designed to be nearly self-sufficient, staffed with a team representing design engineering, materials management, quality, manufacturing engineering, customer service, and field service. A focused factory manager led the team and was responsible for all aspects of focused factory performance.

Although WGEP made changes throughout the plant, our story outlines the transformation that took place in a specific area of one of the focused factories—the bay cable manufacturing cell. This case study demonstrates how one company, through restructuring an organization, implementing lean manufacturing techniques, and tapping into its unlimited human potential, achieved dramatic operating improvements in a short period. The successful transformation of the bay cable manufacturing cell area clearly illustrates the potential and power of change to lean manufacturing.

The Bay Cable Cell Story

The land cable–focused factory designs and manufactures seismic cables. These seismic cables are used in the collection of geological data that energy companies analyze to determine the likelihood of oil and gas deposits in an area. The cables are used in very remote, extremely harsh environments, and are subjected to neglect and abuse by seismic field crews. The land cable–focused factory sold 90 percent of its products internally to Western Geophysical field crews. The remaining sales went to various other seismic data collection companies.

The land cable factory's main products are electrical cables consisting of different numbers of copper wires configured in various arrays and made to assorted specifications. Regardless of design, all cables follow a similar manufacturing process:

1. Bare copper wire is run through a small extruder to make a single insulated conductor.
2. Single insulated conductors are twisted together to make a twisted pair.
3. Twisted pairs are twisted together with strength members to make unfinished bulk cable.
4. Unfinished bulk cable is run through a large extruder, in two passes, to make finished bulk cable.
5. Finished bulk cable is cut to length.
6. The pieces of bulk cable are cut open at various locations, and connectors called "pigtails" are soldered into place.
7. The cable is terminated by soldering connectors at each end of the cable.

8. The takeouts and/or end connectors are then overmolded in an injection-molding machine.
9. The cable is tested.
10. The cable is packed and shipped to the customer.

The bay cable is the largest, most expensive, and most complex cable manufactured in the land cable–focused factory. At 1,250 feet in length, one and one-half inches in diameter, and weighing about 1,500 pounds, the bay cable is used by seismic data collection crews working in shallow water less than 200 feet deep. In the field crews connect an array of cables and drop them from boats, from which they sink to the bottom of the shallow water.

After the crews collect the seismic data for the area, the crews forcefully pull the cables back upon the deck of the boats, thus placing tremendous stress and strain on the cables. The crews then move to a new location where they reuse the cables to collect more data. Failure of the cables is extremely time consuming and costly because the crew has to pull the cable up, repair it or replace it, then re-deploy it. For Western's seismic crews to be profitable, the cables have to be reliable. They were not. Not only were field failure rates high and seismic crew productivity suffering, the bay cable manufacturing process in the plant was in desperate need of improvement in the following other areas:

- Current monthly demand for the cable was 50 percent more than the plant had ever managed to produce.
- First-run yield of the cable was below 50 percent.
- On-time delivery was extremely low.
- Work-in-process (WIP) and raw material inventory levels were very high.
- Material shortages were common, expediting the norm.
- Material handling was excessive and unsafe.
- Material waste and scrap levels were high.
- No master production schedule existed.
- Suppliers were given little or no advance notice of changes in demand patterns.
- Field repair and new cable production were indistinguishable.
- Cable costs were high.

Western management recognized that they not only needed to make changes to the bay cable manufacturing process, but they had to make radical improvements, and they had to make them fast. They had already lost customer orders to competitors because of long manufacturing lead times and poor product quality.

Adopting eight guiding principles for transformation
One of the keys to implementing radical change successfully is adopting, communicating, and *actively utilizing* a core set of guiding principles. WGEP leadership adopted a set of eight guiding principles to help direct the transformation: waste elimination, teamwork, quality, simplicity, flexibility, visibility, customer focus, and measurement. When successfully practiced, these principles lead to competitive advantages in cost, quality, lead time, and delivery.

Early in the change process, WGEP deployed teams to scrutinize all elements of the design, testing, and manufacturing processes. Utilizing the guiding principles, the teams relentlessly focused improvement efforts in six key areas:

1. Product flow
2. Product quality/employee skills training
3. Material waste reduction
4. Visual controls
5. Materials management
6. Performance measurement

Product Flow

The original shop layout was organized in a traditional or functional manner. All unique processes were separated into departments, and products flowed through each department. This layout caused numerous problems during bay cable production such as poor communication between departments and high WIP inventory because of floating bottlenecks. Scheduling the shop floor was a nightmare, and finding out the status of a job without doing hours of fact finding was impossible. Also, a large amount of floor space was dedicated to bay cable storage.

Given the bulky nature of the bay cable, moving the cable presented many problems. First, safety was a major concern. The more the cable was handled, the greater the chance of injury. The plant's safety record was poor, and excessive handling of material was one of the root causes. Also, moving the cables added unnecessary costs to the product. Several full-time material handlers were employed, and hours of direct labor time were consumed in moving the bulky cables around the shop (Figure 11-1 shows the cable's convoluted path). Before improvements were implemented, the bay cable was moved nearly one mile during production. Employees used the slogan, "I'd walk a mile for a bay cable," a parody of the old Camel cigarette motto, to illustrate the absurdity and waste associated with producing this product. With all that walking, it was no wonder the employees were exhausted by the end of the day!

Designing cells with a product-oriented flow
Walking through the shop, an observer would see a plant that resembled an elaborate moving and storage business instead of a seismic cable manufacturer. The new strategy was to redesign the product flow to eliminate unnecessary movement, increase visibility, improve communication, and dramatically reduce manufacturing cycle times.

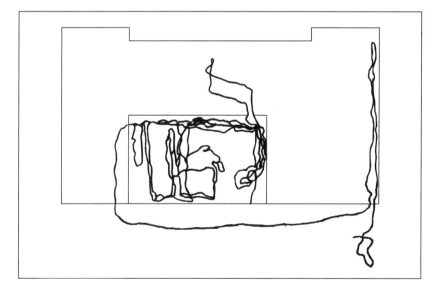

Figure 11-1. Original Bay Cable Production Work Flow

The shop floor was redesigned into manufacturing cells with a product-oriented flow. This included all the equipment required to produce the bay cable. The only machines not moved were the small extruders that manufacture the single insulated conductors common to all land cables. These were kept in their original locations for reasons of capacity and cost, but were connected to the cells through simple, visual material-control systems. Inside the cell, teams designated space and clearly marked it for equipment, supplies, WIP, and anything else required to make the cable; anything that was not required, they removed.

In total, the WGEP reduced bay cable movement over 70 percent from 0.9 mile to 0.3 mile, and floor space by approximately 30 percent (Figure 11-2 shows the much simpler flow). With the use of kanban and visual controls, WIP went from over 60 cables to 12 cables, lead time was reduced from over 30 days to less than 5 days, and material shortages became almost nonexistent. As part of the entire redesign of the land cable–focused factory, WGEP added additional aisles for safety. They eliminated full-time material handling labor and reduced the total time spent moving the bay cable. Reported accidents and lost time accidents dropped (see Figure 11-3). With all

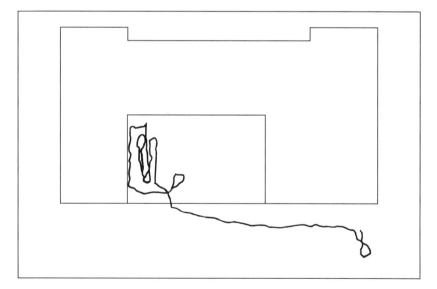

Figure 11-2. Redesigned Bay Cable Production Work Flow

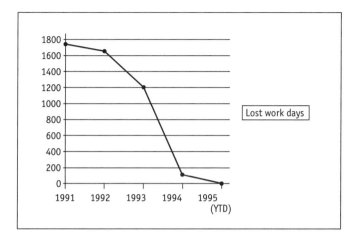

Figure 11-3. Plant Safety Improvement

components of bay cable production under one supervisor and in close proximity, communication and coordination was vastly improved. Bay cable cell employees owned their product from start to finish. Now they could see the end result of all their work, and the new layout enabled them to become a team with a shared mission.

Product Quality/Employee Skills Training

Historically, employees worked on any type of cable at any point in time. Though workers had specialized skills, they had very little understanding of the entire manufacturing process and how their work contributed to the final product. Employees did not inspect or check their own work. In essence, the workers threw their finished work over the wall to the next step in the process. Because of excessive WIP, workers did not usually discover quality problems from previous operations until after they were completed.

John Johnston, the land cable–focused factory manager during the transformation, thought the most profound change took place in the attitudes of the shopfloor workers: "Before, the attitude was that line workers felt no responsibility for the quantity or quality of the product. The products were designed to be difficult to be built. There was absolutely no feeling of responsibility for on-time delivery to the customer."

By redesigning the shop floor into cells, the next step in the process was now located adjacent to the previous step. Because WIP was now small, workers could catch and immediately correct any quality problems. The close proximity of the workers allowed for improved communication, cross-training, and problem solving. Each employee learned the exact requirements for product quality of the next person in the cell.

Brad Piner, the area supervisor during the transformation, felt that the changes gave employees common goals: "If there was a reject, everyone took responsibility. Everybody learned new techniques and taught each other. There was a lot more ownership. They felt part of the decision making. They knew what they had to do. There was a lot more teamwork."

One of the most satisfying moments of the transformation came about two weeks after the move into cells. An employee walked up to the cell supervisor and reported that there was a problem with one of the bay cables. The supervisor asked the employee how she would resolve it. After listening to her answer, he told her to give it a try and to let him know how it worked out.

Prior to the transformation, this supervisor was widely recognized as an "old school" supervisor and one of the premier "firefighters" in the plant. He loved fires and especially loved putting them out. That is why his response was so shocking. If this had happened three months earlier, he would have charged into the fray, taken control of the situation, and put out the fire without regard to the employee's ideas. Instead, he gave the employee a chance to solve the problem. He was giving his people an opportunity to think, to act, to learn, and to grow. Employees were becoming more connected and involved. He was becoming a leader. This was a defining moment in the change process: People's attitudes and actions were changing.

Material Waste Reduction

At each step in the cabling process, extra cable was manufactured to allow for uncertainty in the downstream operations. A long cable could be cut to length, but a short cable was essentially scrap. Therefore, the conventional mind-set was to add a few extra feet of cable "just to be sure." This mind-set, however, was starting to be challenged, and the new guiding principle of eliminating waste was beginning to take root.

WGEP started a project with the goal of minimizing excess cable production while ensuring that they would never produce short cable. For several weeks they collected data. Analysis of the data showed that they were scrapping excessive amounts of cable at tremendous cost. The finished bay cable needed to be 1,250 feet in length, but the two most expensive elements of the cable were being purchased in quantities in excess of 1,450 feet. Through analysis of the gathered data, WGEP determined the actual required length of the expensive elements and adjusted the purchased length. The resulting savings amounted to a 4 percent reduction in the cable cost (several hundred dollars per cable). Based on the projected demand for the bay cable, the annual savings of this one improvement amounted to more than $320,000.

Visual Controls

Given the poor layout of the plant, it was no surprise that workers felt disconnected from the product and the process. They had little understanding of the status of orders, product quality, product cost, or manufacturing lead time. Most had no knowledge of the current or future demand for the product. Visual controls and communication of any type were very limited.

A team of employees, including the supervisors, production manager, and focused factory manager, designed and instituted a visual display system that allowed all employees to understand current and future demand, quality improvements, cost reductions, and any other issues relating to a particular manufacturing cell. The team called this tool a schedule board. Short-term and long-term production schedules are posted and production against the schedule is tracked on an hourly, daily, and weekly basis. Any current issues affecting the cell are also posted, along with any customer-specific information.

Material control became very visible through the use of kanban cards. Kanban is a Japanese word that means "display" or "instruction card." The kanban card acts as a signal for replenishment and provides information about the part needed and its location. (The next section describes in detail the integration of kanban cards into the entire materials management system.) The creative use of visual controls provided employees with simple, yet effective ways to understand current conditions and take corrective action. According to John Johnston, "With fewer and fewer surprises jumping up and grabbing them [the employees], it gave them control of their destiny. I think that simplification [cell layout, kanbans, design, etc.] was key. Visibility brings the cell together. It was clear to them what it took to get the product to the customer. Simplification and visibility are what made it do-able."

Brad Piner agreed with Johnston that visibility and simplicity were key elements in making the dramatic improvements successful: "To be able to see what was going on was very important. When the team didn't do it [make the scheduled production], it was visible to everyone. And if they did do it, they would get instant recognition."

Materials Management

Due to constant internal quality problems, an unreliable supplier base, and an erratic demand pattern, managing materials was extremely difficult. Frequent material shortages were coupled with high inventory levels. Nearly all products required incoming inspection. Since planners had little forward visibility of product demand, suppliers were almost totally blind to future demand.

WGEP undertook a major effort to redesign the supply chain management system. They created a master production schedule to drive requirements for end items, and key team members met for a weekly production meeting. (A pull system for making supplier parts was still not used. Suppliers built to inventory.) They eliminated incoming inspection for all materials for two reasons. First, statistics indicated that inspection did not find quality problems. Second, incoming inspection caused waste through unnecessary labor and needless delays. WGEP supplied key suppliers with a rolling, three-month forecast that was updated weekly. With this information, the key plastic supplier was able to plan future requirements and dedicate inventory at its local warehouse. Plastic was then replenished directly to the shop floor on a daily basis, based on actual production usage.

Using kanban cards

The plastic replenishment system was a model of simplicity and visibility. A kanban card like the one in Figure 11-4 was attached to a corrugated cardboard box full of plastic pellets when the material was received. The kanban card contained all the information the shop needed to receive, store, and use the material. The storage location on the kanban card in Figure 11-4 matched the storage location marked on the floor. After the plastic was consumed and the container was empty, the kanban card was placed in a holder on an I-beam near the point of use. At a specified time each day, a material planner would collect the kanban cards, sum the requirements, and fax a release to the vendor's warehouse. The plant's truck driver would pick up the plastic the next day.

This simple, reliable, and visible system replaced an unreliable, complex, and invisible material resource planning (MRP)-driven system that contributed to endless cycles of acute plastic shortages followed by months of excess inventory. With the new system, plastic shortages were a thing of the past. Inventory turns for plastic increased from about 10 to over 100 turns/year. Material handling, space requirements, inventory transactions, and paperwork were

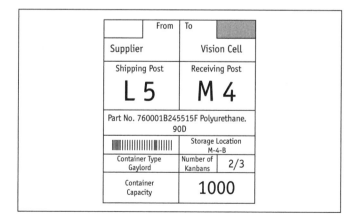

Figure 11-4. Kanban Card

dramatically reduced. Through integrating the daily pickup of plastic into the plant truck driver's daily route instead of having the supplier deliver the plastic, the purchase price of the material decreased.

The most expensive element of the bay cable, the transmission pair, was also purchased based on actual usage. On a specified day of the week, a weekly "pull" signal was sent to the transmission pair supplier. The supplier would then ship the material for arrival at the plant five days later. To increase visibility and eliminate unnecessary transactions and movement of material, WGEP transferred material storage for most items from the stockroom to the floor. Now most of the material arriving from suppliers is delivered directly to the cell into preassigned storage areas.

Now, small inexpensive items (screws, tape, tubing, etc.) are stored in bulk quantities in the manufacturing area in locations near the point of use. WGEP set up a simple two-bin system for replenishment from the stockroom. Employees use material from the bin facing the cell. When the bin is empty, an employee takes the kanban card from the bin and places it in the kanban card post. The employee then moves the empty bin to the outside and moves the full bin to the inside. During the night shift, stockroom employees collect kanban cards and replenish necessary items. The next morning, the card, bin, and parts are waiting in the predetermined location. This system is designed to work like the highly reliable, efficient Federal Express model.

According to Brad Piner, the changes in the materials management system was also a key to making the workload predictable and repeatable: "We were very seldom out of parts and everything flowed. We balanced the line. We went to zero defects in the first seven months. We never ran out of cable. We cut scrap. Having total control made me aware of the entire process. We really had a team. It's one of the few times in the plant I ever saw true teamwork."

Performance Measurement

Prior to reorganizing into manufacturing cells, there was little information available on plant performance. The quality control department kept records of final and in-process inspection results, but little was done with the information, and no one communicated the results plantwide. Customer service intermittently tracked on-time delivery, but the information was used only as a stick to beat on the manufacturing department. Data integrity and reporting discipline were severely lacking in the job-costing system. Nobody trusted the job variance reports. Despite the questionable data, the managers and supervisors continued to spend a majority of their time researching and explaining why there were negative variances.

To avoid the pain associated with negative variances, the supervisors spent time playing a sort of shell game by arbitrarily moving material and labor cost from one job to another. This concealed problems, and made identifying and eliminating waste difficult. All of this variance activity amounted to a lot of effort, frustration, and paperwork, but gleaned no real information to enlighten leadership on performance. Furthermore, instead of spending time improving quality and productivity, supervisors spent much of their time in variance meetings explaining negative variances, or in their offices manipulating numbers in an effort to avoid variance meetings.

To provide focus to improvement efforts, management created a new performance measurement system. The goal was to provide relevant, reliable, and timely information and to communicate this information to all employees on a regular basis. Areas of measurement included the following:

- Quality
- On-time delivery
- Productivity
- Cost
- Safety

The modification of the job-cost tracking system is a great example of the principle of simplification in action. Job-cost tracking was a complex and time-consuming process that was compounded by products with multiple-level bills of materials and long manufacturing lead times. To make a bay cable, for example, more than 75 distinct "jobs" had to be opened and closed. Some of these jobs would be open for two months before they were closed. Tracking and understanding the variances associated with these 75 jobs was absurd and unrealistic, yet expected.

To greatly reduce the number of transactions and to get timely and accurate cost information, the system was radically redesigned. First, the bay cable bill of material was flattened. This immediately reduced the number of jobs from 75 to one. Second, instead of opening a job for each order, each week a job was opened for the cell to produce the required number of bay cables. All cell employees now charge their time to the cell, and all material delivered to the cell is charged to the cell.

Internal kanbans signal any problems within the cell, and problems are immediately visible. There is no need to wait for a report. Each week, management receives a report that provides the total number of completed cables and the actual manufacturing cost of the bay cable (actual labor plus actual material cost). Leadership can readily see whether the cell is profitable or not. Additionally, employees see the results of their improvement efforts monitored and tracked in real dollars. Among other things, they can understand whether or not the cell is profitable.

All performance information is now collected by cell employees and entered into the computer system. The cell supervisor is responsible for compiling and posting the information on the cell performance board. The cell supervisor reviews the results during a daily meeting with cell members and answers any questions.

Leadership Provides a Spirit of Excellence

The results of the bay cable manufacturing cell transformation to lean principles are phenomenal, and they are serving as an internal benchmark for future transformations for the rest of the plant. Results include reducing manufacturing cycle time by 83 percent (30 days to 5 days), improving quality levels from 50 percent to 100 percent, increasing productivity by more than 30 percent, increasing inventory turnover from 2 to 30 turns per year, and reducing material cost by 14 percent (see Figure 11-5). The many positive gains from the "radical" changes in this cell have convinced even the most hardened skeptics that lean works. Downstream customers claim that the cables from the new cell have exceeded expectations and are the finest ever produced. In fact, the on-time

Metric	Before	After
Final yield	75%	99-100%
First run yield	< 50%	> 90%
Hours/Unit	> 100 hours	65-70 hours
Work-in-process	> 60 cables	12 cables
Inventory turns	Unknown	20-30/year
Lead time	> 30 days	5 days
Travel distance	9/10 mile	3/10 mile
Production level	Unpredictable	Steady (15/week)
Housekeeping/Safety	Poor	Good
Bill of material	Inaccurate	Accurate
Employee skills	Single task	Flexible

Figure 11-5. Performance After Cell Implementation

delivery and improved reliability of the cables are two of the reasons that Western Geophysical's seismic crews were able to complete collecting data in the Gulf of Mexico nearly two years ahead of schedule. This early completion contributed greatly to the profitability of Western Geophysical.

Perhaps the most important change that took place, however, is difficult to measure—the remarkable change in employee attitude and outlook. Since the transformation, employees have taken tremendous pride in their work and great personal satisfaction in continuing to make their jobs, and the product, better. Employees, intimately involved and challenged during the transformation, have been taught how to identify and eliminate waste at all levels in the organization. They were challenged to think "out-of-the-box" and to discover creative ways to solve problems. Successes are recognized and celebrated.

John Johnston reports: "After the initial shock that the change was taking place, the people that worked in the cell got into it. The pride and level of teamwork became contagious. It took on a life of its own." Through the efforts of numerous teams rigorously striving toward a common vision, the plant was able to reinvent itself. Brad Piner says that in the process, "People became important." Leadership finally managed to tap into the great potential hidden in the work force.

WGEP leadership, with the help of the Phoenix Consulting Group, provided bay cable team members with a new operating philosophy and a clear vision of the future. By constantly communicating the guiding principles and creating a deep understanding of these principles, team members, when making changes, continually considered the principles of waste elimination, teamwork, quality, simplicity, flexibility, visibility, customer focus, and measurement. The key to the successful transformation in the bay cable cell was the successful internalization and relentless application of these lean principles, principles that not only led to dramatic improvements but that are now spreading plantwide.

The future of the bay cable cell and the entire land cable–focused factory is bright as long as leadership continues to believe in, communicate, practice, and reinforce the guiding principles. But the road to operational excellence is bumpy. New behaviors take time to become instilled habits. Leadership must remember that its ultimate role is to define behavioral expectations, then lead by example. Unclear or misguided expectations result in bad habits. Bad habits yield disappointing performance.

Manufacturing organizations that will thrive in the next century will be those that institutionalize a spirit of excellence. This spirit of excellence is repeatedly demonstrated in all activities, in all places, by all employees. These companies are destined to become the benchmark of excellence.

PART THREE

Managing the
Change Process

Thomas Y. Choi *is an assistant professor of management at Bowling Green State University and a research consultant with the Japan Technology Management Program at the University of Michigan. He received his B.A. from the University of California at Berkeley and Ph.D. from the University of Michigan. He teaches and researches in the areas of supply chain management, total quality management and continuous improvement, Japanese production methods, and organizational change. He has done executive training for numerous companies including Dana Corporation, Samsung Corporation, Lucas Industries, and Korean Airlines. His work has appeared in* Academy of Management Executives, Business Horizons, Decision Sciences, *and* Journal of Operations Management, *among others. He was one of the contributing authors to the book* Engineered in Japan, *which received the 1996 Shingo Award for Excellence in Manufacturing Research.*

The Successes and Failures of Implementing Continuous Improvement Programs: Cases of Seven Automotive Parts Suppliers

12

by Thomas Y. Choi

Editor's prologue: This book has focused on success stories, but not all companies are able to take the first critical steps to lean manufacturing successfully. Tom Choi conducted a systematic comparative study of seven small automotive parts plants that launched continuous improvement programs at the same time. He followed them for the first two years of their efforts. Out of seven, only three had any degree of success, whereas the other four reaped little from their efforts. Tom gives a detailed account of the successes and failures of the companies and extrapolates from their experiences lessons for the implementation of continuous improvement programs. The focus of these companies at the time was on the people systems to encourage continuous improvement. By the time Tom ended his study, even the most advanced plant had a long way to go to implement continuous flow, a pull system, standardized work, and the other technical features of TPS, but at least they were heading in the right direction. There are many ways of starting the lean journey, and getting people on board and active in continuous improvement is certainly critical to long-term success. But beware. Without a total commitment to the CI process, you may find yourself walking down the same old change-effort plank, the one that drops you off where all this began—the need to change your process.

T his chapter addresses the process of implementing continuous improvement (CI) programs in small- to medium-sized manufacturing companies. It illustrates the CI programs of seven companies and draws lessons from their successes and their failures. This chapter may particularly be useful for managers of small- to medium-sized companies, who may be facing the many obstacles inherent in the early process of starting down the path toward lean manufacturing. Such managers may sense the urgency of creating a systematic program to make improvements but find forging ahead difficult because they are constantly in the fire-fighting mode—for instance, with customers who call in for order changes, impose unilateral cost reduction plans, threaten to drop them from the supplier list, or make promises that often go unfulfilled.

The managers of the seven companies presented in this chapter faced such dilemmas. They realized that jumping right into creating a lean production system would be extremely difficult, financially as well as operationally. These managers viewed the CI program, as presented in this chapter, as a low-cost approach to improving quality and productivity that required lots of determination and aspiration but little up-front investment. After all, Imai and Shingo have asserted that CI has been the single most important factor in Japan's manufacturing success (Imai, 1986; Shingo, 1988). According to Imai, CI is "the unifying thread running through the philosophy, the systems, and the problem-solving tools developed in Japan over the last 30 years" (p. xxxii). CI has also been viewed as the Japanese manager's interpretation of Deming's manufacturing philosophy (Suzaki as quoted in Poe, 1991). It also can be used to unleash workers' potential to improve performance in the United States (Schroeder & Robinson, 1991).

The seven companies included in the study are first-tier automotive suppliers in the Detroit, Michigan area. All began to implement CI programs in the winter of 1990, when they became members of a CI training group called the Continuous Improvement Users Group (CIUG). I observed first hand the CI activities at these seven companies for one year. I visited these companies and conducted interviews on a regular basis and also attended all CIUG training sessions, which were held every six weeks.

The chapter is organized into four key sections: Research Background, General Background of Seven Case Studies, Results of CI Implementation Efforts After Two Years, and Pitfalls and Opportunities in Implementing CI.

Research Background

The CIUG was founded in 1990, sponsored by both the Industrial Technology Institute (ITI) in Ann Arbor, Michigan, and Continuous Improvement (CI) Associates in Northville, Michigan. Its primary intent was to help small- to medium-sized companies to "learn and discuss specific issues in CI, using a real-world environment to apply new skills and knowledge" (Fleming & Rother, 1991). The CIUG trained its members in areas such as total productive maintenance, problem-solving techniques, housekeeping and workplace organization, and flow development on the production floor.

The CIUG met on a rotating basis every six weeks at various member locations. The meetings were led by consultants from ITI and CI Associates and Kiyoshi Suzaki, the author of *The New Manufacturing Challenge*. All members were requested to send two participants, one from the shop floor and one from management. At these meetings, participants

- Received training on one specific CI technique, which they called "the focus topic"
- Reviewed and discussed the general work practices of the host company
- Shared the progress they had made in their own company since the previous meeting

The discussion topics ranged from housekeeping and workplace organization to company infrastructure. The three consultants presented a technical topic (for example, identifying waste on the shop floor), and the members applied their practical knowledge in a follow-up discussion. After they completed the training on the technical topic, the participants were organized into three or four small groups, which toured the shop floor of the host company and reviewed actual work practices to seek opportunities for improvement. The small groups subsequently took turns presenting their suggestions to the entire CIUG, including the representatives of the host company.

These seven companies provided a good laboratory setting in which to study the CI implementation process for the following six reasons:

1. They were small (from 25 to 150 employees), thus allowing members to see the effects of CI in a relatively short time.
2. They were well established and financially stable. All had shown profits during the last five years, and most had been in business for many years.
3. They had a record of producing good quality products prior to their joining CIUG (four companies had the status of Ford Q-1 supplier).
4. They were all in the same market niche as suppliers to the automotive industry and were primarily first-tier suppliers.
5. The management of the seven companies felt compelled to implement CI. There had been no direct pressure from the customers to implement CI, but all of the groups believed they needed to make their processes more "lean" to survive in the future.
6. They were exposed to CI at the same time, when they joined the CIUG. So I could compare them from a common starting point.

Methodological Approach

My research approach was to compare the process of implementation across plants by using qualitative methods. This included interviewing employees from each of the seven companies and reviewing the company's internal documents. I first began visiting the company sites in March 1991. At first, my interviews focused on the events that had occurred since October 1990 (when the CIUG was officially launched). In this phase, data mainly came from the respondents' recollection of the events since October 1990. Documents (minutes of the meetings, internal memos, etc.) were collected to cross-check as well as to complement the retrospective data (Fielding & Fielding, 1986).

I first interviewed the CIUG participants in each company. As more people became involved in the CI program, I added them to the interview list. Each visit took approximately one day. My retrospective data collection reached a "saturation point" once the interviewees began repeating the same information (Eisenhardt, 1989), so I visited each site approximately once a month until December 1991, and then once every two months in 1992 until April.

General Background of Seven Case Studies

What follows is a brief discussion of the seven companies: three stamping plants, two fastener manufacturers, one machine tool builder, and one assembly plant. The companies are introduced in the approximate order of how successful they were in their CI programs. I've assigned a pseudonym for each of the seven companies to ensure each one's anonymity. For example, I named one company Progressive Engineering and Manufacturing because it was the most progressive and advanced company. Sunshine Incorporated manufactures sunroofs, and the workers at this company seemed to be more cheerful compared to workers at other companies. Fixer Machine Company manufactures fasteners (i.e., nuts and bolts) and highly emphasizes the explicit justification of their CI changes. Heat Incorporated manufactures heating equipment, and the CI leader at this company seemed always to be taking "a lot of heat" from top management about some of the proposed CI changes. Topheavy Tool and Manufacturing Company had largely focused on training managers for their CI program, and their CI-related committees never included line workers. Small Metal Stamping and Manufacturing was simply the smallest among the seven companies. Mom and Pop Manufacturing was a family-owned company and was described as a "mom-and-pop company" by one of the interviewees.

The period of the study was from the winter of 1990, when the CIUG first started, through April 1992. Thus, we are looking at a two-year window on the activities of these plants. Their key accomplishments are captured in Table 12-1. To assess the level of CI impact in each company, I asked the three consultants that led the CIUG to rate the overall impact of the effort independently. There was a great deal of agreement among the three consultants. The numbers in Table 12-1 are based on an average of their ratings. Clearly, Progressive and Sunshine excelled beyond other companies. In addition to the ratings, I obtained actual data on improvements from the top companies (not shown in the table). At Progressive, internal reject rates and external reject rates improved by more than 400 percent and 200 percent, respectively, after it implemented the CI program. At Sunshine, the internal scrap rates improved by about 250 percent. The productivity improvement at these two companies was modest, however, at 4 percent and 7 percent. This may have resulted from their focus on the issues of housekeeping and workplace organization rather than on the overall work flow.

Progressive Engineering and Manufacturing

As a first- and second-tier supplier, Progressive Engineering and Manufacturing produces various springs for Ford, GM, and Chrysler. The company employs about 40 workers and is the most active in employee involvement among the seven companies. There are several committees, and almost all employees are members of two or more committees. Among these committees are the zero defect quality (ZDQ) committee and the housekeeping and workplace organization (HKWO) committee. The ZDQ committee was organized prior to CIUG, and the HKWO was a direct result of CIUG training.

In March of 1990, the Progressive Engineering and Manufacturing began to promote the participation of workers and started to expose workers to training in empowerment activities, team building, and people-related skills. The ZDQ committee was formed in April 1990. Since then, it has met every week for two to three hours as a forum where workers and managers can discuss

Table 12-1. Summary of CI Impacts

Company	Level of CI impact	Key events
Progressive	5	Shuts down the whole plant to "clean up and throw stuff out." Housekeeping and workplace organization committee organized and given an autonomous budget. Each department is asked to submit CI changes each month. A bulletin board is set up to display change lists and to show quality and production data. The housekeeping and workplace organization committee reviews each department every month and gives out awards. Preventive maintenance training gets underway.
Sunshine	4	Problem board instituted. Involves workers in the new employee hiring. Suggestion program for quality improvement. Scrap reduction group organized. Five CI committees organized and given specific tasks. Plant layout gets a new configuration based on TQM principles.
Fixer	4	Several tool boxes get organized. Setup checklist instituted. Tool staging cabinet constructed. Peg boards for tool organization installed. Generic area tools get labeled. The organizational infrastructure is overhauled.
Heat	2	Internal CI group organized. Suggestion program started. Suggestion reward system instituted. Sets up a display board to celebrate accomplishments.
Topheavy	2	Sporadic meetings Attempts to relocate die racks. Extensive Total Employee Investment training takes place and Employee Involvement structure reorganized.
Small	1	Paints one work room. Dies are color-coded.
Mom and Pop	1	Designs a die chart. Sets up a communication board.

a range of issues such as quality and production problems. Since joining CIUG, the focus of the ZDQ group has been profoundly affected by CI. For example, much of the key vocabulary used in the ZDQ discussion now reflects ideas that were learned through the CIUG (for example, plan-do-check-act cycle, "lowering the water level," etc.).

The HKWO committee was organized in January 1991. It has a unique distinction: Although no managers are members, it has been granted a budget to spend as members see fit. On a monthly basis, the HKWO committee evaluates all the departments' efforts in housekeeping and workplace organization. The committee then recognizes the best department and gives them an award in a monthly meeting.

Sunshine Incorporated

Sunshine Incorporated first began production of sliding sunroofs in the early 1980s in the United States. Its primary customers are General Motors and Chrysler. Its product is a fully assembled and ready-to-install sunroof. The company employs about 60 production workers.

Sunshine Incorporated was previously organized into two independent groups. The primary group of the company included all manufacturing workers and is referred to as Sunshine. The second was a sales group, and it had a different company name; this group handled sunroofs in the after-sales market. The sales group eventually moved out of the manufacturing facility in October 1991. After the departure of the sales group, Sunshine began to organize CI teams that involved its workers.

Prior to joining CIUG, this company had two committees that involved workers in some capacity, the safety committee and merit committee. The safety committee consisted of management personnel only, but workers were occasionally invited to the meeting. Because the safety record has been good (one recorded accident in 1990), this committee has not been very active. In contrast, the merit committee, which was begun in 1989, is still very active. It is a joint committee between management and workers that has developed a review process of worker salary adjustments, which it now oversees.

Fixer Machine Company

Fixer Machine Company is a manufacturer of cold-headed fasteners. It produces fasteners in 100 sizes and in many grades of steel. The operation is based on 29 cold headers, which are supported by grinding and finishing operations. Because the fasteners are small in size, the company uses large-lot production. It will often produce a large lot of one part, keep them in inventory at the customer's request, and deliver portions of the lot as requested. Jobs for General Motors (GM) constitute from 80 to 90 percent of the company's work. The company employees about 110 people.

Worker-participation programs take the form of two committees: the safety committee and the CI committee. Workers can join the safety committee, which existed prior to this company's joining the CIUG, on a voluntary basis, but participation is rotated. The CI committee was organized in January 1991, composed of line leaders and workers, but it was discontinued in August 1991. The CI committee was not eliminated because the company wanted to abandon CI but because it wanted to expand CI companywide. The company subsequently overhauled its infrastructure to make it more participative in early 1992. The key members of the previous CI committee were placed in key positions in the new organizational structure.

Heat Incorporated

Heat Incorporated produces customized heating equipment. Their primary customers are the Big Three automakers. Each customer typically requests the heating machines in different configurations and often for different purposes. For example, one customer may use the machine to inspect parts, whereas another customer may use it to heat-treat parts. Moreover, some customers supply the predesigned blueprint and ask only to have the machine built, but others request the design as well as the machine. Each order, therefore, is treated differently. The work procedure for each order undergoes a customized process.

Heat Incorporated employs about 160 people. About half of the employees are workers in the production department, which is divided into three operation groups. The workers are called assemblers. There are approximately 30 assemblers in each department. There were no employee-involvement programs prior to the company's joining the CIUG. There is now an internal CI committee, composed of managers from one operation group, engineers, and assemblers. The committee has been meeting since January of 1991.

Topheavy Tool and Manufacturing Company

Topheavy Tool and Manufacturing Company is a full-service metal stamping company. It specializes in stamping and the assembling of hood hinges, muffler hangers, and latches. Its primary customers are Ford, Chrysler, and a major Japanese automaker. This company avoids working with GM due to "some bad experiences in the past." Mainly because of its successful relationship with Ford, Topheavy has been encouraged to expand and develop its stamping capability. It has seized this opportunity and is currently undergoing expansion.

About 90 line workers handle shipping and delivery, welding, stamping, maintenance, tooling, and machine repairing. They are represented by the Allied Industrial Workers of America. The only employee-involvement program at Topheavy has been the total employee involvement (TEI) group, which was organized in February of 1989 and oversees the employee-suggestion program. No formal reward structure is in place for suggestions. There have been two internal CI groups, but they have not included line workers as members.

Small Metal Stamping and Manufacturing

Small Stamping and Manufacturing Company produces attaching brackets such as transmission mounting supports, seat-adjuster brackets, brake washers, and air-conditioner and heater brackets. The company's primary customers are GM and Ford. The production volume fluctuates widely from hundreds of thousands of parts per week to only hundreds per month, depending on the order. The size of parts also varies from small washers to transmission supports.

There are about 20 employees at Small. Among them are four managers, two staff, and one engineer. There has been no employee involvement program at this company either before or after it joined the CIUG. One reason for this lack of involvement may be high worker turnover, which was almost 80 percent during the one year of data collection.

Mom and Pop Manufacturing

Mom and Pop Manufacturing is a stamping plant. It typically runs low-volume work associated mostly with repair and service markets. The average number of employees in 1991 was about 70. Some employees are represented by the United Steel Workers.

The formal organizational structure consists of four departments, but another structure is organized around the concept of worker participation. At this company such participation is labeled the quality improvement process (QIP) structure, which is divided into two groups: the quality improvement team (QIT) and the quality work groups (QWG). The QIT is composed of managers, but the QWG is composed of line leaders and workers. This participative approach has been based on the Crosby System. The training has been done by outside consultants.

There were no prior worker involvement programs before this company joined the CIUG. When it joined the CIUG, the training for the QIT had just been completed, and the training for the QWGs was just beginning. This participative structure never really seemed to get off the ground. The communication between the QIT and QWG was extremely poor. The QWGs would submit a proposal for a new project to the QIT, but "would not hear from them for months." The QIT even implemented liaisons to overcome this communication gap, but frequently these liaisons, who were supposed to attend all QWG meetings, could not be found.

Results of CI Implementation Efforts After Two Years

This section describes each company's CI change process over a two-year period from October 1990 when the CIUG was first launched to the end of 1991. The intent of the research was to collect data for at least one year after the companies began to implement CI changes. Although each company participated in the same training through the CIUG, the outcome of this program at each organization was quite different. Each company followed its own unique path to the implementation of CI (or lack thereof).

The following stories describe each company's successes and struggles. They do not always have a clear ending. The stories are an empirical description of initial stages of CI processes and are not meant to show the complete CI process. A table included with each story shows the chronological event history for each company.

The goal of this section is to illustrate some of the many approaches companies can take, good and bad, when implementing a new CI program.

The CI Story of Progressive Engineering and Manufacturing

Progressive Engineering and Manufacturing is regarded by the other six companies as the "model company." Some of the other companies have even taken their employees on a tour of Progressive. At the end of the first year of the CIUG, the six companies voted Progressive as "the company with the best CI practice."

Progressive was the first company to take advantage of what it · learned from the CIUG (see Table 12-2). In December 1990, members from Progressive learned about housekeeping and workplace organization, and during that month they started to work on it. First, the three CIUG participants took a video of their workplace and showed it to all employees. Everyone realized that their work organization needed improvement. Around Christmas time, the company shut down and underwent a major cleanup. According to one manager, "For one whole day everybody cleaned and threw out stuff." Interestingly, after this one month, their quality improvement measures took a quantum leap. Prior to December 1990, the recorded quality problems were about 20 incidents per month, but in the following months Progressive reduced them to about 4 incidents per month. The interviewees explained that because of the more organized workplace, workers seemed to develop a "keener sense" of quality.

What is even more interesting is that this improvement was maintained throughout 1991. This feat was attributed to the continuing effort for improvement under the leadership of the housekeeping and workplace organization (HKWO) committee. It appears that had the level of housekeeping and workplace organization deteriorated, the improved quality level might have also deteriorated. However, the HKWO committee emerged as the most active group, and the workplace remained clean and organized through the committee's effort. The committee rated each department on a scale of 1 to 10 regarding its general housekeeping and workplace organization. Each month at the company meeting the winning department was given an award.

Table 12-2. History of Events at Progressive

Dates	Events
October 1990	• Top manager, a department manager, and a line worker attend the first CIUG meeting. Setup reduction and increasing number of machines per operator chosen as their CI focus projects.
December 1990	• Take a video of the workplace and show it to all employees. Everyone realizes that they need to improve on their workplace organization. • Around Christmas time, the whole plant shuts down and undergoes a major clean up. Internal survey on employee attitudes on quality, management, company ownership, etc. Overall improvement from earlier survey.
January 1991	• Housekeeping and workplace organization committee established, composed of only line workers and office staff. Each department asked to submit a list of its CI changes each month. Lists displayed on a bulletin board. • CI focus projects revised to the reduction of setup time on fourslide equipment and improvement in housekeeping and workplace organization.
March 1991	• Housekeeping and workplace organization committee receives a $6,000 budget from top management to "spend it as it sees fit." • A team is organized to work on reduction of setup time. Team videotapes the setup procedure and devises ways to standardize steps.
April 1991	• Companywide drive on housekeeping and workplace organization in anticipation of the upcoming open house and hosting of the CIUG. At this point, departments actually "compete" against one another for better housekeeping and workplace organization.
May 1991	• A "successful" open house in the third weekend. In the following week, company hosts the CIUG. It is criticized in some areas, but in general it is commended for what the members have accomplished. • A conflict surfaces between a line leader and the housekeeping committee, but they work out a policy as to when workers can leave production to attend meetings.
June 1991	• Each department rated on its general housekeeping and workplace organization practices by the committee. The committee recognizes winning department with an award at the company meeting to celebrate its success.
July 1991	• Steering committee begins to broaden the CI focus regarding preventive maintenance of machines. Training on machine maintenance gets underway.
August 1991	• Machines are put on a preventive maintenance schedule.
September 1991	• A tooling person is hired but is quickly turned into a CI facilitator. He assists the top manager in putting together a CI training course.
October 1991	• There are now CI leaders in all production areas. They receive advanced training 2 hours a day for seven weeks plus 5 hours of general training. CI groups in each area now make up the basic team structure of the company.

Table 12-2. History of Events at Progressive (continued)

Dates	Events
November 1991	• Third wave of the survey is run (first one this year). Workers express general discontentment toward management about singling out one department for a raise. According to one manager, "We just thought they deserved it." According to one worker, "We feel we are in this together. To see one group of people getting a raise and not the rest of us really makes me upset."
December 1991	• A conflict surfaces again surrounding line leaders. Some of them now feel they are "left out of the loop." They feel that they are stuck with production while other workers are making the improvement changes. • Management's plan to minimize goal conflict gets underway.
January 1992	• Company-level goals are stated in a circular, continuous improvement cycle, and all the departments organize their goals stated in a similar fashion. Both are displayed in each department to display continuity between company and departmental goals.

Focus on reduction of setup time

When the company had accomplished a sufficient level of housekeeping and workplace organization, it began to focus on reducing setup time. In March company members videotaped the setup procedures and workers discussed among themselves how better to approach the setup. What emerged from this effort was the standardization of the setup procedures. Once the company felt that it was reducing the setup time and standardizing processes, it moved on to machine maintenance. In July and August of 1991, training on machine maintenance finally got under way. Subsequently, the company made a preventive maintenance schedule for each machine.

The company has involved workers in cross-departmental committees such as the ZDQ committee, HKWO committee, and so on. When the workers became reasonably comfortable with participating (holding meetings, expressing opinions, working on improvements on their own), the company moved on to form more departmental teams within each production area. Workers were trained on more generic topics such as group processes and negotiation techniques; next, they received training on specific production-related CI techniques. Management has shown good leadership, and the workers have cooperated well.

"Rocks" are uncovered

Just as the concept of CI teaches about "discovering rocks when the water level gets low," this company did discover a few "rocks." For example, a few older employees who had been working in this company "longer than all the others, including the president," resisted the changes. According to one manager, "They have the mentality of the old tool maker—he knows where everything is as long as nobody touches it. . . . They don't seem to see the importance of getting organized and standardized." Their refusal to partake in the celebration of change efforts marked a "sad note" when they did not come to the open house party in April of 1991.

Another problem that surfaced was the difficulty that line leaders had in meeting production demands while simultaneously making improvements. During an interview early in 1991, one of the line leaders alluded to the "juggling" that he had to do to meet production despite allowing the line workers to leave for CI meetings. Another described the act of juggling as "an art form." Sometimes the line workers were taken away from production for meetings against the wishes of the line leaders. As the number of workers who wanted to attend these meetings increased, the frequency of line leaders' not allowing them to go increased. One line leader said, "We are responsible for the production deadline, and sometimes we can't afford to let them go." Some line leaders eventually became branded as being against change and improvement. This sort of sentiment left a sense of isolation or loneliness for the line leaders as they felt they were "caught between a rock and a hard place." One worker made the observation that the line leaders did want to work on improvements, but that the line leaders sometimes felt resentful that they were the ones who "got stuck" with production while others were working on the "more fun improvement projects."

Management attempts to address the problems

The management was mindful of this situation. One way they tried to overcome these problems was to lessen the line leaders' production responsibility so they could devote more time working on the improvement projects. They asked the departmental committee leaders to work with their line leaders and to assume some of the production responsibility. The intent was to create an overlapping area of responsibility between line leaders and committee leaders. This did not work out well, however, because there was "no clear way to do this." Nonetheless, the management was still trying, as of January 1992, to lessen the line leaders' production burden through training of the departmental committee members and by aligning the production goals with the improvement goals.

Management stated the company goals in a circular, continuous improvement cycle, and asked all the departments to submit their departmental goals in a similar fashion. Management also asked them to state these goals in terms of how the department could meet the company-level goals. Then, to demonstrate the continuity between what "the company as a whole was trying to accomplish" and how "each department plays a role" in it, management displayed the departmental goals as well as company goals in a circular, continuous improvement fashion in each department, thus showing the synergy between the two.

The CI Story of Sunshine Incorporated

The CI program at Sunshine Incorporated started out slowly but took on momentum with time (see Table 12-3). At first, members seemed to focus on making engineering and administrative changes that were indirectly related to the concept of CI. Toward late summer, 1991, they began to exercise the CI practices they had learned through the CIUG training. By early 1992, the CI program was beginning to develop strong roots in the company.

Management shares information

An essential characteristic of Sunshine provided a foundation for its CI process: management's willingness to share information, whether it was financial or operational. In fact, management encouraged workers to know more about how the company was doing through projects such as "the dollar coin." The production manager would walk around during work and ask workers at random about the operational data posted on the wall. For a correct answer, the worker would get a dollar coin on the spot. This sort of

Table 12-3. History of Events at Sunshine

Dates	Events
October 1990	• Production manager and a line leader attend the first meeting.
December 1991	• CI focus projects—improving the method of applying a seal to glass and improving the assembly of the GM module.
January 1991	• Two people from the production department visit Japanese transplants in Battle Creek, Michigan, with the CIUG group. Both are very impressed with what they saw. • Company starts a suggestion program for quality improvement. A suggestion committee is formed, consisting of workers and managers. If a suggestion is accepted, a monetary reward is given ranging from $10 to $2,000.
February 1991	• Management invites workers to participate in prospective-employee screening.
March 1991	• GM line reorganized. The company ended up moving one person to the Saturn line. With one less person, it maintained the same productivity. • Later this month, company hosts the CIUG. When asked to assist in the company's second focus project, the CIUG makes a few suggestions. However, the problem is later tracked down to the vendor. • Scrap reduction committee is organized to develop ways to reduce scratching of the glass.
April 1991	• One of the line leaders starts a problem-board program for his line. This program eventually spreads into other areas. By July, all three areas have successful problem-board programs.
May 1991	• Production department manager institutes a practice of giving away a dollar coin when an employee correctly answers the productivity data posted on the wall.
June 1991	• GM and Chrysler lines reorganized in an effort to "relocate work-in-process (WIP) inventory." • Production manager puts up the housekeepng board. It displays before and after pictures of changes.
July 1991	• All three production areas hold weekly meetings—"quality meetings." Involves everyone in each area. Discuss topics ranging from tooling issues to vendor quality issues.
September 1991	• A sign-up sheet goes up for the five cross-departmental CI committees—Housekeeping, Training, Service Orders, Process Improvement, and Plant Layout.
October 1991	• All workers asked to turn in proposals for plant reorganization to plant layout committee. A detailed guideline that appears to be heavily influenced by the CIUG training, using jargon such as continuous improvement, horseshoe layout, etc., is issued by management. • "Quality production-tracking boards" are displayed in each area. Quality information had previously been displayed on the bulletin board in the cafeteria area. Now it is displayed "where people work."

Table 12-3. History of Events at Sunshine (continued)

Dates	Events
November 1991	• Bulletin board to show the activities of the five committees. • "Other" company, which deals with after-market sales, leaves the facility and frees up shop-floor space. • Housekeeping committee members take photos of "good" and "bad" practices and displays them on the bulletin board. Process improvement committee focuses on preventive maintenance. Service order committee working on a standard operating procedure (SOP). Plant layout committee moving full steam toward the target to finish reorganization before New Year's Day.
December 1991	• All five committees work together in reorganization process. The housekeeping committee takes care of the details about shop-floor painting. It selects the vendor and the color. Process improvement committee works closely with plant layout committee in laying out production lines. Plant floor undergoes a "total manufacturing layout change." Floor is painted and coated. The production area is marked by yellow lines. All inventory is organized at one central location on one side of the floor. Manufacturing area organized to reduce travel time.

openness from the managers seemed to lead to good communication between managers and workers. Evidence of these attributes can be found in how management handled workers' suggestions for improvement. Workers submitted written suggestions to management, who evaluated them within a week and gave feedback to the workers whether they were going to accept the suggestions and make changes. Workers felt comfortable with this arrangement, and they were happy to make suggestions because they knew that they would hear from management within a week. Subsequently, the work atmosphere at the company was pleasant. Mutual trust was evident even to an outside observer.

Management fails to see the totality of CI concepts

When Sunshine first joined the CIUG, however, its members did not seem to understand how they could take advantage of the CI concepts. They treated the CIUG merely as the source for technical knowledge to solve specific problems. First, they focused on the glass-seal problem. A glass seal was a rubber-based gasket that went around the glass window of the sunroof, and the problem was that it did not make a tight seal when the roof was closed. Next, committee members focused on improving the assembly of the "GM module." In this case, they had to reorganize an assembly line because of the elimination of a subcomponent assembly. One of the three CIUG consultants at the time lamented that Sunshine did not seem to "quite grasp the concept of CI yet." When the two representatives, a line leader and a support person, returned from their field trip to Japanese transplants, realizing "what CI can accomplish for a factory," they excitedly reported this information to managers at Sunshine. Management did not reciprocate this excitement. The two commented, "It was hard for people who haven't seen the place to get fired up about it."

Moreover, in those early months of 1991, management did not seem to grasp the meaning of worker participation. They organized a scrap reduction committee in March and imposed the specific agenda on it of finding ways to reduce scratching of the glass. Although members considered glass scratching "the key cause of scraps," the interest level among them soon dissipated because the topics they could discuss were limited, and the committee eventually became inactive. To give another example: Management tried to involve workers in the hiring process but did not give them the authority to make decisions. Although management encouraged the workers to participate and voice their opinions about prospective workers, the managers still reserved the right to make the final decision. It seemed that management's goal was not to empower workers but to merely utilize workers in the "socialization process" of new workers. As a result, this program, too, did not last long. When the hiring decisions of the workers and managers conflicted, the managers' decision always prevailed. The participating workers consequently felt offended, and the program quickly developed a bad name. On a positive note, a new practice eventually resulted from this program, the so-called "new hire program." As a result, each new employee received a plant tour according to a written agenda, instead of "just getting thrown in there." He or she was also formally introduced to people in the shop as well as the office.

Workers take initiative through problem boards and meetings

The situation began to change at Sunshine in the summer of 1991, when the workers took an initiative to work on their own regarding problem-solving projects through what they called problem boards. They placed a board on an easel in a central location. Whenever a problem arose, workers wrote it down on the board instead of trying to track down their line leader. The goal was to tackle these problems in a more orderly fashion, not as a fire-fighting drill. At first, the line leaders were the only people who would address the problems listed, but eventually the workers began to work on the problems themselves.

The workers of the three manufacturing lines then began to meet regularly. However, there were still conflicting thoughts about the effectiveness of these meetings. One worker contended that the discussions in the meeting were "open and very informal." Another worker argued that "when we are pressed for production we skip the meeting," implying that they should be able to count on having the meeting despite production pressures. In all, the workers wanted to get involved and "do something" about the problems.

Cross-departmental CI committees are formed

By late summer 1991, Sunshine was forming cross-departmental CI committees. Management posted a signup sheet and workers began to volunteer. There were five committees. According to the CIUG training on employee involvement, each committee's proposed tasks were specific. Members of the *housekeeping committee* were to evaluate the general housekeeping practices of all shop areas and make recommendations when appropriate. They charged the *training committee* with devising a detailed training program for the tasks in each shop area. They enacted the *service orders committee* to oversee the process of how to fill out a service order. The *process improvement committee* focused on the production flow, addressing the issues of material handling, production line configuration, work-in-process (WIP) inventory, and so on. The *plant layout committee* was organized more as an ad hoc committee, which was to work on the new layout of the shop floor. Until the reorganization of the shop floor was completed in December 1991, this last committee by far was the most active one.

Proposals for plant reorganization
In October 1991, Sunshine asked all workers to turn in proposals for the plant reorganization to the plant layout committee. Management issued a detailed guideline of considerations in designing the layout. The guideline appeared to be heavily influenced by the CIUG training, and used jargon such as continuous improvement and horseshoe layout. Also in October, rather than displaying the quality-production-tracking boards on the bulletin board in the cafeteria, they were now displayed "where people work." According to one worker, quality consciousness was raised by bringing the quality information closer to "where it counts."

In November 1991, Sunshine posted a bulletin board that showed the activities of the five committees. The housekeeping committee took photos of "good" and "bad" practices and displayed them on the bulletin board. They were now planning to organize floor racks by color coding. The process improvement committee was focusing on preventive maintenance. The service order committee was working on the standard operating procedure for the steps that needed to be taken once a service order came in. The plant layout committee was moving full steam toward the target to finish reorganization before New Year's Day. In December 1991, all committees worked together on the restructuring of the plant floor. The housekeeping committee took care of the details involved in painting the shop floor. They selected the vendor and the color. The process committee worked closely with the plant layout committee regarding the laying out of production lines.

The plant floor underwent a "total manufacturing-layout change." They painted and coated the floor, marked the production area with yellow lines, and organized all the inventory in one central location on one side of the floor. They organized the manufacturing area to reduce travel time. An aspect of this reorganization project amply demonstrated the dedication of a few workers: A few of the plant layout committee members "worked right through the

Christmas vacation . . . up until New Year's Eve" to accomplish the project.

The CI Story of Fixer Machine Company

The top managers of this company were first attracted to CI because they realized the importance of making continuous incremental changes. In the past, they had always focused on making the "home run" type changes. According to one top manager, "We learned from CI that making a lot of [connecting] base hits is a lot better than making a few [unconnecting] home runs. Before, we have always tried make the home runs." However, as it turned out, the company stopped making base hits about halfway through and went for a home run in the end.

Catch-22—Improvements to production vs. production schedule
Fixer set up a CI committee in January 1991, which implemented many incremental changes during the next few months (see Table 12-4). The committee started to meet twice a week and worked fervently to make the changes. The members, nonetheless, began to realize that both meetings and improvement plans often conflicted with the production schedule. As one member put it, "it's a catch-22 thing," implying that they needed to make improvements that would help production eventually but were constrained from making these improvements because of the deadline pressures of the production schedule. For example, workers frequently spent too much time looking for tools when doing a new setup. If they could organize the tools and eliminate the time spent looking for them, they could start reducing the setup time. One member experimented with one of the machines. He set up the machine before organizing the tools, and it took 30 hours. After he organized the tools, the setup time was reduced to 6 hours. Workers could not make this type of improvement if they were pressed to make production deadlines.

This foreboding observation came true in May 1991 when GM's 322 cost-cutting plan got underway. It was a mandatory program imposed by GM on all their suppliers and dictated a 3 percent cost reduction in the first year and a 2 percent reduction

Table 12-4. History of Events at Fixer

Dates	Events
October 1990	• General manager and a line leader attend the CIUG meeting. CI focus projects—setup time reduction and organization of a problem-solving team.
January 1991	• Field trip to Japanese transplants in Battle Creek with the CIUG—"awakened and humbled." • Organize a single CI committee composed of line leaders and workers. Line leader participant to the CIUG personally contacts people who can be "preachers" for CI.
February 1991	• CI committee marks the floor with yellow tape, separating the production and non-production areas; colorcodes generic tools such as mops, buckets, and other tools used by each department; puts up a visual display of skill levels to encourage workers to expand their skills; and makes up a generic checklist to standardize the setup process. Also starts to repair machines with oil leaks. One member explains, "This is an ongoing process because you can't shut down the whole plant to work on the machines."
March 1991	• Installs a buzzer to announce one common time for going on breaks.
April 1991	• Two projects underway as part of the setup time reduction: a peg board is installed for each machine so workers can hang setup tools, and a tool staging cabinet is constructed to stage more generic tools. They run into resistance from other workers. One member comments, "People are not willing to accept the changes when they have been doing their job the same way for 20 years."
May 1991	• Due to production, it becomes difficult to meet as a group. Through sporadic personal efforts, a few members continue to work on standardizing setup procedure and tool organization. CI activities slow down this month.
June 1991	• CI committee no longer meets regularly. It becomes inactive.
September 1991	• Top management recognizes that the CI committee has not been active in recent months and attributes that to the lack of acceptance by the workers at large. CI committee is dissolved.
October 1991	• Management hosts an off-site meeting for managers and supervisors. They set a goal of doubling sales during the next 5 years, from $15 million to $30 million.
November 1991	• All employees participate in the in-house meetings brainstorming ways to meet this sales target. Employees make suggestions, such as to improve communication.
December 1991	• Management hosts a second off-site meeting for the same managers and supervisors. A consultant is involved in this reorganization planning process. The consultant and the general manager "picked most of the members" of this group. Leaders from the former CI committee are drafted to hold key positions.
January 1992	• Reorganization plans are unveiled to the employees.

the following two years. Thus, production overshadowed all other improvement activities. One CI member said, "GM is basically telling us to increase volume and increase efficiency at the same time, and this is getting to be a real struggle." Workers were put on a 10-hour shift. It became difficult for the CI group to schedule a common meeting time. In the following month, members exhibited "frustration over not being able to continue with [the existing] projects, let alone new projects." Production duty was "so overwhelming" that they could not expend their energy on CI changes. One CI member commented, "It's been total helter-skelter around here." Another continued, "We can't work on new projects because we are too busy with production—we have been on a 10-hour shift for the past two months." Another conceded, "We are just spinning our wheels."

One interesting observation based on conversations with the CI committee members was that they tended to overemphasize the justification for changes. They tended to talk down to workers who did not understand the quantitative benefits of the changes. They would say, "[The other workers] resist the changes because they don't see the necessity of making these changes." They focused on justifying changes, and once justified, they showed little sympathy for the other, noninvolved workers' reluctance to accept the changes.

In the fall, top managers contended that the supervisors and workers alike resented the CI members meeting during production time as well as their spending time on implementing changes during production. They argued that this group, though effective in making a number of changes, had worked as "an island" in the company. Management implied that there had not been much integration between the CI members and other workers. Management dissolved the CI committee and instead it planned to completely overhaul the organizational infrastructure so that everyone, not just CI members, could work on improvements. In five in-house meetings, top managers focused on ways to improve "recognition, delegation, and communication." For example, they looked for better ways to transfer information through a new communication structure.

Patience for base hits runs out
In early 1992, Fixer unveiled the plan for reorganization. The company reduced its organizational hierarchy to three levels from six, now resembling a participative-management structure. They were the *synchronous group*, which was a steering committee composed of top management, the *total quality management (TQM) group*, which was an action group that made operational decisions, and several functional committees at the worker level. As of April 1992, however, management was still struggling to "iron out the details" as to how much autonomy they would give to each committee. I stopped collecting data at this point.

In summary, the Fixer Machine Company started its venture into CI because it was attracted to making incremental changes or "base hits." Nonetheless, it made another big home run by completely reorganizing its infrastructure. This company, therefore, offers a story of a home-run hitter who tried to make base hits but ended up hitting another big home run.

The CI Story of Heat Incorporated

The CI process at this company demonstrates one person's struggle against an apathetic organizational infrastructure. The story began when an outgoing top manager who "understood the importance of CI" for the company selected a middle manger to champion the CI program. Meanwhile, the top manager's replacement was less enthusiastic about CI and only reluctantly allowed the CI program to continue. For example, he gave the CI committee little autonomy to make changes; he asked that "all CI changes be cost justified," and that people making such changes follow a formal approval procedure. Moreover, the overall sentiment of the company, including that of most managers and workers, was: "We are doing well, and why should we bother to change?"

Internal political tensions hamper cooperation
The social isolation of the CI program in its present form seemed to be part of a hidden agenda. There are three manufacturing groups in this company—I will call them A, B, and C. The leader of the CI program is the manager of C group, and there seems to be some

tension between this person and the managers of the A and B groups. For example, the other two managers implemented "CI changes [in their areas] independent of the CI program," and they seemed to make it difficult for their workers to attend the CI meetings. There were a few incidents when workers stopped coming to the meetings because they were "suspiciously too busy."

Two factors may explain this political tension. First, at one time there were only two manufacturing groups, A and B. In the past, the C group had been subservient to the A group; also, the manager of the A group had been the boss of the manager of the C group. At this time, the two groups were separate and both managers reported directly to the top manager. Second, after the manager of the A group was publicized in media (trade magazine and training tape of a national manufacturing organization) as the leader of a model manufacturing group, the manager of the C group was appointed as the leader of the company's CI program. Immediately thereafter, the top manager, who was responsible for these events, left Heat, Inc. for a new assignment. Since then, the CI leader, who is the manager of the C group, has been trying very hard to implement CI awareness, conduct training sessions, and make changes, but he feels as if his "efforts are not appreciated."

Because of the change in top managers, the newly appointed CI leader missed the CIUG meeting in October 1990, and began to attend meetings in December 1990 (see Table 12-5). He became the most vocal participant of the CIUG and a vocal proponent of CI within the company. He organized the CI committee and recruited people from other areas of the company, but the other manufacturing groups subsequently gave him "no cooperation" and in fact, hindered the CI process. Frequently, the assemblers that the CI leader recruited from other manufacturing groups had to resign from the committee when faced with "certain political pressures" from their department. Many CI committee members expressed their frustration about the workers' as well as managers' resistance to the changes that the committee was trying to implement. One committee member said, "It has been an uphill battle ever since."

Two examples describe the internal politics surrounding the CI committee in this company. In February 1991, top management

Table 12-5. History of Events at Heat

Dates	Events
December 1990	• Operation manager and two assemblers attend the second CIUG meeting. CI focus projects—fostering awareness in management and promoting employee involvement.
January 1991	• Internal CI committee formed and begins to meet weekly. Suggestion program launched. CI committee sends memos to upper management about proposed changes and asks for responses within two weeks.
February 1991	• Weekly suggestion rates and top-management response rates tracked and displayed on a graph. Top management does not approve the public displaying of these records. It remains in the CI committee "action" folder. • One operational group reduces 12 filing cabinets and 2 storage cabinets to 1 storage cabinet and also forms work teams.
March 1991	• Top management asks the CI committee to evaluate and make recommendations on how the "process lab" sales area can improve its housekeeping and workplace organization practices. They are asked to justify changes in terms of costs benefits. • Committee members generate a five-page document at the end of the month. This report makes no real impact—the manager of the affected area refused to work with the CI committee.
April 1991	• CI committee sponsors an "employee forum" in which workers can discuss the general problems in their areas and offer ideas for improvement. The suggestion rate increases. • "Suggestion challenge project" launched—a project in which each member goes out and verbally urges workers to submit suggestions. The committee, at this point, seeks a reward system for suggestions but gets little response from management. • Bulletin board is used to display the records of workers' suggestions and management's feedback. • By the end of this month, all employees in production and engineering departments have seen the CI training video tapes. Sales department has not shown the tapes to its workers.
May 1991	• Electrical group cleans up the workplace "on their own." Mechanical group devises a tool box under the bench.
June 1991	• CI committee puts up a CI display board that shows the before-and-after pictures of changes. • Company hosts the CIUG. General manager attends the meetings. Apparently convinced of the importance of CI, he publicly expresses his support for CI.
July 1991	• CI Committee proposes a reward plan but it is rejected by upper management.

determined that the process lab within the sales department, where potential customers came to see prototypes, needed to improve their housekeeping and workplace organization. Top management commissioned the CI committee to come up with such a plan. When the report came out, the manager of the lab area took offense and refused

Table 12-5. History of Events at Heat (continued)

Dates	Events
September 1991	• After rejections of several versions in July and August of 1991, upper management finally accepts a suggestion reward program. • CI committee has been working on getting approval of upper management to display the performance data. Finally top management approves a "performance feedback board," but only for one of the operations groups. Shows such operational records as on-time delivery, rework, etc.—the financial records are not yet permitted to be posted.
October 1991	• CI committee focuses on standardizing the assembly procedure for one of the machines.
December 1991	• An assembler, considered the best on one of the machines, finishes writing up standard operating procedures. This effort is met with severe resistance from assemblers. Despite general manager's public praise for this standard operating procedure (the time saving from this could "pay for all CI-related changes"), assemblers win the political battle early next year and are relieved from having to follow the operating procedure: The procedures become obsolete.

to follow the suggestions. The top manager "convinced" him to try a few suggestions, but no real impact was made. The poor housekeeping and workplace organization practices at the process lab persisted as of April 1992, more than a year after the report was filed.

In May 1991, the other two manufacturing groups, A and B, above, made a few changes seemingly on their own. These changes were seen as encouraging signs at first. However, it was later discovered that these changes were politically motivated. Top managers personally asked the operation managers of these two areas to make some of the changes. They reluctantly complied and made a few "CI changes." The two production groups actually made no CI changes "on their own." Despite the apathetic intraorganizational atmosphere, the CI committee tried to remain active under the leadership of the CI-group manager, but as you will see, it was indeed an up-hill battle.

The CI committee promotes awareness, employee involvement, and a reward system

As soon as they formed the committee in January 1991, the committee launched a suggestion program to "encourage employee involvement." To "foster CI awareness," committee members sent memos to all the top management about the suggestions and asked for a response in two weeks. In the ensuing months, in what they called "the suggestion challenge program," each member of the committee went to other workers and verbally urged them to submit suggestions. The members eventually realized that they needed some kind of reward system for these suggestions.

In April 1991, the budget for purchasing a bulletin board to display records on worker suggestions and management response was approved. According to one CI committee member, "It was good that they approved it, but I can't figure out why it took them three months to do it." By the end of April 1991, all employees in the manufacturing area saw the CI training tapes obtained through the CIUG, but the sales group did not agree to show the tape to their workers. In June 1991, the CI committee put up a CI display board that highlighted before-and-after pictures of changes. The changes ranged from a new tool-staging cabinet to a new public announcement system in the cafeteria.

Upper management finally approved a reward system for making suggestions in September after rejecting several versions in July and August of 1991. They coined it the "three-win program," because it included three winners—the suggester, all employees, and the company. The program rewarded the suggester with 5 percent of the savings incurred by the change. Another 5 percent of the savings was placed in a general employee account to be distributed among all employees. The rest of the savings went to the company. The CI committee worked out the dollar limits of the program and was also responsible for reviewing the process.

CI committee attempts to standardize assembly procedures
In last three months of 1991, the committee focused on standardizing assembly procedures for one of the machines. Previously, each assembler used his/her own method for assembling the same machine. Finished machines might meet the same specifications, but their internal wiring and configuration might be different. Standardization would offer the following benefits:

- When customers called with questions about a machine, they would not have to find the assembler who assembled that particular machine.
- The overall time spent on assembly would be reduced if the assembly procedure was standardized to best practice by the best worker.
- The training time for a new worker would be reduced tremendously.

All these advantages were proven in a few pilot projects. In December 1991, the standard operating procedures for assembling one of the machines was completed based on the practice of the best assembler. This accomplishment, however, met with severe resistance from the other assemblers. Early in the next year, 1992, assemblers finally won this political battle and were relieved from standardizing the assembly procedure—thus making the standard operating procedure book obsolete.

The CI Story of Topheavy Tool and Manufacturing Company

Topheavy Tool and Manufacturing Company is a successful stamping company. It has been expanding steadily since 1988, including during this study. It had, however, virtually no employee-involvement programs during the time of this research. Its total employee involvement (TEI) committee oversaw a suggestion program that had minimal impact on the overall company operation. In early 1991, the company formed a CI committee, but it was dissolved "for lack of action" after a few months (see Table 12-6). The second CI committee, called the housekeeping and workplace organization committee, was subsequently formed, but the company also dissolved it for the same reason.

Attempt to build a team with managers only
One critical characteristic of Topheavy that worked against them was the status gap between top managers and the workers. Management appeared very possessive of financial information and rather reluctant about sharing it with workers. Moreover, CI at Topheavy remained a management project, it never really made it to the worker level: The two CI committees never included line workers.

Table 12-6. History of Events at Topheavy

Dates	Events
October 1990	• Operations director and a staff attend the first CIUG meeting. Initial CI projects—quick die change and improvement of employee involvement.
December 1990	• A line leader attends the CIUG.
January 1991	• This line leader assigned to one of Topheavy's sister plants as plant manager. • Staff CIUG participant begins to work on reorganization of dies—paints the racks and relocates them for easier access.
February 1991	• Internal CI committee is organized but includes no line workers.
March 1991	• CI committee members watch the CI training video tapes obtained through the CIUG. These members come up with a handful of projects, but very little implementation is done. • As a side project, management sends one of the CI committee members to one of the two related plants to educate them about CI. He offers ideas about CI-related changes (ie., work-cell organization). The plant subsequently implements "many CI changes."
May 1991	• The line leader who went to one of the related plants in January as a plant manager comes back to Topheavy as a "hero." Based on "what little exposure he had to CI," he has been able to turn that company around. He is made plant manager at Topheavy. • In the last week of this month, the operations director, who was instrumental in joining the CIUG and organizing the CI Committee, is asked to resign. A replacement is hired immediately.
June 1991	• New operations director continues to support membership in the CIUG. However, internal CI committee is dissolved for lack of "focused" action. A new committee is formed, called the housekeeping and workplace organization committee. New plant manager charged to lead this committee. This committee again includes no line workers.
August 1991	• One member assists the operations director relocating and restructuring die racks in plant layout.
September 1991	• New housekeeping and workplace organization committee meets only once. Meetings for this committee continue to be scheduled and continue to be canceled at the last minute due to the "pressing production" schedule. • Management contemplates combining their TEI and CI into one program. • New floor plan instituted. Areas for work-in-process inventory now designated, quality gauges and room brought close together, and obsolete equipment taken out of the plant and stored away.
November 1991	• Top manager announces that "everybody will be involved in CI." After having been in Japan and after visiting other model companies, he decides to adopt the team structure.

Table 12-6. History of Events at Topheavy (continued)

Dates	Events
December 1991	• All employees are trained to work in teams by an external consultant. Employees decide to organize teams by department as opposed to functions. Teams are designated to be "self-directed."
January 1992	• In the third week of January 1992, the plant manager who came back from the related plant as a hero and became the plant manager of Topheavy leaves the company for another job. • Team leaders undergo more intensive training sessions. Management's decision regarding how much autonomy the teams are to be given has not been made.

Early in 1991, one manager explained that the reasons for not including workers in their CI committees was a deliberate strategy to "get the buy-in of managers first and then worry about the workers." This strategy apparently did not work, however, because the CI committee was dissolved for lack of action. In fact, the explanation behind the resignation of the former operations director in May of 1991 (he was asked to resign) was his inability to "build a team" of managers and workers. It was ironic that the second CI committee, the housekeeping and workplace organization committee, also did not include any workers. Members did not meet even once after the first meeting. The suggestions they decided to implement during the kick-off meeting were "never kept up."

Management's reluctance to implement CI
An example of the lethargic activity of the first CI committee is the following: When members watched the training videotape of CI, they typically "ended up watching it only superficially." According to one member, "The energy level was really low. People didn't want to be there, if they could help it." Another member recalls, "We were watching the videotape. A worker came for [a line leader] and he went out for three to four minutes. Then, another worker came for [another line leader] and they talked outside for another few minutes. [One of the managers] then was paged. Then another one. At this point, two or three people there threw up their

pens and said if this isn't a priority, then what are we doing here? The meeting became deflated. People were asking if we are going to do things or just go through the motions. There was lack of commitment." The CI changes made at Topheavy consisted of a few sporadic efforts made by one of the CIUG participants. All the changes he instituted were related to die organization; the other proposed changes suggested by the two CI committees were never implemented.

Another person that top management sent to a sister plant helped make some profound changes in that plant. One manager assessed that he was able to "do more CI at that plant than we did at our plant." The following story of this person's efforts offers another example of Topheavy's reluctance to implement CI.

> He was one of the first CI committee members. He became personally interested in CI and trained himself by "watching the CI tapes" on his own. When he was then assigned to one of Topheavy's related plants as plant manager, he reorganized the plant's work stations into work-cell operations, cut work-in-process inventory, and raised worker morale. He came back to Topheavy after a few months as "a hero." He was then made plant manager at Topheavy and put in charge of the second CI committee, the housekeeping and workplace organization committee. At this point, however, he was bombarded with production quotas. He would schedule meetings for the CI committee, but he would also cancel them at the last minute due to an "emergency." In fact, the committee never met—I drove there to attend the scheduled meeting of this committee on three occasions in the fall of 1991 only to find it was canceled at the last minute all three times. Toward the end of the year, he confided in me, by saying that he was never able to lead the committee "the way [he] wanted to." Topheavy dissolved this second CI committee soon after that time, and after a brief time period, he left the company for another job. Coinciding with his departure was the start of extensive TEI training in late 1991. This was the result of the top managers' mandate that "all employees shall be involved in CI." All managers, line leaders, and workers underwent intensive training sessions. The impact of this training still remained to be seen as of April of 1992.

The departure of two top managers, the operations director and plant manager, occurred right after top management dissolved the CI committees of which they were in charge. Top management asked the operations director to leave the company right after they dissolved the CI committee, and the plant manager left immediately after they dissolved the housekeeping and workplace organization committee.

The CI Story of Small Metal Stamping and Manufacturing

Small joined the CIUG to stop their "sawtooth improvement" and to "share ideas" with other companies. They were "getting tired of" making improvement only to see their efforts decay. Nonetheless, "sawtooth improvement" is all they accomplished in their CI efforts, and they stopped sharing when they became the only company that stopped coming to the CIUG meetings. They made cosmetic changes but they did not process these changes or make them into good standard operating procedures; they were preoccupied with immediate production problems and with "putting the fires out" (see Table 12-7). High worker turnover aggravated the situation. Most of the workers who were involved in the initial CI projects had left the company by the end of my research.

Production gets in the way of the top manager's vision of launching CI projects

Small Metal Stamping and Manufacturing is a family business. The top manager owns the company. One of the three in the next level of managers is his daughter. The top manager makes operating decisions when he is in the shop, but when he is out of the shop, typically for marketing activities, the other three managers make the decisions.

The top manager had a vision of launching many CI-related projects, but production always seemed to get in the way. Small maintained quality through inspections. There was no systematic control for production and inventory. The company had sporadic CI projects, but its CI program was never consistent. For example, when they focused on housekeeping and workplace organization, the managers approached it as a discrete project and neglected the

Table 12-7. History of Events at Small

Dates	Events
October 1990	• Hosts the first CIUG meeting. Housekeeping was pointed out by the CIUG as a major concern at this company. Selects housekeeping and workplace organization as their focus project.
November 1990	• Two workers assigned to the project of die storage and color coding. Specific job numbers also painted in large black letters on the dies. Die racks are then painted with same colors as dies for easy organization.
February 1991	• All of in-house production dies and all die racks are color coded. Remaining dies are service dies, which are to be painted as they are pulled from storage for production.
March 1991	• Company "hits a slow period." Workers are laid off a week, and during that week, shipping and receiving area is cleaned and painted.
April 1991	• Management conducts an internal survey for career development and supervisor-worker relations. It probes for interest and possible areas for training.
May 1991	• Major cleaning effort takes place. Eliminate the pile of wooden pallets in the empty lot between two buildings; clean the floor that has been stained with oil leaks not only from machines but from drip cans at the oil drums; reorganize several pieces of equipment; and install racks to store large bins containing parts.
June 1991	• General workplace organization accomplished last month not maintained. Housekeeping and workplace organization begins to deteriorate.
October 1991	• A janitor hired to maintain a clean shop floor.
December 1991	• No significant CI efforts take place. There is an indication of production and inventory control problem—one month's worth of "raw steel" is sitting on the shop floor.

work process that was needed to maintain it. When sales slowed down in March 1991, they shut down the plant and painted one large shipping room.

New general manager's proposals for CI programs turn into a fiasco
The critical event for CI was supposed to come when they acquired a tool and die manufacturer in 1991. The head of this tool and die manufacturer became the general manager of Small. When Small interviewed the new general manager, he laid out the CI programs he planned to institute. He talked of "housekeeping and plant organization, cross-training programs, standardization of die shut heights, attitude changes," and so on, and the top manager

entrusted him to carry out the CI efforts. In fact, the new general manager was instrumental in a big housecleaning project in May 1991; however, he resigned from his post in June of 1991 and all die makers who had come with him also left the company. Apparently, when he went, all the CI projects he proposed went with him. The top manager later described this venture as a "fiasco."

Small has recovered from this event, but its CI program did not. This unfortunate incident seemed to dampen what little momentum there was for CI. After June 1991 there were no more CI improvement projects. Management merely hired a cleaner to "keep the shop clean." They stopped attending the CIUG meetings toward the end of 1991.

The CI Story of Mom and Pop Manufacturing

There were two sources of employee participation at Mom and Pop Manufacturing: quality work groups (QWG), a result of training from the Crosby System; and the quality die change (QDC) group, which CIUG participants organized, calling it the "internal CI group." Despite the two avenues of participation, the total number of actual changes was dismal (see Table 12-8).

Trying to sell and implement CI changes without management support

The internal CI group was led by three CIUG participants: two line workers and one line leader. All three tried to explain to workers what they learned from the CIUG meetings and to "sell the idea of CI." They were very discouraged throughout 1991, however, that they were unable to make more CI changes "due to the lack of management support." The CI group tried to make changes, but they never accomplished their CI projects. For example, to improve setups, they designed a new die transportation cart. They submitted the design to management and awaited a response to no avail. Their spirits were dampened because this was their first project and they "weren't getting anywhere." This project was subsequently approved by management a year later after one of the CIUG participants brought it up when asked by management about how to gain workers' trust and enthusiasm. The CI project

Table 12-8. History of Events at Mom and Pop

Dates	Events
October 1990	• Manufacturing manager and a line worker attend the first CIUG meeting.
December 1990	• CI focus projects—improving set ups and press loading and scheduling.
January 1991	• Manufacturing manager recruits a line leader as representative of workers to the CIUG meeting. This person ends up playing a leading role in Mom and Pop's CI effort. A worker goes on the field trip to the Japanese transplants in Battle Creek and gets "sold on the idea of CI."
March 1991	• Company hosts the CIUG. At this meeting, management "allows workers to voice their opinions" to the CIUG openly. Two of the most frequently stated sources of dissatisfaction were no knowledge of company's financial status and no established channel for recognition and rewards. • Line-leader participant to the CIUG organizes second quality die change (QDC) group, which consists mostly of hourly die setters. This group considered their CI group.
May 1991	• Manufacturing manager who initiated joining of the CIUG leaves company. General manager assumes his role; no replacement is hired. In the meantime, about 90 percent of workers are now trained in QIP and organized into eight different QWGs. • CI group designs die transportation tray to assist in set up, but it "never goes beyond the blueprint stage." • CI group and a few QWG members put up a communication bulletin board. Overall change efforts remain minimal.
June 1991	• Internal CI group no longer meets regularly, but all three CIUG participants are in leading roles in QWG activities.
September 1991	• QIT develops a recognition board that displays the pictures of QWGs and their progress.
November 1991	• Business is slowly declining, and management starts to lay off people. As people leave, QWG membership shrinks. Many scheduled meetings of QWGs are canceled by management to alleviate production displays.
December 1991	• Because there are fewer workers, management reduces the number of QWGs to three. Instead of electing, they appoint the three CIUG participants to lead their three QWGs.

studied the feasibility of computerizing press loading and scheduling, but the project was never instituted due to high cost. This project was "a management thing." In May, the manufacturing manager, who initiated this company's joining of the CIUG and was instrumental in recruiting the CI participants, left the company "in frustration." The general manager assumed his role, and no replacement was hired.

Communication gap between management and workers worsens
The QWGs were ineffective mainly because of the communication gap between them and the quality improvement team (QIT), a management team. The QWGs met weekly and submitted project proposals to the QIT. Although the QIT was "obligated to respond to all proposals," it responded infrequently. When the responses did come back, they were superficial. To overcome this apparent communication gap, top management instituted "liaisons" between the QIT and the QWGs, but ironically these liaisons were frequently "the hardest people to get ahold of."

The three CIUG participants eventually took over the leadership role of the QWGs. Toward the end of 1991, the company was undergoing a downsizing effort, and as people left, there appeared to be gaps in leadership for the QWGs. Many scheduled meetings of the QWGs were canceled to alleviate production delays. In December of 1991, with a smaller number of workers, management reduced the number of QWGs to three. Instead of electing participants, management now appointed the three CIUG participants to lead the QWGs.

Workers distrust management—us versus them
The CI effort at Mom and Pop was most impeded by management's inability to harness the energy of workers. The workers in general seemed to be more concerned than the management about making changes. There was a clear sentiment among the workers that management was so preoccupied with "firefighting" that the ideas for improvements, whether from the QWGs or the CI group, were a very low priority.

The workers seemed to distrust the top management's commitment to worker participation. Management's commitment appeared moderate in the beginning of 1991, but toward the end of that year they showed little interest. In the early part of that year, one worker voiced concern that "commitment is there but yet not there—things seem to stall out." By summer of 1991, even when the company had eight actively meeting QWGs, another worker still contended, "Management doesn't even seem to understand why we need to make these changes. It takes these suggestions and sits on them." Toward the end of the year, when management began to lay off workers and requested that the remaining employees work on overtime to meet production, there was a distinct sentiment among workers that top managers are "not committed to worker participation, although they say they are."

The "us" versus "them" confrontation was evident in the language that managers and workers used to describe each other. One worker became somewhat hostile in one of the interviews: "They sit there in their cushy offices but understand not a damn thing about what we are trying to accomplish." When management was made aware of this sentiment, the response was rather apathetic: "If they think that way, it is their prerogative."

Pitfalls and Possible Opportunities in Implementing CI

The cases described above represent a range of experiences that a company may undergo when implementing a CI program. Progressive took the most advantage of the improvements in the area of housekeeping and workplace organization. Sunshine first viewed CI as a technical program to solve technical problems, but later began to allow the workers to volunteer and carry out the improvement activities. Fixer approached CI as a tool to increase productivity. To Small, CI was an ideal that it aspired to attain, but it remained only that. At Mom and Pop, the workers seemed to like CI, but to management it was more of a nuisance than anything else. CI takes on different shapes in different companies. Although all seven companies were exposed to the same type of training through the CIUG, events that unfolded in each company were different.

Some approaches to implementing the CI program, however, were held in common. All companies except for Small organized a committee to oversee the CI program. Further, managers of all seven companies tried to offer some type of support, although the level of resources made available for CI activities varied. A group of people responsible for leading the CI effort and management support are the basic conditions necessary for implementing a CI program, without which CI programs cannot even begin.

In the remainder of this chapter, I assume that these two conditions are present in a company—that a company can organize a committee and management is willing to allow a CI program to begin. I then focus on the specific pitfalls (what went wrong) and opportunities (what went right) experienced by these seven companies during the first critical steps of implementing CI programs so you will have the benefit of their experience as you implement your own CI program. Table 12-9 summarizes the key pitfalls and opportunities.

Alienation of the Line Leaders

Progressive asked line leaders to take the leading role in their CI activities, largely because management correctly perceived the shop floor as the center of CI activities, and because line leaders "best know and understand" the shop-floor dynamics. However, the line leaders subsequently struggled because they were in charge

Table 12-9. Pitfalls and Opportunities in Implementing CI: Seven Cases

Companies	Pitfalls	Opportunities*
Progressive Engineering and Manufacturing	Alienation of the line leaders	Quality improvement through housekeeping and workplace organization
Sunshine Incorporated	CI as problem-solving activity	Idea sharing through visibility and feedback
Fixer Machine Company	Alienation of the CI team from the rest of the work force	
Heat Incorporated	Alienation of the CI team from the rest of the company	
Topheavy Tool and Manufacturing Company	CI program initiated as a managerial program	
Small Metal Stamping and Manufacturing	Intermittent efforts to make improvements	
Mom and Pop Manufacturing	CI program perceived by management as "a worker thing"	

*Common opportunities that appeared in almost all companies, the existence of a CI committee and varied management support, are not specified here.

of both production and improvement activities. For the line leaders, it was difficult to make "everyday production goals and make CI changes at the same time." Some referred to this struggle as a "juggling" act. The juggling took place when the leader had to decide whether to allow the workers to work on improvement activities or production activities. The juggling act became even more precarious when the company was behind in production. In fact, it was not unusual to see the improvement activities take a "back seat" to production activities.

In all, there was a deep sense of conflict as the line leaders wanted to meet the production goals and at the same time continue to make improvements. The internal conflict seemed to worsen when they were labeled as "anti-improvement" by the workers. This happened when the company asked the workers to stay on the production line during their scheduled committee meetings. At Progressive, where worker enthusiasm was high for making CI changes, the workers resented being prevented from going to their respective committee meetings. Many workers as well as some managers viewed their line leaders as "impediments" to progress. These perceptions deeply bothered the line leaders. One line leader said, "I am not anti-improvement, and, in fact, I am all for it. It is just that I need to meet production." He summed up by saying that the line leaders are "caught between a rock and a hard place."

CI as a Problem-Solving Activity

During its initial phase of the CI program, management at Sunshine tried to use the CI program as a means to solve specific problems. This approach led to two undesirable consequences: Workers could not differentiate the CI program from other problem-solving committee activities, and the improvement activities became haphazard.

A manager may easily fall into this trap when under pressure to solve problems on the shop floor and maintain production. This type of pressure may be akin to what the line leader of Progressive felt. However, CI should be more than isolated and disjointed problem-solving activities. CI projects need to involve a much larger body of the workers, who need to see how this is a process different from working on specific problems. If management treats CI as a problem solving activity, workers will surely fail to see the uniqueness of this program. CI activities should entail a concerted and systematic approach. As it happened in Progressive, CI activities need to involve the whole organization, and one project (housekeeping and workplace organization) should systematically lead to another (reducing setup time). When CI programs are driven by specific problems, they lose concertedness and become merely "fire-fighting" activities.

Alienation of CI Team from the Rest of the Work Force

The CI team at Fixer initially worked hard to implement many incremental changes, but other workers soon began to resent the CI team members' being relieved from their production duties. When the members heard about this, instead of being conciliatory, they tended to talk down to workers, saying that they did not understand the importance of making changes. Consequently, the CI team gathered little support from other workers, and the changes that they made had only isolated effects.

For instance, one member pushed for a project he was interested in (tool-box organization). Although he was able to demonstrate impressive results (for example, reduced setup time due to organized tools), no one else was willing to duplicate the change, and the effects of the change became limited to his own area. Top managers later conceded that the CI team, although effective in making a number of changes, had worked as "an island" in the company.

Similar to the case of Fixer, the CI team at Heat worked hard to implement many changes but did so in isolation. Unlike the team at Fixer, this CI team was isolated from the rest of the organization, not just from other workers. The source of the problem rested with the CI leader's unstable relationship with other managers.

Top managers seemed to view the CI program more as a nuisance than as a help. A few managers said during the interviews, "[If] we are doing well [financially], why do we need to make changes?" Consequently, CI team members said that making any kind of change was an "up-hill battle." They had to gain approval from management for all proposed changes. A lot of energy went into getting timely feedback from the management. Therefore, many delays were evident in implementing changes, which led to frustration among the CI implementers.

CI Program Perceived as a Management Program

A top manager of Topheavy reasoned that he did not allow line workers in the CI committee because he felt that he needed to get the "buy-in" of the managers first. Consequently, the workers who had attended the CIUG most regularly and were most enthusiastic about CI were bypassed from getting involved in CI activities. Instead, managers who attended the CIUG only sporadically and felt much less enthusiastic were appointed to lead the CI committees.

The company organized two CI-related committees at two different times, but both committees were ineffective and were dissolved. When looking for leadership, management should identify those who are most involved in actual CI training and implementation and appoint those people as the leaders independent of their formal position.

Intermittent Improvement Efforts

Although the managers of Small had earnest intentions to make improvements, they were usually preoccupied instead with meeting delivery deadlines. They did try to make a few changes by cleaning and painting a large area and color-coding the dies; however, these changes were sporadic and unconnected.

In particular, when Small underwent a major housekeeping and workplace organization project in May 1992, managers and workers alike were very enthusiastic about what they accomplished. According to the managers, their quality level went up sharply after this. However, positive feelings and improved quality diminished quickly as they resumed their preoccupation with daily production routines and did not maintain the improved level with continuous incremental changes. In the end, the effects of the change had little immediate impact and no lasting impact.

Perceiving CI Activities as "a Worker Thing"

Much as in Topheavy the worker-manager class distinction was evident in Mom and Pop. As evidence, when Mom and Pop was implementing the Crosby System, it created separate teams among management (QIT) and workers (QWGs). The new structure continued to "manage" the change activities in a traditional top-down way as the QIT controlled the activities of the QWGs.

Quite frequently during interviews, the workers reacted negatively to this separation of status. Referring to managers who were trying to oversee the change activities on the shop floor, workers would typically comment, "We know shop-floor operation [the same way] they know management. How can they tell us what to do and what not to do?" Further, having one group (QWGs) propose and another group (QIT) review and decide added an extra burden to communication. Workers in QWGs would submit proposals, but they did not hear back from managers in the QIT. One line leader commented, "It is like dropping a rock in a bottomless pit. You just don't hear from them."

When the managers were told of these sentiments they responded apathetically: "If they feel that way, it is their prerogative." A group of workers who attended CIUG meetings and were central to Mom and Pop's improvement activities were nevertheless left alone with no concrete support from management.

Quality Improvement Through Housekeeping and Workplace Organization

Opportunities did present themselves at these seven companies during these initial implementation phases. Though housekeeping and workplace organization is perhaps the least glamorous aspect of CI, it appears to be crucial if CI is to get off the ground. For example, the advent of the focus on plantwide housekeeping and workplace organization coincided perfectly with quality improvement at Progressive. When in December 1990 the company began to focus on housekeeping and workplace organization, the recorded quality problems changed from about 20 incidents per month to 4 incidents per month. They maintained this level throughout the following year. Progressive's internal reject rates improved by more than four-fold the following year. The management at Progressive attributes this success to the clean and organized shop floor.

This does not mean that the effects of housekeeping and workplace organization on product quality will be lasting. For example, Small had a similar sort of push for housekeeping and workplace organization. In May 1991, management shut down the plant and undertook a major cleaning and organizing effort. The managers said their quality level went up sharply after this, yet the effects of their housekeeping and workplace activities soon deteriorated, and their short-lived quality increase soon disappeared. Therefore, the key to maintaining the higher quality level is also to maintain good housekeeping and workplace organization. Progressive did this by organizing a housekeeping and workplace organization committee and by granting it decision-making power and an independent budget.

Idea Sharing Through Visibility and Feedback

Initiating a CI program can also enhance or create better communication between workers and management. For example, Sunshine started off on the wrong foot by considering CI a problem-solving activity. When management finally came around to creating an organizational level CI program, workers responded enthusiastically by voluntarily signing up for various committees. Many members of these committees showed a remarkable commitment.

I attribute the success of Sunshine's CI program to the good communication between managers and workers. Managers were always willing to share information with the workers, and workers were always willing to voice their opinions. For instance, Sunshine shared ideas in an open forum through the "problem boards." Unlike Mom and Pop or Heat, when a worker suggested a new idea to the management, he/she always received feedback on whether it was accepted; if accepted, when it would be implemented; if not accepted, why it was not accepted.

What These Seven Cases Tell Us

The continuous improvement program cannot be a management *or* a worker program—it must be one joint program. As long as there is a gap between management and workers, the CI program will not work. Even when management and workers share a common vision for the CI program, the line leader's dilemma and the problem of intermittent improvement efforts will still need to be addressed. These two latter issues stem from the tension between production and improvement activities.

Just as managers and workers need to work together, companies need to conduct production and improvement activities simultaneously. Although this is physically not possible, what is possible is to consider production and improvement activities as two sides of the same coin and to create a new organizational value that holds no difference between the two. If a company can make this happen, your line leaders will not have to choose between the two activities, and the company will not have to abandon the incremental-improvement activities to meet production goals.

A new approach to work routines is required. Traditionally, work routines are viewed as invariant elements of organization. They are the best way of doing a task, and they are something the workers are supposed to abide by whenever they do their work. However, consider the possibility that routines are not something to be maintained faithfully, but rather, they are something that constantly needs to be updated and upgraded. In this way, the routines become more dynamic—they can constantly change, improve, and adapt to circumstances. From this perspective, the production and improvement activities are intertwined and finally can be viewed as one and the same function. From this perspective, you can view the outputs not as a function of static production routines but as a function of *dynamic production routines that embody continuous improvement activities*.

References

Eisenhardt, K. M. Building theories from case study research. *Academy of Management Review*, 14:(4), 1989.

Fielding, N. G., and Fielding, J. L. *Linking Data*. Newbury Park, CA: Sage, 1986.

Fleming, R., and Rother, M. Michigan Continuous Improvement Users Group. Paper presented at A Forum on Leadership, Theory, and Practice. Minneapolis, MN, 1991.

Imai, M. *Kaizen: The Key to Japan's Competitive Success*. New York: Random House Business Division, 1986.

Poe, R. The new discipline: Unleash group intelligence in your company. *Success*, July/August: 80, 1991.

Schroeder, D. M., and Robinson, A. G. America's most successful export to Japan: Continuous improvement. *Sloan Management Review*, Spring: 67–81, 1991.

Shingo, S. *Non-Stock Production: The Shingo System for Continuous Improvement*. Cambridge, MA: Productivity Press, 1988.

Suzaki, K. *The New Manufacturing Challenge: Techniques for Continuous Improvement*. New York: Free Press, 1987.

Yin, R. K. The case study crises: Some answers. *Administrative Science Quarterly*, 26: 58–65, 1981.

Yin, R. K. *Case Study Research: Design and Methods*. Newbury Park, CA: Sage, 1989.

 **George Koenigsaecker's** *background and experience include a unique blend of manufacturing, marketing, sales, and general management with Deere and Company, Rockwell International, and Danaher Corporation. His most recent experiences include serving as president of Jacobs Manufacturing (a subsidiary of Danaher Corporation) and group vice president for Danaher Corporation. He is presently president of the HON Company, a Fortune 500 company.*

Lean Production—The Challenge of Multidimensional Change

by George Koenigsaecker

Editor's prologue: You may have read about George Koenigsaecker in *Lean Thinking*. In their vivid description of the transformation of Jacobs Vehicle Equipment Company ("Jake Brake"), Jim Womack and Daniel Jones described George as one of the executives (actually president at the time) referred to as a "hopeless concrete head" by Mr. Iwata of Shingijutsu (a consulting firm of former Ohno disciples). Although several times Iwata refused to help Jake Brake, George was extremely persistent and eventually convinced Iwata that he was serious about transforming Jake Brake to the Toyota Production System. One of Iwata's requirements was that they do whatever he told them to do. Through this experience, George was introduced to the "just-do-it" mind-set that transformed his outlook on manufacturing. Jake Brake became one of the great American success stories in the transformation to lean manufacturing, and George has gone on to work his magic as the president of the HON Company. In this chapter, George reflects on what he learned at Jake Brake and considers the technical, psychological, and management requirements for successful "multidimensional change."

Throughout this book, the authors stress that top management must be committed to the process of becoming lean if the effort is to be successful. After reading what George has to say about commitment, you may either throw caution to the wind, get "religion" and be challenged to become a "true believer," or you will high-tail it to the mass-production hills of yesteryear and hide there until the day of "true-lean" reckoning finds you.

It must be considered that there is nothing more difficult to carry out, nor more doubtful of success, nor more dangerous to handle, than to initiate a new order of things. For the reformer has enemies in all those who profit by the old order, only lukewarm defenders in all those who would profit by the new.

MACHIAVELLI

After 40 years' success of lean manufacturing, why are there so many "non-lean" operations? The benefits of the conversion to lean production are typically unbelievable to someone who has not experienced the change firsthand. As Table 13-1 shows, by benchmarking the multiyear conversion process in both Japan and the United States, you can predict quantum improvements whether you are starting from batch production or Henry Ford-style flow production.

In 1986, I became president of Jacobs Vehicle Equipment Company ("Jake Brake") in Bloomfield, Connecticut, a producer of diesel engine retarders. Jake Brake was a classic batch manufacturer. Inventory turns were in the high 2's; that is, a little over twice

Table 13-1. Expected Improvements From Lean Over Starting Point of Operation

	Starting Point	
	Batch production	Flow production (Ford system)
Productivity increase	+300 – 400%	+100%
Inventory turns	+1000%	+300%
Defects	-95%	-80%
Lead time	-95%	-75%

per year. The company measured delivery performance in "months past due" and productivity was inadequate at best. Working with former members of the Toyota Group's Production Engineering staff, led by Yoshiki Iwata (formerly of Toyota Gosei), we began the conversion process. Over the next three years we moved from monthly production batches to twice monthly batches, to weekly batches, and eventually to daily batches. The impact of this was to move Jake Brake deliveries from months past due to daily deliveries. Our customers were major truck engine manufacturers, such as Cummins, Caterpillar, and Detroit Diesel, who were building to line set. After three years, we were able to receive orders by fax or phone on one day, produce exactly the product as ordered, and ship it on the following day. By year three of the conversion to a daily production and delivery pattern, we were running multiple consecutive months with zero deliveries past due.

A major financial benefit of the conversion to lean production is the reduction in inventory. This is an automatic benefit of the steps taken to get to daily production/delivery. In the case of Jake Brake, the impact of daily production delivery was to increase total inventory turns (raw, work-in-progress [WIP], and finished [primarily spare parts]) from the high 2's to over 15 turns. By the end of the third year of conversion, 75 percent of the total inventory was in raw material due to the limited number of lean production suppliers available. The total costs of the conversion program had been more than paid for by the cash flow from inventory.

Quality improvement flowed naturally from lean production implementation of concepts such as *one-piece flow* and *poka-yoke* or *fool-proofing*. In Jake Brake's case, the reduction in defect rates was more than 80 percent in the first three years.

The major contributor to the bottom line was productivity growth, which averaged 2 percent per month. This was a rate of productivity growth that I had observed in Japanese companies that had made recent (early 1980s) conversions to the Toyota Production System (lean production) and were able, with a great deal of focus, to stay on this improvement curve. After three years, we had doubled the productivity. After five years of continuous focus, productivity had grown to just under 300 percent of the starting point and productivity was all members—management and production "hours" (management was put in as 40 hours per week; production was represented by time-card hours). The result after five years was a reduction by one-third of the organization hours to produce a unit.

This same magnitude of results has been demonstrated time and time again during lean production conversions. Yet the vast majority of manufacturers (in both the U.S. and Japan) have not yet converted to lean production. Why? The answer is change management.

Change—Just Do It and Then Deal with the Consequences

The process at Jake was not simple, linear, or without resistance. It needed the commitment of top management to prove to middle managers that it could work by just doing it. This change process is well illustrated in the following example provided by my friend and associate Bob Pentland from our days of working together at Jacobs Manufacturing.

> Inventory is evil, always. It hides waste. At Jake we had a very large parts hotel (extended stay) for work-in-process inventory. This hotel was necessary because of the long journey through the plant, and the MRP pushed them out into the plant, whether they were needed or not. We talked and talked about this evil and the need to change. No action. We talked some more. No action. Finally, we said that this parts hotel would face the wrecking ball. Literally. It was a cinder block building in the middle of the plant with the equivalent of 10 percent of sales sleeping inside. Everyone was advised to take their work-in-process back to their respective areas from whence it was pushed. No one—no one!—heeded the message.
>
> D-Day came on a weekend. Saturday A.M. everything was hauled out of the building and just shoved into, and blocking, the aisles. It looked like the DMZ. The three managers of the hotel were horrified. The cinder block walls came down. Dust and dirt were everywhere. The three managers' emotions went from horror to depression to anger. No parts were made Monday, some on Tuesday, etc. One-piece flow was being forced. A ton of waste was exposed, a lot was removed, and progress was made. Performance quickly exceeded our expectations. The for-

merly irate hotel managers had the unmitigated gall to ask: "Why didn't we do it sooner?"

Subsequently, there was the issue of the monumental, omnipotent, one-and-only, centrally located Magnus washer—a big blocker of flow. It was announced that 60 days hence, on July 10 at 7:00 A.M., the Magnus was to become "terminally ill," which meant that all users of the Magnus needed to develop their own right-size, in-line cleaning immediately.

On July 10 at 7:00 A.M., the Magnus died and was removed. The event happened without fanfare.

To manage change, you sometimes have to "just do it" and then deal with the consequences. In this chapter, I would like to share with you some of my reflections on the process of changing to lean—which is a multidimensional process involving people at all levels that reduces waste throughout the value stream. These observations come from over ten years of experience leading change efforts at Jacobs and more recently at the HON Company. I have tried to extract some generic lessons from my day-to-day battles to promote lean that may help others manage the change effort in their plants.

Learning the Principles of Lean Production

Most of the education that we encounter in our business lives is either "formal," that is purely classroom, or it's pure on-the-job-training (if you get lucky you observe something and learn from it). The principles of lean production are fairly easy to learn in the formal classroom. You can have a pretty good intellectual grasp of all of the key principles in one day. No big deal. The problem is that the principle goes against most of what those of us who "grew up" in U.S. manufacturing have been taught from day one. Things like economic order quantity become "non-value-added" concepts when you come to believe that all setups can be reduced by roughly 99 percent. You really only learn how to apply the principles by going out to the factory and working in a small area for a week or more to apply one of the principles. This learning experience then has to be repeated over and over—not just to learn how to apply the principles effectively to the many work areas that you encounter in a plant, but also to give you the personal experiences that eventually culminate in a belief in the new principles deep down in your gut.

Inventory Hides Waste

One of the basic tenets of lean production is that inventory is bad and you should work to minimize it. I had read this for over a decade before I had the opportunity to turn Jacobs Vehicle Equipment Company into a lean production "school" for the members of the Jacobs team. I knew that inventory was bad, but as we set up cells, we had small piles of inventory between each machine. I knew that according to the theory of lean production we should get rid of them, but none of us could quite do it. We had spent our whole manufacturing lives with these little piles of inventory. We knew that they did something for us that we were afraid to do without. We built cell after cell, but we still kept the little piles of inventory. I knew that we would reduce WIP dollars if they went away, but it wasn't that much money—and, and, and. If you take on a lean production conversion, you will eventually hear all of the possible reasons known to mankind for not trying something different.

Our coach visited us from Japan. He made us take out the little piles of inventory. It was pretty clear that we were not going to do it on our own. The result was total chaos. All the downtime that we had hidden with the inventory suddenly would shut the cell down completely. Every tool change would shut the whole cell down. For a month we struggled to solve the problems with downtime, setup times and tool change time. After a month we got to the point that we could say the cell was running, but it was not a pretty sight. Two more months passed before it ran really well. Then it dawned on us that this cell actually ran far better than anything else in the plant. It also dawned on us that the concept of the inventory hiding waste was true. But it "felt" so wrong to go to one-piece flow that it is doubtful if we would have ever tried it if we had not been coerced by our coach. This was not just a management problem. None of the production members were willing to take out the "little piles" either. In fact, after the initial change, the production members were absolutely convinced that we had lost our minds, since the cell could hardly run at all for the first week or so. After a few months we all realized that this did work, and that it had forced us to solve problems we had hidden under the inventory. At that point I became a believer in the principle of one-piece flow and the evil of inventory. From then on, I pushed reduction in inventory with a religious fervor, knowing that it would make us make ourselves better.

Rules of Thumb in Becoming a Lean-Production Manager

The crazy thing about lean production is that most of the principles you must implement, like the inventory example, just feel wrong. The concept of lean is disarmingly simple to understand, but bringing yourself to apply it is difficult. To really believe in the key principles of lean you must consistently apply lean—day after day, month after month. Only then, after years of daily hands-on dedication, will you achieve the performance levels possible with lean production.

From observing many personal journeys over the past 10 years, I have developed some rules of thumb about the training of a lean production manager. The first is that it is a very long journey. I believe there is a limit to the basic learning that exists, but I still find that I learn new dimensions to the process each time I spend time on an improvement team and get onto the factory floor for a week.

My basic rule is that it takes about 12 weeks of full-time kaizen or improvement activity for a manager to learn the basics of the principles. That achievement usually takes a year for very dedicated managers who make themselves spend 25 percent more time at work than normal to be on a full-time shop floor improvement team once a month.

The next rule of thumb is that it takes, on average, about four years of working with the process to become a true believer. A "true believer" is someone who has worked through the learning curves on all the basics of lean production—things like the inventory conversion noted above—and has become convinced that this new way is the right way and will never go back. At this point, they can be entrusted with leading conversion efforts of their own in a remote location. They have also become hard to live with for nonbelievers.

This long learning curve is one of the key impediments to implementing lean production. How many individuals, after 20 years in their careers, want to relearn their jobs totally? How many companies keep consistently on the same path for three to ten years? The good news is that many people in the United States have started their journeys. The bad news is that very few of them have become true believers.

The Change to Lean Production—Impact on Individuals

The individual learning curve (as noted above) is long and occasionally torturous. In addition, over the course of a lean production conversion, every single member's job will change. Every change engenders some form of resistance.

Starting with the Shop Floor

Under lean production, every production member who started as a batch operator will eventually end up as a multiskilled operator running a variety of machines in a cell configuration. This may not seem like a big deal, but people who have operated the same machine for 15 or 20 years have adapted to their situation—and they will find it very difficult to change. When you first form a cell you will hear comments like, "I have lost my job" (which means, "The job that I had for 20 years and developed a strong sense of ownership about has been taken away from me"). This is a traumatic change for the individual. In addition, many production shops move from a batch mode, where members were sitting at benches doing the operation on a batch of product, to a cellular structure, where a single operator not only must operate multiple machines but must now walk from machine to machine all day. This is another one of those changes that is hard to implement. Typically, production members who have been at a seated work station for years will initially have serious pain as their bodies adapt to a walking work routine. It usually takes a month to adapt. The hard part is getting them to try at all. Eventually they will find the walking routine to be healthier and less fatiguing.

If these workers are already in a Ford-type line system, they will still experience change as the kaizen process removes the small waiting periods typical of the usual U.S. production line. In a U.S. assembly line, there is usually a bottleneck station that actually works at "100 percent pace" but all the other stations work at less work content. It is not unusual to find stations with 50 percent work content and other systems at various levels between this and the bottleneck work content of 100 percent. As you apply the kaizen practice, these small wastes are steadily removed. The rule of thumb is to keep working on the problem until the imbalance is down to 0.6 seconds or less. The production members who had less than 100 percent work content may be working harder than the past pace, but they are working more steadily.

Middle Management Has Its Own Issues

There are whole functions, like production control (where I started in manufacturing), that shrink radically due to the flow benefits of visual control/kanban, etc. Managers in these areas are unlikely to be immediate fans of any improvement that will eliminate their positions and make the skills they have developed over many years obsolete. As a conversion gains momentum and the kaizen skills of the organization improve, it is natural to focus on *administrative kaizen*. The basic themes of elimination of waste, building cellular flow, etc., have the same impact on white collar areas. The good news is that productivity per white collar member will go up proportionately to that of production members over the full course of conversion—but every job that remains is substantially different structurally from the initial job. For the individual, this is more unwanted change.

Senior Management Has Even More Concerns

Since many senior managers think they have earned their position and are generally happy with the status quo, they are not necessarily motivated to change their job duties. Yet, the same magnitude of change in job duties happens at the senior level. The plant operations management often moves to focused factory managers with substantially increased authority and responsibility for improvement, but at the same time the staff departments lose some of their authority and manpower to the focused factory. The product engineering department will change from a "throw it over the wall" approach in which there is little audit of the development process, to a structure of cross-functional teams who will seem, at first, to question every decision made by the former development group. Purchasing departments usually shrink by about 80 percent as the release of production material is moved to the shop floor of the focused factory and the vendor base is trimmed down to fewer suppliers (those who are really committed to continuous improvement). All of these changes are major events in the lives of the individual members.

Then You Have the Technical Staffs

On top of all of this change, most U.S. manufacturing operations are wholly understaffed in the technical areas. In the traditional production system, we have far more nontechnical personnel performing non-value-added jobs (like my first production control job of "expediter"; I was paid to spend all day finding lost parts). Improvement in a manufacturing operation takes technical skills. Rearranging machines into cells, redesigning tooling to reduce setup times, building poke-yoke (fool-proofing) devices, etc., requires the skills of maintenance members, toolmakers, and engineers. These technical skill areas are the ones we have traditionally reduced when we had to "cut costs." Over time, these cuts have culminated in a situation in which we are barely able to keep the plant running, let alone improve its operations.

For example, Honda has noted that 80 percent of its nonproduction members focus on making improvements. This includes product design and process redesign, both major and minor (kaizen). They have also noted that 80 percent of their nonproduction members are technical in background. They have a lot of improvement horsepower. At Jacobs we had a major product engineering department and a relatively high proportion of technical members, including maintenance, toolmaking, drafting, etc., and all engineering members. More than 20 percent of our nonproduction staff were in technical roles. By adding to technical staff as we reduced cost, and allowing for all nontechnical attrition, we were able to increase this proportion to almost 60 percent over four years. This gave us the horsepower to drive improvement at a fast pace.

The bottom line is that the organization will need to rethink every employee's role on an almost continuous basis and be willing to change these roles on a continuous basis as they go through this multiyear transition to lean production.

The Psychology of Change

Psychologists have studied the impact of change on individuals and come to some useful conclusions. One of the more helpful models in understanding what is happening in your organization as you begin to change at a more rapid pace is the "sense of loss" model. This model notes that any major change (a job change at work certainly fits this category) results in an immediate sense of loss. Even if this change will ultimately be good for the individual, the immediate impact is a sense of loss. The evidence shows that the individual will, as a result of significant change at work, go into a period of mourning lasting 6 to 18 months.

The period of time that the individual stays in this period of mourning depends upon the magnitude of the change, the character of the individual, and the support for the change in the workplace. In the early phases of a major change, the organization will probably not be very supportive of the individual, because few individuals have a good idea of how they will fit into the new scheme. With lean production this is an especially difficult issue because, almost by definition, few in the organization, if any, have a vision of what the lean production workplace will be like, since they have never been there. One of management's imperatives is to keep the proportion of the organization that is feeling this sense of loss to less than one-third of the organization while still moving rapidly to improve the organization's competitiveness.

Managing the Pace of Change and Resistance to Change

An important aspect of the change manager's job is to stay in close touch with the "level of loss" in the organization. Improvement without change and its accompanying sense of loss is impossible, but there is also a limit as to how much change an organization will accept without a mutiny. The key is to balance rapid change with the pace at which it can be managed. In general, the pace of improvement will be proportional to the pace of change—right up until all improvement stops if the organization rejects the process. Fujio Cho, former president of Toyota Manufacturing, USA, likens an organization to the human body. When a change is attempted, the body generates "antibodies" that automatically grow to fight the change. A lot of management energy and commitment to fight off the antibodies are needed to move change ahead.

Toyota has managed this change process in hundreds of organizations as they converted their own company as well as their supplier base. They have developed a curve that addresses members' attitudes to change. In this curve, the attitude to change is on the horizontal axis and the population of organization members is on the vertical. A normal bell curve is typical. Typically, 3-5 percent of the organization will willingly embrace change. In marketing terms, these are the *early adopters*. They will typically try something new even if it's not a good idea.

At the other end of the curve are the 3–5 percent who are the direct opposites of the early adopters: They will never change but will furiously resist any change. Most change management literature talks about supporting and feeding the leadership group of early adopters. This is essential. But equally essential is the effort to neutralize the antichange coalition. These antichange members cover the spectrum in terms of organizational perception. Many of them will have been excellent contributors under the old system. Many of them will be leadership types in the organization, though they lead to the past. On the balance, if you support the early adopters, the antichange contingent will get energized by their fear of change and will mount a fifth column effort to derail the change. They will spend their coffee breaks undermining the change effort. They will try to convince the organization that the change will "ruin the company," will result in poor quality, will result in an unsafe workplace, and so forth.

From experience, the Toyota Group notes that you must address these members. If they are not addressed, they will offset the efforts of the early adopters and the organization will be in a state of continuous turmoil as the two factions vie for leadership of the informal organization. Toyota demonstrates the necessary action in a new bell curve once the 3–5 percent antichange contingent has been dropped off the curve. Toyota is a lifetime employer so dropping off the curve may amount to special early retirement or a desk facing the wall with no responsibility, but the key point is that, from their many conversion experiences, the organization cannot move ahead until this group is addressed. Of all the things that often derail conversion in the United States, the most common is the failure to address the members who are working to pull the organization into the past. The impact of addressing this group is tremendous. In this change management model, the broad 90 percent of the organization's members in the middle are mostly looking for leadership. When the two factions are vying for opposite directions, middle members do not know which group to follow and consequently they do not move at all.

On the other hand, if the change group is fostered *and* you effectively address the antichange group, then the whole curve shifts toward the new direction as the broad 90 percent begin to follow the change leadership contingent. Identifying and addressing the antichange fifth column is one of the most important issues you will address in implementing any major change. This is especially true in converting to lean production, where the magnitude of change is tremendous. One of the axioms of World War II flyers was that "you get the most flak when you are directly over the target." The same will be true as you address the antichange faction.

One of the tools to manage this process is the idea of the *model line*. The idea of the model line is to take one product family within a plant and work only in this area to implement all the new approaches that are part of lean production. This has two benefits: 1. By containing the change to a subset of the organization, the risks of having the overall change derailed are significantly reduced; 2. With the long learning curve of this approach, the model plant allows a focus on learning and applying many of the tools of lean production in one area, and working out the implementation bugs. When the early improvement results start to flow in, there will be management pressure to accelerate the process. This is the time to keep an aggressive, but steady pace and roll out the change in a way that keeps most of the organization out of the "sense of loss" stage at any point in time.

Multisite Implementation

The various issues noted above are primarily oriented to the experience in a given site or plant. When you are managing a multisite conversion, these issues are multiplied many-fold. The key consideration is that a plant or location will not really be "on the curve" until the unit managers (plant manager, site manager), and the leaders at that location buy into the change. The tricky part is that this is a four-year learning curve process for those who embrace the change. Due to the nature of this learning experience, it is unlikely that a unit manager will embrace the change as well as understand it well enough to manage it unless he/she is pushing up the long personal learning curve by being a team member of improvement teams on a steady basis.

Put Unit Managers on Improvement Teams

One model that has been reasonably effective is to require unit managers to be on 12 full-time, week-long, improvement teams during the first year of conversion. This experience gives them the basic training to begin the process. Another element is to pick the most proactive change agent among your unit managers and start to build that unit into a model plant. By doing this, you contain the change issues and make sure that you are not trying to push change into a unit whose manager is totally opposed to it. This approach then allows you to review the results at the model plant with all units and also allows the other proactive change managers to gradually stand up and be counted. When a unit manager volunteers to join the model plan program, that is the time to throw the support behind the effort. Eventually, the manager who is not interested in taking on the change will either buy in, based on observed results at other locations, or realize that it is time to consider other options. This is a fairly slow startup in larger organizations but in reality it is the only approach that has a high probability of success, given all the change management issues.

Deliver Improvement that Shows Up in the Financial Data

The success of the change process can also lead to trouble. It is unrealistic to expect many people in the ranks of top general management to be able to devote the time to go through their own personal learning curve. It is certainly true that your board of directors will not be able to go very far up this curve. The best you can hope for is to have a general understanding of the principles and the drive for consistent improvement so that support is maintained, based on the numbers. The higher up in the organization the evaluator is, the more likely that the financial numbers will be the evaluation measure. Therefore, part of the change process is to consistently deliver improvement that can be seen in the financial data. Fortunately, with a lean production conversion, this is quite possible. Very early on there should be visible cash flow from inventory reduction and slowly growing expense reduction as a result of productivity gains. Lead time reductions and quality improvements will be apparent to customers, but it will take top management longer to see benefits in these areas.

Keeping the improvement focused in a model line and/or a model plant is important so that you can manage the process of change, but also so that the improvements can generate identifiable bottom line results that buy support at the board level.

From Conan to Coach

In the startup phase of a lean production organization, the only effective implementation model has been a top down model. This is very serious organizational change, and only someone with significant organizational clout is likely to be able to manage the process. The catch-22 comes with the fact that when you start, few, if any, members of the organization really understand what you are going to be implementing. After all, this is the ultimate "learn by doing" school. So by definition there will be lots of "two steps forward, one step back" types of activity. To keep going in spite of the one step back will take top management leadership of a high order. It will be necessary, in many cases, to take the "Conan the Barbarian" approach and just demand that the organization keep working at the process. The tricky part is that the organization really only institutionalizes the process when everyone understands the principles and is involved in the process of improvement. As a manager, the key is to keep pushing the process ahead—aggressively and consistently—while watching for individual subordinates who "get religion."

Getting Religion

There are two phases to "getting religion" in lean production. In phase one, the individual begins to believe intellectually that this is what should be done and will generally work with the process but will occasionally not move past a gut issue (like pulling all the little piles of inventory from between work stations). In phase 2, the individual comes to believe at a gut level in the principles of the system and will willingly put in the effort to apply the principles. When an individual makes it to phase two, the senior management needs to move to the coach role and only help guide the individual's progress. This sounds easy enough, but at any one time there are many individuals at various points on their own personal conversion curve. As a change manager you must identify where they are on their personal development paths and adjust your style so that you are still "Conan" or "coach" when appropriate. One benchmark of lean production maturity is when you, as manager, can be a full-time coach.

What to Expect, Year by Year

At the beginning of this chapter, I mentioned some order-of-magnitude expectations for this conversion process. These are the 5–10 year results that when achieved will typically revolutionize a company's position in its industry. The usual pattern for the first couple of years is not one of consistent progress, however. There are many ups and downs, twist and turns, and unexpected events. In making the conversion to lean production, management will have to keep a stiff upper lip during these early years.

Year One—Maybe This Will Work

During the first year, the progress is slow as most people are being introduced to the principles and are working to apply them in the "two steps forward, one step back" manner that is typical at this point. In fact, there are always a few times when the principles are misapplied due to unfamiliarity with the process, resulting in one step forward and two steps back. This is normal at this early learning stage but very difficult to explain, especially to those who do not want any change to begin with. Although this stage is messy, the stories about improvements on individual projects tend to give management the sense that "maybe this will work."

Year Two—The Jury Is Still Out

Typically, the second year is the riskiest year for the conversion. By this point, the fifth column group who resist change is out in full force—they will be highlighting every instance of one step forward and two steps back and "selling" the organization that it is time to give up this nonsense. On the other hand, those who are working to implement the change will still be novices in applying the principles and will still be making a variety of implementation errors (which are all part of the learning process but difficult to explain). More importantly, the costs of training and implementing the conversion will be readily identifiable to the accounting staff, but things like a 10 percent productivity gain will not have compounded to the point that clearly shows a great payoff. To keep the process moving during the second year it is necessary to continue training and accelerate shop-floor activity, which at this stage of your members' learning curves is still fairly inefficient. By the end of the second year, the "jury will be out" on the conversion. There will be identifiable results, but there will also be identifiable costs—and there will be lots of individuals in their "sense of loss" period. A typical summary comment would be "it seems like a good idea, but I'm just not sure it's working."

Year Three—We Are Making Progress

The third year of implementation is when the compounding of results begins to show in a way that cannot be easily explained away as due to some other cause. The change advocates have gotten more experience and almost always have two steps forward, one step back and begin regularly to achieve two steps forward with no backsliding. Also at this point, the financial numbers are showing net positive results and customers are noticing improved lead times and quality. By the end of the third year, the general comment is "we are making great progress."

Year Four—A Pride Begins to Grow

In the fourth year, the process begins to be seriously institutionalized. Members in the locations, customers, and the board of directors are all convinced that this a good process. The "Big Mo," momentum, is now with the organization—the organization begins to "make its own good luck" and the process has a full head of steam. The largest percentage gains in improvement are often in the third year, but the institutionalization of the process insures that very large percentage gains in all key indicators will continue for several more years. From this point on the organization will continue to outdistance itself from its competitors. Although the change is not complete, members of the organization now find that change is the new norm. They have personally experienced several changes in their work structure and find each new change less stressful than the past. A pride begins to grow in the organization's constant willingness to change and improve. This is when an organization becomes truly dangerous to its competitors.

Think Long-Term and Stay the Course

When considering the length of the learning curve for lean production and looking at the significant issues in change management that are involved, it is not too surprising that most organizations either never really get started on lean production or don't stay with it. Even in Japan, most organizations have not started this process unless they were in serious trouble. Although the process was well established in Toyota by the late 1960s, very few firms outside the Toyota Group were willing to attempt the challenge of change management. Only when many Japanese firms began to face the risk of bankruptcy with the first oil crisis in the 1970s were some organizations outside of the Toyota Group willing to take on the task of conversion.

The greatest success in applying lean principles will come, however, from applying them in a healthy company. The level of improvement available to a healthy company will lead them to a commanding position in their industry. Of course, getting organizational commitment on the need for radical change will be much more difficult in a successful organization.

This conversion process will take from five to ten years. This sounds like an awfully long time to U.S. management, which is typically "quarterly" oriented. The length of the conversion process is actually the good news—once you have the process established, it will generate outstanding improvements in customer and financial performance for the full conversion period. You can do the math yourself on what a doubling or tripling of productivity, a manifold increase in inventory turns, and significant improvement in customer-perceived quality and delivery performance will do for your organization.

The journey to lean is long and at times perilous. For those who are feeling a little faint-hearted and who are looking for an easier route, all I can say is—there isn't one. For those who are willing and ready to take the plunge, revisit the beginning of this chapter and take courage from what Niccolò Machiavelli had to say about change. Nothing of any importance comes easy—especially when you are changing and rearranging the way things get done.

 **Mike Rother** *is manager of Manufacturing Outreach for the University of Michigan's Japan Technology Management Program and teaches in the Department of Industrial and Operations Engineering. His research focus is lean manufacturing and the Toyota Production System. Mike is also a consultant with TWI, a network of individuals who provide support in implementing and understanding lean manufacturing.*

Mike works with large and small manufacturers to introduce lean systems. His work includes shopfloor diagnosis, system design, implementation assistance, and training. He began his career in Germany in the manufacturing division of Thyssen AG.

14

Crossroads: Which Way Will You Turn on the Road to Lean?

by Mike Rother

Editor's prologue: If one were to name places in the country with the most progressive and modern manufacturing practices, the Mississippi Delta region would probably not appear high on the list. Yet this is exactly where a handful of manufacturers are having great success in introducing lean concepts. Mike Rother has found receptive ears from executives who have the interest, drive, and commitment to implement new approaches to manufacturing. Mike shares some succinct lessons regarding the challenges of implementing lean manufacturing, and illustrates his points with cartoons. When all is said and done, to answer Mike's question—"Are you superficial lean or true lean?"—may mean revisiting one of George Koenigsaecker's rules of thumb and asking, "Am I ready to dedicate four years of my life working with the lean process to become a true believer?"

At the Ranchero Restaurant in Clarksdale, Mississippi, the lunchtime rush is in full swing. Plates loaded with "ranch ribs" and fried vegetables slide over the counter as the bell on the entrance door jingles with patrons coming and going. Somewhere a television is on, but what you hear is the sound of lots of conversation.

There are two main sources of the do-re-mi that keeps things swinging in the small towns of the Mississippi Delta region: farming and manufacturing. Farming has historically been the largest source of employment, but today fewer people are needed to work the same land, so manufacturing has grown in importance. Clarksdale sits in the midst of the poorest counties in the United States, where good-paying manufacturing jobs are critical. If one of those manufacturers closes its doors and leaves the Delta, the community ramifications can be serious.

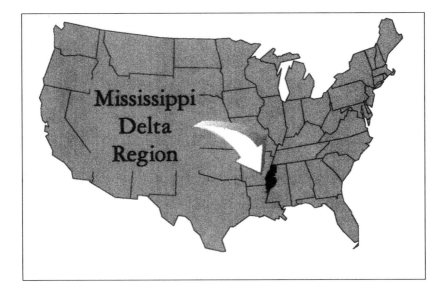

A popular calling card of Delta manufacturers in the past was low labor rates. But customers now want high-quality, short lead time, flexibility—all at the lowest total cost. The Delta, maybe because of the critical nature of manufacturing here, has adapted well. All manner of high-quality, high-value-added products are produced by a work force that values its jobs greatly. The oven in the White House kitchen comes from Greenwood. The bead wire in your tires comes from Clarksdale. The furniture in your boss's well-appointed office comes from Leland. The list is long, but it is not always enough to beat the competition. Delta manufacturers—just like you—have to go further.

Listen carefully to the lunchtime clatter at the Ranchero, at Cicero's in Stoneville, at Webster's in Greenwood, or at any number of Delta eateries, and you might catch some unexpected snippets of conversation: "Toyota Production System," "continuous flow," "takt time," "lean manufacturing." Why? Because lean manufacturing and the Toyota Production System have been recognized as an excellent means to existing-industry development in the Mississippi Delta.

I have had the good fortune to be involved in working with Mississippi Delta manufacturers. The ideas presented in this chapter come from gaining experience together with some hard-working manufacturing people in Mississippi, as well as at plants in my own backyard (the Midwest), and with friends who have worked inside Toyota.

A Program of Lean-Manufacturing Outreach

Formed in 1935, the Delta Council is among the oldest and most respected regional development organizations in the United States. Although the original impetus for creating the council was flood control and water resource management, current programs of the organization include transportation development, farm policy, agricultural research, and industrial and community development. The council serves 18 Delta and part-Delta counties in Northwest Mississippi.

In response to a string of plant closures in the late 1980s and early 1990s, Delta Council's Industrial Development Department initiated a research project to pinpoint differences in high-performance versus low-performance plants. The research, conducted by the Social Science Research Center at Mississippi State University and Dr. Frank Hull of the Stevens Institute of Technology, clearly indicated that lower performing plants were mired in mass production, with heavy emphasis on inspection and controlling labor costs and little ongoing investment in productivity improvement.

As a result of the research, Delta Council has opted to provide hands-on support for the adoption of lean manufacturing in its service area. "Too many companies get training that is heavy on teams and light on doing anything that generates significant, measurable improvement," says Mark Manning, Delta Council's director of industrial development. "To help retain and grow our existing industry, we work with interested companies on lean awareness and education, shop-floor analysis, flow design, and implementation assistance."

Specifically, Delta Council's lean manufacturing activities fall into three categories:

1. *Lean Manufacturing Study Group*. This multi-session seminar for executives and managers is offered once or twice a year. The mission is to help business leaders develop an accurate understanding of what lean manufacturing is, by using the Toyota Production System as a model.

2. *On-site implementation assistance*. Direct shop-floor assistance makes up approximately 80 percent of Delta Council's lean activities. Of the participants in the study groups, some are serious about changing their production systems. These companies receive detailed help from Delta Council via a well-designed process that has started to generate world class results. Delta Council and its client manufacturers together pinpoint improvement objectives, assess whether a lean system will help to achieve those objectives, map the current production system, design a lean production flow to fit the company's situation, and lay implementation out as a series of steps. Delta Council has access to experienced lean-manufacturing specialists who can guide a company through the implementation process for a pilot product line. (It is the company's responsibility to spread what it learns to other lines.)

Because of the intensive nature of this intervention, it is provided only to the most serious candidates. The philosophy: Actually developing lean systems at a few companies is a good way to raise interest among even more companies in the area.

3. *Lean Production User Group (LPUG)*. Every four months or so, Delta Council convenes a meeting of area companies that are working to adopt lean systems and invites a few other companies to attend as well. The LPUG forums involve a presentation of implementation progress by each company and a tour of the host-company's current shop-floor focus areas (the meeting-host responsibility rotates among the user group members). Delta Council also invites other Delta-region companies so they may observe lean practices and learn from their peers. The LPUG forums establish a protocol of progress reporting, celebrate successes, and help spread the word.

Delta Council Defines Lean Manufacturing

Delta Council defines lean manufacturing as "a philosophy that when implemented reduces the time from customer order to delivery by eliminating sources of waste in the production flow." The greatest source of that waste is overproduction, or producing more or earlier than is needed by the next process. In working to eliminate overproduction, Delta Council adheres to a few principles:

- Make only what the customer wants when the customer wants it. The word "customer" also means the next process down the line.
- Develop continuous flow processing wherever possible. Continuous flow refers to producing one piece at a time, with each item passed immediately along from one process to the next—without stagnation in between. Continuous flow is also called "make one, move one."
- Use marketplace-based pull systems to control production in upstream segments of the value chain that cannot be linked to downstream processes in a continuous or FIFO (first in first out) flow.
- Develop the capability to make every part every day. Production processes that involve changeovers should be capable of serving multiple customers via small production lots.

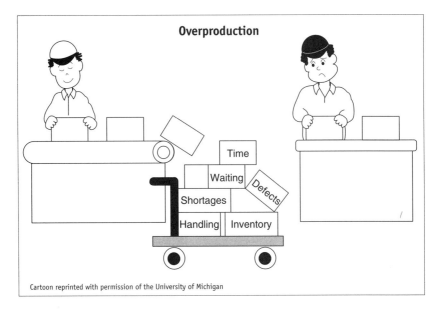

Cartoon reprinted with permission of the University of Michigan

- Facilitate learning through implementation instead of emphasizing classroom training. New concepts can be introduced in
  a classroom, but they are learned through hands-on practice
  on the shop floor.

Implementing Lean Manufacturing at Batesville-American

Overproduction was evident up and down the production stream at
Batesville-American in Batesville, Mississippi, when the company
got involved with Delta Council's lean manufacturing implementation assistance. Producing Batesville-American's line of 30 styles of
metal beds for nursing homes involves the following overall steps:

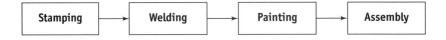

The plant had a history of making many improvements, but
general manager John DeVoe still saw too much waste. Several
weeks' worth of stamped and welded parts cluttered the shop floor,
while the finished goods area was bursting with 10 weeks' worth of

beds that did not match what the customer wanted. Total lead time for steel to make its way through production and be shipped out as a bed hovered around 60 days. In other words, two months would elapse between buying steel and getting paid for products made from that steel. What John didn't want was a superficial solution.

Assembly, welding, and the individual stamping presses each received a build-to-stock production list that was derived from a monthly sales forecast, but this forecast did not match what customers were actually ordering. Stamping and welding also did not produce to the needs of their downstream processes: Each area would look at its own production list several weeks in advance and choose what to make next (see Figure 14-1). These processes made long production runs once a setup for a particular part was qualified. Typical batch sizes were a five-week supply in stamping and two weeks' worth of components in welding. The paint line only ran "bed-brown" on Tuesdays. Assembly had more constraints: It would be instructed to shift from making one bed style to another because trucks arriving at the dock needed specific beds for specific customers. Assembly was the only production area connected, however loosely, to a customer.

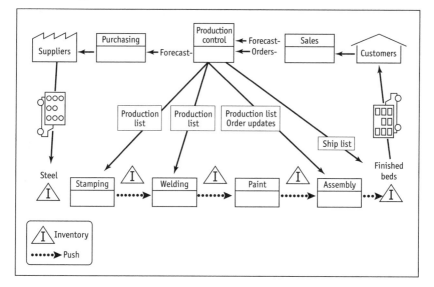

Figure 14-1. Former Process Flow at Batesville-American

Although assembly had already been changed to operate in a cellular continuous flow, its unforecasted jumps from one bed style to another created a choppy demand pattern for the upstream processes. Avoiding shortages of stamped parts was the scheduling challenge. Stamping capacity was occupied with long runs of parts that weren't yet needed, so hot orders were expedited. Otherwise those parts would have to wait in line behind the large batches slowly making their way through welding and painting.

As is typical of mass producers, Batesville-American's processes were functioning as isolated islands, producing large batches ahead of actual downstream requirements and pushing them forward. This overproduction was the cause of the long lead time through the system and generated plenty of non-value-added activity like moving, counting, and storing all those parts that were not yet needed. Quality problems would be obscured by the batches, making it very difficult to trace root causes once those problems did come to light. Ironically, the long lead time through stamping and welding reinforced the paradigm that these operations couldn't be set up to produce to actual customer requirements.

Today Batesville-American is introducing, step-by-step, an entirely different approach to regulating production, which is illustrated in Figure 14-2.

Getting each process to produce only what the next process needs began with scheduling. Instead of the monthly forecast, Production Control now looks at actual shipments planned for the week after next and distributes that production requirement evenly over the coming work week. Some open capacity is included to allow for changes. Customer requirements also determine whether three, four, or five people will be needed to staff the assembly cell. During each day of the work week the assembly supervisor goes to production control and gets only that day's production list, and the assembly operators pull from that list the specifications for three beds at a time. Results: Assembly produces each day an equal portion of the orders that will ship in the following week, and they can easily accommodate short-notice customer changes.

Once assembly was presenting a more level demand pattern to the upstream processes, changes were made to the flow from weld-

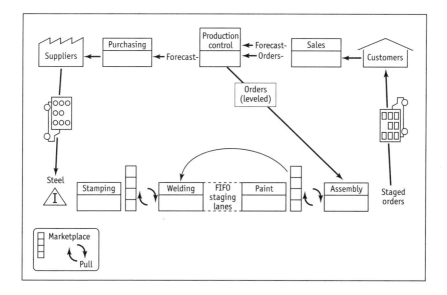

Figure 14-2. Lean Flow at Batesville-American

ing through paint. Bed-brown is now painted twice weekly and welding batch sizes have been greatly reduced. For components with dedicated fixturing (no changeover), the welding batch size was brought down to assembly's average daily usage. Welding is producing to assembly's requirements, instead of the forecast, via a marketplace-based pull system: As assembly withdraws painted parts from the marketplace, welding is triggered to replenish what was taken away.

Batesville-American is now moving its efforts in lean implementation upstream into stamping. It is conducting a process-route analysis for each stamped part to determine lead times and whether they can produce some parts in a continuous flow from one forming step to the next. Producing stamped parts to forecast will then be eliminated. As with welding, stamping production will also be controlled by customer withdrawals from a (stamped-parts) marketplace.

The next challenge for Batesville-American will be to continue decreasing the processing lead times, especially in painting and stamping. Goals include painting bed-brown every day and further reducing the lot sizes in stamping. As smaller lots run through the system, Batesville-American can reduce the quantities held in the two pull-system marketplaces.

Total production lead time at Batesville-American is dropping and the plant is better serving its customers, increasing capacity for new customers, and realizing an improved cash flow. As Lygunnah Bean, Batesville-American's plant superintendent, put it, "The days of 10 weeks of finished beds and all those parts sitting on the floor are over!" For Delta Council, this translates into jobs that have a better chance of remaining in the Delta region.

Two Paths — A Few Lessons Learned in Implementing Lean

Delta Council participates in the lean implementation efforts of several manufacturers, so it is particularly important that its outreach and assistance activities make sense. Toward this end we have agreed on pitfalls to avoid, based on experiences with brown-field plants in Mississippi and elsewhere that are trying to adopt lean systems. One recurring theme in our experience is that there are factories that really work at shifting to a lean production system, and those that try to make improvements in the name of "lean" but actually maintain their traditional, mass-oriented production flow. There is a two-paths-in-the-woods phenomenon going on, but only one leads to the benefits of lean production. We call it *true lean versus superficial lean*.

Although lean implementation efforts will have a different flavor from company to company, and each day we are learning more, I invite you to take a look at some of the pitfalls on our list and consider whether you might be on a true or superficial path to lean manufacturing.

Pitfall Number 1: Confusing Techniques with Lean Objectives

Some companies have vigorously promoted techniques such as work teams, workplace organization (visual factory, 5S), setup-time reduction, error proofing, machine maintenance, and so on as steps to achieving the quality, cost, and lead-time improvements associated with lean manufacturing. The results have been decidedly mediocre. We can now see that it is quite possible, and even likely,

Cartoon reprinted with permission of the University of Michigan

that while promoting individual techniques we still end up keeping our same old wasteful, batch-and-push production flow. In fact, several techniques are more a result of adopting lean manufacturing than a means for becoming lean. Here are three examples.

Technique — Teams

Just trying to establish teams is unlikely to do much for introducing lean manufacturing. Good teamwork on the shop floor does take training and development, but it is the act of developing a lean material flow, moving away from batch-and-push production, that creates both a need and an environment for teams. A lean flow couples islands of work together and creates internal customer/supplier relationships. Continuous flow makes individual processing steps dependent on one another. Producing only to customer requirements takes out buffers and demands attention to making production and delivering high quality. These types of changes lay the groundwork for individuals to become part of groups.

Technique — Visual factory, housekeeping and workplace organization, "5S"

Introducing continuous flow and synchronizing production to the customer-demand rate facilitates improved workplace organization by eliminating accumulations of buffer and work-in-process material. This makes abnormalities more painful and easier to spot—the very point of creating a visual factory. Conversely, trying to introduce organization techniques to a cluttered, batch-and-push-oriented shop floor fails to address the root cause of the waste, and usually the shop floor reverts to the messy state fostered by the traditional mode of production still in place. Cleaning up and organizing a shop floor does not produce a lean flow. Besides, why expend a lot of up-front effort to organize material and information that may not even exist once overproduction is routed out?

Technique—Reducing setup time
Producing to customer requirements means getting batch processes like stamping to produce in small lots. Doing this usually creates a need to reduce setup times. But when we begin instead with reducing setup time as an objective, we rarely go further to change over our equipment more frequently and run smaller batches (see Donnelly case).

The point of these examples is that concentrating on lean techniques first is doing it backwards and won't give the results we want. *Flow comes first* would be another good title for this section, which means developing a production system that gets as close as possible to making only what the customer wants when the customer wants it throughout the production chain. Eliminating overproduction is the primary source of the shorter lead times and other benefits associated with lean manufacturing; it is the pivotal change that "pulls" the adoption of those associated techniques when they are needed to achieve the higher objective. Applying individual techniques outside of this context seldom works, and can be an indication that we either don't know what to do or are putting off real changes to our internal production processes.

A corollary to this pitfall is the theory that starting out with benign, easy-to-understand efforts like visual factory, error proofing, and teams is a good way to ease into lean manufacturing. Experience shows otherwise. The techniques-first approach tends to foster misunderstanding of what lean manufacturing really is and resentment among employees who are pushed into activities that generate little or no measurable improvement. Also, switching from mass to lean production can be a three- to five-year process, but that clock only starts ticking once we begin making real changes to our internal processes. Working on easy techniques does not count toward the three- to five-year timeline. A better way to ease into lean manufacturing is to pick a pilot product line and work to change that one flow to a lean system.

Another related situation is the "we're getting ready" line of thinking. In this case we try to work on process capability or stability as a prerequisite for lean implementation. The problem is that we never achieve the necessary machine up-time because there is little pressure to force rapid and real improvement. In contrast, if we start to make flow improvements—at first in limited segments of the production chain—the need for process improvement becomes painfully clear and such improvements are then approached with much greater urgency.

One reason behind our addiction to techniques may be how we learned about and have tried to reverse-engineer Toyota's lean manufacturing practices. When we originally visited Toyota factories to discover the reason for their high quality and efficiency, we saw well-organized shop floors (color coding, labeling, etc.), people working in teams, error-proofing techniques, short changeovers, and other practices. What was evident to the eye was a collection of techniques. What we couldn't see was the overriding emphasis on a production system that eliminates overproduction in the material flow, which is the driver for when and where you apply the techniques. Lacking the overriding goal, the techniques themselves became our goal and we ended up "cherry picking."

Pitfall Number 2: Expecting Employee Training to Make Lean Manufacturing Happen

There is an implicit belief floating around that if we train our shop-floor operators and supervisors in lean concepts and practices they will get excited about them and the concepts and practices will be adopted. This thinking is probably related to the attractive notion of "self-directed work teams" who drive change from the bottom up. It is all pure bunk.

Communication will not result in the adoption of lean manufacturing. The problems with mass production are fundamental, and shop-floor operators and supervisors are simply not in a position to change them. Shop-floor personnel have a perspective that naturally emphasizes their own work area, while lean manufacturing concerns itself with the entire production flow, or the "production system." Operators are also busy, making a new part every 60 seconds or so. Asking operators to improve when the system is the problem generally just causes people to work harder, faster, and longer, which is even encouraged by our tradition of rewarding overproduction. Expecting the shop-floor personnel to lead the lean charge results in suboptimization at best. More likely, you'll achieve little change but lots of resentment.

Shop-floor personnel work within the prevailing production system and it is management's responsibility to understand and improve that system. The most critical element in changing from mass to lean production is the level of top management's commitment to the change. If a top management person at the factory is not personally involved in mapping out the lean production system and is actively leading its introduction, the effort is likely to fail. We can make many localized improvements without the active involve-

Cartoon reprinted with permission of the University of Michigan

ment of an executive, but changing the prevailing mode of production is nearly impossible in that setting.

The shift from mass to lean begins top-down, with management providing direction. But once some momentum is achieved, the involvement of shop-floor personnel can quickly increase. If a company properly introduces lean manufacturing, people will be involved in changes that affect their work, will be developed as the first-line managers of quality and process improvement in their areas (but only if provided with the necessary support structure), and will be treated as citizens of the company.

Pitfall Number 3: That's Not Lean Manufacturing, That's a Program!

Making a successful shift from mass to lean means spending much of our time on the shop floor—understanding the situation there, making changes there, and checking the results that are achieved there. The superficial-lean route, on the other hand, involves lots of time sitting in offices while analyzing and renaming elements of the Toyota Production System (TPS) and putting them into charts and diagrams—before implementation. TPS can be a program-lover's dream: a proven system with lots of elements to organize.

Program-loving managers are easy to spot. They are the ones presenting on a grand scale what they are going to do (someday), as opposed to showing where on the shop floor they have been able to eliminate overproduction. Lean manufacturing is not a mental exercise. If we find ourselves in endless discussions about whether something like standardized work comes under the heading of quality or JIT in the diagram of our company's lean manufacturing model, we should stop and ask: "Where have we implemented this?"

Pitfall Number 4: Relying Solely on Kaizen Workshops

Kaizen workshops are a popular means of intensive collaboration to achieve visible shop-floor improvements in a short time. Over a period of three to five days of concentrated effort, participants analyze and physically change a particular production process to operate according to lean principles. Results are summarized and presented.

Cartoon reprinted with permission of the University of Michigan

Kaizen workshops sometimes have names like "Kaizen Blitz," and "Five Days and One Night" (you get one night of sleep in five days). Kaizen workshops are useful for establishing an action orientation and for introducing certain changes, like shifting to a cell layout, that would be disruptive to production if dragged out over time.

The popularity of kaizen workshops, however, raises a few concerns. The point to understand is that kaizen workshops have their place, but by themselves they will not build a lean production system for us. Workshops create little islands of improved flow at the process level, but you need to link those islands together in a system-level flow that is improved from door to door, and even extending beyond the plant. Workshops reduce lead time in small areas, but total lead time may still be high. No one has ever blitzed a lean production *system* into place.

Another issue, as shop-floor operators can tell you, is that when the engineers leave after a layout change or line rebalance, there are always dozens of niggling problems that don't surface until after the change. As a result, they are not refined out. In making a shift from batch to flow, cycle times can also take a few days to settle in. How they settle may affect how we distribute job elements. Toyota assembly plants have many team leaders to help take care of this, but most brown-field plants do not. A real kaizen workshop actually goes on for a few weeks because detailed process follow-up and refinement are critical to successful flow changes. Process refinement, which can only happen after the layout change, is what makes the new layout work as intended.

Kaizen workshops are most effective when applied strategically within the context of introducing a lean manufacturing system. Don't begin your lean implementation with kaizen workshops. Start by selecting a family of products based on similarity of processing steps. Then map the current material and information flows for that family, noting customer-demand characteristics, the processing steps, the observed cycle times for each of those steps, where changeovers are necessary, where batches of inventory accumulate, which operations are scheduled, and how they are scheduled.

For each product family you are looking at, someone then needs to have a vision drawn on paper, much like a blueprint, that defines the overall production flow you are working toward. This vision should include takt time(s), where you believe continuous and FIFO flows are possible, where marketplace-based pull systems will need to be used, how the flow will be triggered, and what single point in the flow will get that trigger signal. The vision, which you may refine over time, is thus used as a blueprint to ensure that individual activities, including kaizen workshops, will ultimately fit together. The vision is long term and you don't need to share it with everyone, but whoever is directing the change at your plant needs to have it.

Pitfall Number 5: Quitting After Failures

By now lean manufacturing systems have been proven to work, and our task is to adapt lean principles to our own situation. If it doesn't work at first (and it often won't), then the system is not at fault but rather something we have done, not done, or misunderstood. We may still be tempted to think of lean manufacturing as a theory or say, "This doesn't work here," but in reality the implementation problems we experience result from things we did not anticipate or need to work on some more. This is natural. We need to go back and try again, because learning and refining on the shop floor are

Cartoon reprinted with permission of the University of Michigan

what make lean principles, and lean manufacturing, work. I know that if we avoid this pitfall, our lean implementation efforts will ultimately be successful.

At the Crossroads

Too often we "cherry pick" quick fixes to add on top of wasteful, traditionally run shop floors. Lean manufacturing—because it improves the flow of parts and material in a plant—is a more far-reaching and effective solution to competitive pressures. Lean manufacturing is a strategic choice for manufacturers who face, or will face, serious competition. But it is a choice that the leaders of each manufacturing plant have to make for themselves. Toyota has done it. And many of the companies in this book are becoming, or have become, lean. The results are clear.

Are you still trying to push team training on top of an existing, wasteful mass production system, or will you take a good look in the mirror and rethink your production paradigms? If you opt for the superficial-lean route, you might want to visit the Delta and stop by the Ranchero Restaurant. The leading manufacturers here will buy you lunch and gladly talk with you about true lean.

Note: Seiko Semones drew the cartoons used in this chapter. She is a graphic designer and the principal of S² Design in Ann Arbor, Michigan. Before coming to the United States, Seiko spent 10 years working in graphic design in Tokyo.

15

Conclusion: What We Have Learned about Becoming Lean

by Jeffrey K. Liker

> *If you are looking for perfect safety, you will do well to sit on a fence and watch the birds; but if you really wish to learn to fly, you must mount a machine and become acquainted with its tricks by actual trial.*
>
> WILBUR WRIGHT, *SOME AERONAUTICAL EXPERIMENTS, 1901*

In this book we started with an overview of lean manufacturing, using as our model the Toyota Production System (TPS). We gave example after example of plants that are in some stage of making the "lean leap," in Jim Womack's terms, and in each case obtained outstanding results. We've also heard from some veterans reflecting on their experiences in implementing lean. We provided many individual case studies, each listing their lessons learned, and then provided additional lessons learned in Part Three of the book. Looking across all this information, what have we learned about the process of "becoming lean?"

As a professor I cannot resist giving a test after studying all these rich, individual chapters. It is a simple one-question, multiple choice test, so you either pass or fail. Please answer the following based on what you read in this book.

The implementation of lean manufacturing is:

A. Simple and straightforward once you understand how
B. A quick process—get the system in, then fine-tune it
C. Plannable and predictable
D. Pretty much the same from plant to plant as long as you know the right approach
E. All of the above
F. None of the above

If you circled anything other than answer F, you either read a different book than this one, skipped over everything but the pictures, or thought it was a trick question. If anything is clear from this book, it is that implementation of lean is complex, slow, incremental, and unpredictable, and the process varies dramatically from case to case.

Does this mean that implementing lean is so unpredictable and idiosyncratic that we cannot learn anything at all from other cases? Obviously the answer is no. There are some general points that are clear across these chapters, such as implementing lean is a process, not an endpoint, and lean is a *system* of production. Also, in case you had any doubts, lean is a tremendously powerful production system leading to major leaps in quality, productivity, and delivery performance and to improvements in employee health, safety, and morale as well. And this goes right to the bottom line. For example, Cedar Works took products generating no profits, or just a few percent, up to 20 to 35 percent profitability.

If you have not already committed to "becoming lean," think of it this way: What if your competitors did (or are doing) what the companies in this book reported and were cutting lead times by 90 percent, cutting defects to a fraction of what they were, increasing productivity by 10 or 15 percent per year without capital investments, and reducing total cost of their product by 10 percent per year? These are all readily achievable with lean. Do you think they would beat you if they were doing this and you were not? On the other hand, what could you do with these tremendous advantages in cost, quality, and delivery if you were becoming lean and your competitors were not?

In the end, there is a lot of agreement across these chapters on many aspects of becoming lean that are immensely useful—useful for the beginner and for those who are presently struggling with implementing lean principles. This agreement is remarkable, considering that so many different manufacturing processes and industries are represented by so many different authors. It shows that lean is "a way of thinking." Although some important differences also appear among the cases, these usually boil down to plants' having to ask tactical questions when applying lean principles to their specific work environment: for example, union, non-union companies. In this final chapter I focus on the success factors in becoming lean, looking broadly across all of the chapters.

Success Factors in Becoming Lean

In Table 15-1, I summarize my assessment of the success factors identified across all of the chapters in this book. I say "my assessment" because I did not consult any of the authors in putting this list together. Rather, I went through each of the chapters and wrote down anything that looked like a success factor and compiled a lengthy list. The Ford Production System column is based on my knowledge from public sources. These success factors focused on the process of lean, not the content. In other words, I did not record which specific technical or organizational aspects of lean manufacturing were implemented or even the sequence of their implementation. This is not to say that a solid technical understanding of the elements of lean, such as changeover reduction methods, quality methods, just-in-time methods, etc. is not critical. But in this book we focused on the *process* of implementing the system. Once I had this big, long list, I consolidated it and then grouped the individual success factors into four general categories:

1. *Preparing and motivating people.* How do we get people on board and prepared to contribute effectively to the lean system?
2. *Roles in the change process.* What roles must be filled by able people in order to make the transition to lean?
3. *Methodologies for change.* What methodologies (as distinct from specific tools and methods like mistake-proofing) are used to implement lean systems effectively?
4. *Environment for change.* What environment must exist, or be created, that will be conducive to implementing lean?

Once I developed the list in Table 15-1, I then went through each chapter and asked whether this success factor was in any way emphasized by the authors in the case (shown as check marks in Table 15-1), and if so, whether it was exceptionally well demonstrated by the case (shown as bullets). In some cases I gave a case a check

Table 15-1. Success Factors in Becoming Lean: A Summary

	Auto cases					Non-auto cases			General observations		
	Ford	Delphi Steering	Garden State Tanning	Freudenberg-NOK	Donnelly, G.H.	Gelman Sciences	Cedar Works	Western Geophysical	Choi	Koenigsaeker	Rother
Preparing and motivating people											
• Intense communication	•	•		√	b	√	√				
• Upfront broadcast training	√	√				√					
• Focused training and immediate application	a	√	√	•	•	•	•				
• Compelling need for change (crisis)		√	•	√	•			•		e	
• Visual measurement: Target versus actual	√	√	√	√	√	√	√	√	√	√	
Roles in the change process											
• Informed, active, involved leadership		•	√	•	•	√	•	√	√	•	•
• Bottom-up involvement	•	•	√	√	b	√	√		√		
• Lean experts as coaches	√	√	•	√	√	√	√	√	√	•	√
• Internal lean coordinators	√	√		√	√	√	√				√
• Engineering support	√	√	√	√	√	•				√	
Methodologies for change											
• Guided by systems vision	√	•	√		b	c	√			√	√
• Use of model lines	√	√	•		b		√		√	√	√
• Blitz kaizen events				•	•						d
• Focus on flow		√	•	√	√	c	√	√		√	•
• Go for quick, visible improvements	√	√	√	√	√		√	√	√		
• Action orientation: Just do it!		√	•	•	•		√	√		•	√
• Implementation in steps: PDCA	√	√	√	√	√	√	√	√	√		√
• Problem solving methodology: 5 whys			√		√		•	√			
Environment for change											
• Job security: No lean layoffs	√	√	√	√	√	√					
• Explicit guiding principles	√	√	√		b		•				
• Atmosphere of experimentation	a	√	√	√	b						√
• Flexible union agreement	a	•									
• Build trust	a	√			b						

Blank=Not emphasized in chapter (may still have been a factor though not mentioned).
√Emphasized in case.
• Strongly illustrated in chapter/case.
a These items vary across Ford plants.
b These items were weak in the "stop the bleeding phase" but then became strong under the Donnelly Production System.
c At Gelman, these items were not the focus at first but became so in later phases.
d Best used within the framework of an overall lean-system vision.
e Most often driven by crisis, but advantageous to implement in healthy companies.

mark because of my personal familiarity with the plant, even though the success factor may not have come through clearly in the written chapter. A blank meant the item was not discussed or if it was a success factor in the case, I am not personally aware of it. There were a few other notations used. For example, the Ford Production System is being implemented simultaneously at many plants that differ in their context, and Donnelly and Gelman Sciences used one approach in the early stages of implementation and then made significant shifts to another approach in later stages.

Overall, when we look at Table 15-1 it is clearly densely filled with check marks and asterisks and notes. This is because there was surprising agreement that these success factors were important in becoming lean. In the rest of this section, I summarize what we learned across chapters within each of the four broad categories of success factors.

Success Factor One: Preparing and Motivating People

It is easy to get agreement from managers that the technical mechanics of lean are simple compared to the "people issues." Lean is a system that depends on cooperation across the organization and on contributions by all to continuous improvement. Running over people and demoralizing them is certainly not a good idea. As in any major change project, we should make a major investment up front in training people and communicating to them in detail what they can expect, so there are no surprises. Right? But there were clear differences across the cases in the degree in which companies emphasized preparing and motivating people. In fact, Mike Rother, in his reflections on implementing lean, argues that it is easy to spend *too much* time and effort on up-front training and communicating.

I remember the first time I visited the Toyota Supplier Support Center (TSSC) to interview them about the process they were developing to implement lean in supplier plants. One issue with which they had struggled a great deal was how much training to give up front. They agreed that top management needed to be committed and understand the change and that everyone should eventually understand the philosophy of TPS, but they strongly believed that training without direct experience with

TPS on the shop floor was a waste. For example, they had developed a simulation of lean that was always a great hit with the audience. They knew that if they ran the simulation up front when they first started working with the plant it would get high evaluations by participants. Most of my academic and consulting associates are delighted if they can run an event and get high evaluations, but at TSSC, they believed the participants would still not really understand lean despite their enthusiasm. So they restricted the simulation and associated training to plants that had already gone through some transformation of their model lines. When a plant requested assistance in becoming lean, typically the first thing the Toyota consultant did on his first visit was to give an assignment to change something on the shop floor, not by next month, but by tomorrow. A plant would do a great deal of work on the shop floor before anyone was "trained."

I developed Figure 15-1 after this visit to TSSC to summarize for myself what I believe I heard them telling me. I used the famous pyramid to show deepening levels of understanding as one moves down through the chain of learning—knowledge gets broader and deeper. To the left are the levels of understanding and to the right are quotes to illustrate what the learner is experiencing. I based this model on the assumption that the learner starts with some kind of awareness through training or explanation, then goes through the following stages:

- Seeing a successful application in another plant (for example, a visit to the Toyota Mecca in Georgetown)
- Seeing some plans for applying it to a model line in his/her shop
- Committing to trying it
- Applying it successfully to the model line
- Spreading it to other areas of the plant

At each stage, their understanding is transformed in a fundamental way. So even what the learner thought he or she understood conceptually in the awareness stage is understood in a very different, gut-level way by the end. In the awareness stage, something may make sense in the abstract, but this person would not know

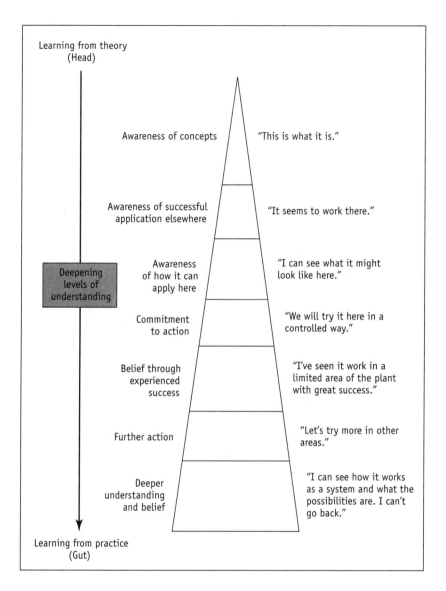

Figure 15-1. Levels of Understanding of Lean Manufacturing

what to do when faced with an actual production line. Even after achieving some limited success in assisting in implementation, the learner may well fall back on old ways in a crisis, for instance, when machines go down or inventory runs out (as illustrated in the Cedar Works chapter).

Learning by doing

This model suggests that becoming what George Koenigsaecker calls a "true believer" takes direct and repeated experience on the front lines implementing lean—learning by doing. When I first heard this at TSSC I found it upsetting because it violated my deeply held belief that training was always good. But lean thinking is in some conflict with much of the wisdom about managing change that says that the more you inform people and train them up front the better. The "just do it!" principle mitigates against spending a lot of time up front on training and communicating. The concept of learning by doing suggests just-in-time training—training people on what they need to know when they need to know it. Most of the important learning and buy-in comes after people experience the system in operation in their plant—the reason for the model line to begin with.

For example, Cedar Works gave a multiweek course to managers and representatives from the model line. The course started with a review of what lean manufacturing is and what the outside consultants' vision of the model line was—where they were headed. Then the course moved to specific training on what was to be implemented, followed by immediate application. To accomplish this, Bill Costantino developed roughly a 50–50 split between classroom training and application on the shop floor. Ultimately, when the model line had progressed, others from outside the model area were bidding to get on the model line, and there was a great demand to "do my area next." Similar experiences were reported in the Donnelly case. Once the model line had progressed significantly there was great interest by others in the plant. So to a large degree, doing needs to precede training.

Sometimes you have to train before doing

The main exceptions to "doing before training" were the large, unionized plants of Ford and GM's Delphi. These companies have a long history of distrust and union-management conflict. In recent times, a lot of effort has been made to overcome that history through focusing on up-front training and communication and employee involvement. No major program that affects the work force will get beyond square one unless management and the UAW work jointly and spend a great deal of time to prepare people, at least getting them to agree to let the "lean experiment" proceed.

The Donnelly Mirrors case is interesting in this regard. This company has been a model of employee participation, positive employee relations, and very open communication for decades. In the "stop the bleeding" phase, the Grand Haven plant believed it was do or die and turned over control of the change process to the "just-do-it!" outside consultants. The result was rapid change, rapid improvement in plant performance, and a near disaster in employee relations. In the next phase, they kicked out the consultants, employees were again heavily involved, and there was a great deal of communication and training. This resulted in the process slowing down considerably, but with far greater employee buy-in. With the successes of the blitz kaizen events behind them, the plant was in less danger of being shut down by Honda and could afford a more gradual pace of change. This case leaves open the question of whether the pressure of impending disaster and the heavy-handed approach of the outside consultants was just what Donnelly needed at the time to push them into the "lean leap." Would they have progressed significantly without this outside push?

There seems to be general agreement across cases that at some point, very focused training, at least for the implementers, followed by immediate application on the shop floor is necessary. The role of lots of up-front communication about changes and lots of training to a broad cross-section of people is less clear.

Crisis motivates change but you don't have to wait for one
How critical it is to have a crisis to motivate the change is also less clear. Certainly a crisis pushed along Donnelly and made Western Geophysical look for outside consulting help. A crisis was also the trigger that led Garden State Tanning to begin work with the Toyota consultants. Delphi Steering had the threat of GM going outside to more competitive suppliers, though how much people in the plant believed this remains uncertain, because GM had always taken care of them before. In all these cases, impending doom certainly seems to have been a strong motivator in moving toward lean.

On the other hand, Ford, Gelman Sciences, and Cedar Works did not face an immediate crisis if they did not change. Forward-thinking managers drove their change effort. As you may recall, George Koenigsaecker argues that healthy organizations can be even more effective in implementing lean. In such cases, the process of becoming lean moved slowly without a sense of urgency to get things done today. For example, Cedar Works took a year and one-half hiatus between the first experiment and the second model line when the outside consultants got busy with their jobs at Toyota.

Measurement as a driver for change

The plants to some degree all used measurement as a driver for change. Ford management believed that this was critical and made a great effort to develop a new set of plant measures to apply uniformly across Ford. Developing these measures, training on them, and implementing them was a significant change effort in and of itself, quite apart from the lean systems. Although other plants did not emphasize this quite so much, all plants posted measures on the shop floor comparing targets to actual performance, and all believe this was critical to their success.

Success Factor Two: Roles in the Change Process

There was quite a bit of agreement on what roles were needed for the change process, particularly in the leadership ranks. All of the plants that have made significant progress were led by informed, active, and involved leadership. Joe Day reports spending 40 percent of his time in the first two years of GROWTTH on nothing but direct involvement in kaizen implementation. As CEO of a $200 million (at first), multiplant company, he spent day after day in the plants with his sleeves rolled up working alongside associates. George Koenigsaecker had a similar level of immersion when he was running Jake Brakes, and he believes the lean production manager should spend 12 weeks on full-time kaizen or improvement activities just to learn the basic principles of lean. To be on a full-time shopfloor improvement team once per month takes years of dedication spending 25 percent more time at work than usual. To become a "true believer," according to George, takes four years of working with the process. At this point you would be ready to lead a lean conversion on your own.

The Delphi Steering process was clearly driven by Mike Husar, who had two years of experience at NUMMI in which he spent all his time, day and night, working to learn the system. Not everyone from GM who went out with Mike to NUMMI made this kind of effort. Mike stood out in his commitment to TPS and in actual application when he came back to GM. When asked about the importance of plant managers' deeply understanding lean thinking and personally leading the transformation, Mike Husar simply says, "It is essential." He explains that the magnitude of the systemic change needed cannot be made without full commitment from the plant manager.

I did not check Ford in this column of informed, active, and involved leadership, not because they do not believe it is important, but because there are many plants with varying levels of leadership understanding and commitment to lean thinking. Ford started out with a set of existing plant managers, not with a Mike Husar or a George Koenigsaecker. In other cases in this book, the plant managers did not start out informed and experienced like Mike Husar but directly involved themselves nonetheless. For example, Bill Costantino reports that the president and owner of Cedar Works attended 80 percent of the training sessions and the vice president of manufacturing attended every class. Attending training is not the level of immersion Joe Day and George Koenigsaecker describe, and the process was perhaps slower as a result, but it was a high level of commitment nonetheless and seen as critical to the success of Cedar Works.

The importance of external lean coaches

Beyond top leadership involvement, all of these cases had substantial outside support from lean coaches. Delphi had less than most because the plant manager, Mike Husar, could act as a lean coach. Garden State Tanning had particularly strong coaches in the Toyota consultants, who clearly took a heavy hand and had clout because the problems were with poor quality and delivery to Toyota. Koenigsaecker's experience with outside coaches at Jake Brake was that the plant needed to be "coerced" by the outside coaches or the plant would not have taken out the piles of inventory on their own. I visited one Japanese company not mentioned in this book with transplant operations in the United States. They specifically requested a Japanese coach known for his relatively *light* touch because their experience with Americans was that they reacted badly to forceful Japanese coaches who loudly and directly criticized problems without praising good practices. We saw in the Donnelly case the negative reaction of employees in a U.S. participative management climate to aggressive outside lean coaches—they threatened to unionize.

Where I come down on the role of the external lean coach is that they are clearly necessary unless the plant is rich with their own coach or coaches that have undergone the kind of four-year training George Koenigsaecker describes—but these are rare individuals. It also seems clear that they cannot just be facilitators who try to lead the plant gracefully from outside to find their own way. The coaches need to take an aggressive role by driving the process more than passively offering suggestions and by making specific technical suggestions. This is a more hands-on and in some cases more directive role than most consultants I know take when working on organizational change projects. As Bill Costantino puts it (Chapter 10): "Very simply, when people are in a process of dramatic change, they need a continuous resource whom they can trust to guide them through the change. Without this resource, there is a high likelihood that the process will either be abandoned or modified to the point that it no longer meets its original purpose."

Lean requires creative engineers
Transformations to lean also require deep engineering skills. If one thing is certain in watching how the Toyota lean coaches work it is that they are excellent engineers. In fact, in the Operations Management Consulting group in Toyota City, consultants commonly come from production engineering. Though I have suggested that the people side of lean is more complex than the technical side, the technical side requires a great deal of creative engineering for lean to succeed. If you visit five top lean plants, you will see no two installations are exactly the same. Ingenious solu-

tions come from all over the place to accomplish quick changeovers, send pull signals (for example, when a long lead time paint operation needs advanced warning before assembly will take place), or mistake proof operations. It is not enough to tell an inexperienced (in lean terms) team to implement pull and then let them struggle to invent solutions. You need as a resource someone who understands lean and has engineering capability to suggest technical solutions. In the case of Gelman Sciences, the effort was led by engineering professor Walt Hancock, who worked with engineering students hired by Gelman. As you saw, there was a great deal of hard manufacturing engineering work to be done. For example, they needed a deep understanding of the sources of product variation caused by the manufacturing process before they could implement appropriate solutions to controlling quality.

Hourly employees need to influence the shop floor
Bottom-up involvement was also evident in all the plants. (I am less familiar with Western Geophysical. Also, it was not mentioned specifically in that chapter.) At Donnelly, the participation of hourly associates was there even in the "stop the bleeding" stage, though the outside consultants were viewed as having their own solutions to problems regardless of employee input. When Donnelly shifted to the continuous improvement team of hourly associates, they were given remarkable power to influence any changes to the shop floor. The most aggressive efforts to involve employees upfront were at Ford and Delphi, the two largest companies. The Delphi steering plant was particularly effective at involving a lot of employees but keeping the process moving steadily toward the overall five-year vision (which was not developed by everyone through consensus). I should emphasize that bottom-up involvement is not the same as consensus decision making. As Mike Rother observed, lean involves changing whole systems and cannot be driven by associates or supervisors who control only a small piece of the system. George Koenigsaecker notes that even with the pressure of top management announcing that the warehouse would be removed and giving a deadline for "removing your inventory," no one took it seriously until the warehouse was destroyed by order from the top.

If we take George's story seriously, waiting for consensus in that case could have meant never moving to lean.

Success Factor Three: Methodologies for Change

All of the plants in this book used an incremental approach to implementation. You cannot implement the whole system at once in the whole plant. You must find a way to divide it into smaller chunks and smaller steps. On the other hand, most plants had an action orientation. You must act and implement and not just talk about it, as Mike Rother notes.

Use a model line

A traditional Toyota approach for helping external suppliers implement TPS was developed through their Operations Management Consulting Group under Taiichi Ohno. The Toyota Supplier Support Center, led by Mr. Hajime Ohba, a student of Taiichi Ohno, uses a similar approach. They begin with a model line for which the goal is to implement as much of the entire Toyota Production System as possible in a relatively short time, that is, months not years. They analyze the model line to arrive at a current state analysis focusing on the current flow of product and information through the system. They then develop a future state vision of what the flow should look like at the end, along with current performance measures and future targets. Though there is some action up front to stabilize the process, the primary focus is on creating continuous flow leading to a pull system and then level production. There is a clear action orientation, and improvements are fast and very visible. Along the way, you reduce setup times, improve workplace organization, and create standardized work, but these are all subordinate to creating flow.

A number of the plants in this book used a similar methodology. Obviously, Garden State Tanning followed this approach as they worked directly with Toyota purchasing and then TSSC. Ford's approach derives directly from TSSC. Mike Husar learned from Toyota directly in his experience at NUMMI and followed a similar approach.

The value of blitz kaizens

The role of blitz kaizen events is less clear. Freudenberg-NOK and Donnelly started out with blitz kaizens focusing on individual projects without a system-level map of the ideal state. Donnelly came to the conclusion that the initial approach to blitz kaizens was okay for addressing the immediate crisis of threatened shutdown by Honda but in the longer term they needed to drive the process by a total system vision. This supports what Mike Rother says about trying to "blitz" your way to lean—it cannot be done.

Focus on flow

Most of the plants focused on flow from the start. One exception was Ford. Ford is progressing through phases, with the stability phase focused on tools and techniques such as total productive maintenance, workplace organization, and setup time reduction with some attention to flow. Gelman Sciences spent an extended period on self-directed teams and stability and took several years to focus seriously on the flow. The main benefits of lean started when they began to focus on flow through product-focused cells.

You need a broad system vision

It seems clear from these cases that a systems vision is important and may be essential, even though the vision cannot be implemented all in one shot. I put a bullet for Delphi, as they had the most clear vision by year of the changes to the plant flow drawn directly on layouts of the entire plant, and they refused to deviate from the plan. The process needs to be incremental, and a good first step seems to be the model line. The model line provides a great opportunity to develop a comprehensive vision of the system for that product line. Of course early, visible improvements are needed to get momentum going, and these may be small steps. But these should be steps along the way toward a future-state vision. Some way of making quick changes on the shop floor is needed, whether it is through blitz kaizen events or weekly training like that used at Cedar Works with activity in between, or an aggressive coach telling you: "Please try this, I will be back tomorrow." Kaizen events provide a focused, scheduled time for study and implementation and evaluation. They clearly have a role, but they should be guided by a broader system vision.

Success Factor Four: Environment for Change

There is less consistency across the cases in the "environment for change" needed for implementing lean. One interesting pattern is that most of these environmental features, like job security, an explicit set of guiding principles, and creating an atmosphere of experimentation, were emphasized in the auto cases, but not outside of auto. With such a small sample size of plants, this may not indicate a pattern, but it may indicate that U.S. auto operations, which are generally large, unionized, publicly held companies, have created a culture that emphasizes attention to the social environment. For example, research has shown that the auto sector has been particularly aggressive in adopting self-directed teams and other innovative forms of work organization (Jenkins and Florida, 1998).

Job security

All of the auto cases emphasized the importance of job security— no one can lose their job because of lean. At Ford and Delphi, it is quite simply a prerequisite for being in the game. By contrast, at Gelman Sciences a number of salaried individuals were mentioned who did not go along with the lean implementation and who are no longer with the company, though no hourly employees lost their jobs as a result of lean.

Using guiding principles

At Western Geophysical we heard of the importance of starting with a set of guiding principles. These were also developed as a matter of course when the lean systems were defined in the auto companies. For example, Ford and Delphi both created sophisticated general training courses on their lean systems that included specific principles and philosophies. At Gelman and Cedar Works, the process of implementing lean was more ad hoc—formal statements of principles were not mentioned.

Building trust

Finally, the importance of building trust was mostly emphasized by Ford and Delphi. They needed to be sensitive in getting the union and employees to buy into the lean systems prior to implementation. At Donnelly, trust was clearly destroyed in the aggressive "stop the bleeding" phase but rebuilt rather quickly after Keith Allman took over as plant manager and worked successfully to involve employees and improve morale. At other companies, like Cedar Works, once the model lines were in place and operating and other employees saw the system working and benefiting everyone, trust was built naturally. Ultimately, trust must be earned through actions, not just words.

A Model of Success Factors in Becoming Lean

Looking across the chapters, Mike Rother and I developed the summary model "Success Factors in Becoming Lean" shown in Figure 15-2. This is a little different from Table 15-1, which is simply an assembly and reorganization of factors identified by authors in the book. Figure 15-2 was developed by stepping back and abstracting from what we had learned. We put the "future state flow" in the middle, because we defined lean as reducing the time line from customer order to production and delivery of goods. Thus, the future-state flow becomes the map for where the plant or model line should be headed. It is critical to develop a fairly detailed model of the future-state flow. We identified four generic technical issues—measuring, stability, approach, and process refinement—and three generic management issues—roles, people development, and environment for change. Of course, the boundary between technical and managerial factors is blurry at best.

We believe all of these factors need to be addressed in some way in managing the transformation to lean, but they also all need to be focused on moving toward the future-state flow. Spending a great deal of time on people development and creating a supportive environment for change will not help unless these activities also achieve the desired flow of product through the production process. We put a question mark after the approach of the "kaizen blitz," because these can easily lead to isolated improvements that do not move the

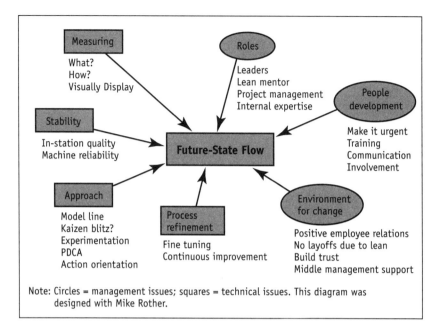

Figure 15-2. Model of Success Factors in Becoming Lean

system toward a future-state flow (see Rother chapter). One issue we added here, which is not spoken about much in the individual chapters, is getting middle management support, particularly from direct line management and supervision. Middle managers are often neglected as we focus on top management and support from workers, but they can easily block implementation of lean if they are not trained and involved in the process. At first it may seem to middle managers that they have little to gain and the most to lose as inventory buffers are reduced and parts shortages occur. Later, they will see the benefits in improved flow and quality.

So What Have We Learned About Lean?

In this book we've learned that the technical concepts are straight-forward, though in practice they require innovative engineering to apply them and are not always intuitive to managers experienced in traditional mass production. We've learned that resistance is natural. We've learned that lean has some characteristics that limit the effectiveness of traditional models of managing change through education, communication, and facilitation. Mike Rother is more direct in saying the notion that you can drive change to lean from the bottom up is "pure bunk." Most fundamental to the shift to lean is an emphasis on flow, and this means moving some equipment around, reducing inventory banks, and increasing changeover frequency, all of which lead to disrupting the mass production system. Operators and supervisors who are responsible for getting production out will not voluntarily agree to anything they fear will disrupt production, particularly getting rid of the inventory banks that have become like a security blanket.

A story comes to mind that I heard from an American veteran of lean manufacturing, Tom Luyster, who was the executive champion for one of the early plants worked on by the Toyota Supplier Support Center. He visited a fairly lean steering gear plant in England where they had moved equipment around to create a continuous flow cell. He noticed that in one of the cells there were six pieces of work-in-process (WIP) that the operators were keeping between workstations even though the workstations had been moved right next to each other. He noticed that each operator watched to make sure they maintained six pieces between stations. At some point Tom, who was only touring, picked up the five extra pieces, held them, and said, "You can't have these." The operators were aghast, but kept working, and the material flowed just fine.

Similar stories abound of supervisors and operators who cannot stand it that the equipment is sitting idle when the maximum inventory levels are met. The mass production philosophy of making all you can when the equipment is running is deeply rooted and very difficult to overcome. The idea that changing over equipment more often leads to greater system efficiency, even though it might cost a little in local efficiencies, is completely alien to mass production thinking. We have a long way to go, and it takes "true believers" who have been through it all before to push us there.

We focused in this book on implementing lean within the four walls of the plant. The case studies all come from U.S. pioneers in lean—pioneers in the country but also pioneers in their own companies. The plants were at various stages of implementation but all were works in progress—as any lean plant is. What's next is the question of how to extend lean beyond the first plant. All of the cases in this book are leaders within their companies; other plants in the same companies still have a long way to go. Moving beyond the model line is the first challenge. Moving outside the plant is the next.

The movement needs to be forward, backward, and sideways. Womack and Jones (1996) tell us that the real challenge is in creating lean enterprises. This means implementing lean throughout the value chain. Working backwards, suppliers must be providing parts on a just-in-time basis, which means they should have lean production systems or they will resort to shipping from large inventory banks. Working forward, customers must be leveling their production schedule to support just-in-time shipments from their suppliers, which means building to a level schedule using a lean production system. And companies must spread lean beyond the model plant sideways to all their plants. Though it was not emphasized, most of the plants in this book have already made great strides in their system for ordering parts via some kind of pull system, dramatically reducing parts inventories in their plant, and getting more frequent (e.g., daily) deliveries from parts suppliers. In most cases the parts suppliers to these plants have not implemented lean systems internally, though in a few cases the lean plants are beginning to teach their suppliers about TPS.

Another issue is keeping the momentum going in the system once it goes through the first big transformation from mass to lean. How do we keep the lean systems operating at a high level of efficiency and continually improving? Without continuous improvement the lean systems will not just stay the same—they will degrade. Continuous improvement requires internal energy coming from all managers, supervisors, engineers, and associates—it cannot be dictated solely from the top. It first became painfully apparent to me when I read Jennifer Orf's vivid description of the Japanese elementary school system that we have a long way to go in this country before we will achieve Japanese levels of discipline and improvement on the shop floor. We saw the struggles most of the plants in Tom Choi's study had developing active CI programs.

Lean manufacturing is being talked about throughout much of U.S. industry. It is being seriously implemented in a tiny portion of U.S. plants. Whether we have any good examples of a true lean enterprise is unclear. Time will tell whether the lean plants we do have can sustain it over the long term.

On the other hand, we do have some excellent examples of plants that are becoming lean. Some are talked about here, others are talked about by Womack and Jones (1996), and there are a variety of other studies, books, and articles that look at this change in America's manufacturing paradigm. The lean pioneers are making great strides and the bottom-line results are nothing short of remarkable. Good luck to their direct competitors! The success stories are mounting in a variety of industries. This is not just an assembly plant phenomenon, or an auto industry phenomenon. Time after time, when manufacturing managers say "this does not apply to me," they are proven wrong. The lean shopfloor revolution is slowly gaining momentum in the United States. For the sake of our national competitiveness, let us hope it continues.

References

Jenkins, D. and R. Florida. "Work system innovation among Japanese transplants in the United States." To appear in *Remade in America: Transplanting and Transforming Japanese Production Systems*, edited by J. Liker, M. Fruin, and P. Adler. New York, N.Y.: Oxford University Press, 1998.

Womack, J. P. and D. T. Jones. *Lean Thinking: Banish Waste and Create Wealth in Your Corporation*. New York, N.Y.: Simon & Schuster, 1996.

INDEX